# SUSTAINABLE COMMUNITIES

# SUSTAINABLE COMMUNITIES
## THE POTENTIAL FOR ECO-NEIGHBOURHOODS

*Hugh Barton*

*Alison Gilchrist, Tony Hathway, Rob Hopkins, Trevor Houghton,*
*Deborah Kleiner, Celia Robbins, Janet Rowe, Henry Shaftoe,*
*Dominic Stead, Murray Stewart and Nigel Taylor*

London • Sterling, VA

First published in the UK in 2000 by
Earthscan Publications Ltd
Reprinted 2001, 2005

A catalogue record for this book is available from the British Library

ISBN:    1 85383 513 7 paperback
        1 85383 512 9 hardback

Typesetting by MapSet Ltd, Gateshead, UK
Printed and bound in the UK by The Cromwell Press
Cover design by Yvonne Booth

For a full list of publications please contact:

Earthscan
8–12 Camden High Street
London, NW1 0JH, UK
Tel: +44 (0)20 7387 8558
Fax: +44 (0)20 7387 8998
Email: earthinfo@earthscan.co.uk
http://www.earthscan.co.uk

Earthscan is an imprint of James and James (Science Publishers) Ltd and publishes in
association with the International Institute for Environment and Development

This book is printed on elemental chlorine free paper

# CONTENTS

## PART I: SETTING THE SCENE

# PART II: RETHINKING THE NEIGHBOURHOOD OPTION

# PART III: COMMUNITY AND SUBSIDIARITY

# PART IV: MANAGING RESOURCES LOCALLY

# ORIGINS

The original impetus for this book came when I moved house in 1994. I found that I was living, for the first time in many years, in a local community – or rather a set of overlapping, interacting communities of varied character, some small and very local, others extending across the whole town and its hinterland. These cultural, social and economic communities all have a strong sense of locale, of connection to place and the people of the place. There are no fixed edges to this 'neighbourhood'. It is part of an urban-rural continuum, offering both a full range of local facilities and open, biodiverse countryside within ten minutes walk. Children growing up in such a place find the opportunity for an integrated social/school life where they are not dependent on parental escort. Old people and others who are home-based can find opportunities for local activities and a rich network of mutual support. This place exhibits some of the characteristics of *social* sustainability, though it also shows certain signs of *economic* decline. It perhaps has the potential, with rail station accessible, safer streets and retrofit of energy and water conservation, to be more *environmentally* sustainable.

My hope is that this book encourages deeper understanding of the nature of local community, and helps to revitalize and legitimize the principles of neighbourhood planning as a means of achieving sustainable development.

Hugh Barton

# PREFACE AND GUIDE TO THE BOOK

There is widespread acceptance of the principle of creating more sustainable communities, capable of providing for local needs locally, but much woolly wishful-thinking about what this might mean in practice. Current reality is more the death of local neighbourhoods than their creation, reflecting an increasingly mobile, privatized and commodified society. This book examines the practicality of reinventing neighbourhoods. It presents the findings of a world-wide review of eco-villages and sustainable neighbourhoods, demonstrating what is possible. Such projects, however, are rare, and the main part of the book is focused on the ordinary localities in which people live, looking at the changing nature and role of local place communities, at the technologies (of energy, food, water, movement) which help close local resource loops, at the potential for subsidiarity in decision-making down to the local level. It expounds the *ecosystem* approach to neighbourhoods, linking this to questions of sustainable urban form, housing need, greenfield and 'brownfield' development, and working towards a theory of neighbourhood design.

The book tries to bridge the gap between environmental and social perspectives on locality in the context of the national and European commitment to sustainable development. It is evaluative and exploratory rather than prescriptive drawing extensively on both research and practice. It is cross-disciplinary, with town planners, environmental scientists, social analysts, philosophers and urban designers amongst its authors.

The intended readership is broad, and the style of presentation therefore accessible. The hope is that the book will inform and motivate practitioners, theorists, students, politicians and activists, so they can observe what is happening to our towns and communities with greater insight, and develop strategies in their own spheres for neighbourhood revival.

The book is broadly structured around four themes: context, neighbourhoods, communities, and resource management.

*Part I – Setting the Scene –* identifies where we are; the problems and the conflicting interests. The opening chapter sets out the dichotomy between the ever-hopeful eco-idealists and the market realists. It carefully defines the key terms of the debate and links the academic research agenda to the policy agenda. In Chapter 2, Nigel Taylor exposes the whole concept of neighbourhood to challenge, showing how far short past attempts at neighbourhood have fallen and doubting whether local place communities still have major importance in people's lives. Then in Chapter 3 Dominic Stead examines the unsustainability of current development trends, drawing on current research work, and provides a review of some of the broad policy issues which are thereby raised. The effect of all three chapters is to cool any premature ardour that assumes the creation of sustainable communities is easy, or the policy solutions obvious. The authors back the need to try, while giving pause for thought about the role of designers, planners and local authorities vis-à-vis the broader market and institutional forces that determine the system as a whole.

*Part II – Rethinking the Neighbourhood Option* – develops theories and principles of neighbourhood planning. In Chapter 4 Hugh Barton systematically reviews the reasons for wanting neighbourhoods, drawing on social arguments to do with health, equity, freedom and community as well as environmental arguments. He also shows that on a purely functional level localities still matter despite the rise in car use. Then in Chapter 5 Barton and Deborah Kleiner examine innovative projects around the world, hoping to find fertile sources of ideas and inspiration for action. The details of their findings are further reported in Appendices 1 and 2, including probably the most complete list of eco-village/neighbourhood projects available, with contacts to allow others to follow their own trails. The overall conclusion of the survey, however, is that there are surprisingly few holistic projects which have actually been implemented.

In Chapters 6,7 and 8 Hugh Barton provides some theoretical underpinning to the difficult task of planning sustainable neighbourhoods. He attempts to give an integrated view, drawing on a wide range of sources from epidemiological studies to urban design principles. Chapter 6 presents the ecosystem view of settlements as applied to neighbourhoods, examining the interaction of social and spatial elements with particular emphasis on housing, employment and water. Chapter 7 applies the theories of sustainable urban form to the local level, while Chapter 8 focuses on the size, shape, linkage, and internal structuring of neighbourhoods, with very clear recommendations for practice.

*Part III – Community and Subsidiarity* – examines the processes of local community change and development in some depth, drawing on several original case studies in the West of England. In some ways it should be read *before* Part II, as it grounds the debate about community, social networks and local decision-making and to a significant extent validates the need for neighbourhood planning. In Chapter 9 Alison Gilchrist examines the changing nature of 'community' and the processes of community development in an inner city neighbourhood. Then in Chapter 10 Janet Rowe and Celia Robbins evaluate the impact of an environmental and a local economic project on local resource use and community capacity building. And in Chapter 11 Murray Stewart takes the theme of community governance, assessing the scope for neighbourhood management and decentralized decision processes.

*Part IV – Managing Resources Locally* – looks at specific topics which illustrate the way in which the eco-system approach and community decision-making might work. It cannot pretend to be comprehensive but does look at resources both in terms of life-support (energy and food for example) and quality of life (including facets such as accessibility and safety). First Trevor Houghton, in Chapter 12, assesses the potential for moving from an energy supply system based on centralized non-renewable resources to one based on community-run renewable resources. Then Rob Hopkins (Chapter 13) advocates and sets out a strategy for local food production and increased community self-reliance. In Chapter 14, Tony Hathway offers a systematic approach to providing for local movement, taking walking and cycling first, then public transport, with the car as a poor fourth. This leads naturally to Chapter 15, by Henry Shaftoe, who examines the theory and practice of creating safe communities, linking back to the urban design issues discussed in Chapter 8.

Hugh Barton rounds off the text, in Chapter 16, by drawing together some of the strands and suggesting steps that could be taken to increase community decision-making and reorientate local and national policy so as to facilitate the creation of sustainable neighbourhoods.

# A NOTE ON TERMINOLOGY

The terms *community*, *neighbourhood* and *village* are notoriously difficult to pin down. In normal parlance and in different academic/professional contexts they can be interpreted very differently. Given the eclectic nature of the book there has been no arbitrary standardization of their meaning, and individual contributors have been free to employ them in their own way. However, the key concepts of community and neighbourhood are examined early in Chapter 1, and further distinctions drawn at the start of Chapter 8. Some simple equations can also be made:

- urban village = neighbourhood
- urban eco-village = eco-neighbourhood
- 'actual' neighbourhood (Chapter 15) = home-zone (Chapter 8)
- place community = local social network

# FOREWORD

*Jed Griffiths – Past President of the
Royal Town Planning Institute*

I was brought up in Honicknowle, one of the 'neighbourhood areas' designated by Sir Patrick Abercrombie in his Plan for Plymouth (1994). It was a very happy period in my life, not least because of the community spirit and willingness of people, both newcomers and former villagers, to come together in developing a lively network of local families and services. Growing up in that lively social environment and witnessing the rebirth of the City of Plymouth convinced me that town planning could improve the quality of people's lives.

Today, many neighbourhoods like Honicknowle are fragmented communities. A range of factors are to blame, not least the advent of the motor car, home-base entertainment and labour-saving gadgets which mean that people no longer have to communicate with others on a day to day basis. At the end of the 20th century the concepts of neighbourhood and community seem to be slipping away.

This book re-addresses these concepts in a refreshing and challenging way. It will be of immense benefit, not only to town planners, but also to all those professional and voluntary groups and politicians who seek to create the new communities of tomorrow. An essential part of the formula will be to apply the principles of sustainability, and the book presents some imaginative ideas for developing neighbourhoods which are self-sustaining and stimulating living environments.

Hugh Barton and his co-writers have done a splendid job and I congratulate them.

# THE CONTRIBUTORS

**Hugh Barton** is a lecturer, researcher and consultant on sustainable settlement planning and environmental decision-making. Originally trained as a town planner at Oxford Brookes University he has worked for many years at the University of the West of England (UWE), and is currently the Executive Director of the World Health Organization (WHO) Collaborating Centre for Healthy Cities and Urban Policy. He has a long standing interest in environmental and community issues, founding the Urban Centre for Appropriate Technology (now the Centre for Sustainable Energy) in the early 1980s. He is co-author of *Local Environmental Auditing* (Earthscan, 1995) and principal author of *Sustainable Settlements: A Guide for Planners, Designers and Developers* (UWE and the Local Government Board, 1995). He is currently completing a book on *Healthy Urban Planning* for the WHO and is leading a project integrating health and equity issues with sustainability and urban design.

**Alison Gilchrist** has been a community worker for many years in inner-city neighbourhoods in Bristol. She has lived in Easton since 1980 and has been involved in community activities both as a resident and as a paid worker. She served on the Executive Committee of the National Standing Conference for Community Development between 1991 and 1998. She is currently a lecturer at UWE, primarily involved in the education and training of community and youth workers. Her research interests include the importance of informal networking within community development, with a particular focus on strategies for achieving equality and empowerment.

**Tony Hathway** is an architect, town planner and transport planner. He is currently employed as a Principal Lecturer in the Faculty of the Built Environment at UWE. Before joining UWE he worked in local government and the private sector on major residential and commercial developments throughout the UK. He has made studies of the travel requirements of low income communities in the major cities of developing countries and explored the successful integration of various forms of non-motorised transport. Recent projects include the preparation of sustainable design guides for new housing schemes and studies of developments which give priority to access by foot, two wheels and public transport.

**Rob Hopkins** is a permaculture designer and is the founding director of Baile D Ira Teoranta, a charitable company working towards the development of The Hollies Sustainable Village near Enniskeane, West Cork. In 1996 he obtained a first-class honours degree in Environmental Quality and Resource Management from UWE. His dissertation, 'Permaculture: a new approach for rural planning', was published and some of its recommendations adopted by UK local authorities. He is also author of *Woodlands for West Cork: A Guide to their Conservation and Management* which was recently published by An Taisce, West Cork.

**Trevor Houghton** has degrees in environmental science and energy policy. For many years he was the Research Director at the Centre for Sustainable Energy (CSE) in Bristol, before moving recently to join CAG consultants. He has contributed some of the key texts on fuel poverty and community renewables, and advises government and parliamentary bodies on energy issues. He coordinated the EU project to prepare Bristol Energy and Environment Plan, which led to the setting up the Western Partnership for Sustainable Development.

**Deborah Kleiner** graduated in Environmental Quality and Resource Management at UWE. She has for the past four years been working at CSE in Bristol. As part of the Research and Implementation Unit at CSE, her main project area since 1996 has been in the solar water heating field. She has been the key person running the Solar Clubs project which enables householders to install their own solar systems at half the usual cost. The project was piloted in Bristol and Leicester and Deborah has been successful in gaining funding for the project to be disseminated nationally.

**Celia Robbins** is a research associate in the Cities Research Centre, Faculty of the Built Environment, UWE. She is currently working on a study funded by the BOC Foundation, assessing the effectiveness of a community development approach to promoting household waste reduction. Using both quantitative and qualitative data sets, this project has generated work on a wide range of topics including participation, local democracy and the creation of local environmental indicators. Other research interests include community capacity and community economic development. Celia has an MA in Environmental Planning from Nottingham University. She has worked in local government as Programme Officer to the Derbyshire Minerals Local Plan inquiry and in central government promoting DETR environmental policy in the East Midlands.

**Janet Rowe** is a Senior Research Fellow in the Cities Research Centre, Faculty of the Built Environment, UWE. Her research interests focus on environmental management in policy and practice. She has a PhD in Biochemical Plant Pathology from the University of Manitoba, Canada. Through her work in the 1970s on cereal diseases in the UK and on forest decline in Sweden, she became an environmentalist. She worked as a natural resource consultant, and as a lecturer and researcher in agricultural and rural policy development at the Royal Agricultural College, Cirencester throughout the 1980s, joining UWE in 1994.

**Henry Shaftoe** is the Award Leader for the Community Safety and Crime Prevention Open Learning Programme at UWE. He also works as a consultant with the Safe Neighbourhoods Unit (a national not-for-profit organization) and undertakes research into many aspects of crime prevention and urban security. With a background in social work, community development and architectural design, he is a proponent of the importance of integrating social and environmental factors in any strategy to create safer communities. This is reflected in the wide range of publications he has contributed to, from a schoolteacher's curriculum pack (*Safe for Life*, Nelson) to a handbook of security detailing (*Design for Secure Residential Environments*, Longman). He has carried out work for the European Commission and government departments in Britain and France and is an expert on comparative approaches to urban security in European Countries.

**Dominic Stead** has qualifications in environmental science and town and country planning. He currently holds the positions of Research Fellow in the Bartlett School of Planning at University College London and Visiting Lecturer in the Faculty of the Built Environment at UWE. His research interests focus on the relationships between transport, land use planning and the environment. Dominic is currently involved in research projects at the European scale and has recently completed his doctoral thesis on the role of land use planning in influencing travel patterns.

**Murray Stewart** is Professor of Urban and Regional Governance in the Faculty of the Built Environment, UWE. He has worked as a civil servant in London as well as at the Universities of Glasgow, Kent and Bristol and at UWE. He has undertaken research for a wide range of organizations including the European Commission, Department of the Environment, Scottish Office, Joseph Rowntree Foundation, European Foundation for Living and Working Conditions, and many local authorities. He is a Trustee of the Lloyds/TSB Foundation, a member of the Bristol Chamber of Commerce and Initiative President's Group, and is a Board Member of the Bristol Regeneration Partnership.

**Nigel Taylor** teaches philosophy and planning theory, and courses on aesthetics and urban design, in the School of Planning and Architecture at UWE. He has published substantial articles on town planning philosophy, theory, professional ethics, and aesthetics in relation to urban design. He is author of *Urban Planning Theory Since 1945* (Sage, 1998).

# FIGURES, TABLES AND BOXES

## FIGURES

# Tables

# Boxes

# Acronyms and Abbreviations

| | |
|---|---|
| CHP | combined heat and power |
| CSE | Centre for Sustainable Energy |
| DETR | Department of Environment, Transport and the Regions |
| DoE | Department of Environment |
| dph | dwellings per hectare |
| GATT | General Agreement on Tarriffs and Trade |
| GEN | Global Eco-Village Network |
| LA21 | Local Agenda 21 |
| LETS | Local Exchange and Trading Scheme |
| LGMB | Local Government Management Board |
| LRT | light rail transit |
| NAP | Neighbourhood Action Plan |
| NFFO | non-fossil fuel obligation |
| NIMBY | 'not in my back yard' |
| pcu | passenger car units |
| PPG13 | Planning Policy Guidance note 13 |
| pph | persons per hectare |
| SVD | selective vehicle detection |
| TOD | transit orientated development |
| TRC | The Recycling Consortium |
| UWE | University of the West of England |
| WAG | Waste Action Group |
| WRCP | Waste Reduction in the Community Project |
| WHO | World Health Organization |

# ACKNOWLEDGEMENTS

I would like to thank all those who have been involved with the creation of this book, including the many colleagues, students, practitioners and friends who have helped to shape its character. I owe special thanks to all the contributors, who kept faith with the project throughout; to Richard Guise and James Shorten, who contributed to the development of ideas; to Debbie Kleiner, whose enthusiasm and commitment was greatly appreciated; to Gill Weaden, for ever helpful and efficient support; and to Jim Claydon and others who allowed me the time and space to complete the work. Thanks also to Val Kirby for her love and support and to Chris, Rachael and Michael for their tolerance at home.

# PART I
# SETTING THE SCENE

# 1    CONFLICTING PERCEPTIONS OF NEIGHBOURHOOD

*Hugh Barton*

*'Unless we are guided by a conscious vision of the kind of future we want, we will be guided by an unconscious vision of the kind of present we already have'* The Edge (1995)

## INTRODUCTION

Neighbourhood is a loaded concept. To some, particularly children and old people, it appears a self-evident reality, familiar and homely, providing daily needs and a community of shared experience and mutual support. Place communities are increasingly recognized by social care and health professionals as important for mental health and social inclusion, and by the police for security. Urban designers are promoting the concept of mixed use 'urban villages', providing convenient, convivial and enlivening pedestrian-scale environments. To others, however, the concept seems *passé* if not faintly ludicrous in the light of contemporary lifestyles. The development industry emphasizes individual consumption at the expense of community cooperation, mobility not stability, internet rather than interplay. Neighbourhood, while in principle a good thing, is perceived as running counter to dominant, multifold trends – a nostalgic concept harking back to a pre-motor, pre-phone age when many people lived out much of their lives in one locality. The social failure of some outlying urban estates built on 'neighbourhood' principles in the mid-century, still suffering problems of isolation, poverty, anomie and decay, is perceived as a cautionary tale for would-be community constructivists. The town planners and the house builders therefore collude in avoiding any hint of community planning even while the politicians appeal to the 'local community' to lend credibility to their pet projects, and the media employ 'community' loosely to draw people into engagement with local stories.

Part of the difficulty in achieving clarity in this tangle of ideas is confusion over concepts. There is a minefield of divergent interpretations, so it is vital to exercise some terminological caution, and recognize the seeds of ambiguity and dissension in words so glibly used: 'neighbourhood' and 'community'. The first section of this chapter draws distinctions between the two concepts examining their professional and academic resonance. The following section then provides an introduction to the equally slippery term sustainable development, and that leads naturally to the question of what might constitute a sustainable neighbourhood or community. Two antipathetic pictures are given: one of which points to an idealized vision of a healthy, ecological, convivial neighbourhood; the other which portrays the reality of current suburban development, where the principle of neighbourhood is almost dead. In this context official policy, albeit ostensibly geared to sustainability, has a hard task. A brief review of European and UK policy is then linked into the prevailing research and professional agenda which, at least from the town planning perspective, has tended to sideline locality. Finally the chapter sets out the agenda which the book as a whole is intended to address.

## NEIGHBOURHOOD AND COMMUNITY

The term 'neighbourhood' has the conventional meanings of 'neighbours' or 'people of a district', or 'the district itself' (Concise Oxford). In its third (and I think dominant) meaning it implies a locality which is familiar or has a particular unifying character, and this is the meaning adopted here. Neighbourhoods have something in common with rainbows. Each person carries around her or his personal image, depending on her own position and experience. Such 'mental maps' are relativistic, individual perceptions which may or may not relate to a *functional* locality – ie the catchment zone of a local centre.

At the professional level 'neighbourhood' has a venerable ancestry stemming from Ebenezer Howard and Raymond Unwin early in the twentieth century, and subsequently gelled by the first generation British new towns. In Harlow and Stevenage, and later Runcorn, the neighbourhood is a discreet residential area with a population of 4–6000 supporting a primary school and a local centre, more or less physically separated from adjoining localities. This concept received a bad press from the social analysts of the 1960s and 1970s who equated it with the idea of social engineering – the artificial creation of a community by design – which they observed did not accord with the reality of individual and social behaviour in an increasingly mobile age, and was based on false perceptions of the designers' role and power (Dennis, 1968; Goodman, 1972). Unfortunately that image of discreet, fixed neighbourhoods, and the subsequent strong reaction against any hint of physical determinism, has tainted academic debate ever since. Theories about neighbourhoods have progressed little since the era of new town plans, and any skills developed then have been forgotten or sidelined.

In practice, in the UK at least, most decisions have been effectively made by the development industry. New residential areas have been, and are being, defined not by any understanding of local accessibility or the pedestrian realm – let alone 'community' – but by market interests and land ownership as mediated by the planning system, creating a fragmented car-dependant pattern.

In *historic* towns and cities neighbourhoods are neither the stylized neat catchment zones of tradition nor the atomized housing units of the house-builders, but something much more organic: neighbourhoods blend into each other as part of a wider urban continuum. There are few firm edges but rather there is permeability between one area and another. Land use and social character are often much more diversified than more recent peripheral estates or new town neighbourhoods.

In this book 'neighbourhood' is defined as a residential or mixed use area around which people can conveniently walk. Its scale is geared to pedestrian access and it is essentially a *spatial* construct, a place. It may or may not have clear edges. It is not necessarily centred on local facilities, but it does have an identity which local people recognize and value. 'Community' is quite different. It is a *social* term which does not necessarily imply 'local'. It means a network of people with common interests and the expectation of mutual recognition, support and friendship. While 'interest' communities of work, school, club or leisure activity normally do have a specific locational focus this is not necessarily the case (witness the rising tide of internet communication) and often that location has little to do with the home base. With high mobility and individual lifestyle choice propinquity is no longer a prerequisite for association. Nevertheless the locality may provide the focus for a number of overlapping and interacting interest communities or activities – children in school, scouts and guides, baby-sitting circles, surgeries, local shops, pubs, allotments, churches – which together with casual public realm meetings make for much more social interaction than the sum of the parts. In some contexts family or specific ethnic connections further reinforce this. However, 'place community' does not imply the existence of the discreet and cosy (or even claustrophobic) close-knit community of the traditional village. Rather a looser network of local association where neighbourhood is *one* of the common factors.

It is worth, then, distinguishing the different facets of neighbourhood. In the first place there is the *functional* neighbourhood: the locality seen as the base for home life, and perhaps for educational, retail, leisure and employment activities. This is typically a town planner's view of neighbourhood. The *loss* of local activity and services is commonly seen by environmentalists, residents and government as a social and environmental problem.

The second perspective is the neighbourhood seen as a *place*, as an aesthetic experience, to do with its historic association as well as its sensuous quality, and linked to residents/users perceptions of their own 'home' territory. This is more the domain of the urban designer. Its importance has been rediscovered in recent years with the renewed emphasis on local distinctiveness and quality.

Thirdly there is the neighbourhood as the locus for *community*. Community is made by people, and people often belong to diverse interest-based communities which barely touch the locality. But many households also have locally-based activities which intertwine to give a sense of a local network of mutual support.

To a significant and damaging degree these three facets of neighbourhood are addressed by separate sets of professionals and separate literature, sometimes exacerbated by national boundaries. For example the American urban designers literature on new neighbourhoods is unfamiliar ground for most British planners, schooled in a more functional perspective which itself has been largely sidelined by market pressures and the sociological critique.

But the reality is that all three perspectives are critically important in moving towards a more sustainable pattern of living. It is part of the purpose of the book to cultivate this more integrated view, grounded in a belief in sustainable development.

# SUSTAINABLE DEVELOPMENT

Sustainable development is a phrase more honoured in the breach than in the observance. It is often used, with casual abandon, as if mere repetition delivers green probity. This is especially the case in relation to land use plans which lay claim to sustainability while promoting a continuation of established development patterns that, as we shall see, belie it. The phrase, 'sustainable development' is itself a paradox. It appears to put together two irreconcilable principles, that of environmental sustainability and economic development. Indeed this tension has led to two interpretations of sustainable development, one *ecocentric*, which puts global ecology first; one *anthropocentric*, which puts human well-being first. An ecocentric view leads to the identification of limits to population and economic growth, in the interest of sustaining and enhancing natural ecosystems (eg IUCN, 1991). Techniques of 'environmental capacity', take this starting point; and one widely-praised planning system – New Zealand's Resource Management System – ostensibly works on this basis, putting biophysical issues first (Barton, 1997).

Conversely the most internationally accepted definition of sustainable development is people-centred: 'development that meets the needs of the present without compromising the ability of future generations to meet their own needs' (WCED, 1987). The UK government puts it even more simply: 'sustainable development is about ensuring a better quality of life for everyone, now and for generations to come' (DETR, 1998d). Such definitions imply that we value the natural world not primarily for any abstract innate virtue it might have but because it is critical to our life support and we gain pleasure from it. So it is in our vital interest to ensure that the Earth's life-enhancing and life-supporting qualities are not compromised.

At the extreme, these two standpoints may rationalize different strategies – contrast for example the priorities of the nature-loving 'eco-warriors' with those of local politicians favouring job creation. Both groups may appeal to sustainable development to justify their stance. But the point of the concept is to avoid polarized options and seek solutions that successfully *marry* human welfare and ecological robustness. The central purpose of this book is to examine the potential for just such a holistic approach at the level of the local community.

Carew-Reid et al (1994) produced a set of six principles which they suggest could provide the underpinning for sustainability laws and policy (see Box 1.1).

## Local Agenda 21

The programme of action towards sustainable development launched by the 1992 'Earth Summit' in Rio de Janeiro under the banner *Local Agenda 21* (LA21) makes considerable play of the role of citizens and the importance of

---

## BOX 1.1 PRINCIPLES OF SUSTAINABLE DEVELOPMENT

- The *public trust doctrine*, which places a duty on the state to hold environmental resources in trust for the benefit of the public.
- The *precautionary principle* (erring on the side of caution) which holds that where there are threats of serious or irreversible damage, lack of full scientific certainty shall not be used as a reason for postponing cost-effective measures to prevent environment degradation.
- The *principle of inter-generational equity*, which requires that the needs of the present are met without compromising the ability of future generations to meet their own needs.
- The *principle of intra-generational equity*, stating that all people currently alive have an equal right to benefit from the use of resources, both within and between countries.
- The *subsidiarity principle*, which deems that decisions should be made at the lowest appropriate level, either by those directly affected or, on their behalf, by the authorities closest to them (though for some transnational issues this implies more effective international laws and agreements).
- The *polluter pays principle*, which requires that the costs of environmental damage should be borne by those who cause them; this may include consideration of damage occurring at each stage of the life-cycle of a project or product.

*Source:* Carew-Reid et al, 1994, as summarized by Selman, 1996

---

drawing all sectors of society into engagement with the goal. LA21 calls for participation of local communities in the process of development. It does not see such involvement going as far as *citizen control* (at the top of the 'ladder' of participation – Arnstein, 1969) but rather a process of devolution taking place within a framework set by the local authority (LGMB, 1992). Selman (1996) suggests that this active citizenship as advocated by LA21 is something of a 'Pandora's box' for government at both levels, having to balance the need for political legitimacy and fairness with real ownership of the process by local people.

Techniques of actively involving local people and businesses, drawing in under-represented groups where possible, in the decisions affecting their own village or locality have multiplied in the 1990s under the auspices of LA21: village maps, community fora, charettes, citizen's juries etc. The 'charette' process, for example, involves bringing all the stakeholders who are affected by a neighbourhood plan together in a guided debate which informs and helps to shape the decisions of the designers, developers and local authority. There are issues here about the degree to which such processes – however sincerely undertaken – raise public expectations of action without establishing effective means of implementation. But the gathering momentum towards such forms of more participative democracy is going to be difficult to reverse.

The essential ingredient for achieving sustainable development on the LA21 model is *partnership*, with effective collaboration between public, private, voluntary and community sectors. But the interpretation of sustainability in practice in a pluralist context is fraught with difficulty. At the local level it is all too easy to equate sustainable development, in knee-jerk fashion, with tokenistic or light green policies (eg bottle banks, recreational cycle routes, dog bans in parks) which, while they are worthwhile in themselves, are peripheral to the main agenda. More incidiously sustainable development can be used to promote *ostensibly* green policies (eg green belts, park'n'ride) which may actually be counter-productive (Barton et al, 1995).

## Sustainability Techniques

There is therefore a widespread recognition of the need for dispassionate, technical processes to inform political debate. Techniques of sustainability appraisal, environmental capacity and ecological footprinting are being developed, and the characterization of elements of environmental and social capital, in such a way that policy-makers understand the complex choices open to them, is gaining sophistication (CC et al, 1998). Simple checklists are widely used as a means of trying to ensure that all important facets of sustainability have been duly considered. Table 1.1 shows a checklist that is loosely derived form the UK government's guidance on the 'environmental appraisal' of plans, extended to embrace some social and economic criteria, and applied to the neighbourhood level.

This is not the place to evaluate the techniques and processes currently on offer, except to recognize that we are on a fast learning curve, and there is a wide gap between best practice and common practice. Perhaps the biggest problem (for people, politicians and professionals) is not the processes but the paradigm shift involved, away from an assumption of competition between interests (in which there are winners and losers) and towards one of cooperation, seeking win-win situations – creative policy-making that fulfils all the criteria: socially inclusive, economically viable, resource-conserving *and* aesthetically pleasing. The well-known trefoil diagram makes the point elegantly (see Figure 1.1).

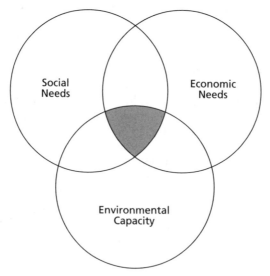

**Figure 1.1** *Searching for Sustainable Development*

**Table 1.1** *A Sustainability Checklist, Applied to Neighbourhoods*

**Global Ecology**
Climate stability
Energy in transport
- Locations that minimize trip lengths, and are well served by public transport
- Design that fosters walking and cycling and discourages car reliance

Energy in buildings
- Energy-efficient built form and layout
- Development of community renewable energy

Biodiversity
- Wildlife refuges and corridors

**Natural Resources**
Air quality
- Traffic reduction and air quality management

Water
- Local sourcing and demand management
- Local surface water/sewage treatment, aquifer recharge

Land and soils
- Higher densities to reduce urban land take
- Local composting/organic recycling schemes

Minerals
- Locally-sourced and recycled building materials

**Local Environment**
Aesthetic quality
- Attractive pedestrian-scale local environment

Image and heritage
- Legible environment with a sense of place
- Design reflecting distinctive landscape and cultural heritage

**Social Provision**
Access to facilities
- Accessible, good quality health, educational retailing and leisure facilities

Built space
- Diverse, affordable good quality housing stock
- Adaptable, good quality commercial/institutional space

Open space
- Accessible, well run parks/playgrounds/playing fields/allotments

Infrastructure
- Adaptable, easily maintained road and utility networks

**Economic Sustainability**
Job opportunities
- Diverse and accessible job opportunities with good local training services

Economic buoyancy
- Encouragement for local offices/workshops, home-working and tele-centres

**Social Sustainability**
Health
- Pollution-free environment facilitating healthy exercise, local food production and mental well-being

Community safety
- Safe traffic-calmed streets with good visual surveillance
- Neighbourhood social balance and continuity

Equity and choice
- Access to housing for all social groups
- All facilities easily accessed by foot or public transport, with special attention to needs of children and the disabled

While from an ecological standpoint this diagram is misleading – in that human society is *dependant* on the global environment for life support (so in a sense the environmental sphere embraces the others), it does provide an apt test of policy. As stressed by the influential *Green Paper on the Urban Environment* (CEC, 1990) it is vital not to treat problems in isolation but to search creatively for integrated solutions that bring benefits across the board. To do this successfully relies on understanding the whole system interactions, in terms of human, and urban, ecology (Hough, 1995; Expert Group, 1995; Tjallingii, 1995).

## Implications

The implications of the principle of sustainable development for locality are fourfold: Firstly, sustainable development demands that we rediscover the link between places and their context, seeing the design and management of every area reflecting its locale in terms of landscape, ecology, water and energy. This is to adopt an *ecosystem* approach to locality. Secondly, the decline in the functional significance of locality, and the concommittent rise in car reliance, is unsustainable in that it means increased transport emissions, health impacts, transport inequities and excessive use of land/energy resources. Sustainable development points instead to *localization*. Thirdly, the locality has a role in maintaining the '*social capital*' of community networks based on local activities and propinquity. Fourthly, under the auspices of LA21 citizens and community groups are being invited to be *partners* in the process of devising plans and programmes for their neighbourhoods.

# VISIONS OF A SUSTAINABLE LOCALITY

In the context of LA21 many local 'communities' are being asked to express their current concerns and future aspirations. It would appear that people involved in this process do value 'neighbourhood'. Visioning exercises experienced by the author suggest that when asked about their ideal living environment, many people belie current lifestyles and conjure up an eco-conscious utopia.[1] This image seems to arise quite spontaneously to the participants – who normally represent quite a range of interests, but are of course largely self-selected. The visioning process is expressly intended as a consensus-building activity between people with different backgrounds from public, private, voluntary and residential sectors, preparing the ground for subsequent strategy-making and partnerships.

Certain attributes of the shared visions are surprisingly persistent: an attractive and green neighbourhood which is safe, pollution-free and uncongested; a sense of local community and excellent access to friends and facilities both locally and regionally. People hope through telecommunications to participate in wideflung networks and activities while (in many cases) living a less frenetic and more locally-based life. When asked what is the first thing heard

---

1 The basis for this claim is personal experience of local events in Southern England in 1996 and 1997, supplemented by conversations in Gloucestershire, Bristol and Somerset with LA21 facilitators, and reinforced by the results of student 'visioning' exercises.

on waking, 'birdsong' is the almost invariable reply. This is altogether very English, hinting at a kind of collective sub-conscious 'garden city' dream. There are sharp divides, however, between those who envisage individual pollution-free vehicles and those who imagine cars banned in favour of foot, pedal, bus and tram. There is also the divergence between those who conjure a rural idyll and urbanites who want a vibrant city life. But the coincidence of values is much more striking than the differences. Both village and city people wish for a place, a neighbourhood where they feel they belong: an attractive, convivial and healthy place that balances privacy with community and local provision with city access. The picture is that of a *sustainable neighbourhood*: emphatically not an inward-looking claustrophobic enclave but rather a local, homely part of the global village.

There is a perhaps surprising coincidence of views between 'visioning' participants and normative ecological thinkers. The rhetoric of sustainability talks of human-scale, mixed use and socially diverse neighbourhoods, providing residents with increased convenience and sense of local identity, while at the same time reducing their ecological footprint. Cogently articulated by radical authors in the 1970s (Ecologist 1972, Boyle and Harper 1972), the essential features have not changed much:

> *'The village would be a balanced community for people of all ages and incomes, where people can live, work and enjoy a vibrant community life, the majority without the need to commute and where everyone could feel a sense of personal belonging. It would provide affordable housing, work opportunities, food production, energy and water conservation as well as self-reliance for its residents in an ecologically aware and sensitive way'.* (Littlewood, 1998)

The internationally-based Eco-Villages Network stresses a *permaculture* approach to the human/environment relationship, and a very high degree of local autonomy for food, energy and water. In the urban (and more mainstream) context similar sentiments are echoed. The 1995 Freiburg Statement on New Urban Neighbourhoods stated that 'the overriding purpose of a new neighbourhood is the care and culture of human beings'. It declares that it is important to learn from the traditional wisdom of city making, and to avoid the errors of modern peripheral urban development. The principles espoused emphasize:

- heterogeneous social composition, with special attention to the needs of children, elderly and low income groups;
- a pedestrian-dominated public realm to facilitate 'good social life' and provide an attractive human-scale environment;
- diversity of use – housing, work, shopping, civic, cultural and health facilities in a fine textured, compact, low rise urban fabric;
- active and frequent participation of all segments of the population in planning and design of the area, thus an incremented not authoritarian design process;
- architectural identity that is rooted in the collective memory of the region, reflecting characteristics most valued by the local community;

- pedestrian, bicycle and public transport networks within the neighbourhood and linking to the city as a whole, discouraging automobile use;
- ecologically responsible development principles consistent with social responsibility and cutting energy use and pollution. (Making Cities Liveable Newsletter, May 1996).

This image is reinforced by contemporary urban designers. The 'new urbanist' designers in the US and the 'Urban Village Forum' in the UK have called for the revival of convivial, convenient, close-knit localities:

> *'The alternative to sprawl is simple and timely: neighbourhoods of housing, parks and schools placed within walking distance of shops, civic services, jobs and transit – a modern version of the traditional town. The convenience of the car and the opportunity to walk or use transit can be blended in an environment with local access for all the daily needs of a diverse community. It is a strategy which could preserve open space, support transit, reduce auto traffic, and create affordable neighbourhoods.'*
> (Calthorpe 1993)

These are reasonable aspirations for a civilized society. Calthorpe emphasizes the desirable physical attributes – in themselves uncontentious but in their implementation problematical. Others stress the social dimension, seeing neighbourhoods as a setting within which people can take control of their own lives (eg Ward, 1976). Tony Gibson, writing for the Town and Country Planning Association, believes a neighbourhood is 'the place, plus the people: one whole which is common ground for everyone living and working in it'. He sees neighbourhoods as cells which help to keep society whole, and advocates self-help at the neighbourhood level which would not only revive a sense of local pride but give some stability to a fragmenting society (Gibson, 1984).

Such views may give inflated importance to locality in an age where local place communities are fading from common experience like the Cheshire Cat's smile, yet are being re-enlivened in the context of LA21. The active involvement of local communities, forming partnership with local government and business, is seen as central to any strategy for achieving sustainable development (DoE 1994b).

## THE DEATH OF NEIGHBOURHOOD

Sometimes local authorities in promoting LA21 have implied that localities possess a power of self-determination which ignores the structural realities. The images of a sustainable neighbourhood are seductive, but run counter to dominant market trends. The question has to be asked as to how far rhetoric with such a strong element of, perhaps, nostalgic idealism can be converted into reality. In delivering low/medium density suburban residential monoculture the market is (presumably) reacting to consumer preferences. People are choosing a particular style of living, heavily car dependent and largely segregated from locality, and may be unwilling to return to a less mobile condition.

How far the prevailing UK development pattern is from the ideal sustainable neighbourhood can be illustrated by the study of a large new residential area on the north fringe of Bristol. Bradley Stoke is a major new northern suburb of Bristol, eventually catering for up to 25,000 people, and developing according to broad design principles set out in the 1986 Development Brief. It had local authority involvement from conception to realization, thus offering a better-than-average opportunity for a coordinated scheme. However the original brief made few stipulations about ecology, local access or character. So within the broad spatial framework the house builders have created the environment they conceive the house buyers want. Adjacent residential enclaves turn their back on each other, with separate distributor access to the main road system and cul-de-sacs off the distributor, creating a fragmented patchwork of housing cells. There is not much variation of housing type or tenure, and there are very few local facilities.

The lack of permeability leads to pedestrian routes that are sometimes twice as long as necessary – whether to local schools, shops or nearby friends in a separate residential enclave. The buses rely on the main roads which, apparently for safety reasons, are shuttered in by six foot high back garden walls, so access to the bus stop, or to the neighbouring areas along this connecting road, involves walking along a heavily trafficked route with little or no surveillance or 'eyes on the street'. Thus outside the small cul-de-sac housing clusters (which some people like for their seclusion and sociability), the scheme has not addressed the neighbourhood scale, and not anticipated pedestrian movement or even the desirability of local services. The atomization of the urban fabric leads to increased trip lengths, increased car dependence, and the reduced viability of local services. The designers' assumption seems to be that in an era of full car ownership people have their social and work life at a distance, and little connection to locality. Rather they parachute in and out of their private home territory barely knowing their neighbours.

What the Bradley Stoke approach does is disenfranchise people who cannot drive or have infrequent access to a car – notably children, teenagers, older people, parents at home. Far from being an escape into freedom, the car-based suburb is a restriction of freedom, effectively reducing the options to walk, cycle, use the bus, use local facilities, instead obliging households to invest in a second or third highly polluting vehicle in order to maintain a reasonable lifestyle.

Other unsustainable practices evident in Bradley Stoke make a familiar litany in common with most new development:

- energy efficiency measures achieve building regulations but do not match best practice;
- there is no attempts to orientate buildings to maximize solar gain;
- roof design militates against both solar collection and roof space use;
- impermeable surfaces impede ground-water replenishment;
- lack of in situ water catchment exports water collection problems elsewhere;
- building materials depend on remote extraction and relatively high energy use.

Bradley Stoke is not exceptional. On the contrary it represents the suburban norm. It helps to emphasize the conceptual distance that large-builders – and many local authorities – will have to travel if sustainable patterns of development are to be achieved. Houses with double garages in a secluded cul-de-sac are saleable to home buyers irrespective of the provision of facilities and the needs of the housing/transport poor. Planning authorities have connived by stressing housing numbers over environmental quality and market facilitation over market guidance. One might be forgiven for suspecting a malign plot to reinforce materialism and consumerism at the expense both of individual choice and local social cohesion.

There is of course an alternative view. The remorseless decline in the significance of locality is a direct reflection of lifestyle changes as people have chosen to buy cars with their increased wealth and diversified their formal and informal social networks. The local place community no longer provides the key social arena for most people, and for some it does not exist at all, replaced by what Melvin Webber (1962) called 'non-place communities' – interest or activity-based social networks centred on work, school, club, historic associations or dispersed extended families. The local facilities that fostered local social networks have decayed, and while that creates problems for the few it is symptomatic of a richer, more diversified life for the many. The change is inevitable and should be welcomed, while at the same time the most vulnerable are protected from its impact.

## OFFICIAL POLICY

European and national agencies, however, adopt neither view, neither seeking to demonize the housing/planning system nor exonerate it. They are strongly influenced by growing concern for healthy local environments and healthy global ecology. *The Green Paper on the Urban Environment* (CEC, 1990) advocated compact, mixed use cities with reduced car reliance, creating convenient and convivial localities. This was followed by the Fifth Environmental Action Programme 'Towards Sustainability', which identified the 'need for a far-sighted, cohesive and effective approach to attain sustainable development' (CEC, 1996). The World Health Organization's European Healthy Cities programme echoes these principles, stressing walking, cycling and pollution-free neighbourhoods in current guidance (1999). The UK Government has accepted the obligation of the Earth Summit accords with its original *Sustainable Development Strategy* of 1994 (impressive in its breadth of vision but short on implementation) and the follow-up *Opportunities for Change* (DETR, 1998d) – which is altogether more adventurous and committed politically.

The recent guide *Planning for Sustainable Development* promotes the idea that planning authorities should develop a 'strategic vision' for existing urban areas, looking 25 years ahead. The importance of neighbourhoods is stressed, and the guide suggests they should have:

• An identified centre, focused on public transport nodes, where new local facilities will be concentrated. A centre will normally comprise shops, a mix of community-based services and some higher density housing. It should be easily reached from surrounding residential areas by foot and cycle;

- Areas of higher density housing close to the centre, which will help to support its range of services, and which will have low car use because those services are close by;
- Their own distinctive character which reflects their history, topography and landscape which is defined by their range and type of housing and by related development. (DETR, 1998c).

The difficulty with environmentally-driven visions and advocacy documents is that they can reflect pious hopes rather than economic and social reality. Sustainable development can become a '"holy grail" ... hallowed by the Earth Summit in Rio 1992, invoked by pundits, planners and politicians to lend credibility to argument and yet – a strangely ineffable concept, hard to pin down, harder still to achieve' (Barton and Bruder, 1995). Local decision-making by people in LA21 collaboration is seen as obligatory, but many of the assumptions of localism are 'shrouded in a good deal of meaningless rhetoric' (Selman, 1996). Marvin and Guy (1997) suggest that in the 'New Localist' faith the 'locality becomes viewed as some sort of container or black box which can be physically and socially shaped to deliver a more sustainable future.' They point to the comfortable myths that have grown up round the idea of sustain-ability – myths that tacitly ignore the central role of national governments and international capitalism and overplay the role of local authorities and design solutions. Their shot across the bows of the LA21 business is well aimed. There is a profound danger of raising local expectations which cannot be fulfilled because of deeper structural factors, and an incipient eco-fascism amongst some activists which would restrict choice and *oblige* lifestyle change.

However, the inflated language and naiveté of some populist advocates of the new localism is no excuse for armchair agnosticism. The evolution of localities in response to market imperatives and state/municipal myopia has contributed to an inequitable and resource-destructive urban environment, and the resulting problems need to addressed. A hopeful sign is the range of social and economic agencies that are beginning to promote an integrated and locally-aware approach. The recent Health green paper, for example, highlights the importance of local communities and the quality of the local environment in targeting healthy lifestyles and mental health (DHSS, 1998). The Social Exclusion Unit set up by the Labour Government is deeply concerned with the lack of effective capacity to tackle problems at the neigh-bourhood level, and programmes such as the Single Regeneration Budget and the 'Best Value' initiative look to the level of local community engage-ment as a criterion for judging success (see Chapter 11). More generally there is growing recognition of the importance of 'social capital', and of the self-reliance of local economies – concepts which have interesting parallels with the principles of environmental sustainability. All this national concern points to the growing centrality of sustainable localities and communities in the policy arena – at least in principle.

## ACCIDENTAL TOWNS

Within the sphere of town planning few UK local authorities are as yet running with these localization principles (McGill, 1999). But there are exceptions, for example, the Hulme project in Manchester, the Ashton Green Development Codes (Leicester City Council, 1998), and the Forest of Dean Residential Design Guide (1998). Elsewhere, Queensland boasts a particularly well developed 'primer' for mixed use development (Morris and Kanfman, 1997), and certain countries, such as Denmark and The Netherlands, are ahead of the game – not only in relation to specific sustainability objectives but in the general orientation and commitment of a wide range of agencies and professions. Even in those states, however, the number of holistic sustainability projects at the neighbourhood scale is alarmingly small, and it is clear there are still barriers to implementation (see Chapter 5).

In the UK policy-makers have been more concerned with the overall pattern of urban growth – preoccupied with high forecasts of new household formation, the consequent fear of the loss of open countryside to housing development, and the pressure to accommodate as much development as possible on brownfield (ie previously developed) sites. Entangled with this political agenda is the issue of sustainable urban form: the advocates of compact urban development (which implies intensification and use of brownfield sites) arguing it out with those who favour new autonomous settlements or suburban restructuring. The empirical work appealed to by the protagonists has been largely about trips and transport energy use, comparing different locational patterns and settlement types (see Chapters 3 and 7).

Seen in the context of economic and social change, the strategic issues of settlement pattern are important. Yet it is arguable that the debates over levels of growth and brownfield versus greenfield are rather artificially generated by the planning conventions of the age, at the expense of a real concern for the nature of the development itself (whether in town or out of town). The development planning end-date of 2011 becomes for all practical purposes a horizon beyond which all problems can be safely ignored. The predicted figures of housing need and housing land, depending as they do on a wide range of assumptions about social trends and policy decisions, may well be fulfilled several years earlier or later than 2011. In that situation a focus on a specific figure becomes largely academic, but this arcane argument has sucked energy away from serious consideration of how new development might contribute to the creation of sustainable communities.

Even more worrying is the *closeness* of the 2011 horizon. It results in a 'hand-to-mouth' approach to housing provision. Local politicians seek to solve the immediate shortfall while ignoring longer term implications. Then the whole cycle of policy review occurs again a few years later with further incremental decisions geared to successive end-dates (2016, 2021). The political pressures in this situation are far from any concern for increasing equity, choice and the quality of life for this and the next generation. Instead they are all about reducing the political fallout from unpopular decisions, trying to minimize the visibility of policy initiatives by cutting the housing total, 'losing' development in-town, and 'spreading the pain' of greenfield development. Particularly worrying is the pressure to find urban development opportunities independently of coherent sustainability plans. Government has set ambitious targets for urban intensification – 60 per cent of all new development on brownfield sites. In searching for urban brownfields, authorities in the south of England (lacking the inheritance of dead industry found in the north) can be driven to compromize other legitimate planning goals. Housing takes over from playing fields, allotments, local small-scale industry and old institutional/cultural buildings which are important to a healthy, diverse, 'mixed use' urban neighbourhood.

The prevailing UK system is thus problematic at two levels: at the strategic level the housing/commercial land allocations are serial blueprints, geared to the spurious certainty of a specific end-date. At the local level the emphasis is all on *whether* a particular piece of land is developed, not *how* it is developed. This approach to land release allows development to occur site by site on a disaggregated basis, often with each development turning its back on its neighbour, lacking neighbourhood focus or the integrated eco-system approach demanded for sustainability.

The system is inadvertently creating 'accidental' towns – socially inequitable and resource-intensive. The interests of people, living locally, are marginalized.

## THE AGENDA FOR DEBATE

It is the purpose of this book to redress the balance and help rehabilitate the neighbourhood scale in relation to both research and policy. The foregoing discussion has raised a series of important questions which need addressing hereafter. It is not our intention to side-step the awkward issues raised – for example about the significance of locality and local communities in an affluent, mobile society – but rather to examine them from a range of viewpoints.

### 1.  Are Neighbourhoods Important?

The significance of locality is stressed by sustainability literature and LA21 but diminished by behaviourist research and tacitly ignored by many planning and development agencies. Most chapters provide insight into the question but Nigel Taylor (Chapter 2) and Hugh Barton (Chapter 4) address it head on – Taylor adopts a consciously agnostic stance, while Barton makes a pro-neighbourhood argument, examining both the *desirability* and *feasibility* of neighbourhoods.

### 2.  Is There a Role for Local Place Communities?

Bearing in mind the distinction drawn between 'neighbourhood' and 'community', there is uncertainty about the relationship between the two. Alison Gilchrist examines the significance of local communities in an inner city locality (Chapter 9). Janet Rowe and Celia Robbins evaluate the effectiveness of community-based initiatives (Chapter 10).

### 3.  *How Far does Current Practice Achieve Sustainable Neighbourhoods?*

Dominic Stead (Chapter 3) shows the degree to which general trends reinforce unsustainbility. Hugh Barton and Deborah Kleiner (Chapter 5) examine a range of innovative projects around the world that break the mould.

### 4.  *What Principles Should Guide the Planning of Neighbourhoods?*

In Chapters 6, 7 and 8 Hugh Barton begins to develop a theory of neighbourhoods as social and spatial entities, taking the neighbourhood as an ecosystem as the conceptual model, then linking that to urban form theory and principles of neighbourhood design.

### 5.  *What is the Potential for Local Resource Autonomy?*

Specific technologies are well developed but have not percolated through to the commonplace. Trevor Houghton (Chapter 12) examines the potential for energy autonomy, within current economic and institutional constraints. Rob Hopkins (Chapter 13) advocates a permaculture approach to local food production.

### 6.  *What is the Potential for Local Health and Safety?*

The pedestrian-hostile environments of some contemporary developments have been stressed. Tony Hathway (Chapter 14) looks at the potential for a pedestrian friendly, traffic-calmed environment. Henry Shaftoe reviews the arguments about community safety (Chapter 15).

### 7.  *What are the Implications for the Decision-Making Process?*

LA21 lays great emphasis on the community approach, but this is not necessarily effective in practice. Murray Stewart (Chapter 11) examines the potential for decentralized and multi-agency decision-making. And in the final chapter Hugh Barton applies this thinking to the development process.

# 2 ECO-VILLAGES: DREAM AND REALITY

*Nigel Taylor*

*'What matters at this stage is the construction of local forms of community within which civility and the intellectual and moral life can be sustained through the new dark ages which are already upon us'* (Alasdair MacIntyre: After Virtue)

*'We should avoid the romanticised view of (local) community which has often surfaced in social analysis ... In the large majority of pre-modern settings, including most cities, the local milieu is the site of clusters of interweaving social relations ... But the large majority of the population were relatively immobile and isolated, as compared to the regular and dense forms of mobility (and awareness of other ways of life) provided for by modern means of transportation. The locality in pre-modern contexts is the focus of, and contributes to, ontological security in ways that are substantially dissolved in circumstances of modernity'* (Anthony Giddens: The Consequences of Modernity)

## INTRODUCTION: VILLAGES, LOCALITIES, AND ENVIRONMENTAL SUSTAINABILITY

There is something new in the proposal for eco-villages (or, for that matter, eco-neighbourhoods), namely, they are *eco* villages (or neighbourhoods).[1] The idea has emerged primarily because of our current concern with the ecological damage being done to the planet and our corresponding concern to construct environmentally sustainable ways of living. But there is also something old in the proposal; they are (eco) *villages*. And, in a world where people have come increasingly to inhabit large towns and cities, the question naturally arises: why propose *villages*? Why not towns, or cities, or metropolises?

---

1 The Note on Terminology at the end of the *Preface* sets out the equivalence of these terms.

One answer is that one way of constructing a way of life which is more sustainable is to construct more local ways of living, for if the inhabitants of an area also work, play, go to school and shop within their locality then, obviously, they will travel less and so not draw on non-renewable and/or polluting energy resources to get around. They can walk, or cycle, instead of going by car or bus. So the idea of the eco-village is really a short-hand for denoting a form of life in which people's activities are based, to a much greater extent than now, in their immediate *locality*.

However, since proposals for what we ought to do must be practicable ('ought' implies 'can'), the question arises as to what are the prospects of feasibly constructing such local forms of life now, in the late 20th and early 21st centuries, when most people have ceased to live much of their lives locally. In this chapter, I subject the idea of eco-villages to critical scrutiny. In contrast to most of the papers in this volume, I shall not start with the idea of eco-villages as a desirable given, and then examine ways in which they have been or might be realized in terms of local water supply and food production, waste disposal and recycling, energy and transport, employment and governance. Rather, I shall raise some uncomfortable questions about the whole idea that the creation of eco-villages is a useful project for those who are committed to the cause of environmental sustainability (and I assume we are all committed to that cause).

Put like this, this chapter could be viewed as voicing opposition to rest of the chapters in this volume. But that would be too hasty. For my argument is not one of outright opposition; it is more complex than that. Indeed, the general project of nurturing local forms of action which contribute to environmental sustainability (and in *this sense* creating 'eco-villages') is one I endorse. But we need to acknowledge powerful tendencies in the modern world which run counter to the project of creating local communities or even forms of life in which people live out much of their lives within a given locality. Because of these tendencies, I think the eco-village project needs to be distinguished – and indeed, uncoupled – from the project of creating local forms of community (and hence eco-villages in the *social* sense). To mark the difference, I suggest that it would be better to re-name the project to encourage forms of environmentally sustainable action which are based on small-scale 'local' areas as one of encouraging the development of 'eco-localities', rather than 'eco-villages'. But, in any case, I shall also argue that locality-based action contributing to environmental sustainability needs to be seen in the context of wider global forces affecting environmental sustainability. Accordingly, I suggest that the main arenas in which the battle for environmental sustainability needs to be fought are at the national and international, rather than the local, levels.

With respect to town planning thought and practice, there has been a long tradition of seeking to create local, village-like neighbourhoods and communities. I therefore begin this chapter by describing this historical background and tentatively suggesting that the idea of eco-villages may represent a continuation of this tradition. If so, then it is important to recall that attempts to create local communities by physical planning have not been successful. It is possible, however, to envisage eco-villages as places where the inhabitants live out their lives more locally but without constituting a traditional, territorially-based 'community'. I consider this possibility and express scepticism with it by drawing attention to some of the 'non-localising' forces of modernity which have not only fragmented local community, but also local forms of life. The arguments above do not lead me to reject the project of planning for environmental sustainability at the local level (the project of Local Agenda 21). But I am led to conclude that we should uncouple the project of working at the local level for environmental sustainability from the project of creating local communities or of trying to plan for life to be lived more locally. In case this conclusion seems a bit downbeat as far as the prospects for environmental sustainability are concerned, I conclude the chapter by stressing that the local arena is not the only, and not even the main, level where the battle for environmental sustainability needs to be fought.

## HISTORICAL BACKGROUND: VILLAGES, NEIGHBOURHOODS AND COMMUNITIES IN TOWN PLANNING THOUGHT AND PRACTICE

The idea (and ideal) of the village (or, in urban contexts, the neighbourhood) and its associated community has exercised a powerful influence on town planning thought, especially in the UK, ever since the emergence of the modern town planning movement in the early 19th century. That movement was rooted in an outrage felt about the living conditions in the cities which emerged in the industrial revolution. This, coupled with a natural nostalgia for the rural way of life and its associated settlements which were being lost under the rising tide of industrial urbanization, led many of the early town planning thinkers in the 19th century to turn their backs on the city and look for the solution to urban problems in terms of more traditional settlement forms, such as the small town or village. As many writers have observed, there has been a powerful current of 'anti-urbanism' running through modern town planning thought (see: Glass, 1959; Foley, 1960; Jacobs, 1961; Williams, 1973; Mellor, 1977 and 1982; Wilson, 1991).

Thus from Robert Owen's project of New Lanark onwards, it was widely assumed by 19th century philanthropists and urban reformers that the village, or something like it, was the ideal settlement for human beings to inhabit, and hence one we should seek to create to replace large cities. In the 19th century, a number of industrial philanthropists followed Owen in constructing planned villages as prototypes of the ideal settlement, eg Ackroyd's Copley and Ackroydon; Salt's Saltaire; Cadbury's Bourneville; Lever's Port Sunlight; and Rowntree's New Earswick. As Tony Scrase (1983) has commented, these 'nineteenth century Utopias are all heavily marked by romanticism, showing a preference for small, self-contained communities and allowing the inhabitants to work for at least part of their time in agriculture or their gardens'.

The 19th century model villages played a key role in shaping town planning ideas into the 20th century. Ebenezer Howard's proposals for garden cities grew out of this tradition. To be sure, Howard was at pains to stress that his garden cities were *cities*, enjoying all the benefits of urbanity alongside the benefits of proximity to the countryside. But the fact remains that what Howard proposed were essentially small country towns, and in this his proposals exhibited an antagonism to the large city. As Jane Jacobs (1961) pointed out in this acerbic comment:

> 'Howard set spinning powerful and city-destroying ideas: he conceived that the way to deal with the city's functions was to sort and sift out of the whole certain simple uses, and to arrange these in relative self-containment... He was uninterested in the aspects of the city which could not be abstracted to serve his Utopia. In particular, he simply wrote off the intricate, many-faceted cultural life of the metropolis. He was uninterested in such problems as the way great cities police themselves, or exchange ideas, or operate politically, or invent new economic arrangements, and he was oblivious to devising ways to strengthen these functions because, after all, he was not designing for this kind of life in any case.'

In spite of this, Howard's planning ideas, together with those of his architectural disciple Raymond Unwin, have had an enormous influence on British town planning thought and practice through the 20th century. As Gordon Cherry (1996) observed: 'The preferred British model remained the decentralist tradition based on Howard's garden city and Unwin's style of cottage architecture...' One of the major pressure groups in the UK for town planning in the early 20th century was the Garden Cities and Town Planning Association, which was founded in 1899 explicitly to promulgate Howard's garden city planning ideas. In 1941 this became the Town and Country Planning Association, and campaigned with considerable success for green belts around major cities and the building of new towns. Patrick Abercrombie's Greater London Plan of 1944 gave expression to these ideas, with its proposal for a green belt around London with a ring of satellite towns – envisaged as Howardian garden cities – beyond it. The aim of planning these new towns as relatively *self-contained* settlements, so that their residents would not only live but also work, go to school, shop and play locally, also illustrated the persistence of the village ideal of a local, relatively self-sufficient community (see also Hall et al, 1973, Vol 2).

Within the context of garden city planning, the idea of neighbourhood planning was another expression of the ideal of creating village-like communities. The idea of neighbourhood planning originated in the 1920s with the work of the American sociologist Clarence Perry (1939), who proposed the division of the city into distinct neighbourhood units, each with its own local communal facilities such as convenience shops, a primary school, a church, a local park. Further, these facilities were to be located at the centre of the neighbourhood so that they would be within walking distance of, and so act as a social focus for, the inhabitants of the neighbourhood. In this way, it was envisaged that the neighbourhood would function as a relatively self-contained unit, and thereby promote local social life, or a local community. As Cherry (1996) observed, neighbourhoods were conceived by town planning theorists as 'self-contained islands for particular communities' – in other words, as 'villages in the city' (Taylor, 1973). Along with Howard's garden city, Perry's vision of neighbourhoods as relatively self-contained local communities also became very influential in British town planning after the Second World War. Thus the neighbourhood unit became a central building block, or structuring device, in the plans for all the post-war new towns, as well as in Abercrombie's plan for London itself.

All this, of course, is just history. But it is a history which shows how the idea of the village, as a physical place and a social community, has exercised something of an hypnotic attraction for town planning theorists ever since the industrial revolution. Against this background, contemporary proposals for planning eco-villages (or neighbourhoods) can be interpreted as a perpetuation of this old ideal of seeking to create small, village-like, relatively self-contained communities. To the extent that there are similarities between traditional town planning ideas of local community planning, and recent conceptions of eco-villages, it is worth reminding ourselves that the attempts to create such local self-contained communities by physical planning have generally failed. They have done so because, as sociologists like Maurice Broady and Norman Dennis pointed out 30 years ago, the main factors giving rise to territorial social communities are social, not physical (Broady, 1968; Dennis, 1968; see also Evans, 1994). In particular, local communities tend to arise where, firstly, the inhabitants of an area lack any real choice to move away from their locality and so come to be acquainted with each other through long-term residence; secondly, where the majority of these inhabitants share a common social position and so tend also to share similar interests, attitudes and values; and thirdly, where the inhabitants of a given area face similar problems and difficulties, and so come to cooperate with each other to combat adversity. Generalizing, local territorial communities have tended to arise in areas where there is the common experience of economic hardship and territorial immobility. Of itself, therefore, the physical planning of distinct territories as neighbourhoods or villages has played a negligible role in fostering territorial or locality-based communities. To the extent, then, that the project of creating eco-villages implies the attempt to create something like local communities (and sustainable communities), then it seems doomed to fail along with its predecessors.

## THE FRAGMENTATION OF LOCALITY-BASED FORMS OF LIFE IN THE CIRCUMSTANCES OF MODERNITY

In response to the foregoing observations about the conditions of territorial communities, supporters of the idea of eco-villages might reply that they do not have to be lumbered with the conceptual baggage of the traditional village or close-knit territorial community. Accordingly (they may say), they can readily discard the traditional 'village-in-the-city' planning ideas as outmoded and irrelevant to current concerns. After all, what they are proposing are *eco*-villages, not just villages as such, and the appellation of the term village (or neighbourhood) is simply a turn of phrase which should not be interpreted as implying anything like a traditional village or community.

Certainly, it is *logically* possible to conceive of districts – termed neigh-bourhoods or villages – which are physically or geographically distinct, and in which the inhabitants shop, play, go to school and work locally in ways which would assist the cause of environmental sustainability, but where these people don't relate to each other in ways which constitute a social community. About this, however, two points need to be made. First, it is extremely unlikely that, *if* the inhabitants of a locality lived much of their life locally, they would not at the same time develop the kind of social relationships which are constitutive of a local social community. For as noted above, one of the preconditions of traditional communities is relative immobility; where people share the same confined territory over long periods of time, they tend to develop relation-ships with each other which are constitutive of community. As Giddens (1990) observes, where 'the local milieu is the site of clusters of interweaving social relations, the low spatial span ... provides for their solidity in time.'

Second, however, even if we can imagine the inhabitants of an eco-village not relating to each other in ways which would form a social community, the idea of eco-villages still presumes that the inhabitants of these villages would engage in more activities, and in this sense live out more of their lives, *locally*, ie in the eco-village itself, or its immediate environs. And if they are doing this, then the inhabitants of eco-villages would, in this respect, be living their lives as people lived them in the traditional village; that is, they would be (largely) tied to their locality. So even if we set aside the idea of trying to create local communities as not relevant to the project of eco villages, we are still left with the project of creating circumstances in which the inhabitants of localities live more of their lives within their locality. We therefore have to consider the feasi-bility of this.

Here again, the prospects for this project are not very encouraging, at least in the developed countries of the western world. For a key feature of urban life in developed industrialized societies in the modern age has been the increasing adoption of spatially extensive ways of life which have loosened people's ties to the localities or neighbourhoods in which they reside. As Melvin Webber (1964) wrote over 30 years ago, urban communities have become 'spatially extensive ... in which urbanites interact with other urbanites wherever they may be... It is interaction, not place, that is the essence of the city and of city life.' Or, to be more precise (since there is no inevitable or timeless essence to cities or city life), interaction has become the essence of the *modern* city.

The trend towards what Webber called the 'nonplace urban realm' began in the late 19th and early 20th centuries, with the development of mass rail transit systems into and out of major cities, and the consequent development of residential suburbs which enabled people to work in the centre of big cities like London, yet live in suburbs 30 or more miles away (see Sennett 1994 for a vivid account of the effects of commuting on social behaviour). This trend has contin-ued to develop throughout the 20th century. In the first half of the century, it was mostly office workers who were involved in commuting from their home-places in the suburbs to offices located in the centres of cities. This was followed, from the 1920s onwards, with the dispersal of light industrial facto-ries to suburban 'trading estates' (see Hall et al, 1973, Vol 1). More recently, traditional city centre activities such as offices and shops have also sought more spacious suburban locations in 'office parks' and out-of-town shopping centres, giving rise to the phenomenon of 'edge cities' (Garreau, 1991).

This loosening of the previously tightly packed pattern of urban land uses, and with it the uncoupling of people's workplaces with their homeplaces, has of course been driven by developments in transport technology, and especially, since the 1930s, the motor car. Thus since the 1960s in the UK, the development of motorways (together with fast inter-city train services) have enabled people to live still further away from their work-place. At the same time, rising material standards of living, accompanied with widening educational and employment opportunities, have further contributed to the loosening of people's ties to place (recall, again, that economic hardship has been a condition of the traditional territorial community). Again in the UK, from the 1960s onwards, an increasing number of people have moved away from their original home places to go to college or seek new work. And even when people do not move because of work or college, increasing standards of living have encouraged people to move their homes more often, so that the home itself is less fixed than it used to be. All this is well known; as is commonly said, we inhabit a 'mobile society'. But it reinforces Webber's contention that people have come increasingly to inhabit a 'nonplace urban realm', and are correspondingly less tied to particular localities or neighbourhoods.

Moreover, it is not just that people are no longer so tied to the localities within which they reside. These localities themselves have been increasingly penetrated by non-local forces and goods, and so are no longer so distinctly local. Thus local shops have given way to national chains of supermarkets selling standardized products, local buildings are often no longer constructed in local materials, even the news in localities is less local and more dominated by news from distant places transmitted by national media. Localities are therefore no longer experienced *as* localities in the old sense; what were once distinct places have become 'placeless' (Relph, 1976). The whole process is vividly described by Anthony Giddens (1990) as one of 'disembedding':

> '*The primacy of place in pre-modern settings has been largely destroyed by disembedding and time-space distanciation. Place has become phantasmagoric because the structures by means of which it is constituted are no longer locally organized. The local and the global, in other words, have become inextricably intertwined. Feelings of close attachment to or identification with places still persist. But these are themselves disembedded: they do not express locally based practices and involvements but are shot through with much more distant influences. Even the smallest of neighbourhood stores, for example, probably obtains its goods from all over the world. The local community is not a saturated environment of familiar, taken-for-granted meanings, but in some large part a locally-situated expression of distanciated relations.*'

In the light of these trends the project of bringing about settlements (eco-villages) in which more people live more of their lives locally is one which runs counter to, and therefore involves a reversal of, modern urban life. In itself, this does not render the project undesirable in principle, and certainly not if the achievement of environmental sustainability *requires* that we live more locally. But the aims we set ourselves must be feasible or realistic in given social and economic circumstances; to prescribe what we ought to do must entail that we can do it. And the fact that the project of eco-villages runs counter to the form of life which has developed in conditions of modernity raises, at the very least, a serious question mark over the feasibility of this project.

To be sure, contemporary life is not inevitably set on a non-localizing, 'disembedding' track. Indeed, some contemporary developments may pre-figure a return to more locally based lifestyles (some of these developments are described in other chapters of this book). For example, the home computer and the world-wide web increase the opportunities for some people to work at home; the radio and recorded music, the television and the video have created a world of entertainment in the home and so reduced trips people formerly took to the concert hall or the cinema; people can even study for degrees now by distance learning. As Giddens has acknowledged, there are 're-embedding' as well as disembedding processes at work in our age; for example, the 'self-same processes that lead to the destruction of older city neighbourhoods and their replacement by towering office-blocks and skyscrap-ers often permit the gentrification of other areas and a recreation of locality' (Giddens, 1990).

However, we cannot necessarily assume that these re-embedding tenden-cies will be sufficient to engender the degree of attachment to locality required to make the creation of eco-villages a feasible prospect. Clearly, there is need for more careful research on this, but already some research findings suggest the need for caution. For example, Owens and Cope (1992) doubt that teleworking is likely to bring about a significant shift to home-based employ-ment. And research by Farthing et al (1996) concludes that increasing the local availability of facilities such as shops and schools does not, of itself, result in a significant increase in local residents walking or using bicycles to get to those facilities.

## 'THINK GLOBALLY, ACT GLOBALLY' (AS WELL AS LOCALLY)

This chapter has expressed scepticism with the project of creating eco-villages. It has done so chiefly by drawing attention to features of our way of life which have loosened people's ties to the localities within which they reside. These facts about urban modernity cast doubt over the feasibility of the project of creating eco-villages in which there would be a significant increase in the numbers of people not only residing locally, but also working, shopping and going to school (etc) locally (not to mention their doing so by environmentally friendly ways of moving such as walking or cycling). To be sure, as noted at the end of the previous section, current trends may not continue, and counter-vailing re-embedding tendencies are possible. But even if non-localizing forces and ways of life remain predominant, what follows from this as far as the project of eco-villages is concerned? And what follows, too, as far as the more general project of creating environmentally sustainable ways of living is concerned?

We can restate the first question like this: if non-localizing forces and ways of life remain predominant, would it follow that we should abandon the project of eco-villages? Certainly, the continuing predominance of these modern forces and lifestyles would undermine the *likelihood of realizing* eco-villages on a significant scale, and so undermine the *feasibility* of the project. But it doesn't follow that we should *abandon* this project. For two reasons.

Firstly, even though, in the modern city, much of many people's lives are not lived in the neighbourhoods in which they reside, it still remains the case that local neighbourhoods exist – if only as distinguishable physical or geographical spaces. And with respect to these areas, it is possible to provide and/or organize things locally in ways which contribute to environmental sustainability, for example, by providing locally-based energy supply systems; local recycling of organic waste and refuse; local traffic restraint measures coupled with improvements to local facilities for walking and cycling; etc. Susan Owens (1986) has pointed to examples of local town councils around the world who have pursued such locally-based strategies (including physical planning strategies), and these forms of local action have made appreciable contributions to reducing energy consumption and emissions. So even if nothing could be done to bring about more local *lifestyles*, there remain environmentally friendly initiatives which can be pursued *at the level of the locality*. In other words, the fragmentation of local communities and local living does not preclude locally-based action of the kind instanced above. And if the eco-village project is reconceived in terms of such local action, it has a part to play in contributing to environmental sustainability.

Secondly, even if non-localizing forces and lifestyles continue to predominate, if these tendencies are demonstrably damaging to ecological stability, and if, too, it is shown that more locally-based lifestyles would be more environmentally friendly, then there remain good environmental reasons for trying to do whatever we can to resist the non-localizing trends of modernity. And developing eco-villages may be part of this strategy of resistance. In this regard, it is worth noting that, quite apart from questions of environmental sustainability, there may be *other* reasons for supporting the project of trying to facilitate more local ways of life. For while the freeing of people from locality which has been such a central feature of modernity may have brought with it some benefits, there are also advantages in living in a locality where one also works, shops, and enjoys much of one's leisure time. As Breheny (1992b) observes: 'advocacy of the compact city rests not just on strictly environmental criteria of energy consumption and emissions, but also on *quality of life* grounds'. To the extent, then, that town planning (together with other avenues of public policy) can foster conditions which encourage more people to live more of their lives locally, then it should do so for these quality of life reasons as well as for any reasons of environmental sustainability. Of course, as this chapter has tried to make plain, the continued predominance of the non-localizing tendencies of modernity diminishes the chances of this project being successfully realized. But the predominance of these forces does not of itself invalidate the project of eco-villages, because there may still be good reasons for *trying* to resist these forces.

But suppose the predominance of non-localizing forces and lifestyles does render the project of eco-villages unrealizable on a scale that would make a significant contribution to the cause of environmental sustainability (not to mention the quality of life generally). Should we be depressed by this? That depends on how significant the project of eco-villages, and more generally of local forms of environmentally friendly action, is to the overall goal of environmental sustainability. And this brings me to the second question I promised to deal with in this conclusion.

We can put that second question like this. Suppose non-localizing forces and ways of life continue to predominate (and thereby render the project of eco-villages unrealizable to any significant degree), is this necessarily damaging to the overall cause of environmental sustainability? No, not necessarily. Consider, here, the well-known slogan of the Green movement to 'think globally, act locally'. This maxim rightly draws our attention to the fact that the carrying capacity of our planet to sustain human life is a global issue. It is global because what is done in one part of the globe (such as polluting the seas or atmosphere) may carry to other parts of the globe thousands of miles away. And it is global because, although the sources of ecological damage are not spread *evenly* around the globe (eg the US, with only about 5 per cent of the world's population, creates something like 20 per cent of the world's greenhouse gas emissions), the sources of ecological damage are, either actually or potentially, *located* around the globe. This being so, the injunction of Greens to act locally is curious. If the causes of non-sustainable development are global, then surely we must find ways of acting globally, not just locally. Indeed, the global reach of the sources of environmental problems makes action at this global level more important than action at the local level. Thus it will be, for example, national and international action which alters the technology of transport, which fosters the development of renewable and non-greenhouse gas emitting sources of energy, which encourages environmentally friendly forms of industrial and agricultural production, which encourages waste recycling systems, and so on, which will make the most significant advances in creating environmentally sustainable ways of life across the globe.

This connects with some of the facts about modern life which I have drawn attention to in this chapter. Increasingly across the globe people have come to live in big cities. And in these cities many live that mobile and spatially extensive way of life which is characteristic of modernity. Given this, it is research and action designed to make *this modern and urban* way of life more environmentally sustainable which will contribute most to the cause of sustainability. Once again, this is not an argument against eco-villages. But it is an argument for seeing that project in perspective. The real challenge facing us is not one of building eco-villages, but of making the modern city, and the way of life lived in it, environmentally sustainable.

# 3 UNSUSTAINABLE SETTLEMENTS

*Dominic Stead*

## INTRODUCTION

This chapter examines why current trends in planning settlements are unsustainable and the lessons that can be drawn if they are to be planned more sustainably in the future. Two main planning trends are examined: the dispersal of population and activities and the centralization of services and facilities. The chapter then identifies some of the environmental consequences of these two planning trends, and discusses ways in which land use planning might reverse these unsustainable trends. The chapter shows how a strategy of decentralized concentration may lead to more sustainable patterns of development, which has a number of implications for the planning of neighbourhoods. Although the focus of this chapter is primarily the UK, many of the trends in land use, impacts and recommendations are applicable in a wider context.

## UNSUSTAINABLE LAND USE TRENDS

### The Dispersal of Population and Activities

Evidence from previous censuses highlights a continuing decline in population in large urban areas and an increase in population in rural areas (Table 3.1). Between 1981 and 1991, the population of London and the metropolitan districts fell by approximately 903,000, whilst the population of the rest of England and Wales increased by approximately 846,000 (Breheny and Rockwood, 1993).

The population dispersal trends between 1981 and 1991 are a continuation of trends over a longer timescale of 30 years or more (see for example Fielding and Halford, 1990). Rural areas have experienced highest population increases in percentage and absolute terms. These changes in population have been accompanied by shifts in employment and retailing but evidence suggests that the dispersal is associated with longer travel distances, fewer journeys by foot or bicycle and the increased reliance on private transport (ECOTEC, 1993). Travel distance in rural areas is more than 50 per cent higher than in large metropolitan areas, whilst travel distance by foot in rural areas is below half that in metropolitan areas (ibid).

**Table 3.1** *Population Change in England and Wales between 1971 and 1991*

| | 1961–1971 | | 1971–1981 | | 1981–1991 | |
|---|---|---|---|---|---|---|
| | Population increase (x 1000) | Population increase (%) | Population increase (x 1000) | Population increase (%) | Population increase (x 1000) | Population increase (%) |
| *London* | | | | | | |
| inner London boroughs | −461 | −13.2 | −535 | −17.7 | −147 | −5.9 |
| outer London boroughs | −81 | −1.8 | −221 | −5.0 | −171 | −4.2 |
| *Metropolitan Districts* | | | | | | |
| principal cities | −355 | −8.4 | −386 | −10.0 | −258 | −7.4 |
| others | +412 | +5.5 | −160 | −2.0 | −327 | −4.2 |
| *Non-Metropolitan Districts* | | | | | | |
| large cities | −41 | −1.4 | −149 | −5.1 | −98 | −3.6 |
| smaller cities | +38 | +2.2 | −55 | −3.2 | +5 | +0.3 |
| *Industrial Districts* | | | | | | |
| Wales and N regions | +118 | +1.3 | +42 | +1.3 | −72 | −2.1 |
| rest of England | +342 | +5.0 | +158 | +5.0 | +59 | +1.8 |
| *New Towns* | +337 | +21.8 | +283 | +15.1 | +133 | +6.1 |
| *Resort and Retirement* | +3461 | +2.2 | +156 | +4.9 | +174 | +5.2 |
| *Mixed and Accessible Rural* | | | | | | |
| outside SE England | +6272 | +1.9 | +307 | +8.8 | +156 | +4.1 |
| inside SE England | +9602 | +2.1 | +354 | +6.8 | +162 | +2.9 |
| *Remote Largely Rural* | +399 | +9.7 | +468 | +10.3 | +328 | +6.4 |
| *England and Wales* | +2629 | +5.7 | +262 | +0.5 | −57 | +0.1 |

*Source:* Breheny and Rockwood, 1993

At the same time as the dispersal of population, employment, leisure and retail developments have moved to outer city locations and to small and medium-sized settlements, although much employment remains within large urban areas. Current flows in population are following a 'counterurbanisation cascade' in which the population is steadily moving from larger to smaller towns and cities and from inner urban areas to peripheral and more remote areas (Figure 3.1).

The development of out-of-town shopping centres and retail parks has added to the use of greenfield land and has also contributed to the decline of

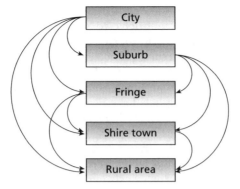

Source: Champion et al, 1998

**Figure 3.1** *The 'Counterurbanization Cascade' of Population*

town and city centres. Large out of town retail centres (those with a floorspace greater than 5000 square metres) covered an estimated 1.4 million square metres in 1985 and almost 4.7 million square metres by the end of 1990, representing more than a three-fold increase in five years (DoE, 1996a). Slower growth in economic activity since 1990 has caused a slowdown in out of town development but the increase in out of town development has continued.

The dispersal of population and activities has clearly increased the development pressure on greenfield land although the use of greenfield land for housing was reduced in the last decade (DETR, 1997c). Over half of the area of new housing was developed on greenfield land in 1985 whereas just under 40 per cent of the area of new housing was built on greenfield land in 1994. The consumption of greenfield land nevertheless continues albeit as a smaller proportion of all land used. The consumption of greenfield land could increase if the supply of brownfield land falls. According to recent government forecasts the increase in new households between 1991 and 2016 may be 4.4 million (DoE, 1996a). Assuming that 40 per cent of these new households are built on greenfield sites at a gross density of 40 houses per hectare (which is well above the average local authority density standard reported by Breheny and Archer, 1998), 44,000 hectares of greenfield land will be required (equivalent to 1760 hectares per year). A similar amount of land may be required to accommodate the development of industry, commerce and transport infrastructure. Despite the introduction of density considerations into Planning Policy Guidance Note 13 (PPG13) in 1994 (DoE, 1995) there are few signs that development densities are increasing (see Breheny and Archer, 1998).

## The Centralization of Services and Facilities

Many different types of services and facilities have been centralized, where fewer, larger services and facilities have replaced a large number of small-scale ones. Examples include shops, schools and hospitals. The total number of retail outlets has declined by more than 15 per cent over the last decade, whilst the number and proportion of supermarkets has increased (Central Statistical Office, 1997). Supermarkets have eroded the profitability of smaller shops and forced some out of business. Many supermarkets are at edge of town or out of town locations which are not conducive to short journeys and encourage shopping by car. Smaller schools have been closed and the concept of school catchments has lessened as a consequence of the increasing emphasis on parental choice (see for example Stead and Davis, 1998). These factors have acted to increase travel distances and increase reliance on motorized forms of transport. Similarly smaller hospitals have been closed because it is claimed that larger hospitals are needed to provide specialized treatment. Elkin et al (1991) argue however that specialized treatment is a small part of medical care and that a larger number of smaller medical facilities would be preferable from the perspective of both patient and service provider.

In addition to the centralization of existing services and facilities, few new services and facilities have been provided in major new residential developments. A study of facility provision and travel patterns in five major new housing developments in the west of England, each containing more than 1000 houses, reveals a paucity of provision (Farthing et al, 1997). None of the developments had their own bank, only one area had a secondary school and two developments did not have a post office or primary school.

Various economic, social and quality of life factors have influenced the land use changes described above but one of the most important factors has been the cost of transport. The real price of fuel and oil fell by almost 8 per cent between 1975 and 1995. The real cost of car travel, including the costs of insurance, servicing, repairs, road tax, fuel and oil, also fell (DoE, 1996b). During the same period the cost of bus and rail travel increased by over 50 per cent in real terms, higher than the increase in disposable income. Thus car travel became more affordable whilst public transport became more expensive.

The dispersal of population and activities and the centralization of services and facilities have clearly influenced the self-containment of settlements. Breheny (1992a) reports changes in the self-containment of new towns in Britain and comparable towns in southern England between 1951 and 1981, showing how self-containment in settlements reached a peak in the mid–1960s before the growth in mass car ownership and how self-containment has since declined. It is likely that land use trends such as the dispersal of population and activities and the centralization of services in combination with increasing levels of car ownership and use have led to the declining self-containment of settlements.

## Summary

The dispersal of population and activities and the centralization of services and facilities has led to a number of impacts on transport and the environment. Many of the impacts on transport have resulted in a vicious circle of decline in which land use changes have increased the need to travel and discouraged more sustainable modes. At the same time, higher rates of travel and car ownership have led to less sustainable patterns of development (Figure 3.2). Furthermore, the dispersal of population and activities and the centralization of services and facilities have led to social impacts such as the increased difficulty of carrying out day to day activities for less mobile groups of society (eg children and the elderly).

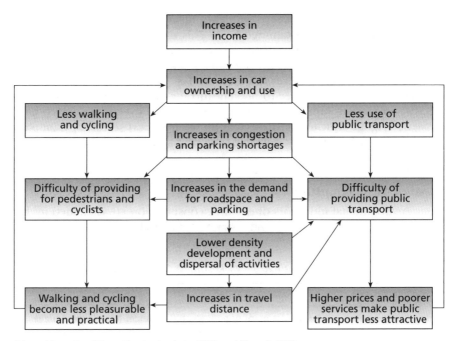

Adapted from: Royal Town Planning Institute, 1991, and Pharoah,1992

**Figure 3.2** *The Interaction of Driving Forces Behind Land Use Trends*

The planning of new development and its associated infrastructure has traditionally been based on a demand-led or 'predict and provide' approach, where trend-based projections are used to plan for future demand. Trends in the dispersal of population and activities and the centralization of services and facilities have occurred due to assumptions about continuing trends in travel and mobility for example. There are however environmental and social problems associated with a predict and provide approach. It assumes that there are no limits to growth and that demand can always be met. There are however clear limits to the growth of development in terms of resource and pollution constraints. The supply of land for infrastructure is finite and therefore limited, and the growth of transport is limited by air quality. There is evidence that there has been some move away from the predict and provide approach in the planning of new development and infrastructure over the last decade (see Guy and Marvin, 1996). A variety of factors have contributed to these changes and include regulatory, commercial, environmental and economic factors. However, the predict and provide approach is still strong in many aspects of the planning process.

## ENVIRONMENTAL IMPACTS OF RECENT PLANNING TRENDS

The environmental impacts of recent planning trends are examined using environmental indicators to illustrate changes over time. There are also social and economic impacts associated with current trends in planning new settlements but these are not examined here. This section focuses on two main types of environmental impacts: *resource consumption* and *environmental pollution*. Most indicators of environmental pollution and resource use represent impacts that have increased over the last decade and which deserve particular attention in order to prevent further increases. Other indicators however represent impacts which have not increased overall, but which have increased significantly in certain sectors (in the transport sector for example). The development of more sustainable settlements must clearly seek to reduce these impacts.

## Resource Consumption

Four environmental indicators of resource consumption are examined in this section: energy consumption, land urbanized, water abstraction and minerals extraction (Table 3.2).

**Table 3.2** *Indicators of Resource Consumption*

| Environmental Indicator | Environmental Impacts |
| --- | --- |
| Energy consumption | • depletion of non-renewable resources (mainly fossil fuels)<br>• emissions of carbon dioxide ($CO_2$), nitrogen oxides ($NO_x$), sulphur dioxide ($SO_2$) and particulates |
| Land urbanized | • depletion of agricultural land<br>• loss of ecological habitats, public open space and biodiversity |
| Water abstraction | • loss of ecological habitats and biodiversity with the construction of new reservoirs<br>• various impacts on the natural and built environment where the water table is lowered |
| Minerals extraction | • depletion of agricultural land<br>• loss of ecological habitats and biodiversity; landscape quality; various types of disturbance (noise, dust, etc) |

## Energy Consumption

Because energy supply in the UK is heavily based on fossil fuels, such as coal, gas and oil, energy consumption is an indicator of the depletion of non-renewable resources and the emissions of pollutants associated with the combustion of fossil fuels (such as carbon dioxide, sulphur dioxide and nitrogen oxides – see the following section on Environmental Pollution). Energy consumption per capita has remained fairly constant over the last decade, although the three main sectors experienced quite different trends. Energy consumption in the industry and commerce sector has decreased, whilst domestic energy consumption per capita have remained fairly constant. At the same time, however, energy consumption in the transport sector has increased. The transport sector is now the largest and fastest increasing consumer of energy, due principally to increased travel distances, the growth in road and air transport and the decline in more sustainable modes of transport such as walking and cycling. Vehicle engines have become more fuel efficient but factors including unleaded petrol, catalytic converters, higher safety standards, higher specifications and performance tended to counter the fuel efficiency gains from improved engine design (DoE 1996b). These factors, together with a fall in the average numbers of passengers per car and a fall in bus use, have caused a reduction in the overall fuel efficiency of road passenger transport. Despite evidence for a certain amount of policy reorientation over the period 1985 to 1995, specifically in relation to increased emphasis on demand management, the effects to date have been limited and there is considerable scope for greater energy efficiency in the transport and domestic sectors (see Chapters 14 and 12 respectively).

## Land Urbanized

The use of land for development is an indicator of the depletion of agricultural land. It is also an approximate indicator of the loss of ecological habitats, public open space and biodiversity. In 1985, over half of the area of new housing was developed on greenfield land, whereas less than 40 per cent of the area of new housing was developed on greenfield land in 1995. Similarly, over half of the area of non-housing development (mainly commercial and industrial property) was built on greenfield land in 1985, whereas less than 40 per cent of the area of non-housing development was built on greenfield land in 1995. The proportion of greenfield land is clearly decreasing but consumption is nevertheless still continuing (albeit at a slower rate). Thus, although a smaller proportion of development is being built on greenfield land than a decade ago, a substantial amount of greenfield land is being used for new development and the rate of consumption of greenfield land could begin to increase again if the supply of brownfield falls.

## Water Abstraction

Water abstraction is associated with environmental impacts such as the loss of land for the construction of reservoirs, and the possible loss of ecological habitats and biodiversity. Water abstraction is also an indicator of various impacts on the natural and built environment, such as species loss or building subsidence, caused by lowering of the water table. Water consumption per capita has fluctuated over the last decade but has overall remained fairly constant in both domestic and industrial/commercial sectors. Increased emphasis on demand management in the water sector appears to have had limited effect to date, and there is considerable scope for more efficient domestic water use, such as the use of 'grey-water' systems.

## Minerals Extraction

The extraction of minerals has implications for the depletion of agricultural land, the loss of ecological habitats and biodiversity, landscape quality, nuisance and disturbance (noise, dust, etc). Roadstone and sand and gravel are both extracted in large quantities in the UK, the majority of which is used in the development of settlements. Roadstone extraction per capita increased by almost one third between 1985 and 1995 as a consequence of increased road building and maintenance. The rate of extraction of sand and gravel decreased over this period. Nevertheless, these trends are unsustainable and substantial amounts of sand and gravel are still required for new development. More sustainable settlements must promote the use of fewer resources in both the construction and maintenance of development. There may be scope to reduce the consumption of consumption mineral resources by reducing the wastage of construction materials and increasing the amount of recycled building materials used.

## Environmental Pollution

Three environmental indicators of environmental pollution are examined in this section: carbon dioxide ($CO_2$), nitrogen oxides ($NO_x$) and particulates (Table 3.3).

**Table 3.3** *Indicators of Environmental Pollution*

| Environmental Indicator | Environmental Impacts |
| --- | --- |
| Carbon dioxide | • global pollution – contributes to the greenhouse effect |
| Nitrogen oxides | • local, national and transnational pollution – contributes to acid deposition and the formation of secondary local pollutants |
| Particulates | • local pollution – contributes to poor air quality and the staining of the built environment |

## Carbon Dioxide

Carbon dioxide ($CO_2$) is the most important greenhouse gas and is thought to be responsible for global warming and consequent climate change. Emissions of $CO_2$ are mainly produced by the combustion of fossil fuels for energy. Thus, $CO_2$ emissions are closely linked to energy consumption. Between 1985 and 1995, $CO_2$ emissions per capita in the UK remained relatively constant, in line with trends in energy consumption per capita (see above). On the basis of current projections, it seems likely that stabilisation of $CO_2$ emissions in the UK by 2000 may be met, but longer term targets of $CO_2$ reduction may be more difficult to achieve, due mainly to the growth in transport energy consumption. Trends in $CO_2$ emissions for the three main sectors (industry and commerce, transport and domestic) experienced different trends over the last decade. Domestic $CO_2$ emissions per capita remained fairly constant, whilst $CO_2$ emissions per capita from the industry and commerce sector fell. $CO_2$ emissions from the transport sector, on the other hand, increased and are likely to continue to increase unless traffic growth is strongly restrained. Economic and land use factors have contributed to the increases in transport-related $CO_2$ emissions (see previous section on Unsustainable Land Use Trends).

## Nitrogen Oxides

Nitrogen oxides ($NO_x$) cause national and transnational pollution and contribute to acid deposition. They also contribute to the formation of secondary pollutants, giving rise to photochemical smog and poor air quality. More than half of all $NO_x$ emissions now originate from road transport. Overall, $NO_x$ emissions decreased between 1985 and 1995. Emissions of $NO_x$

are relatively small in the domestic and industrial/commercial sectors, and both sectors experienced a decrease in $NO_X$ emissions. Emissions of $NO_X$ from the transport sector experienced a rapid increase up to 1989, followed by a steady decrease to 1995. Between 1985 and 1995, the net increase in $NO_X$ emissions from transport was approximately 4 per cent. Emissions of $NO_X$ are expected to continue to decrease beyond 2000 due largely to the reduction in emissions from road transport as a result of catalytic converters. However, $NO_X$ emissions may begin to increase again by around 2010 as increasing levels of traffic outweigh the emission reductions achieved by catalytic converters (see DETR, 1997e). Thus, technology might assist in reducing pollutants such as $NO_X$ in the short and medium term, but other solutions, such as land use planning are also needed to address the problem in the longer-term.

*Particulates*

The majority of particulates, mainly carbon and unburnt or partially burnt organic compounds, now originate from road transport although the domestic sector was the largest source of emissions 10 years ago. Airborne particulate matter is the primary cause of the soiling of buildings and visibility loss on hazy days. The medical impacts associated with particulates include respiratory problems, such as the increased susceptibility to asthma and mortality (Royal Commission on Environmental Pollution, 1994). Emissions of particulates from the industry and commerce sector have remained very low over the last decade. Emissions from the domestic sector have fallen substantially due to changes in domestic fuel from coal to gas, whilst emissions from the transport sector have increased rapidly as a result of the growth in traffic levels and the increased use of diesel which produces more particulate matter. Emissions of particulates, like emissions of $NO_X$, are expected to decrease until around 2010 after which they may begin increasing again as traffic growth outweighs the reductions achieved through technological means. Again, technology might assist in reducing pollution in the short and medium term, but land use planning is also needed to address the problem of particulates in the longer-term.

*Summary*

The indicators of resource consumption and environmental pollution examined above show that a number of environmental impacts associated with existing settlements and lifestyles are worsening, even within the timescale of a single decade. The indicators identify impacts that deserve particular attention if progress towards more sustainable development is to be made. Some of the indicators show that although environmental impacts are not currently increasing overall, certain sectors require particular attention if future increases in environmental impacts are to be avoided (in the transport sector for example). Technology might assist in reducing environmental pollution in the short and medium term, but other means of addressing the problem are also needed to in the longer-term. Land use planning and its influence on various environmental impacts has a role to play in this respect. The externalities of many environmental impacts are unequally spread. Groups who experience most environmental pollution may be those who contribute least. Urban residents, for example, are more likely to suffer from air pollution from transport but produce less pollution from transport than rural dwellers. As Korten (1995) observes:

> 'Although it is true that poor people are far more likely to be living next to waste dumps, polluting factories and other scenes of environmental devastation than are wealthy people, this doesn't mean that they are major consumers of the products in those factories.'

Land use planning offers opportunities to reduce the environmental impacts of settlements and also offers the potential to address the social inequalities of environmental pollution. Acutt and Dodgson (1996) show that land use planning is one of only a few measures that might both reduce travel and also contribute to a more equitable arrangement of land uses (Table 3.4). Furthermore, land use planning has the potential to address the causes of transport problems rather than the effects.

**Table 3.4** *Impacts of Policy Measures on Travel Distance (by Car) and Equity Issues*

| Policy | Travel distance by car | Equity issues |
|---|---|---|
| 1. Fuel taxes | Reduce total | Problems in rural areas |
| 2. Variable car excise taxes | No direct impact | Improvements |
| 3. Scrappage bounties | Small reduction | Improvements |
| 4. Road congestion pricing | Reduction in priced area, but may increase elsewhere | Ambiguous |
| 5. Vehicle use restrictions | Reduction | Ambiguous |
| 6. Parking charges | Reduction in priced area, but ambiguous in total | Ambiguous |
| 7. Parking controls | Reduction in controlled area, but may increase elsewhere | Ambiguous |
| 8. Land use planning | Reduction if policy successful | Possible long term improvement |
| 9. Traffic calming | Reduction in residential areas | Improvements possible |
| 10. Public transport subsidies | Reduce total, especially urban | Improvements |
| 11. Road construction | Increase | Could be negative |

*Source:* Acutt and Dodgson, 1996

# REVERSING CURRENT LAND USE AND ENVIRONMENTAL TRENDS

Strong unsustainable trends require equally strong action to reverse them. This section identifies how a set of land use planning measures, which together form a strategy of concentrated corridor and nodal development, might reverse currently unsustainable trends. A strategy for concentrating development in transport corridors and nodes has the potential to reduce both resource consumption and environmental pollution. A number of complementary land use planning measures are crucial to a strategy for concentrating development in transport corridors and nodes, including issues such as *development density*, *accessibility to public transport*, the *provision of local employment, services and facilities* and *parking restraint*.

## Development Density

There are a number of reasons why development density may promote more sustainable patterns of development. Less land is required for development, there is the potential to use energy more efficiently (by utilizing combined heat and power (CHP) for example – see Chapter 12) and the need to travel may be reduced.[1] Higher density development may also assist the introduction of the other measures that are part of a strategy for concentrating development in transport corridors and nodes (increasing the accessibility to public transport, providing more local employment, services and facilities and reducing the availability of parking).

Research evidence from a number of sources suggests that higher density development is associated with less travel (eg ECOTEC, 1993; Hillman and Whalley, 1983; Næss, 1993; Stead, 1999). Stead (1999) suggests a critical ward-level gross population density of 40 to 50 persons per hectare, at which travel distance is lowest. It should be noted, however, that a gross population density of 40 to 50 persons per hectare requires concentrations or clusters of development *above* this density if employment, services and facilities (as well as open space) are also to be provided locally (see below).

## Accessibility to Public Transport

Ensuring good accessibility to public transport, in combination with the provision of walking and cycling networks, is crucial to reducing reliance on the car and promoting more sustainable alternative travel patterns. Good accessibility to public transport also makes it possible to reduce the amount of parking for development, which in turn may help to promote the use of public transport.

Kitamura et al (1997) report that the distance from home to the nearest bus stop and railway station affects the mode of transport used for a journey. Cervero (1994) shows how the proportion of rail journeys decreases with increasing distance from the railway station. Residents living within 500 feet (approx. 150 metres) of a railway station typically use rail for approximately 30 per cent of all journeys, whereas residents living at a distance of 3000 feet (approx. 900 metres) from the nearest railway station are likely to make only about 15 per cent of all journeys.

The introduction of strict rules for the siting of new development may be necessary to guide new development to more sustainable locations, as in the Dutch ABC policy where the location of development is determined by the use of the development and its accessibility profile (see Chapter 7).

---

1 Higher densities widen the range of opportunities for the development of local personal contacts and activities that can be maintained without resort to motorized travel. Higher densities widen the range of services that can be supported in the local area, reducing the need to travel long distances. Higher densities tend to reduce average distances between homes, services, employment and other opportunities which reduces travel distance. Higher densities may be more amenable to public transport operation and use and less amenable to car ownership and use, which have implications for modal choice.

## Local Employment, Services and Facilities

The provision of local employment, services and facilities may reduce travel distance and increase the proportion of short journeys capable of being travelled by non-motorized modes. By reducing travel distance and reliance on the car, it also makes it is possible to reduce the availability of parking.

Hanson (1982) reports that the proximity to local facilities is associated with lower travel distance. Evidence from research by Winter and Farthing (1997) shows that the provision of local facilities in new residential developments reduces average trip distances. Farthing and Winter (1997) set out a number of recommendations for promoting more sustainable travel patterns through the provision of local facilities, which include:

- clustering of facilities to maximize convenience and market;
- ensuring the most convenient location for facilities to minimize average travel distance;
- giving priority to the design of high amenity footpaths and cycleways, providing direct access to facilities;
- providing high quality environments in centres emphasizing pedestrian comfort and constraining cars.

Some of these issues concerning local employment, services and facilities are explored in more detail in Chapter 6.

## Parking Restraint

Just as increased provision of parking and roadspace has led to difficulties in providing public transport and increases in car ownership and use (Figure 3.2), limiting parking provision might help to promote the use of public transport and discourage the ownership and use of the car.

Evidence from Kitamura et al (1997) shows that the availability of residential car parking is linked to both trip frequency and modal choice. Balcombe and York (1993) show that there is a greater tendency to walk in areas where residential parking is limited. Similarly, Valleley et al (1997) suggest a relationship between the modal split of commuting and parking provision at work. Stead (1999) reports that travel distance is lower in areas where residential parking is limited, suggesting two reasons for this. Firstly, the limited availability of parking may lead to more 'rational' car use as residents seek to reduce the number of journeys and hence the number of times they have to search for a parking space on their return home. Secondly, limited residential parking may also indirectly contribute to less travel by suppressing car ownership, which is a strong determinant of travel patterns (see Stead, 1999).

## Synthesis

Copenhagen provides an example of how the above policies have been put into practice, where development has been concentrated in transport corridors and nodes. The strategy of concentrated development has been used in Denmark for some time to manage urban growth. Since the middle of the century, planning policies in the Copenhagen metropolitan area have encouraged decentralized concentration where population and employment have been guided into clusters along corridors (fingers) radiating from the city centre, whilst retaining green wedges between the corridors. Land-use policies have been used to promote a variety of features associated with more sustainable patterns of land use, such as:

*   new development in accessible locations along public transport corridors;
*   the concentration of relatively self-contained new development at specific points along the 'fingers';
*   retention of public open space and agricultural land in the 'green wedges';
*   allocation of land for allotments and forestry;
*   balancing of population and employment within the metropolitan area.

The 1948 Regional Plan (Finger Plan) for the Copenhagen metropolitan area first set out to achieve a pattern of decentralized concentration, and has since had a decisive influence on the growth of the city region. The plan recommended that the suburbs be developed as small, relatively self-contained communities, linked to the city by the road and rail network. Urban expansion was concentrated along fingers radiating from the city. Since 1948, other regional plans have expanded upon the principles of the original plan. The 1961 Regional Plan proposed the extension of the two western fingers to Roskilde and Køge to cope with rapid urban growth. The three northern fingers were subsequently extended in the 1973 Regional Plan to achieve a balance between urban development to the north and the west of the city. A transverse transport route was proposed to link the five fingers, forming nodes with the radial routes on which to establish suburban centres. The Regional Plan of 1989 focuses on a 'regional localization' strategy, recommending a central city location for certain activities requiring high accessibility and the decentralisation of other types of development, such as local employment and facilities, along the fingers (Figure 3.3).

## Summary
The land use planning measures outlined above can reduce the environmental impacts of development, both in terms of resource consumption and environmental pollution. The measures are designed to reduce the need to travel and

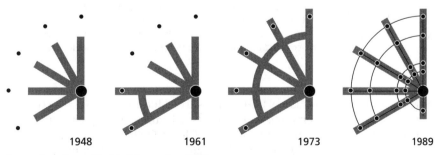

| 1948 | 1961 | 1973 | 1989 |

*Source:* Copenhagen Municipal Corporation, 1993

**Figure 3.3** *Copenhagen Regional Plans: 1948–1989*

promote the use of alternative modes to the car, which can lead to a reduction in transport-related energy consumption and emissions. Higher density development requires less land and has greater potential to use energy more efficiently (eg through CHP – see Chapter 12). Increasing the accessibility to public transport can reduce the amount of land and materials required for roads if it encourages a switch away from the car. Less parking space requires less land and fewer construction materials (Table 3.5).

**Table 3.5** *Land Use Planning Measures to Reverse Current Environmental Impacts*

| Environmental Indicator | Development Density | Accessibility to Public Transport | Local Employment, Services and Facilities | Parking Restraint |
| --- | --- | --- | --- | --- |
| Energy consumption | All four measures reduce the need to travel and promote the use of alternative modes to the car, thus reducing transport energy consumption. Higher density development has greater potential to use energy more efficiently (eg through CHP schemes) | | | |
| Land urbanized | Higher density developments require less land than lower density developments | Increasing the accessibility and use of public transport reduces the amount of land required for roads | | Less parking space requires less land |
| Minerals extraction | | Increasing the accessibility and use of public transport reduces the materials required for roads | | Less parking space requires fewer construction materials |
| Carbon dioxide<br><br>Nitrogen oxides<br><br>Particulates | All four measures reduce the need to travel and promote the use of alternative modes to the car, thus reducing emissions from transport (ie $CO_2$, $NO_x$ and particulates). Very high densities may however lead to high concentrations of local pollutants (see for example Newton, 1998). | | | |

Furthermore, the land use planning measures identified above are complementary and help to reinforce each other (see Figure 3.4). Higher population densities may encourage the provision of local facilities by increasing the number of residents living nearby (although excessively high housing density standards may lead to residential areas being designed to maximize density at the expense of other types of development, such as local employment, services and facilities, unless policies to promote these are also in place).

| Development Density | Higher densities can increase the catchment for local employment, services and facilities | | |
|---|---|---|---|
| Accessibility to Public Transport | Local employment, services and facilities may reduce the need for car ownership and increase the market for public transport | Higher densities are able to provide more people with good accessibility to public transport and provide a larger potential market for public transport | |
| Parking Restraint | Residents of areas where residential parking is limited may prefer to use local facilities to avoid using the car (and a long search for a parking space on their return home) | Lower provision of residential parking allows more homes to be accommodated. Higher densities may also encourage more efficient use of parking spaces | Limited availability of parking may suppress car ownership and/or use and enhance the use of public transport |
| | Local Employment, Services and Facilities | Development Density | Accessibility to Public Transport |

**Figure 3.4** *Synergies Between Land Use Measures*

Higher population density provides a larger potential market for public transport and is therefore complementary to public transport provision (Barton et al, 1995 illustrate how higher development density around bus stops might be used to maximize convenience and accessibility to public transport). Lower provision of residential parking allows more homes to be accommodated per unit area and is hence complementary with increases in development density. Balcombe and York (1993) report that higher densities may also encourage more efficient use of parking spaces and hence reduce the costs of providing parking.

Limited availability of parking may suppress car ownership and/or use, enhance the use of public transport and increase the frequency of public transport services. Residents of areas where residential parking is limited may prefer to use local facilities to avoid using the car (and a long search for a parking space on their return home).

The measures outlined above are designed to reduce the need to travel and decrease the reliance on the car. They are also measures for improving local environmental quality and making urban areas more attractive places in which to live, work, study and spend leisure time. However, other measures for improving urban environmental quality and quality of life may also be necessary if the strong trends away from living and working in urban areas are to be reversed. Other measures might include higher quality urban design (see Chapter 8), improvements in safety (see Chapter 15) and greater access to open space – important factors behind current urban depopulation. The combination of measures identified above may also improve quality of life issues, such as safety, security and vitality (Figure 3.5). Other types of measures, such as economic instruments and regulations might also be used to support and enhance the effect of these land use measures (see for example Stead, 1999).

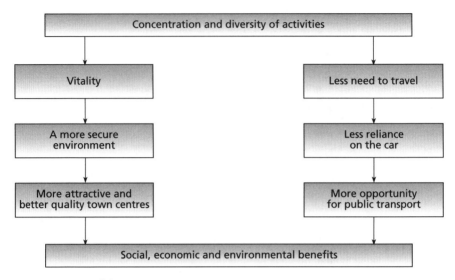

Source: Department of the Environment, 1995

**Figure 3.5** *Benefits of the Combination of Land Use Measures*

## CONCLUSIONS

The dispersal of population and activities and the centralization of services and facilities have resulted in settlements becoming less sustainable and less socially cohesive. The planning of new development and its associated infrastructure has traditionally been based on a demand-led or 'predict and provide' approach, where trend-based projections are used to plan for future demand. The approach has contributed to the dispersal of population and activities and the centralization of services and facilities, with implications for increased travel distance and higher levels of mobility. As a result, there are environmental and social problems associated with the predict and provide approach. The approach assumes that there are no limits to growth and that demand can always be met. It is clear however that there are definite limits to the growth of development in terms of resource and pollution constraints. For example, the supply of land for infrastructure is finite and the growth of transport is limited by air quality. There is some evidence to suggest that there has been some move away from the 'predict and provide' approach in the planning of new development and infrastructure over the last decade. However, current planning policy-making is far from being completely based on a supply-led, or demand managed, approach. More emphasis on a supply-led approach is necessary if development is to be more sustainable (Table 3.6). The concept of environmental capacity and strategic environmental assessment also needs to be used to identify areas where development can be accommodated and, conversely, where the environment cannot support additional development (see for example Barton, 1997; Thérivel, 1992; Thérivel and Partidário, 1996).

**Table 3.6** *Characteristics of Demand-Led and Supply-Led Approaches to Planning*

| From a Demand-Led Approach to Planning | To a Supply-Led Approach to Planning |
| --- | --- |
| Dispersed developments | Concentrated developments |
| Distant employment, services and facilities | Local employment, services and facilities |
| Single-use developments | Mixed-use developments |
| Generous parking | Parking restraint |
| High accessibility by car | High accessibility by public transport |
| Provision of road networks | Provision of walking and cycling networks |

Settlements are becoming less sustainable according to a variety of environmental indicators. Indicators of resource consumption and environmental pollution show that a number of environmental impacts are worsening, even within the timescale of a single decade. In addition, the externalities of many environmental impacts are unequally spread: groups who experience most environmental pollution may be those who contribute least. Some of the indicators show that although environmental impacts are not currently increasing overall, certain sectors require particular attention if future increases in environmental impacts are to be avoided (in the transport sector for example). Technology might assist in reducing environmental pollution in the short and medium term, but other means of addressing the problem are also needed in the longer-term. Land use planning has a role to play in this respect. Land use planning offers opportunities to reduce the environmental impacts of settlements and also offers the potential to address the social inequalities of environmental pollution. Planning has the potential to address the causes of transport problems rather than the effects.

Strong unsustainable trends require equally strong actions to reverse them. This requires action at all levels, including local level decisions about the planning of neighbourhoods. A package of strong, complementary land use planning measures has the potential to begin to reverse the current unsustainable trends and improve quality of life in neighbourhoods. One such package contains measures that address issues of development density, accessibility to public transport, the provision of local employment, services and facilities and parking restraint, which together form a strategy for concentrating development in transport corridors and nodes. The measures may reduce the need to travel and decrease the reliance on the car, whilst at the same time may contribute to improvements in environmental quality, making local neighbourhoods more attractive places in which to live, work, study and spend leisure time (and therefore more self-contained). Other measures for improving urban environmental quality and quality of life may also be necessary if the strong trends away from living and working in urban areas are to be reversed. These might include higher quality urban design, improvements in safety and greater access to open space – important factors behind current urban depopulation. A variety of complementary measures, not just at the local level, might also be used to support and enhance the effect of land use measures.

# PART II
# RETHINKING THE NEIGHBOURHOOD OPTION

# 4   DO NEIGHBOURHOODS MATTER?

*Hugh Barton*

*'No man can therefore conceive of anything but that he conceive it in some place'* (Hobbes Leviathan)

*'Place puts man in such a way that it reveals the external bonds of his existence and at the same time the depths of his freedom and reality'* (Heideggar *Being and Time*)

## INTRODUCTION

This book is premised on the assumption that neighbourhoods matter. Yet, as has been shown in Part I, the concept of neighbourhood has a chequered history, and the significance of locality in people's lives has declined greatly since the seminal Bethnal Green study demonstrated its reality in mid-century London (Young and Wilmott, 1957). It is no longer possible to take 'neighbourhood' for granted. It is valid to question whether planning for neighbourhoods is any longer a relevant ambition, either from the viewpoint of desirability or feasibility.

This chapter therefore seeks to examine whether there is a defensible argument for neighbourhood planning. At the outset it briefly reviews some of the antagonistic trends and highlights their significance by reference to children's schooling – traditionally a locally-based activity. Then it embarks on a review of reasons why neighbourhoods might be a good idea. These range from the impact on global ecology, through social and environmental issues to local politics. This leads to a systematic examination of the empirical evidence as whether, given that we would *like* neighbourhoods, there is any evidence that they can *work*. The issue of practicality focuses on the behaviour of people in localities, in particular their use of and access to local facilities, as this is critical to issues of energy use, pollution, equity, community, health and safety. There are three specific questions:

1   To what extent do people choose to use local facilities?
2   In so far as they do use them, does this result in less motorized travel and a higher proportion of walking/cycling trips?

3  Does the planing and design of localities have a significant impact on people's propensity to use local facilities, and choice of mode to get to them?

These are awkward questions because of the different stances taken by protagonists: urban designers in their writings often take the value of locality as self-evident, while sociologists – suspicious of any hint of architectural determinism – assume personal and social behaviour is independent of place. In this context it is important to draw upon empirical research rather than normative statements. The conclusion is that despite market and policy preferences, neighbourhoods do still matter, and there are compelling reasons why we should reinvent the art of neighbourhood planning.

## LOSING LOCALITY

As Nigel Taylor argues in Chapter 2, the decay of the 'urban place' and the rise of the 'non-place urban realm' reflects profound changes in economic structure and lifestyles. Several factors are influential: the rise in car ownership and use (fuelled by affluence and road construction) which permits increasing trip lengths and dispersed trip ends; the increasing unit size of market and state facilities, which has been facilitated by high mobility; and the post-industrial revolution in markets associated with globalization and deregulation, with associated job insecurity and widening job search areas. The anti-local impact of these factors is well understood in relation to the loss of local shops and jobs, the closure of small hospitals, schools and other facilities, and the increasing danger on the streets.

Stead (Chapter 3) has given an overview of the changing pattern of settlement. Here I focus on one specific issue – that of access to schools – to illustrate local significance. Schools have become bigger, new sites chosen for financial not access reasons, parental choice and car mobility loosening the ties of locality, with the predictable result that the number of UK school children walking and cycling to school has fallen dramatically over the last 30 years. Figures from the Department of Environment, Transport and the Regions (DETR) suggest as much as 20 per cent of peak hour traffic may be associated with escorting children to school. In one locale 44 per cent of primary school children arrived at school by car. Half of those journeys were serving no other function. Three-quarters of them were less than a mile and thus may be construed as 'local' (Osbourne and Davis, 1996). Over schools generally the population of pupils cycling to school is down to 2 per cent, which compares with over 60 per cent in some European cities.

The point of these statistics is show the power of the social, economic and institutional forces: even for an activity mainly local in character the propensity to walk and cycle has fallen dramatically. The knock-on effects are significant. The resulting increase in traffic on local streets is itself acting as a deterrent as more parents consider that the danger to children of walking outweighs the benefits. The traffic also compounds problems of congestion, pollution, severance, resource waste and greenhouse emissions. A growing number of children miss out on the regular exercise of getting to school, at a time when sedentary habits are leading to worrying projections of future prevalence of obesity and heart decease (Roberts, 1996).

The patterns of physical activity established in childhood are a key determinant of adult behaviour (Kuhl and Cooper, 1992). This appears to relate particularly to the habit of cycling where there is talk of a 'lost generation' of cyclists. Outside the school trip the freedom of children to meet casually on the street, in the playground, and to form a community outside the home, is vanishing. One study, comparing the results of children's independent mobility in 1970 and 1990 found a substantial reduction in parental 'licences' for children of any age to go out on their own, and bike use down from 67 per cent to 25 per cent (Hillman et al, 1991). Such declining levels of freedom, however, have not been observed in comparable studies in Germany.

Children walking and cycling locally, to go to school, shops, field or friends are part of the fabric of local community. Parents walking with young children and meeting other parents on the way or at the school gates can be creating local networks of mutual support (see Chapter 9). The rise in car drop-off is symptomatic of the decline of locality and reflects worrying trends towards unhealthy lifestyles and social fragmentation, affecting the coming generation.

The pressures that have led to changed behaviour stem from changed employment and income patterns, the growth of non-local interest communities, perceived street dangers and inappropriate planning/design policies. The question is the degree to which the powerful trends are a matter of conscious individual and social choice, or part of an unintentional vicious circle.

## NEEDING NEIGHBOURHOODS

The example of children's mobility has exposed a number of reasons why it might be appropriate to plan for neighbourhoods. This section sets the reasons out in due order. Note that they are *normative* points about what might be desirable, but say little about whether neighbourhoods are practical. However the justification for each point rests both on common public perceptions and on the statements of public bodies, often backed by empirical studies. The purpose of this synoptic review is not to examine each reason in depth but reflect their cumulative strength. The sequence below moves from environmental issues through health and social inclusion to the more abstract concepts of freedom and community (Table 4.1).

### 1. Reducing Greenhouse Gas Emissions

Ironically one of the key reasons why governments are reopening the neighbourhood option is nothing to do with locality but everything to do with the fear of climate change. Commitments made at the Earth Summit in Rio to reduce the emission of greenhouse gasses have been articulated by Local Agenda 21, the European Union's Framework V programme, and the UK's evolving strategy for sustainable development (DoE, 1994d and 1998d). Global warming is both a huge threat and a likely one. Following the precautionary principle it is therefore logical to do everything in our power to avert it. Planning for transport energy-efficiency is (as shown by Stead, Chapter 3) a

**Table 4.1** *Ten Reasons for Strengthening Neighbourhoods*

| Reasons | Objectives |
|---|---|
| 1  Cutting greenhouse gas emissions | • Reduce the need to travel<br>• Reduce car reliance<br>• Increase energy efficiency in buildings |
| 2  Closing local resource loops | • Reduce demand for non-renewable resources<br>• Reuse and recycling of resources locally<br>• Local water sourcing, treatment and aquifer recharge<br>• Local low-input food production |
| 3  Enhancing local environmental quality | • Promote local distinctiveness and heritage<br>• Create an attractive public realm<br>• Enhance local habitat diversity |
| 4  Creating a healthy environment | • Improve local air quality<br>• Promote an active life-style (especially walking)<br>• Encourage consumption of fresh fruit and vegetables |
| 5  Increasing street safety | • Reduce the chance of vehicle/pedestrian accidents<br>• Reduce the fear of violence |
| 6  Increasing accessibility and freedom of choice | • Choice of transport mode for trips<br>• More facilities accessible locally |
| 7  Equity and social inclusion | • Choice of facilities within easy walking distance<br>• Viability of public transport |
| 8  Local work opportunities | • Accessible jobs for those tied to the locality<br>• Reduce transport emissions |
| 9  Value of local community | • Facilitate accessible social networks<br>• Promote mental health |
| 10  Increasing local self-determination | • Increase user/citizen control<br>• Management of decentralized systems |

central part of any strategy, and since 1994 the DETR has required local authorities to consider how to 'reduce the need to travel' and reduce car dependence without sacrificing levels of accessibility (DoE, 1994a). The rediscovered importance of neighbourhoods – as the location for accessible jobs and services close enough to homes for people to choose to walk or cycle – is a natural corollary, and written strongly into official planning guidance (eg DETR, 1998c).

Low emission strategies in relation to energy supply and use in buildings are also central to government strategy (DoE, 1994d). The 'dash for gas' (replacing old coal-fired power stations with gas turbines) has delivered quick returns but in the longer run reduced heat loss from buildings, and investment in local CHP (combined heat and power) plants[1] using renewable or recycled fuels will be essential. Both energy-efficiency in buildings and CHP benefit from compact patterns of physical development that are compatible with the close-knit neighbourhoods needed for transport efficiency.

---

1 Combined heat and power stations pipe the cooling water from the electricity generating process through 'heat mines' to heat consumers (homes, factories, schools etc) and thus achieve high efficiency in the use of primary fuel.

It sometimes seems the emission targets are pre-eminent in the case for reviving local communities. Certainly global warming constitutes, on our current knowledge, *force majeure* and is politically compelling. But even if global warming suddenly (and improbably) proved untrue, the other reasons for neighbourhoods, and for reducing the need to travel, make a powerful case.

## 2. Resource Use: Energy, Food, Water, Minerals

The 'ecological footprint' of a settlement relates not only to pollutants emitted but also the energy, water and other resources exploited to sustain it. The argument about resource use runs in parallel to that about global warming. In relation to neighbourhoods there are issues about reducing transport energy use, local water management and food production. The relevant resources for transport are not only fossil fuels but also materials used in vehicle manufacture, aggregates used in road construction, and land which is 'lost' to transport needs, including the indirect need for quarrying. The theoretical justification for husbanding natural resources is widely accepted, as part of a strategy for sustainable development. The UK Government, however, speaks with a forked tongue on the issue, backing it in processes such as the environmental appraisal of development plans (DoE, 1993), but largely ignoring it in guidance on mineral policy (DoE, 1994b), or the exploitation of North Sea oil and gas. If the use of transport-related resources is to be cut then it means reversing the trend to longer car-dependent trips, and by implication providing more opportunities to satisfy needs locally.

Water supply and waste water treatment are no longer functions that are assumed to be external to the neighbourhoods that depend on them. The tradition of remote sourcing of water is being challenged for several reasons: objections to more reservoirs in high rainfall zones; over-extraction from rivers threatening both the aquatic environment and security of supply for local users; over-extraction from aquifers leading to falling ground water levels and increased pollution risk. At the same time disposal of grey and black water has become an issue, with distant, end-of-pipe solutions being recognized as problematic. The potential for local sourcing and local treatment is being actively explored (Hough, 1995; EA.UE, 1997).

Turning next to food, research into food production suggests that energy use per calorie can vary by a factor of ten between organic and chemical methods of vegetable growing, and by up to 1000 between organic small-holdings and factory-farming meat production (Leach, 1976). Processing, transport, distribution and storage costs are also significant and favour local organic production, closing local resource loops wherever possible. Beyond direct resource impacts there are indirect ones. The radical environmental tradition sets food production in a global context, stressing the energy-wasteful, highly polluting character of western agribusiness and the exploitative impact of the food trade on people in developing countries. This view motivates the desire not only to change the food industry but to bypass it by growing locally for local use. Vegetable gardens, small-holdings, city farms and allotments are seen as resource-economic, ecologically non-exploitative and convivial (see, for example Ecologist, 1972; Boyle and Harper, 1976). They are also seen as a key to health (see section 4 below).

Clearly there are counter arguments to do with the value of trade and regional specialization. It might be more resource-efficient to import food, for example, from overseas if production there was *extensive* and low energy while production here was *intensive* and high energy. The benefits of localization therefore depend on the nature of food production (etc) processes.

## 3. Environmental Quality

The quality of 'place', the enhancement of 'local distinctiveness', and the desire for a sense of local 'vitality' (people on the street, communicating, enjoying social life) are three themes that are reflected in official documents, such as the Commission of the Economic Community's (CEC) *Green Paper on the Urban Environment* (1990) and the DETR's *Planning Policy Guidance Note 1* (1997).

'Place' is an important element in our cultural identity. People define themselves by the place they live in and value the unique characteristics which give continuity with the past and relationship to the present (Lukerman 1964). It might be argued that a sense of local place can perfectly well occur *independently* of neighbourhood, and clearly that is true, but the quality of place nevertheless is enhanced and even *defined* by people. Real appreciation of place does not come from the person in the car, but from people walking, cycling and meeting, enjoying the sights, sounds, smells, touch and history of the place. This interdependence works both ways. The argument will be made later in the chapter that the pedestrian functioning of neighbourhoods is greatly enhanced by the aesthetic quality of the places people walk through.

Designers have expressed the aesthetic quality of localities in ways that make clear the dynamic, connected experience of townscape (Cullen, 1961; Lynch, 1960). It is the total feel of a place – its noises and scents as well as its visual transitions, its associations as well as its physical presence – that can give enjoyment. Key design principles are diversity, richness and legibility (ie the ability to orientate and find the way). These are not helped by the residential monoculture typical of so many post-war estates. But they are helped by the use diversity that comes with local job and facilities. Urban green space and biodiversity (especially birdlife) are also highly valued as part of the urban tapestry. In the context of planning for pedestrian-scaled neighbourhoods all these elements fall naturally into place.

## 4. Healthy Environment

Deterring car use and promoting human-powered movement are themes which crop up again when considering health. The World Health Organization's (WHO) campaign for healthy cities equates health with general well-being and quality of life and takes the importance of neighbourhoods and local communities as axiomatic (WHO, 1999). EU reports on sustainable cities highlight the importance of health issues such as the provision for basic needs, road safety, healthy lifestyles and air quality. (The EU Expert Group, 1995).

The UK Government's *Health Green Paper* (1998) sings the same tune – representing a radical shift of emphasis away from healthcare fire-fighting and towards a longer term health promotion strategy. The Green Paper targets mental health, accidents, heart disease/stroke and cancer. All four are 'diseases of civilization', reflecting the changing social and environmental pressures of post-industrial society. The character of the local environment and local community are implicated heavily and some of the factors such as accidents, work and community are dealt with later in this analysis.

Three key issues are air quality, lifestyle and food. Air pollution from road vehicles is a prime cause of rising levels of asthma and other respiratory illnesses, particularly in cities. The problem is being tackled in part by technological innovation (catalytic converters) but smoothing the flow and reducing the absolute level of vehicle use remain vital objectives. This means the substitution of non-motorized transport, and the localizing of facilities to increase pedestrian accessibility. Unsurprisingly the promotion of a less sedentary, healthier way of life involves exactly the same policies: reducing the barriers that deter people from walking/cycling; making facilities close so that walking is an efficient means of making local trips; opening options for local recreational trips and sporting activities (especially among the young); slowing, calming, and reducing the capacity for motorized traffic.

The importance of food quality for health is highlighted by the WHO in its 1998 publication *The Social Determinants of Health: The Solid Facts*. Industrialization has brought with it the epidemiological transition from infectious to chronic diseases such as heart disease, strokes and cancer. At the same time diets have changed, with over-consumption of energy-dense fats and sugars, producing more obesity. Social gradients in diet quality and nutrient sources contribute to health inequalities. People on low incomes – such as young families, elderly people and the unemployed – are least able to eat well, and are often tied to their locality (Wilkinson and Marmott, 1998). Dietary goals to prevent chronic diseases emphasize eating more fresh fruit and vegetables, and this can be helped by the availability of local food sources such as market gardens, and a situation where it is possible for people to grow their own fruit and vegetables in gardens, allotments, small-holdings, and city farms. The development of community composting schemes and local food exchange systems can begin to change attitudes and opportunities locally.

The current level of local food production is not great. Estimates vary between 10 per cent and 20 per cent of UK vegetable and fruit consumption. But the potential, given appropriate economic signals and cultural conditions, is illustrated by experience during the Second World War, when the small land proportion of a residential estate that was cultivated (14 per cent) produced 16 per cent more food than farmland occupying the same area as the whole estate, suggesting that garden productivity was eight times higher than farm productivity (Best, 1981). That impressive demonstration of people power does not of itself justify giving urban food production a high priority, given the current EU food glut. But it does add weight to the argument that for health and lifestyle reasons we should keep open options for local growing, and not 'sacrifice' underused allotments to the house builder.

## 5. Safety

Fear of accidents and assault are the biggest barriers to walking and cycling, particularly for the physically disadvantaged, the frail elderly, children subject to parental licensing, and parents with young children. 'Community safety' is now a buzz phrase amongst police, health and social work professionals. Strangely there are two opposing camps on how to promote community safety, one which is effectively anti-neighbourhood, the other strongly pro-neighbourhood. Some police architects advocate 'designing out crime', especially theft and burglary, by reducing escape routes, cutting down on pedestrian connection, making the thief feel exposed and vulnerable in a semi-privatized residential enclave. The logical endpoint of that approach is seen in the US with gated, guarded (and often exclusive) domains where strangers are not welcome and residents come and go in their vehicles.

The alternative view is that put forward with such force by Jane Jacobs in 1962: the streets are safer and welcoming only when there are people walking them and 'eyes on the street' so that the fear (and remote chance) of violence is reduced. Contemporary urban designers follow the latter views, emphasizing the permeability of the urban environment and the convenience of local facilities, together with effective 'natural' surveillance of streets and walkways, and the creation of places people find it pleasant to go to.

There are unresolved questions here. According to some house builders home buyers prefer cul-de-sac positions. Where there are alleyways connecting roads (so contributing to permeability) residents sometimes demand they be closed to prevent children hanging around after school or in the evening. In Chapter 15 it is argued that the solution is not restricted freedom, but better design together with changed attitudes.

## 6. Accessibility and Freedom

Accessibility, like health and safety, is a social issue that goes to the heart of the argument for neighbourhoods. The loss of local facilities within easy walking distance and their substitution by more distant facilities designed for ease of access by car reduces the options open to everyone, restricting choice. It is ironic, of course, that the traditional political rhetoric surrounding provision for the car and the move to edge of town retail/office/leisure parks stresses freedom as the justification – consumer choice, market freedom. But the promotion of such freedoms leads inexorably to the loss of other freedoms. The rationale for neighbourhood is therefore to try to widen choice – not to force a particular brand of behaviour but to facilitate behaviour which currently may be squeezed out by dominant market trends and policy conventions. The accessibility goal is freedom of association and activity. The question as to whether or in what situation, people *use* local facilities, will be examined later in the chapter. The normative principle that it is *desirable* to have local facilities is accepted even by those who have chosen to live in new outer suburban estates designed around car use. Indeed, a survey of a number of such estates, found that the absence of local facilities was a prime cause of dissatisfaction (Farthing and Winter, 1988).

Apart from ease and speed of access another potential accessibility advantage of local facilities is the ability to undertake multi-purpose trips. This depends on the locational pattern and clustering of facilities. The appropriate maximum distance from dwelling to facilities is also a key policy issue and depends on the economic scale of operation and the level of local use as well as the mobility of the clients.

## 7. Equity

Neighbourhoods are also about equity. High car dependence effectively disenfranchises people who cannot drive, do not have a car, or cannot have regular access to a car – typically the young, the old, the relatively poor, parents at home with young families. Conversely neighbourhoods with a good range of local facilities enrich the choices open to the less mobile and help compensate for public transport inadequacies.

The problems of poor accessibility have a significant impact on household expenditure. Studies of car ownership levels amongst the poorest groups demonstrate the degree to which households in low density areas (where on average facilities are further away) find themselves obliged to buy a car to compensate for poor accessibility. In rural settlements, for example, the poorest quintile has 45 per cent car ownership, while in inner urban areas they have 10 per cent (Hillman and Whalley, 1983). While the density measure employed here is not, of course, an adequate proxy for neighbourhood, it does demonstrate the value of closeness.

There are also important social inclusion benefits from effective localities in relation to work, community and democracy.

## 8. Work

It is easy to assume that the high level of mobility enjoyed by many, the trend towards 'out-sourcing', contract work, and job specialization, with consequent wide job-search areas, means that locality no longer has any significance for employment. However, the evidence does not support this (see Figure 4.1). A wide range of empirical and theoretical studies have shown that the local inter-mixture of land uses – specifically housing and employment – is a significant determinant of travel to work distances (Owens, 1991; ECOTEC, 1993; Stead, 1994).

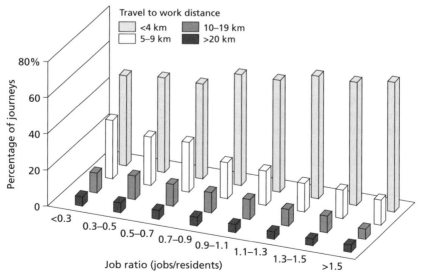

*Source:* Stead, 1994

**Figure 4.1** *Journey to Work Length Related to Ward Job Ratios in Avon, Nottinghamshire and West Yorkshire*

These analyses are based on convenient administrative units, such as wards, which do not necessary coincide with neighbourhoods. It seems quite possible that ward-based analysis therefore underplays the significance of locality. The accident of ward boundaries (sometimes, for example, cutting between a residential and an industrial area) and scale means that it is quite surprising that a clear work trip/job ratio relationship exists. It is therefore possible that the *actual* significance for residents is greater than statistics suggest, though the trend away from local work has undoubtedly continued since the studies above.

The types of people who particularly value local job opportunities are carers, part-time workers, non-car users and young people. The dispersal of appropriate work opportunities to localities goes hand in hand with the local-ization of retail, leisure, health and educational facilities. However, businesses relying on a high degree of specialization, needing to advertise posts over a regional or national area, are not appropriate to dispersed locations, assisting neither local access to jobs nor the reduction of trip lengths.

## 9. Community

The degree to which localities remain the source of community is, as noted in Chapters 1 and 2, open to question. Nevertheless there is widespread belief in the value of the local place community, and recognition that the sense of local community can enrich lives, and assist health. WHO stress local social networks of support as critical to health and well-being (Wilkinson and Marmott, 1998). The UK *Green Paper on Our Healthier Nation* (DHSS, 1998) highlights the value of community networks in combating mental illness. Government backing for the principle of 'urban villages' – illustrated by the Greenwich Millennium Village – is also motivated by a (rather generalized) belief in local community:

> *'The Government wants to herald a new era in community development for our towns and cities by bringing the best of village life into the urban environment.'* (DETR, 1998)

In some settlements, and for some people, local communities are still strong. In Chapter 9 Gilchrist expounds the nature of local support networks using Easton in inner Bristol as an example, while in Chapter 10 the authors show the links between local action and community in Stroud.

## 10. Local Self-Determination

The case for local self-determination has been advocated by a wide range of interests. The official Skeffington Report of 1968 promoted the concept of local community councils as a means of achieving a measure of participatory democracy. The academic Sherry Arnstein placed 'citizen control' at the top of the ladder of participation. Radical environmentalists such as Godfrey Boyle and Peter Harper (1976) put local cooperative decision-making at the heart of their vision of sustainability.

The principles of Local Agenda 21 take the idea politically a stage further. Local communities (of varying scale depending on context) are invited to take some responsibility for their own development, forming partnerships with municipal authorities and businesses. Involvement in such participatory processes is uneven, and general effectiveness may be questioned, but there are sufficient examples of conspicuous success to prove that in some circumstances neighbourhood communities can take control. Coin Street in London is the classic case (Brindley et al, 1989). The next chapter examines innovatory eco-neighbourhoods around the world and concludes that some of the most successful projects involve voluntary/community sector leadership.

Local control may also occur not for ideological or political reasons but out of necessity. Local networks and housing clusters may be asked to take extra responsibility for environmental management as local resource systems are installed which are too large for individual householders, too small for centralized agencies. For example in the field of energy the community management of renewable supply systems is common in Denmark and advocated in the UK (see Chapter 12). Equivalently local control of water collection and sewage treatment is a reality in some rural communities. The idea may spread as the environmental and financial costs of centralized services force new approaches.

## COUNTER ARGUMENTS

Most of the arguments above are based in commonly held values. We perceive health, safety, environmental quality, accessibility and so on as *goods* in their own right. There are nevertheless reservations. Some may take issue with the last two goals: local community and local self-determination. It would be possible to argue, with Taylor (Chapter 2), that local place communities are a concept whose time is past – that not only is it not practicable to create local communities, but more fundamentally people by their actions do not *want* local communities – their lifestyles marginalize locality. Furthermore, it could be argued, there are undesirable aspects to local community and local democracy. Village life, (apparently advocated by the UK Government) may be socially stifling and narrow-minded, invasive of privacy, myopic and self-serving when reflected in local decision-making. Minorities and vulnerable groups (for example gypsies) are often rejected by small communities, so neighbourhood governance, far from reducing social exclusion, might exacerbate it.

There are two responses to these points. First, merely because *many* people by their lifestyles do now marginalize locality it is not logical to infer that *all* people do, or wish to. Evidence to be presented shortly shows the degree to which even highly mobile households living in areas where there is no neighbourhood design still actually use the local facilities. Other evidence shows that in some areas (mainly older places) reliance on locality is surprisingly high. Whether such people feel they belong (or wish to belong) to a local place community is more of a moot point.

The second response is about *choice* – already highlighted as an issue. The case for reinventing neighbourhood planning does not rest on whether or not people now feel part of a local community, but on giving them the option. Recent market led policies of low density car-based use segregation are literally building reduced choice and unsustainability into the urban system. The point therefore is to reopen the opportunity to think and act local, to walk, cycle, meet on the street and in the square. Some people will choose to do so. Others may not.

The third response on local decision-making is more equivocal. Parish councils (the rural equivalent to neighbourhood governance) have a vital role in representing local interests, and may be effective management agents for the local authorities in relation to, for example, parks and playgrounds. But control by parish councils is another thing altogether and raises difficulties of expertise, fairness and representation of non-local interests. This issue of local governance is explored in Chapter 11. The LA21 principle of community involvement and local management is in any case not so much about the transfer of power as about the forming of partnerships so as to engage the active commitment of a range of interests to the overriding project of working for sustainable development.

Taken overall there are, then, convincing reasons for wanting neighbourhoods to exist. But the key uncertainty is whether the reinvention of neighbourhoods is actually a practicable project. Many chapters in the book give insight into this question. This chapter focuses on a few limited but central issues to do with the functioning of neighbourhoods.

## Do People Use Local Facilities?

The answer to this question is critical because so many of the claimed benefits of neighbourhoods rely on the assumption that, despite the evident decline in local facilities, it is still worthwhile to promote them. If it can be shown that people do not use local facilities (choosing rather to get in their cars and go further afield) then the viability of both local facilities and neighbourhoods is doubtful. Examination of the evidence may also tell us the *situations* in which people are more likely to use local facilities, and thus give starting points for design.

There are two levels of analysis: aggregate analysis of travel data and research on specific case studies. Aggregate analysis is inevitably a blunt weapon because of the range of different types and locations of development which may be subsumed under one category, and the arbitrary nature of the boundaries between units, varying widely and not necessarily at the level that matches the issue. Nevertheless there are general patterns which indirectly suggest the importance of local facilities. Density is related local facility provision in-as-much as there is generally more opportunity to use local facilities in higher density areas (ECOTEC, 1993). Studies investigating the effect of density on travel patterns establish a strong linkage: travel distance per person varies inversely with density. Within particular city regions the range can indeed be fairly startling, with outer commuter-zones, typically lacking many local facilities, having more than twice as much personal travel as inner city zones. The debate over density is taken further in Chapter 7, but here we simply note that from the aggregate studies it seems closeness to facilities reduces the need to travel.

So far as neighbourhood case studies are concerned, evidence is accumulating that people do use local facilities where they are available and this results in less travel. ECOTEC (1993) report a clear relationship between the distance from a local centre, the frequency of its use, and average household journey lengths. Hanson (1982) found similarly that proximity to local facilities is associated with shorter average distances, after taking account of socio-economic variations. Interestingly Hanson also found that people living closer to facilities made *more* trips, and this tunes in with the results of Banister's study (1992) comparing settlements in south Oxfordshire. The small town of Henley, with a good range of local facilities, had more *trips* per person but half the total *travel* per person when compared with commuter villages with few facilities.

Winter and Farthing (1997) have made a particular study of local facilities and travel in new peripheral estates in the Bristol sub-region. The design of such estates (including Bradley Stoke which is discussed in Chapter 1) is often antipathetic to pedestrian movement and designed on the assumption of full motorization, with local facilities not planned on any consistent basis. Furthermore such estates are typically chosen by young and mobile house-holds whose lifestyles are geared to car use and the 'non-place urban realm'. So these case studies provide quite a stern test for any theories of neighbour-hood. Nevertheless even in these cases Winter and Farthing demonstrate that local provision has a marked impact(Figure 4.2).

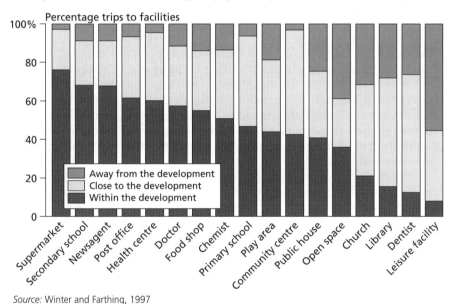

*Source:* Winter and Farthing, 1997

**Figure 4.2** *Percentage of Trips Made to Local Facilities*

The data suggests there are large variations in the degree of local use. Where they exist locally (within the development) supermarkets, secondary schools and newsagents are very heavily used with at least two thirds of trips. Local post offices, health centres, surgeries, food stores and chemists account for over 50 per cent of demand. Local primary schools, play areas, community centres, pubs and public open spaces account for a third to a half. But churches, libraries, dentists and leisure facilities where they exist locally, are only chosen by a small minority of users.

It would appear from these findings that where a given facility is reasonably standard – such as supermarkets, newsagents and post offices – then there is a strong propensity for people to use the closest. Where facilities are more specialized or cannot locally offer a very comprehensive service, then people have to travel to find what they want – for example a specific religious denomination, a larger library, a specific leisure facility. This accords with common sense. But the degree to which people are willing, despite high car ownership, to choose local is still perhaps surprising especially in relation to supermarkets and secondary schools, where retail competition and parental choice respectively might have been expected to result in more diversified choice patterns.

The local effect is even more marked if facilities 'close' but not 'within' the developments are included. Then (for example) 91 per cent of secondary school trips are local, 95 per cent of health centre trips, 86 per cent of food store trips and 93 per cent of primary school trips. These very high percentages suggest that while people may not necessarily choose the closest facility, they frequently find another local option which perhaps suits their tastes better or is more convenient in relation to their normal travel routes. If this is a correct inference then it emphasizes the importance of a local *choice* of facilities, and has implications for neighbourhood design.

These conclusions from study of a particular set of outlying estates are broadly supported by the survey of a more varied set of neighbourhoods undertaken for the Department of Environment (ECOTEC, 1993). The study found that 96 per cent of residents use their local shopping centre at least weekly and 44 per cent use them daily. The range and choice of facilities emerged as a key factor determining local usage. A clear relationship was shown between distance from a centre and the frequency of use. It was also interesting that, as might be expected, certain groups in the population – notably the retired, unemployed and young families – used local facilities much more heavily than some other groups.

Overall, then, it is clear that local facilities do still matter. Where local facilities are available they are used by many local people, though the degree of use varies widely according to distance, quality and the availability of other convenient options. So while the trends are unfavourable, neighbourhoods are far from dead. There is indeed a surprisingly high level of local use even in low density outlying estates occupied by young and upwardly mobile populations. Food outlets, (and perhaps secondary schools?) emerge as key catalysts for locality.

## DOES LOCAL USE REDUCE TRIP LENGTHS AND CAR DEPENDENCE?

While we can conclude quite firmly that local facilities provide (to varying degrees) a valuable service, and that in-so-far as neighbourhoods are about effective local provision they are justified, the other hoped-for benefits of neighbourhoods do not necessarily follow. The reduction of pollution, for example, depends on less motorized travel. Yet as we have noted local provision may well lead to an increased number of trips. So the questions arise:

does the provision of local facilities reduce total mileage? And does it increase the proportion of non-motorized trips?

Both ECOTEC and Winter and Farthing found that local use does (as hoped and predicted) lead to shorter trips and less travel overall. The latter team compared travel behaviour in situations where there were, and in situations where there were not, opportunities of using specific local facilities. The selected facilities were those used on a daily or very regular basis: supermarket, foodstore, newsagent, post office, public house, primary and secondary schools. They found that in every case local provision reduced average journey lengths.

The propensity to walk is of course profoundly affected by trip length. In 1975/76 90 per cent of trips under one mile were on foot (Hillman and Whalley, 1983). However, this percentage has fallen over the past 20 years. From its sample ECOTEC found 53 per cent of trips under one mile to local facilities were by foot, and only for trips of less than 1000m was walking the predominant mode. For all longer distances car use (and in certain places public transport) prevailed. Despite this growing car dependence, however, the inclination to walk remains very strong for trips under 800m, with 93 per cent being on foot.

Winter and Farthing found that where people choose to use a local facility they are (rather unsurprisingly) more likely to walk than if they choose a non-local facility, and for many facilities (not all) walking is indeed the dominant mode. Figure 4.3 shows how walking predominates as the means of access to local open spaces and play areas, and is the main means of access to local schools, pubs and community centres. It also accounts for about 50 per cent of trips to local shops but much less for access to supermarkets where car use is more essential.

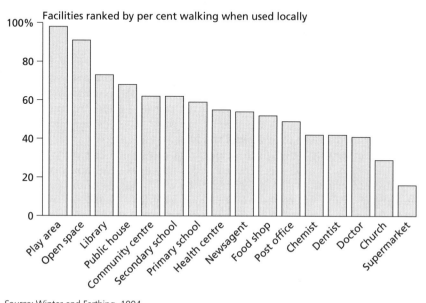

*Source:* Winter and Farthing, 1994

**Figure 4.3** *The Proportion of Walking Trips for Access to Local Facilities*

When they examined the overall impact of local provision on travel, however, the researchers found that the mere existence of a 'local' facility is often not sufficient of itself to affect the proportion of walking trips significantly. Out of the seven facilities studied (see above) only local secondary schools and pubs had a strong correlation with the propensity to walk. Other factors – levels of car ownership and the presence of children in the household – had greater significance (Winter and Farthing, 1997). It seems at first sight rather difficult to square this finding with the observed level of walking to local facilities (well over 50 per cent of trips). But the explanation presumably lies in the overall very high level of car ownership and use in the new estates that were studied, and the fact that some at least of the walking trips may (from evidence in other studies) be 'extra' or 'optional' trips. Further explanation may relate to the way in which 'local' and 'close' were defined in the original data gathering (related not to distance but to a specific residential development) and the small number of case studies from which generalizations are extracted, each with a unique configuration that will have affected the results. So the validity of the conclusions probably needs further testing.

The answers to the original questions, nonetheless, may be stated boldly: local use *does* reduce trip length, and *does* reduce the total amount of motorized travel. Local use for many (not all) facilities also results in more walking trips, especially where those facilities are within 1000m, when walking predominates. However, in suburban locations with high car ownership this does not necessarily result in a significant reduction in car trips, though the trips will on average be shorter. Any action to reduce car reliance will therefore need to combine the promotion of local facilities, opening local choices for residents, with constraints on motor traffic.

## THE IMPACT OF DESIGN MEASURES

Having established the behavioural significance of localities even in the relatively adverse conditions of peripheral estates we now turn to the question: can the design of localities alter the propensity of people to use local facilities, to walk rather than be car-reliant? Like for the previous questions, the answer may appear self-evident, but it is wise to be wary of self-evident truths that actually may be no more than wishful thinking.

The main report which has tackled this question head on is that by ECOTEC (1993). The researchers studied a range of neighbourhoods and innovative projects to establish the degree to which quality of the pedestrian environment could affect the number and length of walking trips. Their general conclusion was that an attractive and safe pedestrian route could encourage (or permit) people to walk twice as much as an unattractive route. Pedestrian behaviour is particularly affected by traffic danger, levels of pollution and noise. Pedestrian priority and related traffic calming measures can improve safety and comfort and hence encourage walking. Similar effects can be observed in relation to cycling. As noted earlier, children's licence to walk or cycle to school/playground/friends is profoundly affected by perceptions (and the reality) of safety on the streets.

It is interesting to note that guidance on the importance of the pedestrian environment comes not only from planners and urban designers but also from contemporary commercial practice. Advice to retailers from their own organization is that design matters: the distance between car parks or bus stops and shopping centre can be effectively 50 per cent longer than normal practice suggests if the pedestrian routes are high quality and safe (Carley, 1996).

At a more basic level the very existence of convenient pedestrian and cycling routes is often an issue. The study of Bradley Stoke in Bristol showed that bad design (based on cul-de-sac enclaves) can double the distance from home to school or shops, and oblige pedestrians to brave intimidating street environments where the homes turn their backs to the street. In a situation where few resident are willing to walk further than 1600 metres, and many rarely walk more than 800 metres, the extra distance, compounded by the poor design, is an effective deterrent. It also undermines the viability of the local services which depend on pedestrian accessibility.

Thus the planning and design of neighbourhoods can have both positive and very negative impacts on the propensity to walk, and directly affect health, safety and aesthetic enjoyment. The absence of effective planning and design restricts modal choice (especially for the more vulnerable groups), restricts accessibility and exacerbates problems of social exclusion. Later chapters on transport and community safety demonstrate ways in which positive design and management of the built environment can reap major benefits for users.

## CONCLUSION

This chapter has shown that there are compelling reasons for reinventing neighbourhoods – reasons that span the breadth of environmental concern from local to global, that emphasize the social potential of neighbourhoods for health, safety, equity, access and community, and even economic justification in terms of capitalizing on the local skills base. Not only are neighbourhoods desirable, but they are also feasible. Even in areas where people live highly mobile lives local facilities, where they are available, are used. Their use leads to less motorized travel as a result of shorter trip lengths and (more equivocally) a shift to non-motorized modes. Contrary to the assumptive world of house builders and trend planners it is clear that locality is far from dead, and that planners can plan to enhance it as part of a strategy for sustainable development and quality of life.

There are two broad questions which stem from this conclusion which subsequent chapters will start to examine. The first is about overall strategy: how do neighbourhoods fit within the general spatial strategy for sustainable development? The second is about design: given the rather mixed achievements of neighbourhood planning in the past, how should we shape the neighbourhoods of the future? The next chapter provides one perspective on these questions by looking at current best practice in terms of specific eco-neighbourhood projects.

# 5  INNOVATIVE ECO-NEIGHBOURHOOD PROJECTS[1]

*Hugh Barton and Deborah Kleiner*

## INTRODUCTION

The previous chapter examined the social and environmental reasons for re-opening the neighbourhood option. But there remains a verifiable suspicion that not much is happening in practice – that economic, political and behavioural constraints are inhibiting the realization of sustainable communities despite widespread support for the principle. There are also reasonable doubts as to whether what is happening matches up to the high aspirations of the eco-neighbourhood movement or the stringent criteria for sustainability as articulated in Chapter 1. We might expect something of a gulf between projects which emerge from idealistic personal commitment and those which are delivered by the market system.

This chapter tests these hypotheses by evaluating current innovative projects. It reports on a search for such projects across the world, it attempts to categorize them and evaluate their achievement so far. Appendix 1 lists the 55 eco-neighbourhood projects that fulfilled the basic criteria, with a brief summary of characteristics. It also gives the initiator and contact point where available. Appendix 2 gives a more detailed analysis of 13 varied projects.

## THE SEARCH FOR EXEMPLARY PROJECTS

This exercise was essentially a search for best practice – seeking to establish what innovative eco-neighbourhood projects currently or imminently exist, how they are being developed and what levels of success they have achieved. The research involved literature and internet searches, personal communication with initiators, and site visits to Little River and Waitakere (New Zealand), Ecolonia (The Netherlands), Kolding (Denmark), Davis (US), Sherwood, Crickhowell, Poundbury and Hockerton (UK).

Overall the survey revealed a fascinating array of different kinds and forms of eco-neighbourhood. There is diversity in scale, location, focus and imple-

---

1 An earlier version of this chapter appeared as an article in *Local Environment* (1998) Vol 3, No 2

mentation. Perhaps the most surprising result, though, was the paucity of really innovative projects at the neighbourhood level – plenty of impressive buildings, but despite the pro-sustainability stances of many governments, there are clearly policy and practical impediments at the meso scale.

The list of projects in Appendix 1 does not claim to be exhaustive, but reflects the main sources that are available. The Global Eco-Village Network (GEN) and the EU-funded project on 'New Sustainable Settlements' (EA.UE, 1997), were particularly valuable. Projects from outside Europe were less easy to trace, and trails often eventually drew blanks. The paucity of projects from developing countries may be more a matter of Anglo- and Euro-centric information networks and cultural assumptions than a true mirror of reality. It is arguable that many rural settlements in Southern Asia, Africa and South America, which are substantially self-dependant for water, food and energy, merit the badge of 'eco-village', but they are not recorded here.

The criteria for inclusion were to do with scale, stage, information and sustainability. Small housing groups and whole cities were normally excluded. The project had to either be already in existence or very close to it. Information had to be available to allow initial appraisal. Sustainability was judged across a range of environmental, social and economic criteria and projects were only included if they rated against several criteria. However, there were cases at the margin where specific schemes have been included because they illustrate an important point. For example Poundbury has been included as an 'urban village' because it does some things very radically and well (high density, mixed use, pedestrian-orientated) even though others (energy, water) are treated purely conventionally. Hockerton Self-build has been included although small because it demonstrates a holistic approach to a rare degree.

## Projects Thin on the Ground

The survey revealed hundreds of eco-village/neighbourhood projects but most were purely at the conceptual stage. In some cases projects with extensive WEB sites and high reputations in the eco-village network proved to be no more than armchair ideas. Eventually only 55 projects around the world satisfied our criteria. It is likely that there are quite a number of others which we have not been able to access or where the response to enquiries has been insufficient to justify inclusion. Even allowing for that, however, the total is disappointing after a decade of international meetings and political hype about global ecological problems.

As illustrated in Table 5.1, quite a number of the projects are small-scale. Over 50 per cent have (or anticipate having) fewer than 300 residents. Of the 14 projects with at least 1000 inhabitants and therefore on a neighbourhood scale, four only are substantially complete or have reached that scale. Those are Lykovryssi in Greece, Puchenan in Austria, Auroville in India and, at the vastly greater scale, Davis in California. Some of the most exciting projects are still on the drawing board: Halifax in Melbourne; Bamberton in British Columbia; Sherwood Energy Village in England. Of the smaller projects (less than 300 people) most are rural eco-villages initiated by the potential residents themselves. Overall eco-villages account for half of the projects and represent a radical approach to rural sustainability and resettlement. The dominance of the voluntary/community sector as project-initiators is striking (Table 5.2).

The urban projects are roughly equally divided between greenfield (suburban) schemes and urban renewal projects. The vast majority are found in Europe. All three sectors – public, private and voluntary – have been active in initiating schemes, though as shown in the case studies later, the successful projects often involve all three sectors. The fair number of sustainable regeneration schemes is worthy of note. In their 1997 review Margaret and Declan Kennedy observed that regeneration policy has normally progressed independently of the sustainability agenda. They found few extant schemes and most of those not very spectacular. Perhaps the extra projects identified here are the beginning of a more integrated approach.

**Table 5.1** *Survey of Eco-Neighbourhoods: Numbers of Projects by Types*

| | Rural Eco-village | Urban Greenfield | Urban Renewal | Town/ Township | Total |
|---|---|---|---|---|---|
| *Population* | | | | | |
| 20–100 | 12 | 1 | 2 | na | 15 |
| 100–300 | 9 | 3 | 4 | na | 16 |
| 300–1000 | 4 | 3 | 3 | na | 10 |
| 1000–3000 | 3 | 3 | 2 | na | 8 |
| 3000–10,000 | na | 2 | 0 | 1 | 3 |
| 10,000+ | na | 0 | 0 | 3 | 3 |
| *Initiator* | | | | | |
| Public Sector | 0 | 5 | 6 | 1 | 12 |
| Private Sector | 1 | 3 | 1 | 0 | 5 |
| Voluntary Sector | 27 | 4 | 4 | 3 | 38 |
| *Stage* | | | | | |
| Mainly built | 11 | 4 | 4 | 1 | 20 |
| Progressing | 15 | 5 | 1 | 2 | 23 |
| Firmly planned | 2 | 3 | 6 | 1 | 12 |
| *Continent* | | | | | |
| N America | 7 | 3 | 0 | 3 | 13 |
| Europe | 14 | 9 | 9 | 0 | 32 |
| Australasia | 5 | 0 | 2 | 0 | 7 |
| Rest of World | 2 | 0 | 0 | 1 | 3 |
| Total Projects | 28 | 12 | 11 | 4 | 55 |

*Note* that where the evidence is not complete for any particular project a reasonable guess has been made to enable completion of the chart.

Three of the four free-standing town projects are in North America. Bamberton in British Columbia is an ambitious but still pending plan for a new semi-autonomous settlement of 12,000 people. Arcosanti in the Arizona desert is a prototype new town for 7000 people designed to illustrate Paolo Soleri's theory of 'archology' (integrating ecology, architecture and urban planning): development has started. Davis is a relatively compact Californian town of 50,000 within Sacramento's hinterland, where a radical, independent civic line has been taken since 1973 on energy, housing, cycling, land use and citizen participation. The fourth project is of a completely different kind: Auroville in India is a rural regeneration and research village cluster of 1300 people, and has ambitious plans to grow into a fully-fledged sustainable town of 40,000. More details and evaluations of Bamberton, Davis and Auroville are given later.

The overall paucity of successful projects, particularly projects of a larger size, seems at odds with post-Rio mood in government and voluntary sectors stressing the need for sustainable development. The explanation would seem to lie not in the absence of proposals but in difficulties of implementation, and in particular the lack of engagement as yet of market interests. The roles of different interests will be further examined in the case studies.

**Table 5.2** *Survey of Eco-Neighbourhoods: Percentages by Population, Type, Stage and Initiator*

| Population | (%) | Type | (%) | Stage | (%) | Initiator | (%) |
|---|---|---|---|---|---|---|---|
| 20–100 | 28 | *Rural eco-village* | 51 | Built (mostly) | 36 | *Public sector* | 22 |
| 100–300 | 29 | *Urban greenfield* | 22 | In progress | 42 | *Private sector* | 9 |
| 300–1000 | 18 | *Urban renewal* | 20 | Planned | 22 | *Voluntary sector* | 69 |
| 1000–3000 | 15 | *Township/town* | 7 | | | | |
| 3000–10000 | 5 | | | | | | |
| 10000+ | 5 | | | | | | |

# CATEGORIZING ECO-NEIGHBOURHOODS

The analysis that follows distinguishes six types of eco-neighbourhood and illustrates them with case studies. The selection is eclectic, to point out contrasts in approach and philosophy. The basis of categorization is first, location and scale; and second, functional or agency characteristics. The location/scale criteria distinguish between rural projects, urban projects and whole-town or township programmes. Within rural the key distinction is between projects based on the land, and those stressing teleworking. Within the urban context the main distinctions are between state-funded experiments (often technology-driven), 'new urbanist' urban villages (aesthetically driven, and market-funded), and eco-communities initiated by voluntary groups (aiming at personally sustainable lifestyles). The town category is not subdivided. Inevitably there is a degree of arbitrariness about the categories and some projects do not fall neatly into one.

## Type I: Rural Eco-Village

These are land-based rural hamlets or villages where the economic *raison d'être* is provided by farming, small-holdings, fuel crops and (stretching a point) on-site tourism, and many energy/water/food resource loops are closed. This image of rural sustainability has been given focus by the theory and practice of permaculture (Mollison, 1988), while at the same time being discouraged by policy guides because of the expectation that land-based employment will not prevent heavy dependence on services, schooling and work at other locations, increasing car emissions (DoE, 1994).

Simon Fairlie (1996) distinguishes two levels of eco-village. One is the 'farm village' (originally a term coined in *Sustainable Settlements*, Barton et al, 1995) where a cluster of farm holdings share childcare, transport and farm/family equipment. The other is the sustainable village, large enough to support basic retailing and social facilities. Such villages are likely to be 'home-grown', with participants having a strong commitment to permaculture or 'low impact' development. Crystal Waters in Queensland is the classic permaculture village.

### Crystal Waters, Queensland

Crystal Waters, initiated by a residents groups in the late 1970s, is a remote land-based village now home to 250 people and still developing. Many residents grow their own food in permaculture gardens. Eighty per cent of the 260 hectare site area is still available for agriculture, forestry, recreation and habitat, with the intention that in the long run the settlement will be resource autonomous. However currently most households rely on non-renewable energy for electricity and hot water. Inevitably in a pioneer village there is limited social diversity with a preponderance of young families. Few residents make a living solely from the land. Many are involved in the building trades or are working from home. There is some limited commuting to Brisbane (1.5 hours drive) and the nearest small town of Maleney (27km). Crystal Waters relies on Maleney for essential retail and health services, but the aspiration is that it should grow sufficiently to be self-reliant for services, food and energy. Management is by a trust fund and residents' co-operative, with ecological and convivial values reinforced by bylaws. The key to village sustainability will be in nurturing not just a permanent agriculture, but a permanent culture as well (see Appendix 2).

In the UK the eco-village ideal was pioneered in the 1970s and 1980s by groups with specific philosophies and economic rationale: the Centre for Alternative Technology in Wales (visitor centre); Findhorn in Scotland (spiritual growth); and Botton Village in Yorkshire (for the mentally handicapped). The concept of a permaculture village was expounded (but never realized) by the Stroud Sustainable Village Project in the 1980s. Tinkers Bubble (Somerset) is an existing low impact rural resettlement project; it is also very small. The ten pioneers are currently in temporary shelters but have won planning permission to build accommodation on the small-holdings they farm. The aspirations of pioneer groups are often frustrated by regulation and difficulties in securing land. While the largely unfulfilled intentions of pioneer groups are an inspiration, the image of the rural eco-village and 'low impact rural development' may also be perceived as a cover, as the case of West Harwood illustrates.

### West Harwood, Lothian (See Figure 5.1)

This is perhaps the most significant current UK local authority project for low impact rural development. It is called Lowland Crofting, but that is misleading, as it is really very low density housing with extensive woodland development (Fairlie, 1996). The scheme has been devised to reclaim a depopulated and deforested landscape. The existing farms are being divided into three parts – a minimum of 30 per cent planted with trees, some farmland retained, and the remainder being sold off as 'crofts' to pay for the extensive landscape improvement. The resulting smallholdings may be 0.25 hectares in size, and have permission for one house plus

**Figure 5.1** *Lowland Crofting at West Harwood*

outbuildings as a base for a small business. The very real benefits of the scheme are in terms of landscape, biodiversity and carbon-fixing. The problem, however, is that the plots are essentially being occupied by affluent urbanites, with consequent high car use and emissions. The so-called lowland crofting is in effect likely to be low density out-of-town commuter development, and as such does not fulfil basic sustainability criteria (see Appendix 2.).

The essence of rural sustainability is a local land based economy, but this is difficult to sustain. New dwellings permitted for agricultural workers tend to transfer to non-and-based occupants within five years. The legal agreements obliging land-working will therefore need to be strong if new eco-villages are to remain true to their original tenets. Rural pioneers, as in Tinkers Bubble, would welcome such agreements as a safeguard for themselves (Simon Fairlie, 1996).

## Type II: Televillages

'Televillages' do not necessarily claim to be land based, but rely on telecommunications and the Internet to foster home/locally-based work, geared to 'remote management', out-sourcing and freelancing. The electronic exchange processes may be supplemented by more traditional rural crafts and local workshops. Such televillages are more likely than the true rural settlements to be provided by the market. For example, in the small Welsh market town of Crickhowell, within easy walking distance of the centre, is Acorn Televillage, a group of some 30 energy-efficient homes built partly of locally sourced materials, for sale to telecommuters, with a shared telecottage and small offices available for rent (see Appendix 2). There are few other examples, however.

Most of the rural telecentres so far are outposts of universities (eg Plymouth) or local offices offering telecommunications services to residents.

The idea of televillages is seductive, but there is little evidence as yet as to whether they – or home-working – reduce overall travel demand (Gillespie, 1992). On the contrary, if televillages are given permission in rural settings rather than closely tied into the towns, on the unproven assumption that telecommunications substitutes for not only for commuting trips but trips in general, then they could well prove to be 'Trojan horses' in rural sustainability strategies.

### Little River, New Zealand

This is a community-led scheme of a rather different nature. Little River is a small dispersed village on the Banks Peninsular within striking distance of Christchurch. The residents, with local authority support, are planning to expand by 50 per cent from 400 to 600 people. They intend to create a relatively compact settlement centred on a research out-station of the local university and an improved range of local facilities, together with localized schemes of sustainable food, water and energy provision. The hope is that commuting will be minimized by both local job opportunities and teleworking, with connection into global research communities. Locally-produced goods will be marketed with the aid of a distinctive eco-quality stamp if they meet certain standards. The development project is partly the result of a community empowerment and design programme funded by the Banks District Council. Children as well as adults are involved in a bottom-up decision-process that is helping to give the village a strong identity (see Appendix 2).

The Little River project is innovative and exciting but may not be easily reproduced elsewhere. It is on a scale sufficient to generate some economies of scale and to support shop, primary school and leisure facilities. Active involvement of local people gives hope for effective implementation. The issue of resource autonomy is considered by residents to be central. The professional design team is willing and able to work in collaborative style. However, progress waits on funding organizations, and time will tell if the project is essentially sustainable.

### Type III: Urban Demonstration Projects

A wide range of experimental projects, often initiated as part of a competition or for research purposes, have been promoted by local and national governments. Normally they fall into the 'architectural' category, with technical innovation or demonstration being the driving force, and are located on suburban sites. In the UK the Milton Keynes 'Energy Park' is perhaps the best known example. Kennedy (1994) lists several European projects, including Ecolonia, Alphen aan den Rijn, in The Netherlands.

### Ecolonia, Alphen aan den Rijn

Ecolonia consists of 101 residential units, planned by NOVEM (The Netherlands Agency for Energy and the Environment) and part funded by the Dutch Government. A wide range of architects were challenged to create solar, energy-efficient, healthy houses, with maximum durability and recyclability of building materials and effective provision for water collection, use and on-site drainage. The scheme claims a good level of success in showing that sustainable buildings are both technically feasible and commercially viable. However, subsequent monitoring has also shown that technical innovation by itself is not enough. It needs to be accompanied by resident commitment and understanding if the full benefits are to be realized (see Appendix 2).

Such demonstration projects are valuable in breaking new ground and helping to win public and commercial acceptance for new concepts. They are typically rather limited in the range of issues they aspire to deal with, and may risk giving the impression that sustainable equals new build, and that sustainable architecture is idiosyncratic. While the best examples are well integrated into their urban setting and are admirable trail-blazers, the scale of projects is often not sufficient to support local services, and schemes can fail to address the issue of high transport energy costs.

Projects demonstrating ecological renewal, and located in inner more accessible zones of cities, are in many ways more important than greenfield new-build. So far the number of such projects is small – sustainability and regeneration programmes have been rather separate. But a conspicuous exception is the Kolding Ecological Renewal Scheme in Denmark.

## *Kolding Ecological Renewal Scheme, Denmark (See Figure 5.2)*

A high density block of courtyard housing (over 150 units) close to the town centre has been renovated, with grant assistance, to save energy, increase solar gain, catch roof water, recycle grey water and treat black water in an eye-catching pyramidal greenhouse, while upgrading the quality of the housing, the semi-private open space, and diversifying ground floor uses to create local facilities for the wider area. This scheme is nearly complete, and an environmental and social success. While the glass pyramid is not in itself economic, it demonstrates the potential for ecological inner city renewal in vivid style (see Appendix 2).

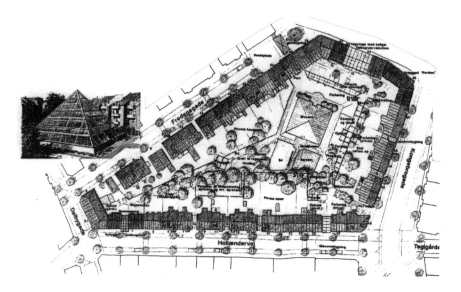

**Figure 5.2** *Plan of Kolding Ecological Renewal Scheme*

Exploratory subsidized projects are important in order to convince consumers and the development industry that radical solutions can work, and be economic in operation if not construction. Almost inevitably, however, they cannot easily be reproduced elsewhere.

## Type IV: Urban Eco-Communities

While the demonstration projects are technologically-led the urban eco-communities are inspired by social ideals of conviviality and mutual support. Early variants were often driven by housing need, such as housing co-operatives eg the Eldonians in Liverpool. Recently ecological motivation has combined with social to shape a new form called 'co-housing'. This started in that most libertarian of countries, Denmark. Co-housing schemes, typically of 20–30 units, combine private ownership of individual dwellings with shared ownership of a communal house, open space and essential infrastructure. Shared facilities bind the community together (especially where people choose to eat the evening meal together) and provide mutual support (eg shared transport, crèche arrangements) and increase life-style options open to residents (privacy *and* community).

Co-housing – as a way of building a closely knit ecological community – has stood the test of time in Denmark, but despite enthusiastic promotion has yet to prove itself in the UK. Co-housing could be expected to facilitate reduced car reliance but this has not been assessed. One great potential strength is that it offers a means of motivating people to jointly manage local community energy/water/sewage/composting/transport schemes which could in their turn increase ecological sustainability. Such small, close-knit communities can be linked together into larger projects, as in the case of Ithica Eco-village in New York State.

### Ithica Eco-Village, New York State (See Figure 5.3)

This eco-village is being created on 70 hectares two miles from the centre of the city of Ithica. When complete it will have five small neighbourhoods clustered around a village green. Each neighbourhood is intended to be a co-housing scheme and the whole is organized by prospective residents as a grass-roots project. The housing will be ultra energy-efficient, and water, wildlife, woodland and food growing are being planned following organic/permaculture principles. The short distance from the 'village' to Ithica centre means that non-motorized transport is an option.

While Ithica is a greenfield project, the next two examples are redevelopment projects: the first in the heart of a major, energy-profligate city; the second rejuvenating a small ex-mining town.

### Halifax EcoCity, South Australia (See Figure 5.4)

The Halifax EcoCity Project is being co-initiated by a community non-profit organization Urban Ecology Australia Inc. It is to be located on a brownfield site in the centre of the city of Adelaide and is claimed to be the 'world's first piece of eco-city'. The design is for a community of up to 1000 people, with commercial space and community facilities as well as housing. It will be a relatively high density, three to five storey development with pedestrian streets, squares, courtyards and roof gardens. At

**Figure 5.3** *Part of Ithica Eco-Village*

the same time, as part of a two-pronged programme of urban redevelopment and rural renewal, at least one hectare of degraded rural land will be restored to effective use for each person living in the EcoCity development. The scheme has a comprehensive approach to materials reuse, energy-efficiency, water catchment and reuse and local habitat creation. The process of planning and design involves cooperation between the professionals and the incoming residents. Subsequent land ownership control will be vested in a community-owned company. According to the architect, Paul Downton, the main hurdles the project has to overcome are not financial but bureaucratic. At present it is premature to reach conclusions about the economic and social practicality of the scheme (Urban Ecology Australia, 1995) (see Appendix 2).

## Sherwood Energy Village, Nottingham

Sherwood Energy Village is to be developed by an Industrial and Provident Society on a 60 hectare disused colliery site a few hundred metres from the centre of the small ex-coal town of Ollerton in north Nottinghamshire. It is an example of 'eco-renovation' and aims to improve the quality of both the physical and social fabric of local communities by increasing resource efficiency, reducing pollution, and through the provision of jobs, education and leisure facilities alongside housing.

The village is to be energy autonomous with net zero $CO_2$ emissions (though excluding transport emissions). This will require local renewable energy generation and the provision of super insulated buildings with efficient electrical appliances and solar electricity generation. Autonomy will be further developed by independence from mains water and sewerage, and encouraging local food production and local employment provision.

The Industrial and Provident Society is run by local people committed to the regeneration of the town and is strongly supported by the Newark and Sherwood District Council. At every stage in the development of ideas

**Figure 5.4** *Image of Halifax EcoCity (John Downton)*

the town community is actively involved. The biggest motivation for redevelopment is jobs, not homes. Funding for £3.5m worth of site recovery and infrastructure work is coming from a range of EU and UK government sources (Crawford, 1998) (see Appendix 2).

These three emerging schemes in three separate continents demonstrate the potential of voluntary sector initiatives. All are impressive inasmuch as they are working with sustainable development as holistically as possible, encompassing energy, water and mineral resources, economic activity and social structures. All are located close to urban facilities. They vary in the motivation of their promoters, Ithica being created by the residents for themselves, Halifax and Sherwood being planned as key parts of a wider community regeneration programme. High costs and bureaucratic hurdles are the bugbear of such projects, which may help to explain why few have yet been realized. Certainly the Sherwood initiative group are achieving progress only by dint of persistence, political wheeler-dealing, flexibility and patience. Yet from what evidence exists there is a potentially large untapped market for such ecological development which could in time trigger a private sector response.

## Type V: 'New Urbanism' Development

Whereas all the previous categories involve projects on a modest scale, each with less than 1000 dwellings, the last two categories are mostly on a bigger canvas, and necessarily involve partnership between the local planning authorities and the development industry. In the US the 'new urbanism' designers have promoted the concept of TODs (transit orientated developments) – compact pedestrian-scaled neighbourhoods focused on transit stations giving high level of local accessibility by foot and of regional accessibility by public transport. TODs are typically more dense, socially diverse, and mixed in use than the suburban norm, and carefully designed around a system of public spaces that help create an attractive living and working environment (Duany and Plater-Zyberk, 1991; Calthorpe, 1993). They may or may not incorporate special energy/water/wildlife features. TODs in Portland and San Diego are a surprising switch in development conventions and provide an enticing new image of urbanity in a land that had forgotten its value. The concept is also being adapted to other political and cultural systems:

### Waitakere, New Zealand *(See Figure 5.5)*

In the Western suburbs of Auckland, Waitakere City Council has picked up the idea of TODs and in a context of sprawling car-based suburbs is reinventing town centres (notably Henderson and New Lynn) around

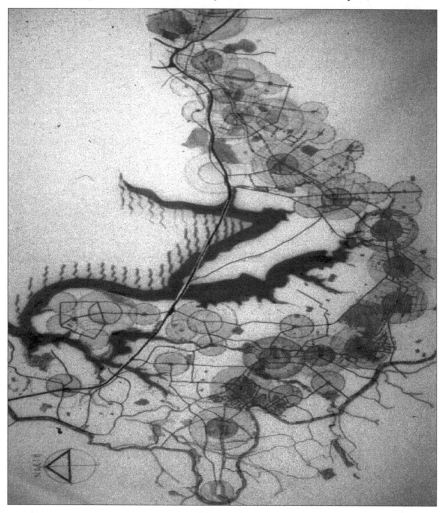

*Source:* Ecologically Sustainable Design Ltd, Auckland

**Figure 5.5** *Waitakere: Intensification Nodes*

potential LRT stations. These TODs are the focus not for greenfield but for brownfield reuse where old industries have died. The planning strategy of intensification, doubling or tripling the original four-dwelling-to-the-acre standard of the first suburbanites, is finding a ready response from the market and the electorate. The town centre has at the same time been revitalized by establishing pedestrian priority and traffic calming.

TODs are an appropriate and marketable response to American and Australasian conditions of generally low density dispersed suburban development, in that they begin to focus the decentralizing forces of the market on transit-accessible locations, but they are very much a compromise position: they are inevitably only islands of relative transport-efficiency in a sea of wastefulness, and the intensive commercial developments that are part and parcel of urban TODs typically will serve wide hinterlands predominantly reliant on car access except along the one transit corridor. The Waitakere strategy, like its precursors in Portland and San Diego, could be pilloried as too little, too late. Car use is very high by European standards and still expanding faster than population. But these transit/town centre revivals sow the seeds for more radical change in urban structure – if and when governments recognize the costs of pollution/congestion and changes the fiscal messages to travellers.

In the UK the Urban Village Forum shares many aims and values with the New Urbanists. The dominant motives are aesthetic and cultural rather than ecological. Poundbury, the growing new suburb of Dorchester, is the most conspicuous realization so far.

### *Poundbury, Dorset* (See Figure 5.6)

Poundbury was initiated by Prince Charles on his own land and designed by Leon Krier, with effective support from the local authorities in the process of implementation. It is built at nearly twice the normal greenfield density, with terraced housing, mews, streets, squares and courtyards providing an attractive pedestrian environment. Housing types and tenures are varied. Small-scale employment and social facilities create a patchwork pattern of land use. Poundbury belies house-builder marketing presumptions by selling well. Residents so far are satisfied and environmental care is excellent despite the density. Nevertheless by the exacting standards of sustainability Poundbury falls down. It adopts relatively conventional approaches to energy and water resources, and is far from ideal for bike and bus efficiency. Its greatest importance lies in confounding assumptions of house purchaser conservatism, and pointing the way to much more efficient and effective use of greenfield sites.

'Urban villages', like TODs, are normally envisaged as part of urban regeneration and restructuring, though development on brownfield sites. The high profile stance of the British Deputy Prime Minister John Prescott in relation to the Millennium Village has helped to ensure that the Greenwich brownfield project has much higher sustainability aspirations than Poundbury.

### *Greenwich Millennium Village*

The consortium, led by Countryside Properties and Taylor Woodrow, who have won the Millennium Village competition, propose a high density, low rise, pedestrian-friendly scheme on the previously contaminated site next to the River Thames. There will be 1377 flats and town-houses, 80 per cent for

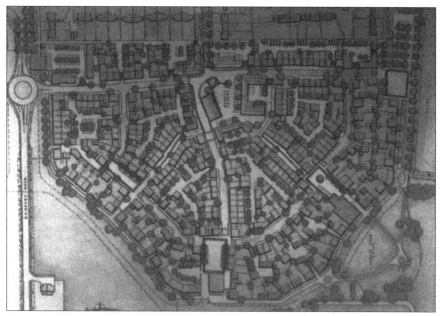

*Source:* Duchy of Cornwall; *Poundbury Philosophy*

**Figure 5.6** *Plan of Poundbury's First Phase*

sale and 20 per cent for shared ownership with housing associations, giving a total population of about 3000. The scheme boasts quite a number of innovative features: highly adaptable manufactured buildings with low embodied energy; a CHP plant providing 60 per cent of heating demand (viability assisted by the mixture of uses on site); reuse of grey water and visible water management systems in the 'ecology park'; communal garden courts reminiscent of London squares but without the cars; and the whole well served by light transit route and bikeways. Cars will not be encouraged, but neither will they be actively deterred – in the interest of saleability (Garlick, 1998). The village will thus challenge lifestyle and development conventions in many ways. The most risky design element is the extent of semi-private shared open space – something the Danes are more familiar with than the British. Taken as a whole the scheme is a bold pilot sustainability project. But given its likely attractiveness as a leisure/tourist haunt, living there could be a bit like living in a goldfish bowl. And it will be interesting to see if all the much-vaunted sustainability features survive the implementation process.

## Type VI: Ecological Townships

The new urbanist neighbourhoods treat transport energy efficiency, environmental quality and the creation of community as key goals but are usually non-specific about important ecological aims. They are also, as noted, only small parts of the urban whole. The objective, clearly, is that *whole* urban neighbourhoods, townships, towns and cities are evolved towards sustainability. Many historic towns in Europe have made courageous steps in the right direction: for example Delft, in The Netherlands, with a comprehensive bike/

walking network and enviable urban environmental quality; Frieburg, in the Rhine rift valley, with a comprehensive transport strategy; Odense, in Denmark, with an impressive energy system based on combined heat and power. Very few urban authorities, however, have been in a position to adopt an integrated sustainability strategy and implement it. One possible exception is Davis City in California.

## Davis City, California

Davis, an agriculture and university-based town of 50,000 people in the hinterland of Sacramento, has been developing on eco-conscious lines from before the first oil-price hike in 1973. This has led to a pedestrian/bike friendly environment, high energy and water efficiency, progressive reduction in wastes, and the integration of natural habitats with the human habitat. It is a safe and friendly place to live and work. The local plan requires that every new development shall have a mix of housing, designed both to ensure the availability of low cost homes and to avoid ghettos. It does remain, nevertheless, a relatively privileged ex-urban town dependent on Sacramento for higher level services. Ironically its very success has led to above average house prices which may have excluded some less affluent potential residents.

The most distinctive feature of Davis' achievement is the process by which it has got there. The town has a thorough going democratic approach encouraging the active participation of citizens in the decision-making process through (at the last count) 376 volunteer committees or commissions. Consensus building can take time and frustrate innovation, but in this city the ideals of Local Agenda 21 have been realized to a surprising degree. Few other towns, though, can boast the same high level of educational attainment in its residents (City of Davis, 1996).

Idealistic newbuild schemes abound, but few reach the implementation phase. Particularly impressive is one proposed on Vancouver Island in Canada.

## Bamberton, British Columbia

The South Island Development Corporation had bought a 640 hectare site, formerly a cement works, above a tranquil fjord 20 miles from Victoria. An intensive programme of community meetings led to the planning of a 'traditional' pedestrian-scaled town of 12,000 people that could be a model of ecological probity. Development is to occur 'organically' over the period of a generation with investment from trade union pension funds interested in long term returns. The Bamberton Code, which anyone involved is invited to sign, sets out principles of community life, economic self-reliance, and ecological stewardship as the basis for detailed design guidance on incremental decision-making. The inspiration for Bamberton is much more than purely environmental, more about realizing the potential of human beings (Dauncey, 1996).

Spiritual values even more explicitly underpin the development of a town in a completely different physical and cultural setting, as illustrated by Auroville in India.

## Auroville, South India

Run by the residents as an independent trust, Auroville was founded in 1978 and 20 years on has 1300 people, drawn from many countries, though with a strong Indian contingent. The denuded landscape has been revived by good water management and extensive tree planting. Sustainable agriculture forms the basic activity, and the settlement is still a cluster of linked villages rather than a town. Auroville provides health, education and agricultural services to nearby rural settlements, and undertakes crop and ecology research. It plans to grow eventually to an urban community of 40,000 (Martin Littlewood, personal communication, 1998).

While there are therefore a few bold and innovative town-scale projects spanning the full breadth of the sustainable development agenda, it is impossible to be sanguine about achievements so far. The larger the scale of eco-neighbourhood the greater the complexity of interdependent issues and the larger number of stakeholders who need to be involved. It is rare to find sufficient unanimity amongst partners, or sufficient concentration of benign power, to allow effective progress on all fronts.

**Table 5.3** *Eco-Neighbourhood Case Studies Classification and Agencies*

| Scale and Location Lead Sector(s) | Rural | Urban Greenfield | Urban Brownfield | Town |
|---|---|---|---|---|
| Voluntary | Crystal Waters ✔ Eco-village | Ithica ✔ urban eco-community | Halifax ? urban eco-community | Auroville ✔ new town |
| Voluntary/ Public | Little River ? Televillage | | Sherwood ? urban eco-community | Bamberton ? new town |
| Public | | Ecolonia ✔ demonstration project | Kolding ✔ demonstration project | |
| Public/ Private | West Harwood ✔ Eco-village | Poundbury ✔ new urbanist plan | Greenwich ? new urbanist plan | |
| Private | Acorn Televillage ✔ Televillage | | | |
| Public/ Private/ Voluntary | | | Waitakere ✔ new urbanist plan | Davis ✔ existing town |

*Notes:* ✔ = project completed or being completed
? = project at planning stage and still uncertain

# EVALUATION

The typology above makes no claim to be exhaustive. It is more a reflection of where we are at present. The fact that the projects listed are still innovative and exciting to us is a sad comment on the slow progress of the past 20 years – since the first British eco-village was founded at Llyngwern Quarry near Machynlleth (the Centre for Alternative Technology). However, there is now, in the atmosphere of millennial idealism, a burgeoning interest in eco-projects, and growing evidence both that the technologies are robust and that there is an enthusiastic (largely untapped) market.

The categorization above highlighting contrasts of scale, focus and implementation, makes clear the sheer diversity of existing eco-neighbourhood projects. Table 5.3 acts as a summary, distinguishing different degrees of sectoral partnership.

Table 5.4 provides an overview of the strengths and weaknesses of the projects. Like all such summaries it should be treated with caution since it necessarily involves a level of simplification which at the margin can be arbitrary. The Freiburg objectives (see Chapter 1) have been adjusted to assist clarity of judgement, and supplemented by criteria on green economic activity and the recycling or restoration of land and buildings. If the list of criteria is accepted then the contrast between projects becomes startling. While Bradley Stoke (as the example of contemporary suburban development discussed in Chapter 1) clearly does worst, the eco-neighbourhood projects range from Acorn (achieving only three criteria unequivocally) to Auroville (achieving 10 out of 12). The differences are in part accounted for by divergent implementation contexts. West Harwood and Acorn are both primarily market-driven, (though the former initiated by the local authority) and limited by what affluent 'rural' consumers will buy. Waitakere and Davis are municipally led and achieving surprising levels of success in relatively hostile social and economic environments. Of the government-inspired projects Kolding is a bold consciousness-raiser and Greenwich promises much. Generally speaking the projects led by community non-profit trusts – such as Little River, Ithica, Halifax, Sherwood and Auroville – are able to be the most radical, relying strongly on the personal interest and commitment of residents, and less trammelled by bureaucracy or profit-takers.

As *exemplary* projects all the schemes reviewed are admirable. However in absolutist terms their success is open to question when set against the sustainable transport requirements. Most are too small to qualify as independent settlements, lacking the population to support local health, educational, leisure or retail facilities, let alone a good range of work opportunities.

In the urban areas the projects need to be seen not as semi-autonomous enclaves but, rather, as part of the urban continuum, woven into the physical fabric of the town and sharing facilities with adjacent localities. While that is not the image purveyed by some advocates (Ecologist, 1972; Littlewood, 1998), many of the selected projects do exemplify it. The urban brownfield schemes in Kolding, Waitakere, Greenwich and Ollerton (Sherwood Energy Village) all see the new eco-neighbourhood as fully integrated with the town and encouraging its regeneration. Even Acorn Televillage is very much part of the small town of Crickhowell.

Moving up the scale the TODs and eco-towns are generally large enough to support a fair range of local facilities. The TODs are also being marketed as suburban locations for city-wide businesses, (Calthorpe, 1993) even though the resulting dispersed trip patterns are likely to be energy-intensive. The argument is put that such a policy prepares the ground for an energy-constrained future – where people will be motivated to localize their job-search areas – while at the same time providing a focus for the decentralizing tendencies of the market (Waitakere, 1997). In other words current *certain* inefficiency (driven by pragmatism) is being traded for future *possible* efficiency: a Faustian bargain.

**Table 5.4** *Eco-Neighbourhood Projects: Evaluation*

| Category | Project | Heterogeneous social composition | Land use diversity (local work and facilities) | 'Green' economic activity | Distinctive, pedestrian-scaled public realm | Effective ped/bike/p.t. networks linking to the wider area | Private motor use discouraged | Ecologically responsible energy strategy | Ecologically responsible water strategy | Recycling of land and/or buildings | Ecological landscape/local food | Community/user involvement | Sustainable management |
|---|---|---|---|---|---|---|---|---|---|---|---|---|---|
|  | Bradley Stoke | ✗ | – | ✗ | ✗ | ✗ | ✗ | ✗ | – | – | ✗ | ✗ | ✗ |
| I | Crystal Waters | – | ✓ | ✓ | ✓ | – | ✗ | – | – | – | ✓ | ✓ | ✓ |
|  | West Harwood | ✗ | ✓ | – | – | – | ✗ | – | – | ✓ | ✓ | – | ✓ |
| II | Acorn Televillage | ✗ | ✓ | – | ✓ | – | ✗ | ✓ | – | – | ✗ | – | – |
|  | Little River | ✓ | ✓ | ✓ | ✓ | ✓ | ✗ | ✓ | ✓ | – | ✓ | ✓ | – |
| III | Ecolonia | – | – | – | ✓ | ✓ | – | ✓ | – | – | – | – | – |
|  | Kolding | ✓ | ✓ | – | ✓ | ✓ | ✓ | ✓ | ✓ | ✓ | – | ✓ | ✓ |
| IV | Ithica Eco-village | – | ✓ | ✓ | ✓ | – | ✗ | ✓ | ✓ | – | ✓ | ✓ | ✓ |
|  | Halifax EcoCity | ✓ | ✓ | ✓ | ✓ | – | – | ✓ | ✓ | ✓ | – | – | – |
|  | Sherwood | ✓ | ✓ | – | ✓ | – | ✗ | ✓ | ✓ | ✓ | – | ✓ | ✓ |
| V | Waitakere TODs | ✓ | ✓ | – | ✓ | – | ✗ | ✓ | – | ✓ | ✗ | ✓ | – |
|  | Poundbury | ✓ | ✓ | – | ✓ | ✓ | ✗ | – | ✓ | ✓ | – | ✓ | ✓ |
|  | Greenwich | ✓ | ✓ | – | ✓ | ✓ | – | – | – | – | – | – | – |
| VI | Davis City | ✓ | ✓ | – | ✓ | ✓ | ✗ | ✓ | – | ✓ | – | ✓ | ✓ |
|  | Bamberton | ✓ | ✓ | ✓ | ✓ | ✓ | – | ✓ | – | – | – | ✓ | – |
|  | Auroville | ✓ | ✓ | ✓ | ✓ | – | – | ✓ | – | ✓ | – | ✓ | ✓ |

*Notes:* ✓ = aims to achieve;   – = unknown or imponderable;   ✗ = militates against

Conversely there are risks associated with rural projects. If truly *land-based*, and capable of being maintained as such when families mature and property is sold, then their benefits in terms of rural revival could be great (Auroville, at this early stage in its development, perhaps shows this). If on the other hand rural eco-villages in reality provide for people with an economic and social base in the city, then car ownership and transport emissions are likely to be very high and the overall footprint heavy. Even Crystal Waters, with its strong base, is parasitic on urban areas.

## CONCLUSIONS

There are several general conclusions from the analysis of current projects. First, the 'technology' of sustainable development in relation to energy, water, buildings, organic growing, and wildlife diversity is very well demonstrated. The processes of building partnerships, engaging the local community and working towards commitment are quite widely practised. But there is sometimes an element of wishful thinking about human behaviour over time – how residents and businesses react to changing opportunities particularly in relation to access and movement. It is not normally appropriate or possible to create cosy self-sufficient neighbourhoods or villages.

Second, despite the buzz surrounding the concepts of eco-villages and eco neighbourhoods, surprisingly few are as yet being realized, and this reflects the inertia of public and private agencies. Many excellent schemes, promoted by local groups, are frustrated by outdated public policies and conservative fund-holders.

Third, some of the innovative schemes laying claim to the sustainability mantle promote certain facets of the sustainable agenda to the detriment of others. This applies particularly to some small scale rural projects, technology-based demonstration projects, and 'new urbanist' schemes.

Fourth, nevertheless, there are developments that are putting together the whole integrated concept of sustainability at the settlement level or contributing to the regeneration of existing towns. Successful projects typically demonstrate the value of partnership, with the voluntary sector providing the inspiration, the private sector providing development funds, and the local authority facilitating the process. The most successful schemes involve active participation of residents, if not project planning and subsequent management by users and residents. The basic principles of LA21, drawing all groups into engagement and commitment, working towards sustainable development, are demonstrated by these projects.

Finally, the significance of successful trail-blazing projects is that others should follow the trail. The idea of eco-neighbourhoods is of general application. While in the UK government guidance and the emerging new generation of development plans put sustainability centre stage there are very few signs of change on the ground. Most new developments repeat the pattern of the recent past, facilitating car use, disenfranchising the non-car-users, providing the essential services of water, sewage treatment, gas and electricity on demand rather than managing demand or achieving local autonomy. Only when the mainstream development agencies alter course is the first battle won, so perhaps the most optimistic sign that can be extracted from the case studies is that in some projects the private sector is actively engaging with local authorities, finding markets for high density innovative schemes that begin to change the nature of the development game.

# 6 THE NEIGHBOURHOOD AS ECOSYSTEM

*Hugh Barton*

*'An ecological system is healthy if it is stable and sustainable –
that is, if it is active and maintains its organisation and autonomy over time, and is resilient to stress'* (Constanza et al,
*Ecosystem Health: New Goals for Environmental Management*)

## INTRODUCTION

Planning neighbourhoods is a suspect activity. It went out of fashion in the
1970s as a result of the social scientists', and then the Thatcherites', critique of
physical planning. But now there is the recognition that the laissez faire
approach to localities had produced an atomized, disfunctional, unsustainable
and often unappealing residential environment. Residents, through LA21
processes, are voicing their demands for something better. Government is
advocating design for quality and sustainability. Urban designers are recover-
ing their self confidence. However, the majority of planning and architectural
professionals do not have expertise in the field, and the literature is slow to
respond to new demands: plenty of advocacy but little analysis.

Chapters 6 to 8 begin to rekindle a theory of neighbourhood planning.
They take as a platform the conclusions of the previous two chapters, namely:

* there are good reasons to try to reinvent neighbourhoods;
* despite high mobility and poor design, localities are still important in many
  people's lives;
* local planning and design (or its absence) affects behaviour;
* there are innovative and exciting neighbourhood projects around the
  world which demonstrate what is possible;
* such projects remain the exception, not the rule.

The task, therefore, is to articulate principles for the planning of neighbourhoods which do not rely on exceptional commitment for their implementation,
but which rather could be applied generally. The key is a philosophy of *integration*, not *fragmentation*.

# THE ECOSYSTEM APPROACH

Urban development in the late 20th century has arguably happened as a piece-meal, disaggregated process. Despite the existence of planning systems which are designed to provide coordination, the reality has often been that of varied public and private agencies making disparate decisions according to their own remits. Housing, commerce, transport, recreation, energy and water have not only been 'planned' without adequate cross reference, but within each of those spheres there are divided approaches. For example the energy supply indus-tries (oil/gas/electricity/coal) are geared to maximizing market share and increasing their turnover, while governments are ostensibly promoting energy-efficiency. Potential synergies with waste, water and sewage functions have been underdeveloped. The result has been progressive urban disconnection, fragmentation and fission, with growing ecological and health impacts.

The problem is to find a widely recognized philosophy and rationale to counteract the piecemeal process, capable of fulfilling technical, design and political needs. In his book *Good City Form* (1981) the urban designer Kevin Lynch examines the relationships between human values and the physical form of the city. He evaluates some of the favoured concepts of the day: the city as a machine for living in, the city as an organism. He eventually rejects both of these as inadequate, concerned more with image and metaphor than actuality. Tjallingii (1995) has observed that in the world of designers concepts play a large part, often to the suspicion or irritation of researchers. So what is needed is a 'scientific' alternative. But while scientific and technical research, adopting the reductionist method, is providing insight into many separate facets of urban development, designers regard this as piecemeal, in danger of reinforc-ing the atomized view of the world that has failed.

Lynch's solution to the design/science dilemma is the theory of the ecosys-tem. This theory, applied to human settlements, recognizes the complexity of an open system with living and non-living elements, cyclic processes and a complicated network of relationships. It is not a metaphor: it is a useful means of describing settlements and has both explanatory and normative power. It provides grist to the scientific mill but also a satisfying and useful motivating image for designers and politicians.

Interestingly the ecosystem theory was used by Brian McLoughlin in *Urban and Regional Planning: a Systems Approach* (1968) which launched a period of technocratic urban model building in the UK. That is a cautionary tale we should learn from. The theory was and is convincing. The resource-greedy systems models are often not. They necessarily involve simplifying assump-tions which reduce their reliability as decision tools. They also can be used (unintentionally perhaps) to conceal rather than reveal key policy assumptions and choices.

The principles flowing from the new ecosystem approach have an inher-ent value-structure missing from the older set. They start from the premise that it is good, other things being equal, to increase local self-sufficiency:

> 'A *home, an estate or a town is an* eco-system *in the sense that*
> *to provides the essential local habitat for humans, creating its*

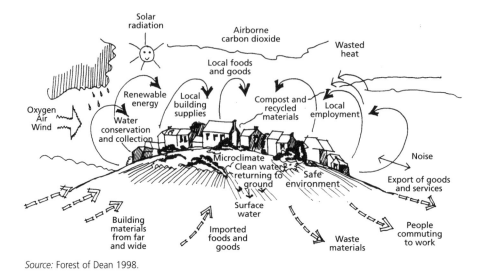

*Source:* Forest of Dean 1998.

**Figure 6.1** *Small Settlement as an Ecosystem – Emphasising Resource Loops*

*own microclimate, and should provide as far as possible for their comfort and sustenance ... At every level the designer or decision-maker should be attempting to maximize the level of autonomy of the eco-system while enhancing its life-giving qualities'* (Barton et al, 1995).

The EU Expert Group on the Urban Environment points out it is neither appropriate nor possible to treat a settlement as a *closed* system, but a number of useful techniques including monitoring/quantification of resource flows, indicators and performance criteria, energy and water budgets, ecological footprint studies and state of the environment reports – demonstrate the technical and scientific value of the concept (EU Expert Group, 1995). Often the concept is considered particularly relevant to bioregions and river catchments (Tomatty, 1994).

Much discussion about settlements as ecosystems tends to imply (as above) that we are interested only in physical systems. However, it is the *human* habitat, and therefore human need, which provide the focus here. The ecosystem approach is potentially compatible with the anthropocentric Brundtland definition of sustainable development, but the alternative construction promoted by environmental and wildlife interests provides a more explicit connection:

> *'Sustainable development is about maintaining and enhancing the quality of human life – social, economic and environmental – while living within the carrying capacity of supporting ecosystems and the resource base.'*

In that context the approach has the express purpose of improving quality of life as well as the quality of the natural ecosystem.

## Basic Principles

If the eco-system approach is applied to neighbourhoods, then there are a number of key principles.

### 1. Increasing Local Autonomy

Where it is technically/socially/environmentally feasible the needs of residents should be met locally, reducing inputs necessary from the wider environment or outputs which might poison it. This principle most obviously relates to energy, water and wastes, but could also extend to work and services to a significant degree.

### 2. Increasing Choice and Diversity

Human beings come in all sorts and sizes. The neighbourhood as ecosystem should permit options and choices so that different needs, incomes, preferences can be locally satisfied. Key spheres for choice are movement, home, work, services and open space. Choice of movement mean that 'weaker' transport modes are protected from domination by 'stronger modes', and a permeable environment gives access options. Housing choice suggests a range of locations should be available whatever the household's needs and means. Work choice involves support for home-based work as well as small-scale commerce and industry, but also critically involves maximising non-car-based job search areas across the city. Facility choice requires design that creates local options for shopping, school and socializing without recourse to the car. Open space choice means good access for residents to the full range of provision from pocket park to open country; and, on another plane, to habitat diversity as well.

### 3. Responsiveness to Place

The land is the basic resource being managed by planning policy. Development should be responsive to the particular geological, landscape, hydrological, biological and microclimate conditions. In so doing it can increase its level of autonomy and robustness. It will also have unique characteristics, distinguishing it from neighbouring places.

### 4. Connection and Integration

Connectivity extends into the purely human domain. The housing cluster is interconnected with other clusters. One neighbourhood links to another in complex ways, and to the town or city region as a whole. The local activities gain strength from association with each other, permitting dual or multi-function spaces and multi-function trips which benefit providers and users.

### 5. Flexibility/Adaptability

The precautionary principle is reflected in design for the built environment by keeping options open where possible, and managing resources so that future, potentially desirable options are not prejudiced. This means buildings designed for use change, houses easily extended for evolving family circumstances, spare capacity in infrastructure provision, multi-functional open space and social space provision.

## 6. User Control

Centralized market or bureaucratic control tends to limit diversity and can make for insensitive or inappropriate decisions that ignore special needs and stymie creativity. The general principle of subsidiarity – that decisions be taken at the lowest appropriate level – should apply to neighbourhoods, and to individual households/firms within neighbourhoods. This could relate, for example, to the management of local parks by a neighbourhood council; the management of an estate water/sewage system by a residents' company; and the availability of self-build plots.

The ecosystem approach thus strives to achieve the complexity, richness and robustness of a climax culture with each neighbourhood linked and a part of a wider urban system. It seeks to reduce the ecological footprint of each neighbourhood while providing more choice and opportunity for local people. It looks to local resources where possible, but recognizes the reality of inter-dependence with wider areas and communities.

The sections which follow start to apply ecosystems thinking to various elements of localities, initially concentrating on social and activity systems, then progressing to local resource management. The topics are chosen not only because of their innate importance but because they complement topics covered in other chapters.

# SOCIAL CAPITAL AND HOUSING MIX

Basic human needs such as access to housing, and access to networks of mutual association and support, are central to eco-neighbourhood planning. This section links together questions of social capital and community with the issue of housing mix and socially balanced neighbourhoods. Social capital is concerned with the network of personal relationships and associations that helps to give meaning to people's lives and provides mutual sustenance and support. It embraces both the casual daily meetings that give some stability and sense of belonging and the formal groups (toddler groups, sports clubs, school parents associations, local work groups) that provide shape to life and a source of friendship. Social capital is recognized as important for guiding adolescent behaviour and for maintaining health and happiness. It is particularly highlighted by the recent health green paper as a bulwark against depression, loneliness and mental illness. (DHSS, 1998).

'Social mix' is one of those principles that seems to polarize views, a traditional planning goal reaffirmed by contemporary neighbourhood designers (Duany and Plater-Zyberk, 1992) but rarely achieved in practice and rather scoffed at by many practitioners who see it as flying in the face of a status-conscious housing market. Academics too are suspicious of the concept, suggesting there is little sociological basis for it and linking it with residual notions of determinism present in the architectural profession (Bishop, 1986; Breheny et al, 1993). Despite these doubts about social mix, however, social monocultures have few friends.

The single status suburban estates of both private and public sectors that have been the predominant form of residential development over the last few decades in the UK are accused of aesthetic monotony and excessive residential social polarization. Such polarization is associated with the problems of ghettos, the labelling of areas and resulting exclusion of specific ethnic or social groups from wider employment and housing markets. As a result housing mix has returned to the government's agenda, especially in relation to affordable housing, as a means of ensuring improved access to housing for all groups. Increasingly it is becoming standard practice for urban development briefs and village plans to specify a percentage of social or cheap/accessible housing. In pursuance of this philosophy of 'choice' Milton Keynes goes a stage further and aims for a degree of balance in every grid square, giving affordable housing at least a share of the prime sites (eg lakeside positions). This social mix policy has been an accepted element in the planning strategy for a conspicuously success-ful city. (Milton Keynes Development Corporation, 1992).

The concept of a socially-mixed neighbourhood is often equated with that of the planned *community*, and both seen as goals of 'traditional' neighbour-hood planning. It is important, however, to distinguish clearly between the two ideas. The people who developed the neighbourhood principle were not suffering false illusions: Frederick Osbourne, one of the fathers of the new town movement, was sceptical about the use of architectural means to create communities, observing 'community life in a new town is of the interest group pattern, not the neighbour pattern – except in the very earliest days, when everybody is uprooted. I doubt if you can *create* a strong neighbourhood consciousness, though you can provide neighbourhood *convenience*, and that produces just a little such consciousness' (quoted in Ward, 1993). Frederick Gibbard, the designer of Harlow, echoes this, though confusingly using 'neigh-bourhood' to mean 'local community':

> '*It is people who make neighbourhoods and none of us were under the illusion that these planning ideas would automati-cally generate neighbourhoods. But the evidence is they have encouraged this*' (Gibberd et al, 1980).

Jeff Bishop's survey of Milton Keynes residents gives some further credence to this last point: the grid 'villages' are a very significant focus for household activity, and also a source of identity – places to which people feel they belong. (Bishop, 1986).

Mixed neighbourhoods, then, do not rely for their rationale on the assumption that they generate community, though the sense of a place commu-nity is likely to be assisted by shared local facilities and the casual meetings that occur in well-used streets and squares. And no more is housing mix justi-fied by some principle that different classes should live cheek by jowl to cajole them into friendship. Rather the key arguments concern equity, economy and environment. The equity argument is that housing mix is desirable to free up various housing markets (social housing/rental/first time buyers/mid range and executive buyers, etc), so that in every part of the town there is some accom-modation appropriate to the needs of any particular household. This increases the locational choices open to all groups, but particularly to the most finan-cially constrained, and thus it is an important equity consideration. When there are such options, then people tend to identify locations that maximize family convenience and reduce the cost of travel (Hillman and Whalley, 1983). So the added benefits are a reduction in the need to travel and a reduction in environmental pollution.

The second argument relates to age groups and family status rather than income bracket, and is about avoiding the syndrome of the social wave, whereby almost all the initial residents of an estate are one family status – young parents with babes and toddlers – leading to uneven demand progressively for child clinics, nursery education, primary schools, secondary schools and so on right through to sheltered accommodation and undertakers (GLC 1965). A variety of accommodation, together with a slow build up and conscious second generation provision, can help avoid the peaks and troughs of demand for local facilities, thus saving money, and avoiding a series of socially damaging crises of deficit and surplus. The range of age groups can also be important to provide continuity in behaviour patterns (particular in the teens) and increase opportunities for family support and neighbourliness (eg real or acting grannies assisting young families). The richness and significance of such networks should not be underestimated.

The third point is about skills and jobs, and relates to a scale rather larger than one locality – more the district or township. There is a benefit to local business and households if the full range of common trades and skills are accessible, available to be called on. This particularly relates to the availability of a local pool of part-time workers – often carers who cannot travel far because they need to get back quickly. The benefits here, again, are not only social and economic, but environmental as well, because there is less need to travel.

These arguments clarify the kind of social mixing that is needed. Within a residential area there could be provision for different tenures and markets, for the full range of household size, and for special needs. The UWE/LGMB guide *Sustainable Settlements* goes further in recommending provision of space for less obvious choices which at present are largely excluded – for example craft houses, co-housing schemes and self-build sites (Barton et al, 1995). The guide also calls for diversity in home/garden matching. As in many old towns it should be possible to have a small terraced house with a large garden, or a large house with a small garden. The essential rule is that of opening up choice *for everyone*. People then have the option to choose which is best for them, and the planner can simply hope (and trust) that other community and environmental benefits will follow.

This is a far cry from the crass social engineering of some architects of the 1960s, trying to impose their tastes and their behavioural theories on others – like Stirling's award winning Southgate Scheme in Runcorn, which has since been demolished. But neither are we accepting the armchair agnosticism of the sociologist critics (see Ward, 1993, p11 for a marvellously paranoid example, and Ward's robust comments on it!). As demonstrated in Chapter 4, the influence of design on behaviour can be malign or benign. But influence there certainly is, at the most mundane but vital levels: the distance a child has to go to meet a friend; or get to school; the real and the perceived personal safety of the child's journey; the ability of a 17 year-old to find separate accommodation from the family, but still close; a pub and a post office in walking distance, along a pleasant route; the opportunity for a family to survive on one car because they can find a house within easy cycling distance of the househusband's part-time job; the availability of sheltered accommodation in the familiar neighbourhood; the opportunity to build your own home in a convenient location.

Design for these things is not delivered by the market unassisted. It relies on a clear, integrated policy and determined implementation: the determination that physical design be used to open doors, to provide options, to safeguard the environment locally and globally, and facilitate the development of community. The 'new urbanist' designers, and the DETR too through its advice, are recognizing the degree to which the planner has an obligation to reveal the significance of possible design decisions to the local authorities, the developers, and to the local community affected.

## ACCESS TO WORK AND SERVICES

Personal transport to employment, education, retail, health and leisure facilities accounts for a substantial and growing proportion of total energy use and related pollution (see Chapter 3). At the same time non-car-users are being disenfranchised by the increasing distances involved in reaching facilities and by locational patterns geared to the car. So for both ecological and social reasons the reversal of the trend is paramount.

A fundamental problem is the increasing unit size of facilities (notably shops, offices, schools, hospitals) with hinterlands commensurately extending. Increased size may be economic from the operators' viewpoint but is often not economic in overall social or environmental accounting terms. It has led to the decay of neighbourhoods. If the project of reinventing locality is to be successful, the key is probably the cost of travel. If the EU and national governments increase the friction of distance with a carbon tax on fossil fuels then the economics of unit size will be tilted back. At the same time governments could alter institutional remits (of health, education and other public services) so that externalized household costs and pollution costs are part of the formal auditing and accountability process.

The dispersal of job opportunities into local areas is particularly problematical. The value of local jobs has been noted in Chapter 5, but creating job opportunities locally can be a thankless task when, as with village workshops in Cornwall, most of the opportunities are taken up by outsiders, often reverse commuting from the towns (Pinch, 1994). The key issues are good matching of local employment needs to local job opportunities, and the tolerance of non-noxious employment uses within or near residential areas.

In relation to facilities generally there is less equivocation. Where there *are* local facilities there is a propensity to use them and, in varying degrees, to walk to them (see Chapter 4). However, in an increasingly privatized economy it is often not possible or appropriate to define specific catchments for specific services. The principles of consumer choice and the fact of mobility means that a flexible approach to facility provision is necessary. The population needed to support a given quality of service can change, and there is no common catchment population that can be equated with a fixed neighbourhood. Table 6.1 illustrates the range of possible local facility catchments, based on new town standards and 1990s housing estates. Note that in some older

**Table 6.1** *Possible Local Facility Catchments*

| Catchment | Population |
|---|---|
| Primary school | 1:2500–4500 |
| Secondary school | 1:7000–15,000 |
| Doctor's surgery | 1:2500–3000 |
| Public house | 1:5000–7000 |
| Corner shop | 1:2000–5000 |
| Local shopping centre | 1:5000–10,000 |
| Post office | 1:5000–10,000 |
| Health centres (4 doctors) | 1:9000–12,000 |
| Library | 1:12,000–30,000 |
| Church | 1:9000 minimum |
| Community centre | 1:7000–15,000 |
| Youth club | 1:7000–11,000 |
| Sports centre | 1:25,000–40,000 |
| Superstore/district centre | 1:25,000–40,000 |

*Note:* Caution – this list is indicative only, and based on city-scale not small towns. Catchments may vary from place to place and over time.
*Sources:* Coombes, Farthing and Winter (1992–94) Greater London Council (1965) Milton Keynes Development Corporation (1992) *Source:* Barton et al,1995

urban areas certain catchments are off the end of the scale: pubs, corner shops and churches in particular occur in greater profusion than theory would suggest. Such areas may provide models of locality that planners can learn from. Both the variation in catchment for specific services, and the variation between services, have implications for the spatial planning of neighbourhoods that will be explored in the next two chapters.

People's willingness or ability to walk to local facilities varies with both user and use. As yet empirical evidence is rather sparse. In general users are prepared to walk further for a higher quality of service – for example 300–400m to a bus stop but 600–800m to a light rail station (White, 1995). A 400 or 500m standard is widely applied for access to local neighbourhood services as well as bus services (in British and Dutch new towns, American TODs). The recent study of *Sustainable Residential Quality* in London suggests what it calls 'ped-sheds' around suburban town centres and transport interchanges of 800m (Llewelyn-Davies, 1997). The *Sustainable Settlements* guide attempts to relate standards more flexibly to likely catchment populations: the distance suggested for primary schools is 400–600m; for local shops 400–800m; for park and playing fields 800–1000m; for secondary school 1500–2000m; and for district centre and leisure centres 1500–2000m (Figure 6.2).

Many existing suburban areas fail to achieve such standards. Local accessibility is apparently not a high priority for service providers. If urban planners and designers are to promote better access they will need to not only persuade decision-makers about the essential logic and reasonableness of such standards but also work to create an urban form where it is natural (and indeed economic) for business and state-providers to *think local*. This could rely on reinforcement by fiscal policy and institutional remits.

The other key spatial issue affecting local service autonomy is *connectivity*. Figure 6.3 illustrates connections between housing, local facilities and

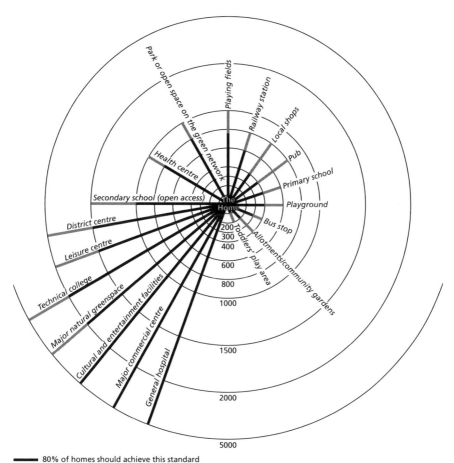

■■■ 80% of homes should achieve this standard

■■■ All new dwellings in urban areas should achieve this standard

*Source:* Barton et al, 1995

**Figure 6.2** *Possible Standards for Accessibility to Local Facilities*

open space on several levels. First there are potential economies from the dual use or combined of space. For example the school might share a hall, playing fields or hard pitch with the local community. Then there are benefits from close physical association: the viability of local shops is increased if there are other reasons such as school, bus stop or surgery – why people might go there. Then there are varied access requirements: sheltered accommodation should be close to shops and bus stop, for example, but children can walk a little further to school. While there is work on connectivity by urban designers, including a book by Robert Cowan (1997) *The Connected City*, the empirical research side is very thin. There is a need for observation and measurement of the way people behave and move and use facilities locally.

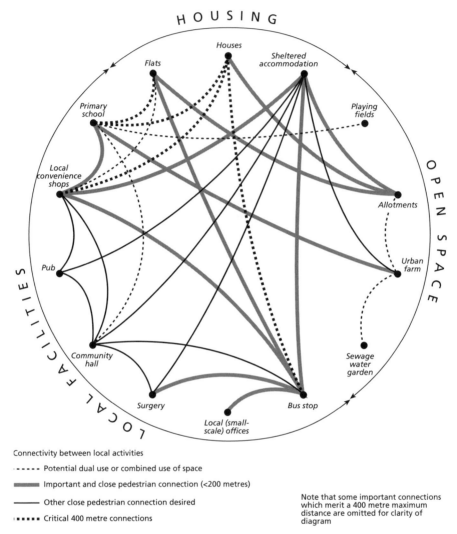

Connectivity between local activities

· - - - - - Potential dual use or combined use of space

▬▬▬▬ Important and close pedestrian connection (<200 metres)

——— Other close pedestrian connection desired

ı ▪ ▪ ▪ ▪ ▪ Critical 400 metre connections

Note that some important connections which merit a 400 metre maximum distance are omitted for clarity of diagram

**Figure 6.3** *Connectivity Between Local Activities*

## Home Working

One sphere where the trends are positive is home working. In some countries the rise of the post-industrial economy means home working is a major sector. In Australia 21 per cent of all businesses in 1993 were home based, and this was rising fast. In the US 37 per cent of dwellings already have a home-based business, and this could be 50 per cent in only a few years (Kemp, 1993, reported in Morris, 1996). The EU's working group on home working was (rightly) concerned with issues of worker conditions, morale and level of autonomy. It tended to see home working as a problem reflecting increased flexibility and sub-contracting in the market, often leading to exploitation of low status employees. The growth of freelance, home based teleworking has been made possible by the advent of fax, desktop publishing, e-mail and the world-wide web. One survey of 400 freelance home based workers in publishing found that most were educated women, who almost invariably had trained previously in-house and still worked on a contract basis for the same employer. While enjoying the independence and sense of freedom of self-employed status, these teleworkers experienced financial insecurity, very uneven work pressures and social isolation (EU 1994).

The implications for the future role of neighbourhoods if home working continues to increase are significant. First, the locality may become *more* important for work than it is now, reversing a long trend. Given the feeling of isolation it is likely that some home workers will seek compensating activity locally – lunch in a pub, meeting friends, going for a walk – which would not be possible if they still worked elsewhere. Telecottage type activity (sharing facilities and services) could grow further (though equivalently the spread of home based internet connection could render telecottages a passing phase). Such workers are likely to make off-peak trips to meetings with clients, often widely dispersed. But the net effect locally would be valuable spin-off for local businesses and, perhaps, social capital.

There is every reason to expect that home working *will* increase. The technology and internet access is spreading fast. The shift to sub-contracting looks set to continue. More people are living alone or in households without children, and space standards per person are rising as household size falls, so the practical difficulties of home working are reducing. If the friction of distance rises, then the economic incentives to homework become greater. The disincentive of loneliness is real, but new social conventions locally might mitigate this. My conclusion is that better neighbourhoods could benefit the home worker greatly, and conversely, home working will help regenerate neighbourhoods.

## MOVEMENT AND THE PUBLIC REALM

The residential, economic and community activities within neighbourhoods are interlinked by footpaths and streets. This may seem a statement of the obvious but has been largely forgotten in car-orientated layouts that are designed primarily for exogenous trips: travellers dropping into the area for a special function, or making a quick escape from it to external attractions. This approach represents the triumph of the goal of motorized mobility over the goal of accessibility. For some people design for mobility has indeed meant a *decline* in accessibility, where walking, cycling and public transport trips are actively deterred by inconvenient routing, danger and intimidation.

Provision for movement is not purely functional. The roads, paths and squares that allow movement impact on the network of social connections and activities, and are the *main* ingredient of the public realm and therefore a key expression of urban art and culture. Movement should be a delight. Local movement plans could also be a means of reducing social exclusion. The groups in society who have been disenfranchised by current car-dominated designs include parents with babies/toddlers, children and adolescents, adult carers and elderly people without access to a car, the infirm and disabled. These are often also the people who are more neighbourhood-bounded, and have a major interest in local social networks. Planning to increase opportunities for such groups necessarily means working towards a safe, attractive, convivial and convenient pedestrian realm.

The ecosystem approach makes considerable play on the principle of choice: trying by design to ensure that everyone has the real and practicable possibility of choosing to walk, cycle or use public transport for the vast majority of trips. That means that traffic is tamed, so that it does not prejudice the other options. Some environmentalists of course would like to go further and ban the car altogether. The logic for that in small areas is very strong in-so-far as some households may actively *choose* to live there (eg a car-free housing cluster, as in Edinburgh – see Appendix 1). But across a whole neighbourhood such an approach prejudices choice and could well lead to social polarization as those who continue to rely on their motors move elsewhere.

Walking – and in some flatter settlements, cycling – dominates intra-neighbourhood movement. Reorienting neighbourhoods around people not cars means adopting design principles that stress safe, traffic-calmed streets, permeability, variety and richness of streetscape, effective surveillance and the creation of activity hubs/meeting places that engender a sense of urban vitality and community. Later chapters explore aspects of this agenda in detail.

Public transport needs to be in a position to challenge the car for inter-neighbourhood trips. Very few urban development schemes in the UK have been designed around public transport. Runcorn new town was a conspicuous exception, which sadly has not been emulated since. Runcorn's master planner recognized that:

> '*In many post-war new towns and suburban extensions the tendency has been to design the road layout for private vehicles and then route buses along the most appropriate roads. This has led in some instances to minimum use of public transport which has made it uneconomical to provide socially convenient services. It is considered that the contribution of public transport to a (new) town is of such importance that it is essential to plan for it as an integral part of the town structure and not to provide it as an afterthought*' (Ling, 1967).

Ling's solution for Runcorn was a linear structure of neighbourhoods – a 'string of beads' along a busway thread. The linear form was twisted round into a figure of eight pattern that elegantly incorporated existing development and located the new town centre at the crossover.

Recent practice guides for sustainable development in the context of a deregulated market also emphasise that public transport is not a bolt-on extra, left to operators to provide if they will. Rather planners and developers can effectively predetermine the viability of public transport by the disposition of roads, footways and land uses. Achieving the most effective public transport configuration should be given pre-eminence in the design process and closely specified by plan and development briefs. 'Different land uses should then be 'hung' on the public transport network. The network becomes a starting point, not an afterthought.' (Barton et al, 1995, p121).

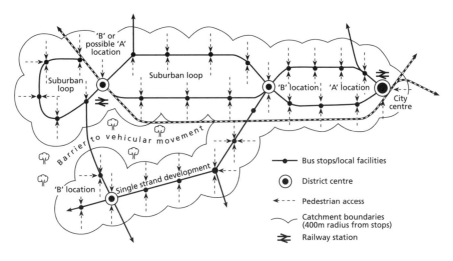

*Source:* Barton et al, 1995

**Figure 6.4** *Principles of Public Transport Planning*

Figure 6.4 illustrates some of the principles of public transport planning. It does not show the internal structure of neighbourhoods but how neighbourhoods may be strung together along bus routes within a sector of a city. The development area is directly related to pedestrian catchment from bus stops. The linear form makes for operational efficiency and higher quality of service. Transport nodes provide the locus for commercial centres. Open space creates a barrier to all vehicular movement between adjoining radials, helping trip concentration so that the buses have a good chance of successfully competing with private car use. These spatial principles tie in closely with concepts of density gradients and 'twin-track' linear development discussed in the next chapter.

## LOCAL RESOURCE MANAGEMENT

In conventional, segmented thinking the social activities of a locality are seen as independent from the provision of basic infrastructure. Utilities such as water supply, waste treatment and energy supply are taken for granted, the functional backcloth to the drama of human existence. But the 'joined up' thinking that typifies the ecosystem approach recognizes the interplay between people and infrastructure and the potential value of its transforming power. When energy, food and water are simply there to be plugged into, purchased from a superstore or turned on, then ecological realities are side-stepped. Conversely when energy comes from a community-owned wind farm, some food is home-grown, water caught on the roof and, after use, treated in the local sewage garden before being returned to its natural cycle, then synergy is evident. Local economic and leisure opportunities are enhanced and the potential for the development of social capital increased.

The financial and social practicality of local resource management can be problematic: for example the community wind farm may not be viable; few residents may want to grow vegetables. But in many spheres it is the inertia of inherited investments and the dissected organizational structures that inhibit recognition of the opportunities. In the sphere of energy, for example, different companies, often trans-national in ownership, are competing to sell a variety of fuels; and while in the UK the regulators do oblige the companies to promote energy-efficient products it is still in the context of trying to persuade consumers to buy more. Neither the energy supply companies nor the various regulators (OFFWAT, OFFGAS) have the remit to form or force partnerships with, say, local authorities, to invest in combined heat and power schemes. The system is one of competing to consume, rather than cooperating to conserve. The contrast with Denmark, where there is an integrated national policy and strong obligations on municipalities to produce local energy conservation strategies, is marked. The result at neighbourhood level is that whereas in Denmark community-led renewable/CHP energy projects are common, in the UK they are extremely rare.

Application of the ecosystem approach to resource management has been called the 'principle of least effort... It involves the idea that from minimum resources and energy, maximum environmental, economic and social benefit are available' (Hough, 1995). In developing countries amongst the rural and urban poor, economy of means, maximizing local production, reuse and recycling, is critical to survival. In Denmark the strategy of reducing energy consumption has produced the win-win situation of very low heating costs (before tax) and the absence of fuel poverty. In the UK the decision to let road verges flower has both contributed to biodiversity and cut maintenance costs. It is only by taking problems out of individual pigeon-holes and looking at them together, in the round, that such solutions are found. The ecosystem approach involves reducing resource imports and pollution exports from any town or neighbourhood, and instead relying on ambient and recycled resources. When old buildings are reused, or their materials recycled, then the demand for potentially damaging quarries elsewhere, and the impact and cost of subsequent transport, are reduced. When buildings are ultra energy efficient then the emissions (local or at distant power stations) are cut and less carbon dioxide destabilizes the global climate. It is a question of reducing the extraction rates to levels that do not impoverish subsequent generations (or through unequal trade impoverish other communities), and reducing emission rates to levels that can be satisfactorily absorbed by the environment.

Technical choices for energy, waste, materials and water supply are not independent of each other. The most environmentally-benign solutions seem to occur when individual technologies are seen in a systematic context. So in Figure 6.5 the interplay of services makes a complex pattern. Sewage disposal, for example, is linked to drainage and water supply quality; sewage sludge can be treated with other compostables and make a contribution to local food and energy production; it affects air quality, and can affect the design of buildings. The consequent impact on land needs and on layout is far from simple. People are currently so acclimatized to external sourcing and end-of-pipe solutions that the spatial significance of incorporating green technologies remains uncertain. The technologies now need to be integrated and applied more widely so

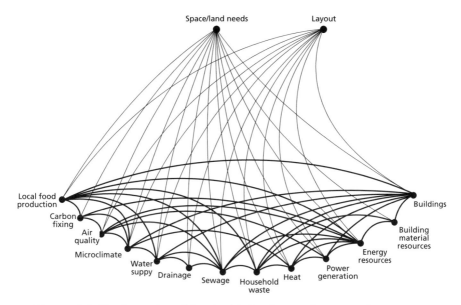

**Figure 6.5** *The Interplay of Service Technologies, Resource Management and Spatial Planning*

we gain the experience on which to base firm spatial design principles. Solutions which are adopted need to be capable of flexibility of operation, extendibility, and reuse. Houses, for example, could have central heating systems (if they require any at all) capable of adaptation to district heating, and roof orientation, tilt and construction to facilitate solar cell retrofitting and use of roofspace. Ecosystems and settlements by nature are dynamic, not static.

## Water

Water is one of the obvious dynamic elements and, with food, clean air, and energy, critical to life. The natural hydrological cycle is interrupted by human settlements as they catch it for use, deflect it with impermeable surfaces, pipe it, treat it, dump it (Figure 6.6). In applying the ecosystem principle water is a useful metaphor for other resources. The natural self-renewing cycle is under threat both from increasing demand for water in urban areas and from inappropriate methods of disposal. Excessive demand is justifying unsustainable extraction rates from aquifers (resulting in the water table falling and becoming more prone to contamination), increased demand for remote sourcing (eg from reservoirs in the Welsh Hills) and energy-intensive transfer costs between regions. At the same time infiltration and aquifer recharge is reduced by the loss of permeable surfaces (replaced by tarmac etc), increased speed of run-off increasing the risk of flood. These factors are exacerbated by other land use changes: building on flood plains, canalization of rivers and excessive use of agricultural fertilizer. The effects on water are closely paralleled by effects on wildlife, with impoverishment of habitats.

These problems could be effectively combatted at the levels of neighbourhoods and individual projects. Every new/renewed area could be obliged to

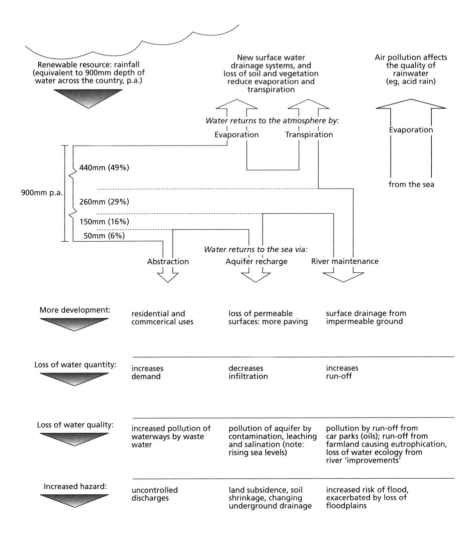

Source: Barton et al, 1995

**Figure 6.6** *The Effects of Development on the Hydrological Cycle*

achieve substantial or complete water-autonomy. Part of this strategy would be in-situ water collection. It would be perfectly possible to require all new developments over a certain size to catch their own water on the roofs and purify it through a sand filter before use. The Vales' house in Leicestershire demonstrates the practicality of this on a small scale. The Kolding renewal scheme in Denmark (see Chapter 5) illustrates a solution at a bigger scale in a high density, urban context. Both projects also involve the in situ recycling of grey and black water.

Disposal of 'black' water (ie sewage) has become a matter of out-of-sight, out-of-mind. But the energy/materials costs of end-of-pipe solutions are often greater than the cost of local sewage treatment by 'reed-bed technology'.

Reed-beds and 'sewage gardens', however, do take space. Systems vary, but at a standard two square metres per person a new estate for 1000 people would require at minimum a fifth of a hectare, probably more. The need for a location downstream of the development is also an influence on the design of the estate.

If such systems are to be put in place there are profound implications for attitudes. Residents and businesses have to accept responsibility for their own wastes, and robust local management systems devised. This could be difficult in a techno-fix society but immensely healthy as more ecocentric values are induced and the philosophy of local resource autonomy gains confidence. The local management of resources offers other desirable changes: a greener environment with more water-related ecological niches; extra justification for open space associated with constructed pond and wetland systems; more tree cover helping reduce wind speed, moderate temperature, absorb pollution, sequestrate $CO_2$ and encourage birdlife; frost pockets in low-lying areas excluded from development. Perhaps most significant of all, local black water treatment systems could encourage the reuse of the sewage sludge for composting, and could reinforce the potential for local organic food production (Chapter 13).

## Functional Integration

The sections above have reviewed the activities and infrastructure of neighbourhoods, and some of the design implications. The interplay of the elements, and the consequent interdependence of decisions by a range of agencies is clear. It is easier to handle that interdependence in relation to activity linkage, *or* movement choice, *or* technology, than when all are combined in one complex web. Figure 6.7 show these three determinants of local space needs in a relationship to each other. Local activities, the basic ones of living, working, playing, generally require dedicated spaces set aside for them. Movement is about getting from one space to another by a variety of modes, and requires channels/networks. The technologies which support human activity also need both spaces and channels.

Some functions quite naturally overlap two or even three of the spheres. Local composting and food production is both an economic and a recreational activity and an important resource provider. Teleworking relies on advanced technology systems but is also a subset of work and a potential substitute for travel.

Local Planning policy has conventionally focused on the space needed for discreet activities. *Sometimes* it has planned accessibility and movement – rather than simply providing a road network. Rarely has it paid much attention to the infrastructure technologies, which instead have been taken for granted. But we have seen in this chapter how activities, public realm and infrastructure might be looked at in the new eco-system approach, stressing human values and integrated design. The sustainable technologies, if they are to be adopted, imply change not only to design but management structures as well. If housing clusters, or whole neighbourhoods, are to be semi-autonomous for

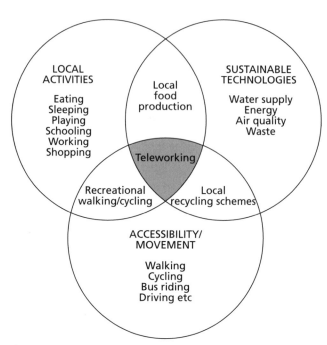

**Figure 6.7** *The Determinants of Local Space Needs in a Neighbourhood*

water, sewage and energy then merely providing land or technology is not sufficient. Local decision and implementation mechanisms have to be capable of managing them.

# 7 URBAN FORM AND LOCALITY

*Hugh Barton*

## INTRODUCTION

Since the Earth Summit in Rio questions about sustainable spatial strategies and urban form have become increasingly central to planning policy debates. They also loom large in academic inquiry. There has been a deepening and broadening of work in the field. The new environmental agenda has brought together academic and policy interests that previously had little contact, and according to Breheny there is an 'integrity of effort' that has not been witnessed for a long time (Breheny, 1992a).

Yet it is still difficult to find clear and unequivocal messages coming from the academic research community to the practitioners and politicians. There is disagreement between researchers about, for example, the significance of density, the validity of the compact city strategy and the appropriate role for new settlements (see the different views in Jenks et al, 1996).

In this context the present chapter is an attempt to focus the urban form debate as it impinges on the character and location of neighbourhoods. Much of the academic discourse is driven by concern for global warming and the desire to reduce transport emissions. To that is added, in the political sphere, the issues of housing forecasts and greenfield protection. The discussion both academic and political is predominantly on the strategic plane. Small-area policy issues are side-lined. So the purpose of the chapter is first to reorientate the strategic questions towards locality, and second, give due weight to non-transport issues.

The urban form debate is pursued in relation to four interlocking dimensions of form, which are discussed sequentially in the chapter. It is rather easy to become confused over the arguments because of the way evidence relating to one dimension ties in to the others. The first dimension is about the degree of dispersal or concentration. At one extreme there is dispersal into hamlets and villages, while at the other extreme is concentration into dominant cities. In between there are 'dispersed concentrations', equated with polycentric regions such as West Yorkshire or a city region with expanding suburban towns. This dimension guides the *location* of neighbourhoods.

The second dimension is the degree of segregation or intermixture of urban activities. This particularly concerns the way in which industry and commerce is located, both within centres and within the urban area as a whole. The current thesis is that mixed use is preferable, but there is little consensus about what mixed use actually means, or how much mixed use should occur in neighbourhoods.

The third dimension is about settlement density. The question of low versus high density is sometimes confused with dispersal versus concentration. The confusion occurs because density statistics are often aggregated and used at the level of whole administrative districts, many of which are only partly built up, and thus density becomes a proxy for degree of concentration. But within the *aggregated* density figures the actual density of built up areas may diverge. It is quite possible for small historic towns in apparently low density areas to be at quite high densities, while city suburbs are low density. Here the focus is the appropriate density of neighbourhoods, both in terms of *net* density (ie just the housing area) and in terms of *gross* density (ie housing plus local facilities/employment/open space).

The fourth dimension concerns shape. The designers of new towns mid-century distinguished three basic types, depending on transport emphasis: stellar, grid and linear. Even more simply there are nucleated and linear forms. Shape relates to whole towns or cities – as in the case of Copenhagen, illustrated in Chapter 3 – but neighbourhoods are the building blocks which combine to create the wider pattern.

# DISPERSAL VERSUS CONCENTRATION

## Rural Autonomy

The ongoing arguments over dispersal versus concentration pit the eco-idealists and market realists against the urban revivalists and transport researchers. The eco-idealists expound an ecosystem approach to settlements partly justified by the hope of social transformation. Ecologically and socially they consider 'small is beautiful' (Schumacher 1972). They picture small-scale self-sufficient communities repopulating the countryside, relying on locally-grown food, ambient sources of energy and water, linked to the global village by internet, fax and viewphone: as the influential *Blueprint for Survival* put it 'broadly speaking, it is only by decentralization that we can increase self-sufficiency – and self-sufficiency is vital if we are to minimize the burden of social systems on the eco-systems that support them' (Ecologist, 1972)

The idea of decentralized self-sufficiency has been recently enlivened by Mollinson's persuasive guide to 'permaculture' (1990), which has helped to spawn the active world-wide movement for eco-villages noted in Chapter 5. In the UK Simon Fairlie has articulated the hopes of the rural dispossessed and eco-idealists with Low Impact Development (1996). Fairlie's vision is of a rejuvenated rural economy based around sustainable, organic use of the land. By giving people the opportunity to live in the countryside, in low impact dwellings and pursuing a low impact lifestyle, he believes the planning system could create richer and more diverse rural communities.

Ironically the image, if not the substance, of this supposed rural idyll also reflects the aspirations of the consumer society. Many people want to live in the countryside, and the cost of country cottages reflects this. Attempts made to keep agricultural dwellings tied to agriculture, or to provide village-based rural employment, have been distorted by the buoyant rural housing market. Market pressures for village/small town development, following the rural dream, have reflected commuters preferences. This dispersal is part of an energy-intensive trend, exacerbating problems of social polarisation as well as climate change.

Even where there are express planning or ownership controls to try to ensure permanent eco-sensitivity (as Fairlie proposes) there is no guarantee. Restrictive covenants decay in application over time. People's behaviour tends towards societal norms. This is well illustrated by the changing fortunes of an original 1900s eco-village. Whiteway in Gloucestershire was set up as a Tolstoyan settlement – self built from renewable sources, self reliant in most foodstuffs, energy, water, local schooling, crafts and community culture. While something of the original atmosphere still remains by virtue of the buildings, large gardens and community association, the ideal of self-sufficiency has evaporated. Households have two or more vehicles and workers commute to the towns. The prices of plots ensure exclusivity. The friction of distance would need to increase dramatically to force any general move towards rural self-sufficiency, and the substitution of telecommunications for travel. For the moment at least the promotion of rural settlements will simply promote the further urbanisation of the countryside.

## The Compact City

At the other end of the spectrum are the 'urban revivalists' who advocate the compact city. They are represented pre-eminently by the EU Commission (the *Green Paper on the Urban Environment*, 1990) and the Government. The 1998 White Paper *Planning for Communities of the Future* puts in place the targets and decision processes intended to foster urban regeneration and increased urban density as the sustainable alternative to greenfield development. Other advocates include Sherlock (*Cities are Good For Us*, 1991) and Elkin and McLaren (*Reviving the City*, 1991). The researchers whose work underpins this strategy are primarily in the transport energy field and may be represented, for example, by Newman and Kenworthy, whose seminal work *Cities and Automobile Dependence* (1989) looked at the relationship between modal choice, trip generation, density, centralization and transport systems. Their evidence suggests that concentration leads to lower fuel consumption than dispersal, and that the average density of an area (where density is a proxy for degree of concentration) is a key predictor of energy use – at least as significant as social variables such as income and car ownership. The level of significance has been subject to considerable debate (eg Gordon and Richardson, 1990; Jenks et al, 1996) made complex by the interdependance of social and physical variables.

When they assessed intra-regional movement Newman and Kenworthy found surprising variations, for example a five-fold variation between transport energy use in central New York and in the commuting hinterland. Earlier analysis of UK data by Hillman and Whalley (1983) also shows very significant variations, with not only car use but also car ownership varying inversely with density, even when socioeconomic variables are held constant. In other words even the poorest households find they cannot do without a car in dispersed areas, while conversely in accessible inner urban areas some of the richest households choose not to own a vehicle (or not to invest in a second one). Hillman and Whalley show how accessibility to facilities varies greatly with location, with trip lengths for rural dwellers (<5pph gross) being four times the trip lengths of higher density urban areas (>90pph gross).

While such data is 'fairly unambiguous' showing a 'strong inverse relationship between urban density and energy consumption for transport' (Owen, 1992), there are suspicions that in recent years the significance of location has reduced as levels of mobility have increased. However, as far as the advocates of the compact city are concerned the benefits are not only reduced emissions and resource consumption but also social, economic and environmental benefits. The compact city is seen as offering the opportunity for creative and dynamic activity, the revival of a rich and diverse cultural life:

> *'The enemies of this source of creativity are, on the one hand*
> *undifferentiated suburban sprawl in quasi-rural settings which*
> *isolate the individual; and highly specialized land use policies*
> *within cities which create functional enclaves and social ghettos*
> *... Re-creating the diverse multi-functional city of the citizen's*
> *Europe is thus a social and economic project for which "the*
> *quality of life" is not a luxury but an essential'* (CEC, 1990).

The compact city strategy implies a particular vision of neighbourhoods strongly at odds with the self-sufficiency of the eco-idealists. It implies the kind of close-knit, mixed use, higher density pattern exemplified within many European cities (Bologna, Amsterdam, Paris) but also in historic towns in the UK (York, Bath, Chichester). The difficulty of transferring densities typical of Italian and Dutch cities, with their high proportion of flat living and low open space standards, to UK situations in order to achieve the desired urban vitality, are often underplayed. Breheny has criticized the idea of higher density compact cities put forward by the European Commission as neither practical nor desirable. He argues that people have been actively choosing the lifestyle of the lower density suburbs in preference to survival in declining urban cores; pointing out that... 'the large majority of Europeans live happily in the very kind of suburb that the Commission designates as 'sprawl'. (Breheny, 1992a)

Developing the same theme the Town and Country Planning Association gives an image of revitalized low density cities, with town and country interpenetrating, a sustainable local ecology and relaxed lifestyle: Michael Dower (1984) asks rhetorically:

> *'Why should we green the cities? Because man needs beauty: he*
> *needs nature, trees, greenery, birds, squirrels, the changing*
> *seasons, the links to the soil. Because we need space for leisure,*
> *to recreate mind and soul, to run, play, fish, cycle, relax and*
> *socialize ... Because the green can be productive of food, of*
> *timber, of energy, of pure water, of benign microclimates.'*

In such a 'thinner, greener' city, Colin Ward sees the opportunity for more user or resident control, more individual initiative (Ward, 1989).

### The Feasibility of Urban Intensification

Despite such arguments the dominant mood favours intensification. The refocusing of development potential into the towns and cities is seen as promoting economic, social and physical regeneration while reducing the requirement for greenfield development (DETR, 1998a). The central policy question is no longer *whether* to intensify but *how* to intensify – particularly how to intensify without sacrificing environmental quality and householder/market freedoms. There are distinctions to be drawn between old industrial cities with ample supply of brownfield sites (though sometimes they are contaminated) and historic towns and suburban centres with a very limited stock of brownfield sites. In the case of the former – eg Glasgow, Manchester – brownfield development and urban renewal provide options for intensification. But in the case of the later urban capacity studies suggest that the speed of change, given current market conditions and environmental policies, is not sufficient to achieve much intensification or to avoid further urban spreading (West Sussex, 1997; Baker Associates and UWE, 1999). The danger is that the constraints on greenfield development together with higher urban land prices force unacceptable losses of allotments, private open space and old employment sites in favour of housing, destroying the mixed use pattern that is a valued sustainable characteristic of older settlements. Conversely some studies point to the willingness of the market to entertain the notion of higher density development (Fulford, 1996) and the increased densities which can be achieved, with benefit, if some current planning constraints – such as car-parking standards – are relaxed, and effective design guidance is introduced (Llewelyn-Davies, 1994 and 1998). Certainly it is possible to find successful case studies of intensification (eg Johnson, 1995), and the growing proportion of small, childless households points to the market potential for more flats and fewer houses. But overall the jury is still out on the practicality of compactness. Intensification is a process which needs to be promoted, but handled with great care, and its effects monitored in each settlement. Figure 7.1 indicates the kind of close-knit perimeter block development that may be needed.

## THE LOCATION OF NEIGHBOURHOODS

The conclusions of the concentration versus dispersal debate so far are *first*, that a dispersed pattern of development, except for land-based activity, is not sustainable because of the high level of transport emissions and the low level of accessibility; *second*, that the compact city and a strategy of urban rejuvenation have much to commend them but raise questions about lifestyle choices, policy/market feasibility, and the practicality of the kind of ecosystem approach advocated in the previous chapter. One of the limitations of much of the urban form debate at the academic level is its reliance on statistical averages across a wide range of different settlements. It is often difficult to know what weight it is valid to put on the conclusions so this section looks more closely at the evidence in relation to specific case studies.

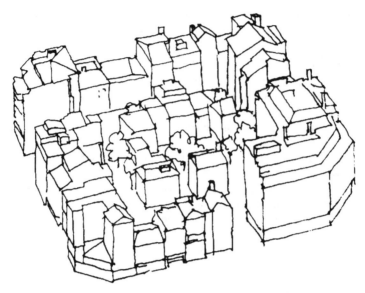

*Source:* Barton, Davis and Guise, 1995

**Figure 7.1** *Mixed Use, High Density, Low Rise Inner City Block: The Image of the Future?*

A number of studies have compared residential areas which, while socially and physically similar, have very different locations. Where similar residential developments are located in-town as opposed to out of town, then transport energy use can vary by 100 per cent (Birley, 1983). The same pattern is evident when looking at whole small settlements. Banister found over 100 per cent variation between commuter settlements without local facilities and a small town with a good range of facilities. People in the small town in fact made *more* trips, but they were shorter, and much more likely to be on foot (Banister 1992).

Hedicar and Curtis's 1995 study of 1980s residential estates in Oxfordshire reinforces the argument further. The research examined the strategic location of housing and its relationship to travel behaviour. The five case studies (at Botley, Kidlington, Bicester, Didcot and Whitney) are at varying distances from the central city (Oxford). They have very similar socioeconomic profiles – young, relatively affluent households with high car ownership – and the physical characteristics of the estates are also similar, so it is the significance of location and the relationship to the main settlement that are on test. The survey reveals wide discrepancies in car use. Indeed the lowest average figure of 65 car miles per adult per week is only 38 per cent of the highest at 172 car miles. Kidlington – the lowest car use – benefits not only from being close to Oxford but also having a fair range of local services and a good bus service into the city.

Of the outer locations Didcot, which is walking distance of high quality train services to London and Oxford, has only 63 per cent of the car miles of Bicester and Whitney (average) despite the highest proportion of residents (27 per cent) working in London. The particularly high car miles of Bicester residents is partially explained by the closeness to the M40 motorway, and it is

**Table 7.1** *Distance Travelled by Location: A Study of Oxfordshire*

| Survey area | Botley | Kidlington | Bicester | Didcot | Witney | All |
|---|---|---|---|---|---|---|
| Total distance (miles)* | 123 | 94 | 182 | 145 | 162 | 142 |
| Number of return journeys | 7.6 | 7.8 | 7.2 | 7.4 | 7.3 | 7.5 |
| Per cent car journeys** | 78 | 67 | 96 | 82 | 85 | 81 |
| Car distance (miles)** | 97 | 65 | 172 | 102 | 152 | 108 |

*Notes:* * All regular journeys – including mixed mode and multi-purpose journeys
** Does not include mixed mode or multi-purpose journeys
*Source:* Curtis, 1996

noticeable that the estate, despite being physically part of the town, does not seem to be psychologically part of it. The residents are more footloose and relate to a wider region. The local town does not benefit as much as might be expected from their patronage. Since according to the research households claim to be locating to maximize accessibility this re-emphasizes the problems they have in finding suitable accommodation close to Oxford or London. Of course it also reflects the low friction of distance, very high car availability, and for some households the divergent work locations of household members.

Rather similar lessons can be gained from the study of a very different area, Leicestershire, which is much less influenced by metropolitan overspill (Breheny, 1996). In this case trip distance varies strongly between the urban areas of the city (Leicester, Oadby and Blaby) and the more outlying districts. Energy use per person in the outlying district of Harborough is 260 per cent that of Leicester itself, where walking and cycling account for a much higher proportion of trips. In this study socioeconomic factors were not held constant and the data set had some limitations, but the scale of variation is great and emphasizes again the dangers of 'overspill' settlements beyond a green girdle.

These studies have implications for the urban form strategy of *dispersed concentrations* (Owens, 1986). While some authors have equated dispersed concentrations with dispersal into neighbourhoods (and this is discussed in the next section) it is more commonly seen as a larger scale polycentric struc-ture. The Oxfordshire strategy of constraining the central city while boosting the satellite towns should, the theory goes, result in less travel as those towns increase their level of autonomy, particularly if higher energy costs deter travel. However, in the current dispensation quite the reverse is the case. Building new estates in the satellite towns increases the distance travelled and the level of car dependence. It would appear that the towns (with the possible excep-tion of Banbury) do not have the level of services to catch and hold new households which in any case have established connections with Oxford or other main centres.

There are important conclusions for the location of neighbourhoods. We have seen in relation to a range of scales from large city down to market town how dispersal, even into relatively compact (smaller) settlements, leads to increased emissions and less transport choice. In principle, therefore, any new neighbourhoods should be located as close to the town or city that is generat-ing the household growth as possible. The link with employment and major service provision is critical. The allocation of 'footloose' housing developments

**Table 7.2** *Energy Use Data for Leicester and Surrounding Districts*

|  | Trip distance (km) | Energy use per trip (M) | Trips | Energy use per household (M) | Energy use per person (M) |
|---|---|---|---|---|---|
| Leicester | 5.89 | 10.55 | 3700 | 52.32 | 18.62 |
| Oadby | 6.94 | 13.63 | 1096 | 108.22 | 37.84 |
| Harborough | 13.17 | 25.88 | 990 | 125.00 | 48.63 |
| Blaby | 7.85 | 15.12 | 292 | 93.90 | 35.70 |
| Charnwood | 12.72 | 24.63 | 288 | 118.22 | 42.29 |
| Overall | 9.31 | 17.96 | 6366 | 99.53 | 36.62 |

*Source:* Banister, 1996

to exurban towns or villages should be resisted. That is not to say there may not be some need for housing locally because of the settlement's *own* dynamic – but this needs to be scaled and angled to the local market.

Essentially, therefore, the concentration (though not *necessarily* high density) strategy is justified. Decentralization, at current energy prices, does not work. The sequential test for housing land allocation put forward by the DETR (in *Planning for the Communities of the Future,* 1998) is sensible: first, accessible brownfield sites; second, accessible peripheral sites linked to public transport investment; third, new or expanded settlements well served by rail.

## MIXED USE DEVELOPMENT

This section looks more closely at the way human activity is reflected in land use patterns within settlements, and the degree to which different land uses/activities should be spatially interspersed. Again the urban form literature provides a rich vein for tapping. Urban form researchers are almost unanimous in suggesting a move away from the prevalent system of segregated land uses to one where activities are more integrated throughout the urban area to allow more local access, with some clustering of facilities to permit multipurpose trips and provide an effective demand base for public transport (eg Owens, 1986; Barton, 1992; Breheny and Rockwood, 1993). Government, too, has caught this idea and is promoting the principle of mixed use development (DoE, 1994a). City revivalists such as Sherlock (1990), Elkin and McLaren (1991) take mixed use as almost axiomatic, and local authorities are beginning to follow suit, despite reservations about local environmental impacts.

It is by no means clear, however, that there is a consistent view as to *what* is being interspersed, or over what *scale* mixed use should occur. The strategy of *dispersed concentrations*, applied within cities gives one specific shape to the mixed use principle. It would suggest a decentralized pattern of townships, with jobs and services concentrated in mixed use district centres. Cervero (1989) has shown convincingly that mixing uses in this way significantly increases the viability of public transport and permits multi-purpose trips as people walk between work, shop and leisure activities. This strategy also has the benefit of providing a focus for the decentralizing forces of the market. It accords with the multi-focal model of urban form.

Recent commentators have expressly linked this apparently robust strategy of dispersed concentrations with the idea of neighbourhoods (eg Breheny and Rockwood, 1993; Jenks et al, 1996). But this equation raises some awkward issues to do with the friction of distance, the activities being dispersed, and the scale of the dispersed concentration.

First, while the theory works well (ie reducing energy use/emissions and maximizing accessibility) when the friction of distance is *high*, it can be counterproductive when the friction of low (as now in most European countries). The value of interspersion can only be realized if people choose to use facilities that are close to them. In her study of a Norfolk town and its hinterland, Owens (1984) found that when the deterrent effect of distance was strong the best solution was one that mixed employment and housing in each settlement. When the deterrent effect was weak then larger and more distant centres became relatively more attractive than small local ones. Furthermore, if the viability of public transport is taken into account then the best option is not necessarily that involving the minimum home/work distance even *with* high fuel costs: a partial concentration of jobs allowed more effective public transport access, reducing car reliance and hence emissions. Similar patterns have been observed in more urban settings, and by Cervero in the 1989 study noted earlier.

Putting it more directly, if jobs/services are distributed across a large number of neighbourhood centres, and mobility is high, the resulting pattern of suburb to suburb trips is anathema to public transport and inevitably leads to high car-dependence. So the equation of dispersed concentrations with locality or neighbourhoods as people normally define them is inappropriate. Such concentrations need to be on a bigger scale.

The second point flows from the first: the effectiveness of dispersal depends on *what* is being dispersed to *where*. An obvious distinction needs to be clearly drawn (often in the literature it is not) between activities that are essentially local in character, with a limited catchment area (eg local shops, playgrounds, post offices, primary schools, pubs) and those that have a much broader catchment for employees or clients (eg superstores, hospitals, universities, office centres). Clustered dispersal into neighbourhoods is entirely appropriate for the former, but as we have seen, not for the latter. The art is to find ways in which the planning system can discriminate. The Dutch ABC strategy of the 'Right Business in the Right Place' suggests a particular framework for decisions. Here it is adapted and extended to encompass all facilities (Table 7.3). What it does is provide a graded set of locational criteria related to public transport, lorry and pedestrian accessibility.

While the Dutch system can make such distinctions routinely, in the UK system at present the distinction between local and city-wide, and between people-intensive and freight-intensive, is confused. The General Development Order B1 use class encompasses a very wide spectrum of business activity, and development plans fail to differentiate.

If Table 7.3 provides an acceptable rationale for what *should* be happening then it gives structure to the concepts of dispersed concentration and mixed use. Polycentric patterns are defined by the location of 'A' and 'B' centres (ie existing/proposed centres with high levels of public transport accessibility). 'A' centres (with good intercity rail connections) in addition serve whole town or

**Table 7.3** *The ABCD of Facilities Location: Derived from Dutch Practice*

|  | Category of Business | Accessibility Requirements |
|---|---|---|
| A Locations City/Town centre Major secondary centres in conurbations | Major Regional Trip Generators • Large offices/business centres (distinguished by size, no. of employees and no. of visitors) • Specialist/durable goods shopping centre • Major cultural/leisure attractions • Universities • Regional hospitals • Any B location activity | • Within 400–800m of the entrance of a railway station providing fast and regular services • With centrality in relation to good quality urban public transport services, which should be adjacent or close to the station • Easy, safe and convenient movement by foot and bike around the centre and to nearby residential areas |
| B Locations District centres Centres of small towns | Major Town/District Generators • Small offices, eg up to 500–1000m$^2$ • Convenience shopping centres, including superstores and DIY warehouses • Leisure centres • Technical colleges • District hospitals • Intensive manufacturing (with high employee density and frequent visitors) | • Within 400m of an urban public transport hub providing good level of access in most directions • Safe and convenient access for pedestrians and cyclists • Embedded within the built-up area, not on its edge |
| C Locations | Heavy freight generators • Regional warehouses • Distribution centres • Manufacturing (where employees and visitor density is low) | • Within 2km of direct access on to the national road network (normally motorway or dual carriageway) without passing through residential areas • Direct access on to railways, waterways or coastal shipping – or the potential to achieve direct access in the future |
| D Locations | Local generators • schools • parks and playgrounds • local shops, post offices • pubs, clubs, community centres • health centres | • clustered in local centres or along high streets at the heart of residential areas • majority of catchment population within 400m • close to a good bus service linking to higher tier centres |

*Source:* based on Barton et al, 1995

city regions. 'B' centres provide, or are capable of providing with further planned development, a fair level of choice in job and services for broad parts or sectors of the city, while still being interlinked (by public transport services) with the wider city region community and contributing to diversity of services across the whole area. For the sake of argument I will call these incipient dispersed concentrations *townships*. Research on levels of settlement autonomy suggest that in the UK towns need to have a population of at least 25,000 if they are to maintain/achieve a reasonable level of self-sufficiency (Breheny et al, 1993). Analysis of facility catchment populations seems to confirm this figure. At 25,000–40,000 a town or urban township is capable of supporting two or more secondary schools, a district shopping centre including a superstore, a leisure centre and local library, plus a good range of work opportunities (see Table 6.1).

In major cities such townships may be at the upper end of the population spectrum, reflecting their interdependence and interpenetration. In rural areas it may be that some towns of 10,000, plus their hinterland, can support appropriate levels of service. It is noteworthy, for example, that in Bannister's study of South Oxfordshire, Henley – which has about 10,000 population – emerges as surprisingly self-sufficient.

Within such towns/townships urban form theory suggests a rough balance of population, jobs and services. Mixed use, in this context, is not about intermixing along a street or even within a neighbourhood – though there may be benefits in this – but at the level of the township. In-so-far as neighbourhoods are localities with a range of services to which most people can easily walk they are not normally the same as townships. Several neighbourhoods may constitute a township – though even to refer to them both in this way gives an impression of fixed entities which may be false. The next chapter will expound on form and structure.

What this section has argued is that there are virtues but also dangers in the principles of mixed use and dispersed concentrations. The concepts have been used without precision both in the literature and (in the case of mixed use) in practice. The significant scale for dispersed concentration, ie areas with the capacity to achieve a fair degree of autonomy when the friction of distance is high, is not the pedestrian-scaled neighbourhood but the town or urban township. The mixing of uses is most relevant at that scale. But there are dangers in applying the dispersed concentration model while car travel is very cheap because the resulting dispersed pattern of trips undermines public transport and is highly polluting. There are also problems if activities that provide employment or services for a *whole* city region are located in townships lacking adequate regional public transport services. The ABCD framework for job/services locational decisions offers a logical means of managing these problems, but does challenge the UK to update its market-orientated General Development Order.

## LOCAL DENSITIES

Up to this point the chapter has set localities in the context of urban form theories and empirical evidence about travel behaviour. Density has been seen as a key aspect of this discussion and treated at the aggregate level, allowing broad generalizations about trip lengths and modal choice. This section looks at the density of specific development areas at a local level, drawing out the land needs implied by the eco-neighbourhood principle. It contrasts the competing advantages of higher and lower densities and puts forward a strategy which maximizes both.

Urban density is a critical issue because of its relationship to questions of *urban capacity*. In discussions about urban intensification the arguments often turn on the acceptability and practicality of higher net densities. In other words, how far would people accept flat living, smaller gardens, less space for cars, and is there the realistic prospect of the market being able to deliver intensification? These are key issues, but what the debates tend to ignore is the significance, in sustainability terms, of the non-residential land uses that contribute to the gross density and therefore affect urban capacity. Indeed old industrial areas, underused allotments and surplus hospitals or schools are often allocated for housing as a matter of priority in order to avoid spilling over into 'greenfields', undermining the principle of mixed use.

The main functional justification for promoting higher densities is shorter trip lengths in order to reach a given range of jobs, facilities and social contacts. The lower the density the less likely it is people will choose (or be able) to walk to facilities and the higher the proportion of motorized trips. The effect on bus viability is significant. White (1995) and Addenbrooke et al (1981) both suggest that contemporary densities are low for efficient operation of buses, falling below a desirable threshold of around 100 persons per hectare (40+dph). They also suggest density banding within any average figure. The maximum proportion of people should be living as close as possible to public transport, so flats and close-knit terraces cluster around the stops and stations, while lower density housing is further away. It is noteworthy that this kind of density gradient can be observed out along the radials in many UK cities, where the original 19th century development close to the tram route is at a higher density than the interwar or postwar development of the backlands.

We noted earlier (Chapter 4) that people tend to use local facilities if they are available. The level of density that allows facilities to be close enough to encourage most users to walk is therefore important. If the catchment population needed to support a primary school is 5000, and 600 metres is taken as a threshold for walking to school, than that implies a gross density of about 45 pph minimum, other things being equal. If the post office catchment population is 7000, then using the same accessibility standard implies over 60pph gross. Such calculations of course beg questions of user choice, behavioural variation, and also of the uneven distribution of facilities which tend to occur in reality. Choice emerged as a significant factor affecting the propensity to use local facilities in the analysis in Chapter 4. Higher densities, equivalent to Dutch or Italian cities or inner urban areas in the UK, are necessary in order to support a good choice of facilities within easy walking distance, and overcome problems of uneven distribution. Those higher gross densities imply economy in the land demands of the local facilities themselves. Market or institutional preferences for single storey development (eg schools) or land-hungry car parks (eg offices, shops) need reviewing and vertically mixed use considered.

The other key arguments for higher densities relate to energy. Higher net residential densities force the adoption of energy-efficient built-forms such as flats and terraces, and deter single storey and detached forms which are innately less efficient (Building Research Establishment, 1975). So long as higher densities do not involve high rise, then there are also advantages in terms of embodied energy: shared walls and shorter infrastructure lengths mean less building materials needed (Wright and Gardiner, 1980). The potential for district heating schemes attached to combined heat and power stations is also affected by density. Precise thresholds, such as the 50 dwellings per hectare suggested by one official study (Combined Heat and Power Group, 1979), are rather arbitrary. Viability is also dependent on the location of main users (ie a mixed use pattern) and the level of take up from consumers, as well as competing supply costs. But generally a compact, high density form is necessary.

Conversely some energy-related objectives point to the need for lower densities. As densities rise overshadowing becomes an increasing problem for solar layout. The key is whether winter sun (or at the very least spring and autumn sun) reaches ground floor windows. On flat land *maximum* densities are around 40dph (Roth, 1977) or 50dph (Turrent et al, 1981). As important as solar access is shelter from wind. To be effective shelter belts should be quite thick (around 10 metres) and occur at regular intervals, therefore occupying a significant amount of space. They can double as wildlife corridors, enhancing local biodiversity.

Other key resources of water and food, if managed and produced locally, require land. Water catchment can be on the roof, but treatment – while possible in high density developments such as the Kolding renewal scheme (Chapter 5), is easier and cheaper if land extensive. The standard two square metres per person, for reed-bed sewage systems, could however amount to only about 2 per cent of the housing area. The need to maintain the natural ecology and hydrological function of streams (rather than culvert them) is probably more significant. However, if the opportunity for local food production is valued, then the impact on density is on a different scale altogether. The 'Greentown' proposal in Milton Keynes, designed for high levels of energy, food and water autonomy, was nine dwellings per hectare (Greentown Future Residents, 1981). Typical interwar and 1950s estates, at about 25dph, give a fair opportunity for home growing (demonstrated by wartime productivity). On the other hand 1980s estates averaging 32dph generally do not, and are criticized by some householders for that reason (Farthing and Winter, 1988). Moderate densities such as this could, in the context of falling household size, embrace a higher proportion of one/two person flats so that more houses could have decent-sized gardens. Though given normal market equations where plot size is related to cost this risks frequent mismatch between home growing inclinations and opportunity. Allotments can provide a viable alternative. But allotments as normally provided (often far from homes) do not encourage recycling of home organic waste. One practice guide suggests a maximum home to allotment distance should be 200 metres, an easy barrow distance (Barton et al, 1995).

So there is no simple answer to the question of density. On the one hand the transport, accessibility, built form and CHP arguments strongly favour higher densities. On the other hand the solar power, food, water and urban wildlife arguments favour lower densities. However, detailed evaluation of these issues does begin to show a way through. Table 7.4 draws the distinction between net housing density and gross density – any neighbourhood strategy has to deal with both. The chart shows that the fairly stark choices between higher and lower net density can be mitigated by taking a broader view. If

**Table 7.4** *Net and Gross Density: Typical Areas*

| Objectives | Net Housing Densities | | |
| --- | --- | --- | --- |
| | Current greenfield average 25dph | Current major new estates 35dph | Possible higher density standard 50dph |
| Encourage more terraced development | ✗ | ? | ✔ |
| Deter single storey development | ? | ✔ | ✔✔ |
| Encourage solar design and layout | ✔✔ | ✔ | ? |
| Encourage home growing/larger gardens | ✔ | ? | ✗ |
| Minimize embodied energy cost | ✗ | ? | ✔ |
| Promote DH/CHP | ✗ | ? | ✔ |

| | Gross Density Levels | | | | | |
| --- | --- | --- | --- | --- | --- | --- |
| | Lower 17dph | Current 20dph | Lower 20dph | Current 25dph | Lower 28dph | Current 35dph |
| In situ water supply and treatment | ✔✔ | ✔ | ✔ | ? | ? | ✗ |
| Safeguarding ambient energy supply | ✔✔ | ✔ | ✔ | ✗ | ✔ | ✗ |
| Increasing local allotment provision | ✔ | | ✔ | ✗ | ✔ | ✗ |
| Providing shelter belts and local biodiversity | ✔✔ | ? | ✔ | ? | ✔ | ✗ |
| Viability of local facilities | ✗✗ | ✗ | ✗ | ? | ✔ | ✔✔ |
| Encouragement of walking trips | ✗ | ? | ? | ✔ | ✔ | ✔✔ |
| Improving bus viability | ✗✗ | ✗ | ✗ | ? | ✔ | ✔ |

*Notes:* ✔✔ = strongly positive; ✔ = generally positive; ? = equivocal; ✗ = generally negative; ✗✗ = strongly negative

more space is allowed for local allotments, water management, shelter belts and greenspace, while average *net* housing densities – and job/services density – are increased, then we have the best of both worlds, creating suburban variegated urban environments ranging from high intensity along public transport routes to low intensity around water courses, woods and hillcrests. The town sits within the landscape. And this density gradient is over a quiet modest scale, commensurate with easy pedestrian access to local facilities and to open space. It occurs within neighbourhoods and gives shape and purpose to local land use plans.

# CONCLUSION: LINEAR CONCENTRATION

At the start of the chapter four key spatial issues were identified: dispersal versus concentration, high versus low density, segregated versus integrated land use patterns, and nucleated versus linear form. Drawing the previous discussions together, there is a clear but quite complex line emerging which can help provide the strategic framework for neighbourhood planning.

On the first issue urban dispersal is rejected as a sustainable solution even though, ironically, many environmentalists advocate it. Concentration is *de rigeur*, but comes in two broad variants: the 'compact city' model and the 'dispersed concentration' model which can be equated with a polycentric city or cluster of linked towns. The compact city performs well empirically in relation to transport and accessibility criteria but above a certain size less well in theoretical tests assuming an energy constrained future. Dispersed concentrations should not be equated with neighbourhoods but with towns/townships large enough and economically attractive enough to support a good range of jobs and services. The mixed use centres of such townships should be locally accessible by non-motorized modes but also tied into the rest of the city or urban cluster by high quality public transport to avoid the necessity for car use while retaining city-wide choice. Mixed use does not imply a dispersed pattern of activities. Rather it is highly structured at both the neighbourhood and the township level. Variations in intensity of use give the framework for locational decisions. Higher intensity activities should cluster around public transport routes, with net housing densities sufficient to allow energy, access and community benefits to be realized. They are complemented by quite extensive open space networks providing the lungs of the urban area and often based on water courses.

The linear networks of water and public transport thus give the frameworks on which diverse urban land uses are hung. Even where a compact city solution is appropriate it is yet important both to maintain/enhance green parkways and to maximize public transport accessibility. This may lead to compact linear patterns for any necessary greenfield development rather than simple annular expansion. Put more pointedly, amorphous suburban sprawl is out, but it is not suburbia *per se* which is wrong – it is its lack of shape.

Linearity is a long standing theme of urban planning and research, so I will end the chapter by rehearsing some of the lessons of that work as a precursor to the consideration of neighbourhood form in the next chapter. The concept has been around a long time. For example Patrick Geddes (1915) advocated a star-like urban form, with wedges of open space, as a means of bringing nature back into the city. The Stockholm plan consciously attempts this, and sees linearity as helping to dissipate the urban pollution dome (Stockholm, 1998).

Linear development can come in a variety of forms: ribbon development, 'beads on a string', and 'linear band'. The first two suffer from long trip lengths, and are part of a dispersed rather than concentrated pattern. Rickaby (1985) tested a spider's web of development along country lanes and ribbon development (200 metres deep) along main radials out from a town, concluding that neither pattern was energy-efficient. Conversely the more concentrated linear band can offer short trip lengths and short trip times, with low infrastructure costs and high public transport efficiency (Jamieson et al, 1967).

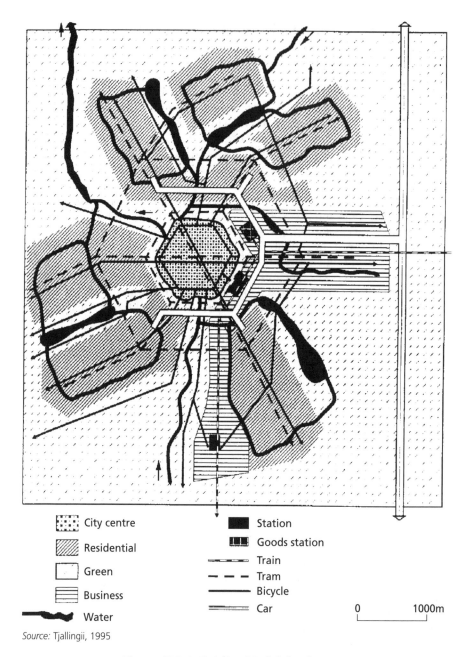

| | | | |
|---|---|---|---|
| City centre | | Station | |
| Residential | | Goods station | |
| Green | | Train | |
| Business | | Tram | |
| Water | | Bicycle | |
| | | Car | 0    1000m |

*Source:* Tjallingii, 1995

**Figure 7.2** *A Guiding Model for the City*

The advantage that linear form gives of good access to open space and countryside, together with the potential for local food production and recycling of organic wastes, is widely recognized. Services can be distributed along public transport spines in local centres, with major facilities clustered at nodes to produce counter-magnets to the main city centre and balance tidal

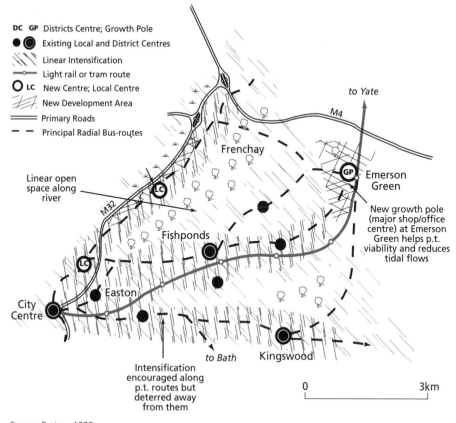

DC GP Districts Centre; Growth Pole
● ◉ Existing Local and District Centres
Linear Intensification
Light rail or tram route
O LC New Centre; Local Centre
New Development Area
Primary Roads
— — Principal Radial Bus-routes

to Yate

M4

Frenchay

Emerson Green

Linear open space along river

M32

LC

New growth pole (major shop/office centre) at Emerson Green helps p.t. viability and reduces tidal flows

Fishponds

LC

City Centre

Easton

Intensification encouraged along p.t. routes but deterred away from them

to Bath

Kingswood

0      3km

*Source:* Barton, 1988

**Figure** 7.3 *Linear Principles Applied to a Sector of Bristol*

flows (Barton, 1987). The experience of expanded/new town designs employing linear principles (Ipswich, Runcorn, Peterborough, Central Lancashire) suggests that linearity should not ideally take the form of stellar or radial growth – which can put undue pressure on congested radials – but rather adopt a tangential or loop pattern.

The emerging picture chimes in with the 'twin-track' approach advocated in The Netherlands. Tjallingii (1995) gives a picture of ecologically-sound urban development with the residential neighbourhood accessed by tramways, bike routes and roads complementing the water-based urban open space network (Figure 7.2).

Given a desire to intensify the use of existing urban areas to save greenfields and achieve regeneration, the linear model can give a rationale to *where* and *how much* intensification. Not by accident are there existing zones of higher density in many UK cities along the old radial tram routes. In certain cities (eg Oxford) the space between has never been built on and so the twin track system is already visible. In other places it would be possible over a long time scale to reinforce existing divergent densities within the city to create the two networks (Figure 7.3).

So in principle the linear band option can be applied in a range of circumstances. In practice it is liable to require a high degree of technical and political commitment and effective collaboration between diverse agencies if it is to succeed. It provides the broad framework which can help give shape and linkage to eco-neighbourhoods.

# 8   The Design of Neighbourhoods

*Hugh Barton*

## Vexed Terms and Traditional Concepts of Form

The focus of this chapter is the spatial form of neighbourhoods. Drawing on principles established in the previous chapters, it sets out the different ways in which neighbourhood form has been conceived in terms of identity, size, differentiation, density and access. The objective is not to provide a guide for urban designers – though the new urban design wisdom of permeability, streets and perimeter blocks is highly relevant – but to assess the options at the level of local planning. The chapter concludes with a case study of one of the largest neighbourhood renewal projects in recent years: Hulme in Manchester.

The studies which underpin the discussion come from the *UK* new towns on the one hand and the new urbanist designers on the other. The former offer a rich vein of creative spatial analysis, largely treated as purely historic by late 20th century market-orientated planners. The latter, with their concern for the human and physical context of development and the recreation of vibrant urban life, represent perhaps the shape of things to come. However, neither new towns nor new urbanists grapple fully with the issues of resource sustainability. Whereas the urban design principles have largely been applied in the inner parts of major cities, this paper is as much concerned with the shape of the suburbs and the evolution of smaller towns.

For the sake of clarity some key terms are defined at the outset:

- *local catchment area:* zone of good pedestrian accessibility to local services such as primary schools and shops, normally defined by threshold walking times (five or ten minutes) or distance (400–800 metres). 'Neighbourhoods' are often presumed to coincide with catchment areas but this is by no means always the case.
- *ennvironmental area:* zone where through traffic is excluded and the quality of the local environment takes precedence. Routinely achieved in new development through careful planning of road hierarchies. The term was coined by Buchanan's 1963 report *Traffic in Towns*.

- *neighbourhood:* an area of distinctive identity, normally named, which may coincide with either a local catchment area or an environmental area, or both, and is geared to pedestrian/cyclist access.
- *township:* larger area (over, say, 12,000 population) often embracing a number of local catchment areas, providing for some more specialized or larger catchment services such as leisure centre or superstore, plus a wider range of job opportunities.
- *home-zone:* a specially coined term referring to a cluster of dwellings often developed at the same time, with shared identity or character, usually grouped around a common access: eg a street, square, urban block or cul-de-sac. Other terms used: residential unit; housing cluster. Note: *home-zone* can be used to refer explicitly to zones where pedestrians and cyclists have priority over other traffic, eg a Dutch 'Woonerf' (DETR, 1998b).

## Concepts of Form

Neighbourhoods come in many shapes and sizes. The original concept in modern town planning can be traced back to Ebenezer Howard's ideas for the internal structuring of towns around school catchments. Subsequently the trail of the concept can be followed from the Garden City movement (of which Howard was the father) through the American planners Wright and Stein who were influenced by it. They devised the Radburn layout, with residential enclaves giving access to a segregated pedestrian network leading to schools, shops and playgrounds without risk from traffic. The Radburn principle equated local catchment areas with neighbourhood units. The catchment-based neighbourhood was gelled in official UK planning guidance at the end of the war when the London new towns were first planned:

> 'A neighbourhood is formed naturally from the daily occupa-
> tions of people, the distance it is convenient for a housewife to
> walk to her daily shopping and, particularly, the distance it is
> convenient for a child to walk to school. He (sic) should not
> have a long walk and he should not have to cross a main traffic
> road. The planning of a neighbourhood unit starts from that'.
> (Boyd et al, *Homes for the People* HMSO 1945)

In both *Homes for the People* and Radburn we get the idea not only of local catchment but also of an environmentally protected area. Both principles have functional implications that help determine appropriate size of neighbour-hoods. The traffic management implications were later developed by Buchanan in *Traffic in Towns* (1963), with maximum traffic flows on residential streets within a defined 'environmental area' being 300 passenger car units. The population implications of different catchment, density and access standards were usefully explored in *The Hook Book* (Greater London Council, 1965). Table 8.1 demonstrates the wide degree of variation across these characteristics even within the UK new town tradition. It also shows how closely *new urbanist* design in the US relate to that tradition. Ensuing discussion on neighbourhood form focuses on two issues, size and identity, which draw in all the other design elements.

**Table 8.1** *Characteristics of Idealized Neighbourhood Designs*

| Design | Identity | Population/ density | Facilities | Accessibility | Shape |
|---|---|---|---|---|---|
| Harlow *Gibbard* | Well-defined neighbourhoods linked to form districts | c.4000 population districts 15–20,000 | Local centres on distributor roads District centre at major intersection | 400m to local centre; 1000m to district centre | Dispersed concentrations – varied in detail |
| Runcorn *Ling* | Very clearly delineated separate local networks | 5–6000 population | Local centres on bus-way at heart of neighbourhood, off main roads | 400m to bus stops | Linear single-strand; beads on string |
| Milton Keynes | Very clearly delineated by grid roads | c.4000 population | Local centres on grid roads *between* neighbourhoods | 500m to local services and but stop | Dispersed grid with nucleated localities |
| Hook (inner town) *Greater London Council* | Not clearly bounded – part of urban continuum | 170 persons per ha, or 53dph net at planned average household size of 3.2 | Linear concentration along pedestrian spine | 400m max. to primary school and local facilities | Compact linear form |
| Peterborough Townships | Neighbourhoods with defined character but integrated in the wider township | Neighbour-hoods variable, c.2000; Township 20–30,000 | Wide range of services on township high street, accessible to all neighbour-hoods | 400m to bus stops on spine road | Linear single strand but quite concentrated |
| TODs (Transit-Oriented Developments) *Calthorpe* | Distinguished by density and character, but integrated into wider district | 44dph net density est. 4000 population | Clustered near transit stop and arterial road | 600m max to transit stop | nucleated half-circle |

# NEIGHBOURHOOD SIZE

The size of a neighbourhood may be defined by reference to population and/or access. The catchment population required to support a primary school and local centre is one key criteria. For example Runcorn has a string of neighbourhood 'beads', each with about 5000 population, along its integrating bus-way. Almost every house in the neighbourhood is within easy walking distance (conventionally defined as five minutes or 400m) of local facilities.

However the size of neighbourhood varies widely. For 'transit oriented developments' (TODs) in the US, the maximum walking distance is recommended as 2000 feet (600m) and densities set at a minimum average of 18dpa (44dph or about 100pph) in order to generate sufficient demand for a light rail station (Calthorpe, 1993). Ironically, given the half circle shape of TODs the population ends up as rather less than Runcorn 'beads on a string' despite the larger catchment distances. The recent study of Sustainable Residential Quality in London selects 800 metres (ten minutes walk) as the critical threshold for pedestrian access to district centres (Llewelyn Davies, 1997) – the same as that adopted by Redditch new town corporation some decades earlier; and the key walking distance in the aspiring eco-city of Waitakere in New Zealand is taken as 1000m. By contrast the Peterborough neighbourhoods in the Bretton township average 2000 people, and are more about identity than they are about discreet local services

This range and variety gives the designer pause for thought. While the general principles are clear the justification for specific standards and sizes is often obscure. There is sometimes an element of slight of hand. The 400m/five minute standard is probably pretty robust, recommended by public transport operators in the UK (Addenbrooke, 1981), and quoted in several continents. Interestingly it is advocated in The Netherlands, where the quality of public transport is legendary. With very fast efficient public transport services people are generally, however, willing to walk further. In relation to the London underground 800m marks the significant fall-off in ridership. Obviously local conditions will vary, and sensitivity to those conditions is essential.

The degree to which people choose to use local shops, schools, surgeries and clubs also depends on quality and diversity to match diverse needs in the population, in competition with other facilities in less accessible locations which may offer more. The limited range of services (even in ideal circumstances) that can be supported by a small neighbourhood catchment has led a number of planners to emphasize a higher tier. The classic plan for Harlow, for example, groups neighbourhoods together into loose townships, of up to 20,000 people, and ensures the township centre is highly visible on the main road network, able to attract trade from further afield as well as locally. The plan for the Peterborough townships goes one stage further, scaling down neighbourhoods and integrating them along a bus spine with a distinct high street offering a wide range of employment opportunities as well as services. According to one study Peterborough's townships offer a much better level of local accessibility than that achieved by the neighbourhood pattern in Milton Keynes (Potter, 1990). The size of the townships and their linear form (ideally suited to public transport operation) probably account for this result. The population of, say 30,000 people, is equivalent to a small town. As noted earlier 20–30,000 represents a threshold level for some key services – superstore and district centre, leisure centre, technical college, library, maybe a cinema, that gives the opportunity for a reasonable level of local autonomy (Breheny et al, 1993) (see Table 6.1).

In general, then, there may be good arguments for planning townships as the key level of local provision. Consumers have gained mobility and discrimination and as a result the large 'district' centres offering wider choice have often thrived while smaller local centres and the corner shops have suffered. It would be perverse to expect this trend to reverse. But the problem of relying on district or township centres is that trips by whatever mode are longer, and the incentive or need to indulge in healthy walking activity is reduced.

## NEIGHBOURHOOD IDENTITY

Creating local identity had long been a central theme for urban designers. Gibberd, designer of Harlow, considered it vitally important that each place should have its own character distinct from other places (Gibberd 1955). Kevin Lynch (1960) stressed people's perception of a locality, the image of a place, and importance of clear boundaries to assist orientation and the sense of belonging. Krier (1984) suggested 'every city quarter should have its own centre, periphery and limit'. Prince Charles encapsulated the feelings of many when he called for the development of *urban villages* in the UK to reintroduce human scale, intimacy and a vibrant street life ... to help restore to people their sense of belonging and pride in their own particular surroundings (HRH The Prince of Wales, 1989).

While the sentiment is widely shared the approach to achieving it is quite varied. Studies of perception show the degree to which each individual carries round their personalised image of 'their' neighbourhood, depending on what they feel is home terrain, and identified by landmarks (church, pub, supermarket, dual carriageway). Urban designers therefore try to create a *legible* environment which residents and visitors can find their way around, with key nodes marked by distinctive public spaces, vistas, higher buildings, public art. The recent reinforcement by government of the importance of *local distinctiveness* in PPG1 (DETR, 1997f) is part of this movement. Design guides now emerging are stressing responsiveness to local culture in terms of materials, built form, landscape and urban morphology – making places appropriately different from each other (Essex County Council, 1998; Forest of Dean District Council, 1998). The main contrast of approach is perhaps between those who believe that clear edges and physical separation help neighbourhood identity (eg Gibberd, Krier) and those who believe permeability between localities is vital, and the city is a seamless web (eg Bentley et al, 1985; Calthorpe, 1993).

The permeability philosophy is in the ascendant on the professional plane, but, as noted in Chapter 1, the development industry has for its own convenience and marketing reasons adopted a bowdlerized version of the 'clear limits' philosophy, producing a fractured pattern with each safe home-zone too small and too cut off to function as the whole or part of a neighbourhood. The real difference between the market and the designers is one of mode of transport: car or foot. For the designers it is the place as experienced on foot that matters, and their attempts to fabricate a physically distinctive neighbourhood identity are predicated on the assumption that people will choose to be pedestrians.

It is not only the physical identity which is valued. For some the potential for the local body politic is critical. Moughtin (1996) examines the unit size that might foster participatory democracy noting that Plato, using the model of the Greek City state, cited the figure of 5040 voting citizens. Given that in ancient Athens only free men were citizens (ie women, children and slaves were excluded) that figure would have been multiplied several times to equate with population. But with universal suffrage 5040 votes equals say 6200 population, ie in the centre of the traditional range of neighbourhood size. Alexander, on the other hand advocates identifiable spatial units no more than 300m across and with 500 people maximum (1977). He had in mind a community where everybody can know each other and participate actively in decision-making – perhaps relevant to the scale of home-zones rather than neighbourhoods.

Even in the age of Local Agenda 21 such intensely localized democracy is something of a dream. Nevertheless these ideas (Platonic or Alexandrian) are a stimulus to the argument. New localized systems of technology point to greater local control. Chapter 11 looks at how far devolution and subsidiarity can go. It seems logical that where possible town or parish councils should coincide with identifiable neighbourhoods or townships.

## SOCIAL IDENTITY AND HOME-ZONES

There are also community and health reasons for being concerned with local identity. There is widespread agreement that local social networks and the 'supportive environments' that enable those networks to function effectively are important to mental health (Halpern, 1995). The social identity of the local area – in terms of social class and ethnic group – help to determine feelings of security (or fear). An enormous range of evidence, according to Halpern, suggests that 'where group concentration at the local level falls below a certain critical mass, the level of mental ill-health found in that group markedly increases.' At first sight this seems to undermine the principle of social balance within a neighbourhood which was espoused in Chapter 6 as a means of reducing social exclusion and increasing the efficiency of resource use. However, the key issue is the *scale* over which a degree of social homogeneity is desirable: it would seem from the research to be very local, at the level of the street or the cul-de-sac – hence the term home-zone: home in the sense of home territory, socially and environmentally safe, the scale the house builders recognize as critical to their sales-pitch.

Thus the home-zone becomes the essential building block of the town. Within it social diversity is consciously limited, extraneous traffic excluded or calmed, and clear physical identity established. The neighbourhood is made up of a number of such home-zones, and the town a mosaic. Milton Keynes has pursued this kind of strategy with success. Every grid square neighbourhood of 2000–4000 people has a mix of housing (Table 8.2).

The home-zones were developed by different agencies or house-builders, and in the following example (Figure 8.1) they range from 9–130 units. The pattern of housing within the grid squares is designed to ensure that the elderly, disabled and those least likely to have cars are conveniently located at or near a local centre. To attract the more affluent residents the high priced dwellings are located to ensure an attractive approach and the opportunity for larger gardens.

There are interesting parallels with experience in America. The new urbanists Duany and Plater-Zyberg also believe in the value of socially diverse

**Table 8.2** *Broad Housing Mix of Two Contrasting Grid Squares in Milton Keynes*

|  | Shenley Church End | Crownhill |
| --- | --- | --- |
| Rent/shared ownership | 388 (28%) | 383 (39%) |
| Lower priced | 484 (35%) | 370 (38%) |
| Higher priced | 422 (30%) | 139 (14%) |
| Plots (very expensive) | 93 (7%) | 90 (9%) |
| Total | 1387 (100%) | 982 (100%) |

*Source:* Milton Keynes Development Corporation (1992)

neighbourhoods. In their terms every urban village should have about five different building types at different densities satisfying the needs of a variety of income groups. Their experience has shown that the different income types may be mixed successfully in adjacent streets. The density gradation from central public space with fully built-up street frontages through to low density pavilion (ie detached) dwellings on the outer edge also helps to emphasize the identity of the neighbourhood and blend it with its surroundings (Duany and Plater-Zyberg, 1991).

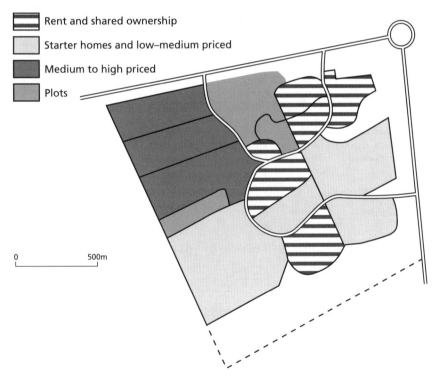

- Rent and shared ownership
- Starter homes and low–medium priced
- Medium to high priced
- Plots

0      500m

*Source:* Adapted from Milton Keynes Development Corporation, 1992

**Figure 8.1** *The Patchwork of Housing Sites in Chepstow Drive Grid Square, Milton Keynes*

# OPEN AND CLOSED NEIGHBOURHOODS

The master plans created by the British new town designers worked from the premise that neighbourhoods are stable and fixed. This assumption sits uncomfortably with contemporary life-styles and economic restructuring. It also, arguably, contradicts what can be observed in the evolution of older towns. Its persistence may be part of the reason why neighbourhood planning has lost credibility.

Where new neighbourhoods are bounded and discrete this may assist the sense of an identifiable community, but too often the range of shops developed in the initial flush of incoming families subsequently falls off, leaving empty units and declining turnovers as those families grow up and spread their wings. This pattern is particularly visible in suburban council estates suffering from an ebb of fortune and estate 'labelling'. The isolation of the estate contributes to a downward spiral as residents experience exclusion.

The fixed, delimited, neighbourhood also is ill-adapted to the variation between facilities. Table 6.1 showed typical catchment populations for a range of local facilities, derived from traditional standards and empirical observation of service levels on new suburban estates. There are no clear thresholds to equate with a specific neighbourhood size (Figure 8.2). Indeed it is likely that forcing catchment conformity on the range of services will increase operating costs for some, and threaten their local viability.

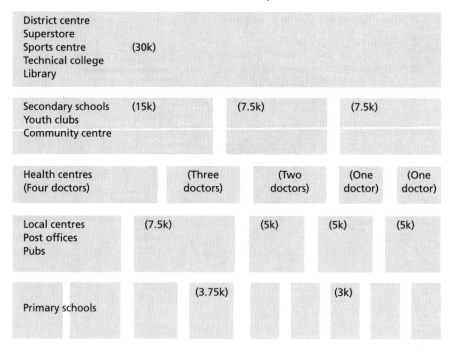

Source: Barton et al, 1995

**Figure 8.2** *The Variability of Local Catchment Populations for Different Facilities*

Furthermore neighbourhoods, and local services are not static. The spatial patterns give a misleading impression of being forever unchanging. On the contrary, populations evolve with household size and status; operational needs of businesses react to wider economic and social change; social preference and behaviour alters.

Taking each of these factors in turn: the population capacity of an area alters as one and two person households occupy dwellings previously lived in by families. Rising incomes allow people to buy more space. Unless more units are constructed to compensate, the population falls and local businesses find their market shrinking. The economic unit size and the service requirements of enterprises also changes: for example, educational policy has led to bigger schools; doctors are often grouped in threes and fours rather than ones and twos; the breweries demand bigger pubs and close small pubs; local butchers and bakers have lost out to the supermarkets. Consumers have also become more discriminating: in some spheres (such as in relation to dental treatment or church-going) they are less than likely to choose local even when local is available. In this situation of flux it is unrealistic to expect preconceived residential catchments to remain valid indefinitely. The physical form of neighbourhoods needs to be able to respond to social and economic change, not prejudice it or be prejudiced *by* it.

Runcorn provides an example of an *inflexible* design. The neighbourhoods protectively cocoon their local facilities, hiding them away from view, resisting sharing. It would be interesting to investigate the quality and quantity of local facilities *vis-à-vis*, say, Harlow, which has a more open and varied approach (Figure 8.3).

The design for Milton Keynes, and the TODs of Peter Calthorpe, demonstrate a particular strategy for avoiding inward-looking, closed neighbourhoods. That strategy is simply one of *visibility*, inviting people from other locations to make use of local facilitates and thus reinforce their viability. In the case of Milton Keynes local centres are located at the edges of the neighbourhood block as defined by the grid roads. Shops and pubs are visible from the main road (and the bus stop) and vehicle access is encouraged. In the Milton Keynes context this encourages car-based trips and contributes to emissions; and the local centres still have rather a fixed local hinterland, and varying success. The TODs, also, align their commercial zone in highly visible sites alongside the highway and adjacent to transit stops. The urban TODs are expressly designed to cater for commercial services in excess of those justified locally, satisfying a more general market demand for decentralised employment and services (Figure 8.4). Much of that demand relates, however, to car-based clients, unless an effective public transport orientated land use strategy (such as the ABCD strategy) is enforced.

The general lesson from the closed versus open neighbourhood question, as from the review of social identity, is that planners cannot 'buck' the market, but they can help shape it. The 'market' in these cases is 'the community' – people individually and in social and economic groupings. The closed neighbourhoods have a limited life before they become out of joint with social and economic needs. The open forms are more robust, though involve (on the examples above) environmental costs, and may still have restrictions on catchment flexibility.

**Runcorn**

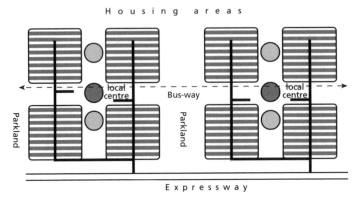

**Harlow**

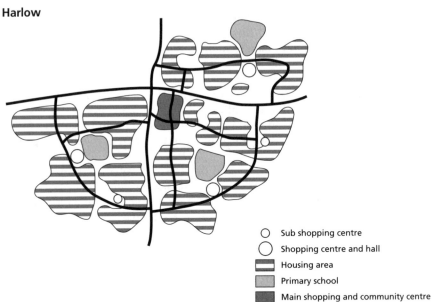

**Figure 8.3** *Runcorn and Harlow Neighbourhood Structures Contrasted*

The market in the sense of the housing developers needs effective public guidance if it is to deliver distinctive home-zones within the neighbourhood in a way that achieves social inclusion for all sectors of the housing market, and avoids the physical and identify fracturing of the neighbourhood observed in conventional estates.

## THE URBAN CONTINUUM

The traditional pattern of neighbourhoods in older settlements is not normally one of discreet enclaves but of interconnected districts – more an urban continuum than a series of cells (Breheny et al, 1993). The urban continuum has the

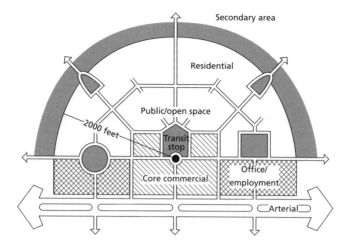

**Figure 8.4** *Transit Oriented Developments (TODs)*

major but unsung advantage of allowing the very flexibility of catchment size over time and space that the neat, stylized neighbourhoods of planning convention inhibit.

The structure of service provision, reflecting market conditions before universal car ownership, has lessons for us now, trying to recover the pedestrian/tram-based city. The trams and buses provided the connections between localities and the natural foci for pedestrian movement. The shops and services grew up along the tramways, often creating a pattern of radial high streets out from the heart of the city. Densities were highest close to the high street and graded down away from them, reflecting both the sequence of urban development and the relative market values. Identifiable, named neighbourhoods are *bounded* by the high street or *centred* on it (depending partly on the degree to which the road is heavily trafficked and impedes free pedestrian movement). These 'fuzzy' neighbourhoods often merge into each other with no clear edge but high permeability. This is particularly so in the 18th and 19th century environments. Lynch (1981) advocates neighbourhoods bounded by main streets, which he called 'uniting seams', on the basis that people walk to the services provided and mingle with people from nearby areas, but rarely carry on beyond the main street unless for some specific purpose, so their familiar territory is all to one side. The neighbourhoods in the Peterborough townships follow this pattern.

So local high streets typically provide the social meeting places between residential neighbourhoods, the place for exchange of goods and services but also where the locality meets the town and connects with the city. Instead of neighbourhoods being conceived as inward-looking villages – a kind of nostalgic image of rural community falsely transferred to the town – the neighbourhood becomes a more fluid medium for local and city-wide contact, facilitating diverse forms of place and interest communities.

The high street is a series of activity generators – bus stops, supermarkets, clusters of civic/community buildings, cafés, shops and local offices. It is not normally uniform in use and level of activity, nor in property values. There are prime, secondary and tertiary locations, with the latter locations providing a useful habitat for more marginal users – the low-key (often charitable) office, the independent retailer, the garage workshop, recycling shops – and also for higher density residential accommodation – blocks of flats, sheltered housing, flats over shops. The variety of uses along the high street is reflected in variety of built form and public space. Three and four storey blocks – the limits of walk-up access – with side alleys and courtyards at the prime zones to increase frontage, may be complemented by broader promenades, market squares or parks breaking the longitudinal pattern.

Such high streets are not static. They are organic structures that can absorb a considerable amount of change over time, responding to altered market conditions and catchments. The drawback is the traffic. High streets have in a sense been the victim of their own success. The combination of transport functions can range from street parking and bulk deliveries through to primary route and public transport spine. In the same space cyclists and pedestrians want safe and convenient environments, and the street acts as a series of casual meeting places, where the interests of conviviality should (but rarely do) take precedence. Pedestrianization, even where it is feasible, is not necessarily the answer. The essence of the high street is that it is bustling with activity – the focus for a number of residential areas that are placid by comparison. So the removal of traffic is only appropriate where pedestrian activity is high and the space limited. In most situations the cars, bikes, buses and delivery vehicles contribute to the sense of bustle, provide vital access, and assist the natural policing of the streets after hours. But traffic does need to be 'calmed' if the pedestrian users of the street are to hold sway. Buchanan (1963) suggested that the environmental capacity criteria for shopping streets should be the ability to cross the road without undue delay, and the ability to converse at normal volumes – admirably humane criteria. He equated these criteria with a maximum of 600pcu per hour each way.

## SHAPING NEIGHBOURHOODS

The trick for urban planners is to realize the advantages of traditional inter-connected urban districts and high streets without the accompanying disadvantages – principally traffic dominance. The planners of Hook – in North East Hampshire ten miles south of Reading – were unimpressed by the cellular structure of earlier new towns and argued for interconnection. Hook was perhaps the most innovative and 'sustainable' of UK mid-century new towns but sadly was never built. It involved quite high density development based on an excellent pedestrian/cycling system and compact form. Figure 8.5 shows the way the pedestrian spine was to be the focus for activity in much the same way as traditional high streets. The key difference was that the traffic and buses were segregated onto a separate system and made to go the long way round. The criticism that can be levelled at the scheme is that which is made often about pedestrian schemes in old high streets: they remove key sources of vital-ity – especially important during evening or times of low pedestrian activity – which contribute to the sense of street safety.

## Hook: concentration of meeting places on a central pedestrian way

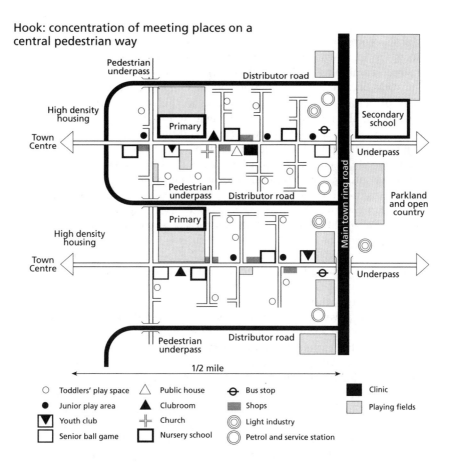

| | | | |
|---|---|---|---|
| ○ Toddlers' play space | △ Public house | ⊖ Bus stop | ■ Clinic |
| ● Junior play area | ▲ Clubroom | ▬ Shops | ▢ Playing fields |
| ▼ Youth club | ✚ Church | ◎ Light industry | |
| ▢ Senior ball game | ▢ Nursery school | ◯ Petrol and service station | |

## Peterborough: Bretton Township, neighbourhoods integrated into the township by the multi-purpose spine road

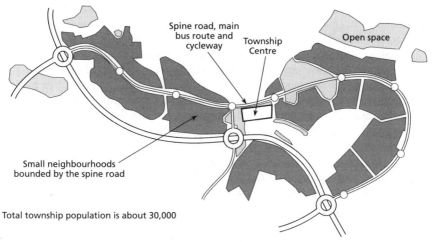

Total township population is about 30,000

**Figure 8.5** *Linear Concentration: Hook and Peterborough*

Peterborough's new townships are at a more modest density, so except at the district centre do not generate the level of local pedestrian activity envisaged in Hook's inner town. But the township spine road is multi-functional like a high street, combining traffic distributor, bus route, main cycle and pedestrian way. It works because of careful design and the exclusion of non-township traffic.

The principle of planning high streets at the core of urban districts or townships has the advantage over the nucleated model of service centres in that it can provide continuity between new and old areas. It is not a matter of rejecting the traditional form but making it work. Even in the small towns and low density suburbs of the US and Australasia the linear commercial strip and 'main street' provide starting points for gradual evolution into public transport/pedestrian-oriented high streets. The Auckland authority of Waitakere sees its main commercial strip, currently experiencing burgeoning growth because of improved car access off the motorway, as a major long term asset in enhancing the role of public transport. Linearity is the key. Progressive intensification and redevelopment of short-life retail sheds can be designed to foster a future LRT link along the wide boulevard, and create a pedestrian-friendly environment, out of what is currently a pedestrian nightmare (David Meade, personal communication).

Few recent developments in the UK have adopted the principle of high streets. Even in the Peterborough townships the high streets are truncated. The absence of high street schemes is partly a reflection of inertia and conservatism on the part of local authorities, developers and designers, but also a matter of development density and commercial viability. The inertia stems from the conventional wisdom of (in particular) retailers and planners that major facilities such as supermarkets and multi-screen cinemas, which are key trip generators, are by nature surrounded by car parks. Even if located on a shopping street such car parks break the continuity of the frontage (thus deterring linear pedestrian movement) and invite people to parachute in by car rather than walk or cycle. However, the viability of local services, even assuming pro-pedestrian development schemes, is a more profound problem. Typical UK suburban densities, even more North American or Antipodean densities, are not sufficient to maintain the wide variety of local services implied by the term *high street*, within the accessibility standards suggested by Figure 6.2.

Taking 400m as the key threshold for easy pedestrian access to local shops, pubs, primary schools and bus stops, and a *gross* density of 40 people per hectare (20 dwellings per hectare with an average of two people per household), then a nucleated catchment area has a total population of 2000 – probably insufficient to support all but the most rudimentary services. Hence the invalidity, in suburban areas, of cellular-type neighbourhoods. With a linear core of, say, 1000m (which is functionally rather ambitious given the likely absence of a frequent and cheap bus service) the population rises to 5200, ie comparable with traditional neighbourhoods. This is *perhaps* sufficient to support a primary school, local centre and post office, but does remain at the margins of viability given current consumer patterns. Indeed the Post Office, health authorities and breweries are all now expecting bigger threshold populations before they will invest. So unless there is reliance on (motorized) customers from a wider hinterland, the high street will have but a sprinkling of low key facilities, and local people will go further afield. The interests of environmental and social sustainability will not be served.

Conversely, if gross densities of at least 100 people per hectare can be achieved (assuming 50dph), as in some low rise renewal schemes such as Hulme in Manchester which is described later, then the situation is transformed. The nucleated 400m catchment then has 5000 population and the linear catchment area has 13,000. That is sufficient to support a good range of facilities including a diverse shopping centre, banks, several pubs and cafés, health centre, community centre and secondary school, plus perhaps a library and church. At this density also it is normally possible to run a frequent public transport service which facilitates movement along the high street as well as to the wider city. If, furthermore, densities are graded, with the main open spaces away form the core, then viability is further enhanced and the high street perhaps begins to hum with activity. (Note, of course, that we assumed a 1000m high street only for the sake of argument).

Clearly reality might be somewhat different. These are theoretical models geared to specific sustainability criteria. But the difference between prevailing suburban patterns and traditional European cities, where densities are comparable to or greater than the high density version above, is eloquent. Indeed in places such as Bologna and Athens or parts of Amsterdam, there are often criss-crossing high streets, supplemented by corner shops on other streets, which give a remarkable sense of local accessibility.

In the UK gross densities of 100pph are high where a significant proportion of homes with gardens is required, but 100pph *net* can be achieved in the context of a socially balanced area. Reasonable densities, of course, are a *necessary* but not *sufficient* catalyst for a sustainable pattern of local facilities within neighbourhoods. The local authorities and development agencies also have to create a situation where public, private and voluntary agencies will *want* to locate within a locality. There are a number ways of achieving this:

- a layout that encourages a pattern of movement – particularly a concentration of pedestrian trips – so that specific allocated sites are attractive to shops, cafés, pubs etc;
- the clustering of uses to gain benefits from association and multi-purpose trips;
- negotiation with service providers (eg education authority, library services, clubs) to reinforce the clusters and gain economies of shared use;
- the creation of an attractive, safe and convenient public realm;
- a layout designed to maximise the efficiency and accessibility of bus services from the outset (not an afterthought);
- good public visibility of key sites to a wider community – ie car and bus travellers;
- flexibility in the location of small-scale facilities (eg hairdressers, playgroups) so that local initiative is not frustrated.

# THE OPEN SPACE NETWORK

Whereas pedestrian access and public transport routes provide the structure for higher intensity development, water courses and hill crests offer a logic to the organization of open space. In 1963 Sylvia Crowe anticipated the creation of an urban parkway system linking residential areas to the countryside and encompassing a wide range of recreational needs. She advocated the parkways to bring the green into the town and provide for round walks, parks, playing fields and allotments.

Such landscape concepts have been influential in new settlement design but not in urban planning generally. Suburban open space increments have been provided on a disaggregated and discontinuous pattern. Yet, as we saw in Chapter 7 in relation to the Dutch twin-track approach, the arguments for a linked system are powerful. In Leicester the driving force was ecology. Leicester City Council have devised a 'green network', involving the protection and enhancement of open space and linear habitats both for biodiversity and residents' delight. The strategy is based around the extensive network of rivers, canals and wetlands, and incorporates woodlands, farmland, and formal recreation space. It provides a marvellous system of strategic green routes for walkers and cyclists. It also protects the wildlife capillaries of hedgerows, ditches, railway lines and road verges and, on another plane, moderates microclimate and assists pollution absorption. The intimate relationship between natural land/drainage systems and urban space makes for the uniqueness of any place. The landscape is recognized as providing the form within which a neighbourhood may lie. Human activity responds to and reflects the landscape that nurtures it, and in its turn shapes the landscape itself.

The interplay of function is illustrated by Figure 8.6 which gives one model for the transition between housing and a narrow greenway alongside a main road, emphasising the importance of supervision of the cycleway and illustrating the multi-functional role of the open space: windbreak, noise baffle, particulate absorber, $CO_2$ sink, energy source, wildlife haven, aesthetic pleasure, movement and recreation.

Milton Keynes Development Corporation (1992) demonstrates the way such greenways link together with formal and informal open space along river valleys and hill crests to create a network accessible to all residents. According to Barton et al (1995) elements of this network should be within 800 metres of all dwellings, with some playgrounds, parks and allotments closer, within the residential area. In the long run the potential value of the open space network for local food production, energy crops and water treatment together with associated economic and social functions is impossible to calculate. But the existence of ample open space within towns gives ecological resilience and increased structural flexibility, as well as delight and pleasurable exercise to the citizens.

Such principles can be incorporated into new development if local authorities have the wit and will. But it is clearly difficult to retrofit existing urban areas, not only because of the slow rate of change but because of financial constraints and pressure on brownfield sites. The financial cost of purchasing brownfield sites for open space could be met by a hypothecated greenfield

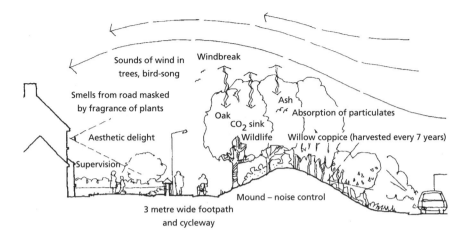

Sounds of wind in trees, bird-song

Windbreak

Smells from road masked by fragrance of plants

Oak
$CO_2$ sink

Ash
Absorption of particulates

Aesthetic delight

Wildlife

Willow coppice (harvested every 7 years)

Supervision

Mound – noise control

3 metre wide footpath and cycleway

*Source:* Barton et al, 1995

**Figure 8.6** *The Interrelated Functions of Urban Greenways*

development tax, equitably redistributed between authorities. The pressure for housing development in-town, on every spare site, could be managed by a coherent twin track strategy, offering opportunities for intensification away from the green network.

## CONCLUSION: CELLULAR AND FUZZY NEIGHBOURHOODS

The traditional planning models treat the neighbourhood as a *cell*. Cellular neighbourhoods come in three distinct forms. The *single cell* model, with the nucleus of services at its heart and limited main road or public transport connectivity, risks isolation for the transport poor and non-viability for local businesses. The *interlocked cell* model (as in Milton Keynes) solves the problem of the visibility of local services, but there is tension between the grid square neighbourhood defined as an environmental area, and the catchment-based neighbourhood which is split by the main road barrier. Neither of these forms is innately very adaptable because of catchment limits. The *cell cluster* model, illustrated by Harlow, has more openness and flexibility. The cluster of cells equates with a township, supporting a wider range of relatively local services. The cluster can work well where the possibilities of interconnection are high and transport links directly between nuclei.

The urban continuum pattern of older towns, with linear high streets serving overlapping neighbourhoods and providing both local and township services, offers an alternative to the cellular model. Essentially neighbourhoods in this context have fuzzy edges. Residents may define *different* neighbourhoods depending on their personal location and associations. Even where there are recognisable boundaries (such as railway lines or rivers) the

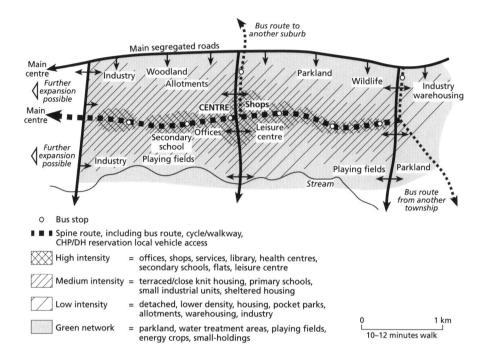

**Figure 8.7** *Idealized Model for a Linear Township of 30,000 People*

fuzzy neighbourhood model emphasizes permeability. These neighbourhoods (following the Peterborough idea) should be environmental areas of distinctive character. But because they are not tied to catchment populations they can be widely varied in size, responding to local conditions, increasing diversity. Each neighbourhood should consist of a number of home-zones, each of which may be socially quite homogeneous, but together bringing social heterogeneity to the neighbourhood. The diversity of home-zones creates a residential mosaic combining, it is hoped, security with social inclusion.

The high streets become the places where residents from different neighbourhoods can meet, though there may also be very local facilities within neighbourhoods which provide local focus. The high streets also provide connections by cycle, bus/tram and foot to the rest of the urban area. Car access is normally permitted but 'calmed'. All this assists vitality and viability, with catchment populations able to vary between activities and over time. Average densities are generally significantly higher than the current UK norm, and the density gradient reinforces access to the core. The integrated township – which can provide visual coherence and political identity – will normally consist of a number of fuzzy neighbourhoods and a *minimum* population of circa 25,000, sufficient to support key facilities such as superstore and leisure centre. The obverse of the transport-centred township is the water-based system of green spaces which percolate into the town to give good access to all, and allow the town to breathe. The linear urban concentrations can be one strand (one public transport route) or two strands wide, can be looped or truncated, radial or orbital or grid based. Figure 8.7 shows the basic one-strand model.

One grid-based urban neighbourhood in the making, or remaking, is Hulme in Manchester. It has been chosen not because it illustrates all the points above or can lay special claim to sustainabiliy, but because it is one of few major UK examples of the 'new urbanist' thinking. It demonstrates the practicality of the high density, mixed use neighbourhood integrated into the inner urban fabric and creating a permeable people-friendly environment.

# Case Study of Hulme, Manchester

## Richard Guise

Hulme is located immediately south of Manchester city centre and has suffered from severe surgery in the postwar era. Its grid of 19th century working class terraced streets was cleared in the 1950s and 60s to be replaced in the early 1970s by a townscape of concrete tower blocks and multi-storey deck access crescents and terraces with extensive ill-defined grass spaces between. The morphology of the street pattern was virtually ignored except for the odd remnant pub. Indeed the main shopping artery of the Stretford road was swept away with most businesses disappearing from the area. The density of development was, at 37 dwellings per hectare gross, only a quarter the density of the terraced development it replaced. The familiar story of technical and social failure in the new developments ensured their unsustainability barely one-third of the way into their 60-year design life. By the early 1990s the area was flattened for the second time in living memory, to start again.

As a result of winning a City Challenge bid Hulme Regeneration Ltd was set up as a joint venture company, a partnership of the City Council and AMEC plc to manage the regeneration. The plan is to build up to 3000 new homes over five years in an area of over half a square kilometre at densities of 75–87 dwellings per hectare (over twice that of the 1970s scheme).

Hulme Regeneration produced an excellent *Guide to Development* in 1994 which sets out a well argued urban design agenda owing much to the *Tibbalds Ten Commandments* (Tibbalds, 1992) and such gurus of urban design as Jane Jacobs and Kevin Lynch.

To paraphrase the main points:

- the area is to be redeveloped as a network of streets and squares conceived as a setting for urban life, not just as traffic conduits;
- the streets should contain a rich mix of uses and tenures allowing as much integration and adaptability as possible;
- high densities are considered as crucial to sustaining the uses and services deemed essential to the area;
- Hulme needs the best possible links through the area, and to the area from the rest of the city. It needs to be permeable, connected and 'legible' ie easily read by residents and visitors alike;
- the new district needs to develop a sense of identity or place deriving from the retention of its landmarks and the creation of new nodes of activity;

*Photos: Richard Guise*

**Figure 8.8** *Images of Hulme: Reinventing Streets*

- the area should feel owned by its residents having a stake in its maintenance;
- it should be sustainable – socially as well as environmentally – through energy efficiency, alternatives to the use of the car, adaptable long life buildings.

The Guide develops these aspirations in some detail with much emphasis on good street design as a key to achieving these. Thus there is guidance on active street frontages, public and private realm, informal surveillance of the public realm through having rooms facing the streets, height of buildings related to width and function of the streets and focal point buildings at major corners. The grid layout is reinforced by the visual advocacy of cross road intersections which help direction finding. In order to achieve the high densities required buildings are to be between three and four storeys high with a minimum car parking allowance of 50 per cent per dwelling. It is envisaged that much parking will be on-street. Special provision is being made for cycle routes away from major streets. Bus stops should be safe, well lit and related to nodes of action.

Finally guidance is given on energy, targeting a minimum National Home Energy Rating of eight, to ensure the affordability of heating bills. Housing should also attain a 'good' rating on the Building Research Establishment Environmental Assessment Method for assessing $CO_2$ emissions, choice of materials, etc.

The impact of the early stages of development is now being seen as grid blocks are being completed. Townscape is beginning to emerge which – whilst often in familiar brick and pitched roof – is clearly of the late 20th century. There is variety, but also a grammar of strong corner elements, with neighbourhood shops or other services at ground floors, front doors close to the pavement and an absence of garages on the frontages. Building heights are probably averaging at three to four storeys with some two storey blocks. A landmark mixed use development containing shops, workspaces, café, a minor theatre, and housing, rises to six storeys around a shared landscape courtyard.

Is the new Hulme likely to be a sustainable neighbourhood? If aspirations for the physical fabric of the district can be used as a measure then these incorporate much of present day good practice and should have a better chance than conventional development of being sustainable. However the guidance document is a set of headline aims and it relies on successful negotiation with developers to achieve these aims in reality. It also relies on an infrastructure of community and commercial services to be established as soon as possible and for people to adopt the lifestyle of working, shopping, learning and spending much of their leisure time within walking distance of their homes. A public transport infrastructure must also be in place which provides an attractive alternative to the car. If all these aspects can be established in addition to the physical fabric Hulme could become a vibrant and sustainable neighbourhood.

# PART III
# COMMUNITY AND SUBSIDIARITY

# 9 Design for Living: The Challenge of Sustainable Communities

*Alison Gilchrist*

## Introduction – The Changing Nature of 'Community'

The word 'community' resonates throughout our lives. It embraces a quality of life that seems universally valued: a sense of belonging which absorbs some of the stresses and strains of an increasingly fragmented existence. Community refers to that layer of society in which interaction takes place between people who are neither close family and friends, nor yet total strangers. Community is neither private nor fully public. It shapes our social identity and helps us make sense of a complex and dynamic world.

This chapter explores the impact that the built environment has on our experience of community, focusing particularly on the functions of social networks and voluntary associations within urban settings. It argues that the diversity and intensity of connections formed between residents in a given locality is enhanced through opportunities for conversations and casual interchange. Our sense of community emerges from this web of informal interactions and is crucial to how we interpret and integrate experiences at local level. By helping us to understand the issues and anticipate how people are likely to react, community networks enable us to mediate disputes within and between different groups. Interpersonal links act as bridges of mutual trust and respect so that wherever possible conflicts can be resolved positively, rather than through antagonistic confrontation. Community members use informal networks to mobilize for collective action and to influence politicians and planning officers. Whilst it might be assumed that an emphasis on locality overlooks the substantial changes that have occurred in the way many people live their lives (see Chapter 2), nevertheless the vision of eco-neighbourhoods needs to recognize that personal networks add a vital dimension to community sustainability and collective empowerment. The three examples in this chapter illustrate how the residents of one inner city neighbourhood organized themselves to work in alliance with the local authorities and other partners to enhance the quality of community life. With support from paid community workers, they set up self-help groups to run community activities and campaign for better local services and facilities. As a consequence, they were able to achieve major improvements in the physical environment, which in turn have strengthened local solidarity and commitment.

Much has been written about the fuzziness of the term community and there have been countless studies of different kinds of communities, observing and analysing the 'everyday lives of ordinary people' (Crow and Allen, 1995). For a time sociologists argued that the word has become so over-used that it has lost its meaning (eg Stacey, 1969; Bell and Newby, 1971) and yet in common parlance as well as government policy, the desire for community endures. There is a growing body of evidence suggesting that there are advantages in being well-connected into strong social networks. Membership of social networks promotes physical and mental health (Pilisuk and Parks, 1986; Argyle, 1996). Individuals benefit in terms of their happiness, their resilience to misfortune and resistance to disease. They gain access to resources, practical assistance, emotional support and advice. At a collective level, community organisations and informal networks are a way of managing shared facilities and promoting social solidarity. This is especially important for people struggling at subsistence level or living in situations of great uncertainty.

Levels of violent crime and vandalism also appear to be reduced by strong community participation (Worpole, 1998). Informal exchange mechanisms amongst friends and neighbours mean that people make less demands on non-renewable resources, using these more efficiently through borrowing, bartering and sharing. People use conversations and personal contacts to gain the advice and information they need to make decisions rather than relying on their own feelings or the biased opinion of close family. Informal networks that reach into other experiences and perspectives help an individual to broaden their horizons so that they are less likely to make wasteful or distressing mistakes.

In addition to informal patterns of interaction, many communities organize collective activities through formal associations, constituted around shared values and interests. Community groups, voluntary organizations and campaigning bodies are an important aspect of civil society, allowing people to express their sense of mutuality and to participate in democratic processes. In the UK today organizations are based on people's political and spiritual beliefs, as well as meeting their social, cultural, health and recreational needs. The voluntary sector contributes vital services to our welfare system, through self-help and philanthropic organizations. Over the years, voluntary organizations have pioneered innovative and challenging ways of responding to and articulating the needs of people who are disregarded by mainstream state provision. National bodies have acquired major influence and funding, whilst small, community-run groups continue to provide important resources, often with a focus around a particular culture, impairment or sexual identity (Chanan, 1992). As well as developing more experimental and specialist services, these groups are frequently involved in advocating for improvements or changes in policy on behalf of their members or users.

Whilst it is true that community involvement may no longer involve participation in *local* activities, nevertheless the desire to be connected with others remains an important motivation in many people's lives. Inner city localities and outer urban estates are becoming more diverse, reflecting different patterns of employment, migration and gentrification. Even rural villages, the embodiment of the traditional community, have changed. Young people leave home to find jobs and a chance of independent living, and their places are taken by commuters, teleworkers or those enjoying retirement.

For many individuals, the place where they live has only a limited and transient significance. They are less dependent on neighbours for support or entertainment and are likely to have little in common with those living in the immediate vicinity. Technology and increased mobility (most notably telephones and car ownership, but also more recently the Internet) have meant that people are able to communicate easily with one another world-wide. Many people also now enjoy a higher level of disposable income and more leisure time. They choose to spend time with people who share their hobbies and interests. They may develop links with people with whom they share common cause, for example on the basis of a political commitment. These social networks, based on chosen connections rather than residential proximity, have been termed 'communities of interest or identity' (Willmott, 1987). They incorporate a growing awareness of social oppression (around race, gender, disability, sexual orientation, etc) and greater flexibility in lifestyles.

The 20th century has witnessed fundamental changes in the ways that people live. Shifts in the global economy and technological developments have restructured the labour market, destroying occupational communities (such as around the mines and cotton mills) where people worked all their lives alongside their neighbours and relatives. Communities are still based on attachments and shared identity, but they are more geographically scattered with people making use of new forms of communication to stay in touch and to organize collective action (Castells, 1996). People are less reliant on informal modes of exchange to meet their material needs. The welfare system continues to provide some residual and targeted services, but generally market forces now cater for many leisure, health and care needs. In some areas LETS schemes and credit unions have been established to provide semi-formal, non-profit making mechanisms for exchanging and sharing skills. Although they aspire to the values of community, they do not rely purely on informal trust relationships. Instead they use token currencies and record-keeping to keep track of exchanges and ensure that there is equivalent benefit for all participants.

Globalization has meant that economic, social, political and cultural networks are becoming international. Horizons are expanding and, through the Internet and mass media, we have increasing access to other experiences, markets and traditions. The social and environmental costs of this are gradually being acknowledged, with a growing opinion that we should strive to live our lives more locally, making better use of the human and natural resources that are around us.

How is it possible to reconcile these divergent trends? How can we develop a society that is adaptive, integrated *and* diverse? Sustainability does not mean isolated self-sufficiency. Eco-neighbourhoods are as much about the renovation of community, as they are about recycling and energy conservation. Strong, flexible informal networks and self-managing voluntary associations are indispensable to these new forms of governance and mutuality.

## Complexity and Sustainability

The notion of community is inextricably linked to sustainability. Voluntary associations and patterns of collective organizing evolve in response to global and local changes. Traditional forms of organization are adapted and new ones developed. These processes of experimentation and evolution ensure that the community as a whole is able to adjust to changes in the environment and learn from its collective experience. Personal ties between individuals, groups and organizations create a robust communications network through which information and ideas flow across the whole community. People talking together develop a collective intelligence, a form of 'communal wisdom' which integrates past, present and future experiences into a coherent, but flexible model of the world. It is these informal networks that sustain a dynamic and creative community, and promote social cohesion.

Complexity theory offers some useful insights into the development of collective action within complex societies (Eve et al, 1997). For our purposes, the emergence of community can be envisaged as a way of managing the complexities and uncertainties of human society. Voluntary associations, community groups and social networks represent stable (but not static) patterns of interaction through which joint activity is coordinated so that the whole system is able to maintain some kind of equilibrium.

Communities that are well-connected and contain a good diversity of ideas and experience are better able to synthesize these to generate creative solutions to problems which arise in their environment. Networks allow complex systems to respond flexibly and innovatively to changes in the prevailing conditions. Particular cultural and organizational arrangements survive if they have the right combination of skills, energy and commitment to fill a particular niche in the social environment, using resources within (or within reach of) their networks. Just as ecological communities require biodiversity to be sustainable over periods of change, so too can human communities flourish on socio-diversity if there are robust mechanisms for symbiotic integration and flexible adaptation. How can this be achieved in a society dominated by competition, rigid institutions and discrimination of all kinds?

Community can be envisaged as the experience of social inter-connectivity. It represents the collective consciousness (which some people might call 'community spirit' or solidarity) emerging as a result of the myriad of personal and local interactions which occur in the course of our everyday lives. A sense of community affects our behaviour, feelings, judgements and expectations. Whether we like it or not, we are influenced by the decisions and actions of those around us, especially those for whom we have some emotional attachment. This is particularly true if we focus on those aspects of our lives which we consider to be about free will, personal choice and voluntary association. These influences are by no means always positive. Unfortunately, we are constrained by jealousy, fear, resentment and suspicion, as much as we are inspired by love, compassion and respect.

We experience community through a shifting and multifarious pattern of relationships and interactions. Informal networks are simultaneously idiosyncratic and collective. We use them to pursue our own self-interests, but also to contribute to a shared mutuality (Burns and Taylor, 1998). The web of relationships connecting us with each other, and with society as a whole, provides an important resource which enhances and regulates our lives. Some communities find it more difficult to establish and nurture networks which are diverse and flexible. Consequently, individuals experience 'network poverty' (Perri 6, 1997) and the collective population suffers from social exclusion, internal conflicts and an inability to adapt. The community is unable to manage itself without external interventions or statutory controls. Community sustainability requires both formal organizations and informal networking, with a constant interplay between these two aspects of community life. Voluntary associations emerge from and are sustained by personal links between individuals, which weave in around the more formal structures.

The development of community can be seen as an active process of network construction and maintenance, using a variety of spaces, reasons and activities to promote and support local interactions. Cultural symbols, myths and rituals help to identify boundaries and affirm membership (Cohen, 1986). Community represents a sense of mutual pride and commitment, keeping people together and in touch. It bestows both rights and obligations, promoting active citizenship and communal responsibility (Etzioni, 1995). For many people 'community' significantly improves the quality of their lives. For some, the practical and emotional support it provides is essential for their survival.

Most people experience community as a positive expression of their own identity. It provides social significance for the individual and collective solidarity (Clarke, 1973). Community networks, such as the grapevine of gossip, can also bring pressure to conform, through unofficial mechanisms of surveillance, stigma and social sanctions. Informal networks are used to suppress 'deviant' behaviour and uphold standards of 'respectability' (Tebbutt, 1995). Communities which are too homogenous and insulated from the outside world lose their ability to assimilate new ideas and to adapt to changes. Eventually their traditions and beliefs become obsolete or redundant, and the community either disintegrates through unresolved internal tensions or simply dissolves into the wider society.

Despite the rather romantic view of 'community' presented in the popular imagination, the actual lived experience is rarely harmonious. Nor can it be artificially constructed or imposed by external bodies. The development of community is a long-term, organic process which emerges from the complexity of micro-interactions as a sustainable means of managing diversity and controversy. Even within an apparently stable, mature community, there will be power differentials requiring continual negotiation and debate. Social inequalities, caused by oppression and exploitation, are unsettling and disrupt cooperation and communication. Sustainable communities require reciprocal and reliable relationships which are based on trust, equality and the honouring of diversity. Different needs are recognized and met, but it is expected that favours will be returned and assistance rendered on a basis which is mutual and equivalent.

Assets and opportunities are not evenly distributed within social networks. Some individuals have higher privileges and status, whilst certain sections of the population are advantaged in their capacity to influence events and decisions. Informal processes usually operate to the detriment of people already on the margins of society. In order to achieve a community based on social justice, the influence of these traditional structures may need addressing through formal regulations, such as equal opportunity policies and anti-discrimination legislation.

## THE DEVELOPMENT OF COMMUNITY

Community spirit is rather like a sense of humour. It is generally seen as desirable, its absence is lamented and yet it evades attempts to analyse its existence or function. The limited consensus that exists within sociological theories suggests that community is associated with mainly beneficial social interaction and the coordination of collective activities. Friendship and family networks have been identified as a source of welfare and support (Bulmer, 1986; Willmott, 1987) and attempts made to co-opt them into government community care strategies (Trevillion, 1992). Urban development programmes have similarly endeavoured to develop community participation in planning decisions through the involvement of local people in regeneration partnerships, such as the current fashion for Community Development Trusts. It is assumed that the community can take on these responsibilities as if it were a single entity and speaks with one voice. In reality, communities are only superficially homogeneous or united. Government policies which emphasize community involvement must first acknowledge and then cherish the differences amongst people as a necessary condition for developing a shared consensus and commitment.

This chapter argues that the development of community is essentially about supporting and extending opportunities for informal networking. Community development is both a professional practice and a policy strategy. Primarily it assists people in their efforts to create and maintain forms of collective organization, and is often targeted at disadvantaged or 'hard-to-reach' sections of the population. A community development approach does not attempt to impose solutions using the professional 'know-how' of external consultants. Rather it encourages local people, the experts in their own living environment, to define the nature of the problem and to determine, so far as is possible, the solution.

Many individuals perceive themselves as belonging to several communities, arising from different aspects of their social identity. Personal interactions and communal activities create and trace 'pathways for living' through which we organize our lives (Finnegan, 1989). A pattern of ties is woven and reinforced by the exchange of nods, smiles and greetings as we go about our daily routines. Through convention and convenience some of these links gradually develop until familiar strangers become casual acquaintances, and eventually perhaps our friends or more intimate companions. The initial encounters are not necessarily planned. They take place in quasi-public spaces, often when we are waiting for, or on our way to, something else. They occur on the street, at the bus stop, in the local playground, the staff canteen, the pub, the corner shop or whilst queuing at the post office or job centre. It is often only when an additional connection has been discovered that these informal exchanges acquire a greater significance. People build affinity by disclosing things about themselves and discovering a common interest or complementary ways of meeting each other's needs (Duck, 1992). Community is developed in the same way, building up connections through a kaleidoscope of habitual and happenstance exchanges.

Whilst the separate strands of community are spun from incidents and conversations between individuals, the web itself is suspended from fixed points in the social landscape: the afternoon pick-up outside the school gates, Friday gatherings at the mosque, the regular darts match, the youth club. These places and activities provide opportunities to chat and pass the time of day (or night). The resultant patterns of interaction and dependency are partly strategic and partly serendipitous. The networks are not static. They reflect the local environment and the changing circumstances of people's lives. Neighbours come and go, friends fall out, partnerships dissolve, jobs change, children grow up, people develop new interests or they may become ill and less mobile. Social divisions and antagonisms are part of the pattern. When people bemoan a perceived 'loss of community', they are often referring to an apparent decline in the range and quality of their informal relationships, or the lack of opportunities to work with others for mutual benefit. Increasing heterogeneity and transience within the local population is sometimes resented, especially by those unwilling or unable to adapt to change. Alliances of 'us' and 'them' are formed, often on the basis of ethnicity or class, which seek to defend the status quo or to promote a particular interest. Diversity enriches the social environment, but it also generates stress and occasionally outright hostility. Community is clearly not a passive experience, nor always comfortable.

Communities need to find ways of managing these tensions and tackling local issues without necessarily relying on external forces. Many societies have evolved traditional and/or democratic mechanisms for dealing with internal conflicts and making decisions about public matters. Their exact form varies from one community to the next, but they are generally sustained through a combination of informal networking and formal structures (Gilchrist, 1995).

Studies of successful partnerships indicate that communities which achieve their goals and are able to adapt to changing circumstances are rooted in a long tradition of collective organizing (Taylor, 1995). They sustain and are sustained by strong local networks. At their core there is often a small group of well-motivated and resourceful activists, who have good personal links with one another and also with outside agencies. Even when not involved in campaigning or running voluntary organizations, they tend to remain in touch informally through social activities (Melucci, 1996).

If community is that collective sensibility which emerges from the interconnections between individuals, then it can be enhanced by increasing the quality and diversity of these interactions. The professional intervention of paid community workers can assist people in making and maintaining their own connections by maximizing opportunities for networking and suggesting useful contacts. This approach strengthens and diversifies social networks so that it becomes easier to mobilize people and resources for collective action. The three examples of community organizing given below illustrate how a well-connected community, with community work support, can obtain and manage a major collective asset (a community centre), work in partnership with the local authority, and mount a campaign to resist an outside threat.

## *Places for Networking*

As indicated earlier, the nature of the built environment has an important influence on how people interact and communicate. Local shopping facilities are obvious meeting places. These can be made attractive and accessible so that residents visit them frequently and on foot. Wide pavements, traffic calming and pedestrian precincts mean that children need be less closely supervised and allow people to stop and chat.

Public places can be designed to encourage people to linger in them, enjoying the possibilities of happenstance encounters with fellow residents or visitors (Landry and Bianchini, 1995). People do not generally have to negotiate or justify their presence in these places, though young people gathered here are often unjustly regarded as a nuisance or a threat. These places feel relatively safe, at least to locals or regular visitors. They are not alienating in the way that a large windswept expanse between tower blocks or an out of town hypermarket might be. They have local atmosphere, a sense of place which reflects the lives and traditions of the people that use them. If that space feels congenial, convenient and comfortable, people are more likely to spend time there, increasing the probability and quality of social interchange.

Community represents the capacity, sometimes referred to as social capital (Putnam, 1995), which is created through personal investments of time and emotion in networks of overlapping relationships. Being well-connected enables people to respond more confidently to uncertainty, change and conflict. They are able to cope with scarcity and crises on a more collective basis. Through their informal networks people receive advice and guidance. They check out their knowledge and update information. Resources are borrowed and shared. People exchange skills and favours. Informal networks and voluntary associations enable people to learn from one another and to cooperate without the need for formal contracts. Social ties can also create a confidence and solidarity which empower people to challenge injustices and to organize collectively to promote and defend their interests. Communities operate best when they are in a state of dynamic equilibrium, capable of responding to changes in the environment and embracing ideas which challenge out-moded traditions and prejudices. Studies of modern organizations indicate that flexible networks provide the most appropriate and effective form of organizing in a fragmented and tumultuous world (Hastings, 1993). Society at the turn of the millennium offers just such an environment, and community networks ensure a sustainable balance between individual autonomy and collective responsibility. People may be connected, but they are not controlled. The resilience and creativity of well-connected communities depends on both chance and choice, otherwise the whole system freezes into rigidity and is incapable of adaptation or innovation.

# Case Study of Easton, Inner City Neighbourhood

A few examples of recent community action may help to bring the theory to life. They are drawn from the author's experience of living and working in an urban neighbourhood at the heart of Bristol. Easton scores high on all indices of social deprivation and stress. Rates of unemployment, poverty and crime are amongst the highest in the country and levels of mental illness, disease and disability are significantly above the national average. Nevertheless Easton accommodates a rich diversity of cultures, originating from India, Pakistan, Africa, the Caribbean, China and points closer to home. There is a good variety of people from different class backgrounds, including university students and middle class professionals. It is a typical, perhaps more than usually impoverished, inner city community, which enjoys a reputation for getting things done whilst accommodating the different experiences and traditions of the local population.

A major contribution to this process was the establishment, after a decade of lobbying and fund-raising, of a purpose-built community centre, which is managed by the local Community Association. The building was designed with an interior layout which allowed maximum flexibility and encouraged interaction amongst people using the centre. It has provided a base for a number of groups and voluntary organizations to meet and run services, such as play schemes, youth clubs, adult education classes and social activities for older people. It has also created a much needed focus for political campaigning and community events, including an annual summer festival.

In areas like Easton, the development of community participation and common ownership is not straightforward. Over the years public meetings and working parties have tackled local issues, including problems thrown up by competing demands made on the centre itself. These sometimes emerged as conflicts of interest or attempts to exclude certain sections of the population who didn't 'fit in' so neatly to the overall strategy. Despite a strong equal opportunities policy and a firm commitment to 'inclusivity', there were tensions amongst the different groups wanting to use the centre. These arose between the generations and between different ethnic groups. One example will indicate how potential conflicts were averted or resolved using public discussion and informal networking.

## Managing a Shared Facility

Within a year of opening the Community Centre became a popular venue for late night socials. There were problems around traffic and loud music, particularly in the early hours of Sunday morning. These events were often hosted by African-Caribbean organizations. Local white residents, understandably annoyed at this regular disruption to their night's sleep, laced their complaints with veiled racial stereotypes. This was despite the fact that many white people attended the dances and contributed equally to the disturbance. The Community Association organized a public meeting to consider their grievances, hoping to find a way forward which was both feasible and diplomatic. After much debate, it was agreed to introduce a number of measures to address the problems of noise and parking. Years of working with residents from all sections of the community meant that the Community Association was able to consult effectively with all concerned and to develop a solution which satisfied most people. This was made easier because of the tolerant and friendly relationships that had been developed between individuals in the various groups using the centre. The Community Association was trusted to deal with a difficult situation and had earned some respect over its years of campaigning and arranging local events. Supported by its community development workers, the voluntary management committee had worked hard to be welcoming and responsive to the needs of different cultures, age groups and abilities. Rather than imposing an artificial 'unity' on its residents, Easton Community Centre embraces many traditions. Diversity is viewed as an asset, not a source of division. Local networks ensure that news, ideas and shared concerns are able to cross the boundaries of faith, social identity and ethnic origin. Consequently people with very different lifestyles are able to enjoy a fairly harmonious co-existence and have developed collective strategies for responding creatively and constructively to opportunities and threats which appear in the environment.

## Working in Partnership

Easton has been favoured with substantial investment from government funding to regenerate the local economy and improve the built environment. A ten-year programme of neighbourhood renewal schemes has included the upgrading of streetscapes and major refurbishment of many houses. A team of City Council officers was based in the area and regular consultation was organized (such as public forums, questionnaire surveys, exhibitions) for residents to find out about the programme and contribute their ideas. 'Planning for Real' exercises were used to identify specific local problems and generate suggestions as to how these might be solved.

A local shopping area, St Marks Road, has been transformed from a row of dilapidated shops to a lively thoroughfare well used by residents and visitors from outside the area. Each shop front has been given a facelift with distinctive signage, indicating the nature of their business (chemist, barbers, grocers, etc.) and a section of the road itself has been made one-way, allowing pavements to be widened and better parking arrangements introduced. Many of the improvements can be attributed to the efforts of local traders, the imagination of community artists and funding from the Council's renewal programme. This partnership was embodied in the Easton Renewal Forum which held open meetings in the Community Centre and published a regular newsletter. By developing a shared commitment to the scheme, which incorporated residents' suggestions and concerns, the resulting improvements have generated a real sense of local pride and promoted the multi-ethnic character of the area.

## The Community in Action

The ability of a community to take action does not necessarily involve cooperation with the relevant authorities. Indeed, the history of community action in the UK includes many examples of campaigns which have challenged decisions by council committees or private companies. On the fringes of Easton a former railway embankment had become overgrown, creating a much appreciated area of greenery within an otherwise urban landscape. Planning permission had been given for housing and the site sold to a private building firm. On hearing this, the local wildlife trust alerted supporters living in the area and opposition was swiftly mobilized against the proposed development. Initially the campaign was based around a small group of activists who tried to persuade the council (which had originally granted planning permission) that the area should become a protected habitat. When this approach proved ineffective and the bulldozers were about to move in, more confrontational direct action tactics were adopted. Informal networks were used to mobilize sympathetic residents and at short notice a crowd of mainly local people assembled to occupy the land, preventing clearance of the site. Eventually the plans to build houses were abandoned and the embankment has since reverted to a wildlife corridor linking the inner city to open countryside. It continues to provide a natural amenity for the whole community.

### Local Links and Liaison

Over the years Easton, which actually consists of a number of overlapping and intersecting communities, has developed a positive identity as a multi-ethnic and well-integrated neighbourhood. Despite continuing economic problems, it is seen as a strong and vibrant community, attracting residents and visitors from many backgrounds and cultural traditions. The ideas, imagination and initiative of local people constitute a major resource for urban development, which is frequently overlooked by planners or environmental campaigners. Because community involvement is usually on a voluntary basis, considerable skills and sensitivity are required to sustain and coordinate this complex mosaic of individual motivation and collective effort. Professional community workers can help people to develop the necessary abilities, awareness and confidence to collaborate in joint ventures.

In Easton community participation is underpinned by vigorous and imaginative networking, which has enabled local people to manage divergent interests and tensions. There has been an emphasis on diversity and social integration, using positive action strategies to tackle inequalities and to support cooperation across traditional organizational and 'identity' boundaries. The aim was to break down some of the prejudices and animosities which can occur within mixed communities, and enable people to learn from one another in a spirit of mutual respect and growing trust. The Community Association organized activities which would be attractive and accessible to a range of people. They were fun, but also functional in providing ample opportunities for informal networking within a safe and inclusive environment.

### Networks as a Community Resource

In Easton residents organized themselves collectively in order to make changes which would meet their own needs and benefit the wider community. For individuals voluntary collaboration is a risky strategy, requiring a trade-off between the costs of participation (in money, time and effort) and the anticipated gains. Many people are deterred or prevented from contributing to community initiatives because they feel excluded, disempowered or lacking in self-esteem. Before individuals will commit themselves to collective action, they need to feel that they have a stake in the community such that their needs will be recognized and their efforts rewarded. Informal networks help to build this sense of belonging and foster loyalty and respect, the emotional building blocks of community.

Many successful community projects originate in informal conversations amongst people who are in regular contact and who share a common predicament or vision. An initial idea is shaped until it can be formulated as a firm proposal for consideration through local meetings and wider discussion. In the first phase of development, the core group will often be well acquainted with one another and new members tend to be recruited by word of mouth. Once the project has gained commitment from a critical mass of supporters and potential contributors, a formally constituted organization may need to be established in order to attract funding and membership. In their formative stages, voluntary associations are often sustained primarily through emotional attachments and a common understanding. This 'soft' infrastructure of personal relationships enhances people's sense of community and helps people to cooperate without recourse to formal structures or bureaucratic procedures (Thomas, 1995). There is a danger, however, that organizations which are over-reliant on informal networks become 'cliquey', excluding people who have a right to participate or who may have useful experiences to offer.

## COMMUNITY GOVERNANCE AND DEMOCRATIC RENEWAL

In addition to performing vital welfare functions for their members and users, voluntary associations and community self-help groups constitute an important layer of civil society. They contribute to and facilitate the democratic processes of consultation between government institutions and citizens. Community acts as the interface between the state and people's private lives. It provides a forum for public debate and decision-making. The value of community networks lie in their capacity to hold divergent opinions, integrating and articulating a multiplicity of perspectives without suppressing minority views. They are therefore important vehicles for anticipating and resolving disputes within and between different communities, and maintaining a dialogue between 'ordinary' people and the politicians.

Recent policies on urban management and regeneration emphasize the importance of community involvement in inter-agency partnerships. The different partners (local authorities, private companies and community representatives) do not, however, have equal power in these arrangements and often find it difficult to work together. This can produce conflict and frustration for all concerned. Deprived communities have low expectations of their ability to effect change. They may need support in imagining, let alone implementing a vision of how their lives might be improved. The barriers to participation can be overcome through training, team-building and resources, especially if these are used to build personal links and relationships (Skelcher et al, 1996). Regeneration programmes often include funding to develop community capacity, but this is usually interpreted to mean enhancing the skills and confidence of individual community leaders. An alternative approach is to invest in opportunities for local networking, thus increasing people's ability and willingness to communicate across organizational boundaries, particularly with those who don't necessarily share their outlook and interests. This is a challenging, long-term and somewhat risky strategy in that it is difficult to predict outcomes or to assess its impact through specific performance criteria. Ultimately community capacity depends on shared energy, commitment and expertise percolating beyond a central core of 'activists' and 'social entrepreneurs' (Stewart et al, 1995; Hastings et al, 1996). Local authority funding for capacity-building can support this to a limited extent, but sustainable regeneration will only be achieved through the participation and empowerment of substantial and diverse sections of the whole community.

In urban neighbourhoods, where the population tends to be more differentiated and often materially disadvantaged, planning for sustainable development must reflect and champion local diversity. Communities of interest and identity (the connections people make through work, leisure, political and spiritual activities) transcend geographical boundaries. They allow ideas, experience and resources to be shared and exchanged between people with a common experience but who live in different areas. Activities in which people find a common enjoyment and interest provide vital connections for shared learning and discussion. Neighbourhoods benefit from amenities and events which encourage visitors and support cross-fertilization between different communities.

## Participatory and Inclusive Planning

Where effort is made to accommodate different views and experiences, local people can be effectively involved in planning through formal membership of consultative committees. Such bodies are, however, rarely representative and the way they operate (evening meetings, formal procedures and documents written in official jargon) tend to discourage all but the most determined and articulate residents.

Established voluntary organizations and paid professionals are likely to be crucial in this respect. They provide a pivotal role between local people and government or private agencies. By building on past traditions and current initiatives, local synergy can be harnessed towards sustainable regeneration. It takes time, patience and wisdom to combine different views, skills and resources to achieve a shared vision. Mutual understanding and respect are generated, weaving the neighbourhood into a community and linking it into the world beyond. Decent relationships and open dialogue are just as important to the long-term success of eco-neighbourhoods as environmental improvement schemes. Community management of these, through residents' cooperatives or whatever, will be a vehicle for the development of social networks, but it is only through old-fashioned virtues of trust, mutuality and tolerance that the real complexity and dynamism of community life can be invigorated and sustained.

# 10 LEADING FROM BELOW: THE CONTRIBUTION OF COMMUNITY-BASED INITIATIVES

*Janet Rowe and Celia Robbins*

## INTRODUCTION

The aim of this chapter is to examine, through the use of two contrasting case studies, the potential contribution of community-based initiatives to sustainability. It examines the goals and programmes of the case study initiatives, and how they relate to various aspects of community sustainability. It identifies the kinds of achievements within each which might comprise 'success' in the context of sustainability, both for the communities themselves and in a wider context; and examines their contribution, transferability and potential.

The first of the initiatives we examine is the Waste Reduction in the Community Project, which ran in local communities in Bristol and South Gloucestershire between mid-1995 and 1998. It was initiated and managed by a formal voluntary sector organization, The Recycling Consortium (which grew out of community and environmental activity in the early 1980s), committed to the general issue of waste minimization, and had the goal of stimulating genuine grassroots activity within the communities in which it was working. The second initiative is a Local Exchange and Trading Scheme (LETS), an example of a community of interest and identity (Wilmott, 1987) which has spread from Canada through the US, New Zealand and Australia, the UK and much of Europe and onto the Internet, representing, according to Albrow (1996), a global 'socioscape' of like-minded people. Here we reflect largely on Stroud LETS, but draw also on experience in and around the Bristol area and elsewhere. Our LETS case study material comes from the work of O'Doherty, Purdue, Durrschmidt and Jowers, and we are particularly indebted to Derrick Purdue for his contribution to this chapter, although the views expressed here remain our own. The account which follows represents 'work in progress', but we hope it will be of interest in the light of the current debate about Local Agenda 21 and the role of the individual within, and collective responsibility towards, sustainability as expressed in UK Government documents of 1997 and 1998 (DETR, 1997b, 1998 a, c, f).

# The Community Context: Capacity Building

The contemporary slogan 'think globally, act locally' is at the heart of Local Agenda 21 and community based environmental action. The idea that community equals locality however is already outdated. Gilchrist, in the previous chapter, reflects upon the recent changes brought about for some sectors of society through increased disposable income and mobility; and the concurrent shift in emphasis for these sectors from communities of place towards communities of interest and identity. Hoggett (1997), quoting Castells (1991) points out that whilst increased choice and mobility is a reality for some parts of society, those who are 'excluded' are increasingly tied to place.

The assumption which tends to be implicit in many programmes of regeneration, that 'community development' will somehow supply the social cohesion and 'improvements' in behaviour which cannot be delivered directly by the state, may be seriously questioned. While we may all approve of the neighbourhood Scout group out planting trees of a Saturday morning, some of us may not approve of community action to save local green space which is wanted by developers and which may 'bring jobs'. Fewer of us still may support the anarchistic 'direct action' interest community. Thus the attempts to persuade 'the community' to participate in self-management towards the greater good of the majority, upon which current Local Agenda 21 strategies are largely predicated, fly in the face of democratic probity: the majority may not wish to pay the price of the collectivist policies which sustainable development implies. Thus exercises such as 'Choices for Bristol' (Burton, 1997) and the Bath and North East Somerset Local Agenda 21 Issue Commission (Rowe, 1998), designed to engage widely with geographical communities and to lead to consensus on ways forward, tend to engage only with certain interest groups.

Policy-makers and decision-makers must be prepared to take an objective view of what various kinds of communities of interest and identity and of locality can deliver in terms of local sustainability. This is the concept of community capacity, which is gaining currency in policy circles. Community groups may be defined as loose organizations which are unpaid; parochial rather than strategic; and neither representative nor accountable, although they are often perceived as being so (Percy-Smith, 1998). These inherent characteristics mean that the incorporation of community-based initiatives into public policy is fraught with difficulties. Firstly, the 'output' measures to which public funding is generally attached tend to make a mockery of community-based initiatives: organic growth can rarely be predicted, and community groups often will not have the right type or level of capacity to achieve pre-set policy goals. Secondly, it is increasingly recognized amongst decision-makers that it is the voices of proxies which are generally heard during exercises of community engagement. Thus, if such communities become involved in the decision-making process, they do not necessarily have a channel of communication back to their localities or to the wider community. Stewart and Collett (1998) point out that the empowerment and inclusion of the community sector in formal partnerships bring responsibilities which include the need for clear lines of accountability. The bureaucracies of accountability may, paradoxically, make activists and leaders less effective by taking them away from the community work they are good at. Lastly, projects which originated within communities may come to be managed on behalf of those communities, and attached to agendas which are not necessarily those of the communities. The 'public policy community' has a long way to go before it may acquire the confidence to allow true community development its place in the strategic agenda of sustainable development.

## The Changing Nature of Community

Local authorities have been given the key role by government for implementation of Local Agenda 21, which seems to be predicated largely upon communities of place. However, as discussed above, large numbers of the population expect to live and work in localities which are geographically separated, and to change both of these several times during their lives. Their relationships with place are thus quite different from those which appertained a generation or two ago; and the structures of local governance (including local authorities) tend to appear, to many people, unconnected with everyday life. The personal milieu, which may be defined as the immediate social world a person inhabits and can affect (Purdue et al, 1997), is changing. It includes face-to-face relations with a wide variety of individuals, and may extend far beyond through electronic media. Individuals may use globally disseminated ideas, eg environmentalism and forms of self-expression derived from international cultures, to define the meaning of their own lives.

Purdue et al (1997) describe the links in the South West between members of LETS and veggie box schemes and festival goers, referring to their extended milieu as 'DIY culture'. Such milieux validate new identities and facilitate their maintenance in a sometimes hostile and indifferent society. They may also form the links through which more 'grounded' local networks respond to the challenges of global issues. A recognition of this potential has produced the shift in emphasis towards local action which has characterized the environmental pressure groups since the early 1980s. The programmes of The Recycling Consortium (The Recycling Consortium, 1999) in Bristol, of which the Waste Reduction in the Community Project (WRCP), our first case study, is most recent, are illustrative. However, communities of locality have traditionally organized around their immediate needs rather than around general issues. Threats to the survival of traditional local features, as described above, have created cohesive community action which may not outlive removal of the threat. The extent to which the members of the TRC themselves form an interest network seeking to root itself in locality is explored further below.

## The Policy Context

As examples of community action, our case studies may be set within the broad policy context of the New Labour administration's drive to reclaim the credibility of local government and advance participative democracy (DETR, 1998c). The emergent themes of Blair and Clinton's 'Third Way' politics are also significant in that they include a shift of responsibilities to the individual in the context of a reinvigorated democracy; and the renegotiation of rights and responsibilities between the individual, the community and the state (Giddens, 1998). The policy direction has been described as leading towards 'community-owned government' (Hambleton, 1997), which we might equate with reaching the top of the 'ladder of citizen empowerment' proposed by Burns et al (1994). However, while community empowerment, as opposed to consultation as window-dressing, might be universally applauded, serious questions arise about the capacity and even willingness of communities to engage in local democracy to the extent which is implied.

Sustainable development is one of the most widely expressed aspirations of current public policy throughout the EU. While the breadth and all-embracing nature of the concept creates huge practical difficulties for both policy generation and implementation, there are root problems which lie far deeper. The greatest is that of establishing cause, effect and significance, of the many environmental consequences of human activity. Although scientific consensus is increasing in some fields, the mechanisms for allocating responsibility for preventative action to levels of government and to the community are fraught with difficulties. The second is the inherent dichotomy, experienced at the local as well as the national level, between the traditional policies and practices of economic growth, which stress competitiveness and exploitation of 'free goods' (both environmental and social), and environmental and social well-being. The key driver of traditional economic growth is collective consumption predicated upon feeding individual desires and aspirations rather than community or individual needs. It is unclear to what extent responsibility for the maintenance of environmental and social goods can and should be borne by any locality and /or community. Much work remains to be done on the extent to which a balance may be achieved between general well-being and individual choice in a system striving for accountability.

## Building Towards Community Sustainability

It might be argued that, while community-based initiatives may have different emphases, to make a true contribution to sustainability they should to some degree demonstrate that they promote the closing of resource loops; reduce the community's impacts upon the environment; contribute to community development; and build capacity, in order that activity and action can be sustained without continuing external inputs. Thus, the parameters by which 'success' might be measured are wide. The framework for assessment which was developed for the WRCP included aspects of personal, organizational and collective development in both the project communities and their support networks, as well as effects on the waste stream. We have adopted a normative approach based on the above criteria in interrogating our case study material, as follows:

- *closing resource loops:* we ask where, how, in what ways, and to what extent, resources were used more locally, and whether this was a temporary output or (may) contribute(d) to a longer-term outcome of the initiative. We distinguish between natural and economic resources and the 'soft' resources of knowledge, skills and labour;
- *reducing the community's impacts upon the environment:* we ask whether such effects were identifiable; what form they took and how and by whom they were experienced; and whether they were, or could be, evaluated;
- *community development and capacity building:* we have taken as our starting point that, if these inter-related processes are to be 'real' and

lasting, they must originate within the community, as a function of it, and be particular to the characteristics, needs and goals of the community.

In analyzing our case studies, we have addressed a series of issues. We ask where the initiative came from, and what was the impetus behind it. We examine goals, and how these were arrived at (the roles of leaders and facilitators). We ask who devised programmes, and what methods were used (to what extent they drew on existing 'home-grown' networks and activities). We examine how the initiative evolved, what were the outputs and outcomes (within the limits of our study period) and what benefits were accrued by whom and/or what. We also explore issues of cultural sustainability, asking questions related to equity and futurity.

## CASE STUDY 1: THE WASTE REDUCTION IN THE COMMUNITY PROJECT (WRCP)

WRCP was initiated by The Recycling Consortium, a not for profit organization lobbying for sustainable waste management, in April 1995. Financial help was received from the Environmental Action Fund of the (then) Department of the Environment which funded a dedicated full-time development worker. Waste Action Groups (WAGs) were set up in five local communities in the unitary areas of Bristol and South Gloucestershire, and the development worker worked with these groups over three years (until April 1998) with the aim of reducing waste through facilitating community development. Four of the communities were selected for their contrasting characteristics, while the fifth (Patchway) was included by its own request. Community boundaries were set by the groups themselves. They comprised:

- *Easton*, a multi-ethnic inner city district of 2000 households (WAG name EARTH, Easton Area Recycling Together);
- *Hartcliffe*, an outlying council estate of 4000 households (WAG name HEROES);
- *Westbury Park*, an affluent urban residential area of 2000 households (WAG name WORM);
- *Patchway*, an urban fringe residential area of 4000 households (WAG name Patchway Recycling Group);
- *Hawkesbury Upton*, a rural agricultural and commuter village 20 miles from Bristol and 34 from Gloucester, of 330 households (WAG name HURG, Hawkesbury Upton Recycling Group).

The WAGs were not formally constituted. Their focus was a monthly meeting facilitated by the development worker at which current projects were discussed and tasks allocated according to each member's capabilities, with additional support as required from the development worker. The active membership of the groups varied from three to ten, with a wider support group of around 20 others. The network of WAGs was supported by a monthly newsletter, regular activity days at Bristol City Council's Environment Centre for information-sharing and workshops on creative uses of waste materials, and organized visits to places of interest such as a paper mill, recycling projects and landfill sites. Following the three years of supported development, the groups were offered ongoing help, at a reduced level, if they wished to continue work.

A two-year study of the project (April 1997 to April 1999) was funded by The BOC Foundation and carried out by the University of the West of England. The research study analyzed data from the refuse and kerbside recycling collections in these and control areas selected for similarities in their socio-economic characteristics, attempting to identify trends or changes in waste management behaviour which might be associated with the project. The activities of the WAGs were closely observed in relation to aspects of community development, and at the end of the three-year period a series of group and individual interviews was carried out in which members reflected upon their progress and feelings, and how they thought they would proceed.

## Outputs of the WAGs

The WAGs differed greatly in terms of membership and programmes, and the progress they were able to make over the three years of the programme. In brief, outputs included:

*Easton:* although existing community networks provided initial contacts, EARTH developed largely independently of other organizations within the community. A small core of two or three members attended the monthly meetings while a wider transitory group became involved in particular projects. Notable outputs were a waste directory *101 Things to Do with a Dead Anything*, and a 'Reduce/Reuse/Recycle' display for local public places made from timber salvaged from the destruction of a local dog track to make way for a multinational retailer which had triggered considerable local opposition. Towards the end of the three-year period, a series of awareness days was run with the Asian community to spread the waste minimization message more broadly.

*Hartcliffe:* here there were few informal community networks into which the WAG could tap, nor community activists with the capacity to take a lead in the initiative. HEROES developed largely as a network of community development and environmental professionals working and/or living in the area, including the publicly funded voluntary sector body Hartcliffe Health and Environmental Action Group and the manager of the local city farm. Activities included initiating composting at the local city farm and influencing Bristol City Council policy to ensure the installation of a mini-recycling centre at a block of high-rise flats.

*Westbury Park:* here community activity was already relatively well developed, current foci being the community association and the annual festival. An active group of local professionals, some retired, formed the core of WORM. A three-dimensional 'scrap-map' was produced from waste materials for public display in which each waste-reducing home and local business could be identified. WORM stickers were designed and placed in windows and on recycling boxes;

local shop keepers were encouraged to commit themselves to the project and to display certificates in their windows; and a *WORM-a-Fax* directory was produced of local waste reduction, reuse and recycling activities.

*Patchway:* the WAG developed with the strong support of the clerk to the Town Council and the Town Council itself, in parallel with a strong conservation group dedicated to environmental improvements. The focus was a community composting unit alongside the local allotments and public open space, which, although designed for garden waste, attracted green contractors' waste and reduced significantly fly-tipping in the neighbourhood. Towards the end of the project, landfill tax funding was secured through South Gloucestershire Unitary Authority to support the maintenance of the composting unit although responsibility for its management remained with the WAG. A large 'Reduce, Reuse, Recycle' mosaic was constructed in a local park with input from across the community, including schools, youth clubs, community groups and elderly persons' dwellings.

*Hawkesbury Upton:* HURG was set up by a small group of women who were home-based and/or working part-time. Some of the core members were already friends while others had been promoting recycling in the village individually, and were brought together by the initiative. Prior to the WRCP members of the group had independently been instrumental in arranging the location of recycling banks next to the village hall. The group had excellent relationships with much of the local community. The focus of HURG was also upon building and running a composting unit. As in Patchway funding was secured through the local authority to support the unit's maintenance during its second year of operation. Other activities included the creation of a large mosaic in the school grounds depicting 'Reduce, Reuse, Recycle' in relation to local children's sense of place.

## Closing Resource Loops

The overall aim of WRCP was to reduce, reuse and recycle waste by using the skills, knowledge, labour and enthusiasm of local communities of place, ie it aimed to influence the flow of both 'hard' and 'soft' resources within its target areas. 'Hard' resources comprised those materials which might be reclaimed from the waste stream and invested with value through reuse or recycling. The initiative influenced these both through the ongoing diversion of specific materials, eg through both community and individual composting, and through the one-off use of items in specific projects, eg waste tiles in creating community mosaics. The initiation of community composting was the most visible of the initiative's successes in diverting elements of the waste stream and in minimizing the use of imported materials. HURG packed the end product into fertilizer bags to be used by individuals in place of bought compost. In Patchway, large quantities of mature compost were made available to the local conservation group and allotment holders and to the parish groundsperson for the maintenance of local parks, gardens and conservation sites. While the magpie instincts revealed by WAG members in making use of waste items on a one-off basis in community arts and other publicity campaigns were of marginal significance in quantitative waste reduction terms, the symbolic significance was self-evident.

That the initiative depended upon the soft resources of each community and WAG – knowledge, enthusiasm, skills and labour – was quite clear. In some instances, eg in the building and management of the composting units, this became over time a very large donation of labour to the public good. It is unlikely that this sort of activity would have been sustainable without the intervention of the local authority. The role of the development worker was in facilitating the conversion of the soft resources into better waste practices in the community at large. Information which existed in the community was collected and disseminated, eg four WAGs created new resources in the shape of waste directories. A WORM member who was a retired chemist learned about pyrolysis and anaerobic digestion at a consultation meeting held by Bristol City Council on future options for waste disposal, and passed on this new-found knowledge to the community through the local newsletter.

WRCP also provided opportunities for the application of skills locally in ways which reinforced the development of a local economy, eg in Easton an EARTH member successfully used the initiative as a way of seeking employment opportunities locally: as a carpenter and woodworker who was new to the area, his work for EARTH brought him into contact with other community and environmental groups from which he started to pick up commissions.

## Reducing the Community's Impacts Upon the Environment

WRCP impacted upon the environment in terms of: changes in the behaviour of individual members; the effects of practical projects run by the WAGs; and influence on the behaviour of the wider community. Individual members were often active waste managers prior to their involvement in the initiative. However, a significant feature of the meetings in all WAGs was the exchange of ideas about reusing items such as plastic containers and information on where to recycle items not collected by the recycling round. Evidence that this concern was translated into action is anecdotal, eg a WORM member claimed that she had started to forget the day of the household rubbish collection because she had so little to put out; but it is significant in that it seems to reflect a positive shift in activists' attention from recycling to waste reduction. A vital role of the monthly meetings was to provide support and validation for these attitudes.

That only the community composting activity is likely to have impacted significantly on the quantities of waste generated locally has been noted above. In Patchway, the reduction of fly-tipping of green waste on open spaces may have been more significant. Clearance of this waste had often been the task of the conservation group, which was thus freed to undertake other more positive environmental improvements.

It is difficult to isolate any impacts the WAGs may have had upon the wider community's waste management behaviour from those other influences acting upon households over the lifetime of the project. The analysis of refuse and recycling data from all the five project areas showed that increases in the frequency of kerbside recycling produced the biggest impact on the waste stream. However, two WAG areas did demonstrate particularly good recycling performance in relation to their control areas. In Hawkesbury Upton, the members of HURG were both very active and well linked with a small, relatively homogeneous and closely-knit community, eg a key feature of their activity was the inclusion of a piece in every edition of the parish magazine. A survey of households carried out in late 1997 found that 80 per cent of residents were aware of the activities of HURG; and this is likely to have impacted significantly on waste management behaviour. In Westbury Park, a much larger community, awareness of WORM was also high at 52 per cent. The relatively close-knit nature of the community and the presence of WORM stickers and certificates throughout the area, along with regular publicity in the local newsletter, were thought to be factors.

## Community Development and Capacity Building

It is quite clear that the impetus for the WRCP came from the community of interest represented by TRC rather than from the communities of locality themselves; but that, in all of the localities, the project was able to pick up on, and give expression to, existing individual concerns about the environment and specifically the issue of waste. Significantly, the two WAGs which were (apparently) most effective in terms of an increase in local recycling activity (WORM and HURG) were based in communities which had a relatively strong sense of local identity, shared values and existing capacity. In Patchway, the WAG was able to provide the Town Council, and others with an existing public remit and commitment, with a mechanism for engagement with the local community towards a Local Agenda programme. Here the capacity provided by the local authorities fed the project and was likely to help to sustain continued activity. In Hartcliffe, HEROES provided professionals, some of whom lived in the area, with a mechanism through which they could both work together and draw in some extra support in the form of the development worker and other project resources. Although this was not the original aim of the project, it could be viewed as a significant contribution to ongoing community development. In Easton, while existing community activity was diverse but fragmented and EARTH continued to rely heavily on the development worker's inputs to make progress, nonetheless the initiative provided a bridge between different ethnic groups.

The goals of WRCP were holistic in that TRC's network, with its roots in the environmental pressure groups, had drawn on long and wide experience in how behaviour might be changed towards environmental goals. However, in order to fulfil the funder's expectations, certain targets had to be met within the three years of the project. TRC inevitably had to engage with performance indicators (eg numbers of events run, numbers of WAG members active in various ways) and inevitably these influenced to some extent the development worker's activities.

Community development might be divided into personal aspects, which embrace relationships and skills, and organizational aspects which concern group capacity, local networks and inter-relationships with other groups. The WRCP produced positive outcomes on each count in that there was, in all groups, a noticeable increase in the course of the project in confidence and skills of both individual members and the groups collectively, on a broader scale than their grasp of waste issues. The groups also achieved a degree of community ownership of waste issues, represented by the waste directories. WAG members identified their personal gains from the project as including: enjoyment, meeting new people, the opportunity to develop existing skills and learn new ones, often practical eg making mosaics and composting but also more generally applicable skills such as making presentations.

The development worker actively sought members for the WAGs in the early stages of the WRCP, and here existing community networks proved invaluable. The Easton, Patchway and Hartcliffe groups remained closely linked to other community groups throughout, and their work and longer term sustainability became integrated with these groups following the initial three years of the WRCP. However, the groups (WORM and HURG) which operated largely independently of other networks and publicly-funded organizations within their communities and did not receive support from these, depended for their vitality on the number of individuals who remained active and their degree of commitment to the project. The larger size of the WORM group (at six to ten members) compared with four key members in HURG, made for a looser network and greater robustness. At the end of three years the core of HURG had diminished through two members moving away, underlining the vulnerability of a small group. In all of the groups, few new members had been recruited after the initial impetus provided by the development worker, and the need to boost numbers was an ongoing source of concern.

## CASE STUDY 2: STROUD LOCAL EXCHANGE AND TRADING SCHEME (LETS)

LETS comprise one of several forms of local economy which are distinct from the national sterling economy (see eg the review by North, 1998). Members trade goods and services using a locally defined currency, units of which generally bear a name chosen by the participants. Thus, 'Strouds' are traded in Stroud, and 'Thanks', 'Ideals', Beets', Squids' and 'Tots' in various parts of Bristol. A directory of members' names and contact numbers, often sectioned by the type of goods or services being offered, is collated and distributed by a core management group, which is also responsible for the recording of trades and publication of accounts. An explicit purpose of LETS is to keep currency circulating locally so that the benefits of trading are felt in the local community, rather than leaking away into the global economy; and the intention of members is often to support a lifestyle which is less dependent on the global market, to which many have ideological objections (Purdue et al, 1997). Many schemes mimic the mainstream economy in assigning monetary values to tasks, provoking arguments over the values of trades undertaken, quality of work, and failures to meet commitments; but LETS survive primarily because of the value their participants perceive in belonging to a community of like-minded people.

LETS in Stroud, Gloucestershire, was one of the earliest schemes which proliferated in the UK in the early 1990s. It was examined as part of a two-year research project investigating environmental and cultural innovation and networks within the South West of England. Stroud itself is a medium-sized market town, eight miles from Gloucester and 30 miles from Bristol with a population of 104,205, 46 per cent economically active and 5 per cent unemployed. Its situation in a Cotswold river valley provided water power for a manufacturing boom in the 1800s, and Stroud District has retained a higher level of both manufacturing and engineering businesses than other areas in the South West, although the overall shift in the UK towards a service economy is also evident here. It has a long history of environmental and cultural innovation and elected the first Green Party local councillor in the UK.

In the study reported here, a mail survey was carried out of the 300 active members of the LETS scheme, of which 32 per cent responded. Face-to-face interviews with a sample of members of the LETS were also carried out. Members were questioned as to what goods and services were offered and exchanged within the LETS scheme; how recruitment to the scheme was carried out, and how and why they had themselves joined; and what they perceived to be the advantages and disadvantages of the scheme. Goods and services offered within Stroud LETS were reviewed in the context of other LETS schemes in the UK and in The Netherlands as evidenced by their directories, and found both to be fairly characteristic and to shed some light on the interests, skills and preferences of the LETS members. Alternative health care comprised 25 per cent of the Strouds offered and 31 per cent of Strouds consumed. However, while other services offered comprised home and domestic care at 17 per cent, professional and business skills also at 17 per cent and arts and crafts at 14 per cent, other consumption focused mainly on repairs and manual skills at 16 per cent, and food at 13 per cent. When asked to identify what characteristics they would most like to find in their LETS, the majority of members cited 'better quality'.

Recruitment to the LETS scheme was generally found to have taken place by word of mouth. Seventy-seven per cent of respondents were recruited through personal contact and 44 per cent had friends who had subsequently joined the scheme. 84 per cent felt that LETS contributed to their sense of belonging to the local community. Thus, while Stroud LETS encouraged participation from all within the locality, in practice those who joined belonged to existing social and interest networks. It was shared values and like-mindedness, rather than the mere fact of physical proximity, which drew the LETS members together and underpinned their commitment to the scheme. Geographical boundaries of the LETS were defined loosely in relation to networks.

The reasons given for joining the Stroud LETS reflected the sense of shared values. While 25 per cent had joined to save money, 20 per cent became members for purely ideological reasons and 33 per cent cited attachment to the local community. Thus, in Stroud, LETS replaced in a more formal way the informal give and take which existed in traditional communities. It is notable in this regard that formal LETS schemes even in the inner city of Bristol have very low recruitment of ethnic minority communities where the informal exchange of goods and services often continues to thrive.

### Closing Resource Loops and Reducing the Impact of the Community on the Environment

Local supply of local needs underpins many of the campaigns which have sprung up around the ethic of sustainability, eg *Local Food Links* (Bristol City

Council, 1998), and indeed LETS schemes are predicated upon the prevention of leakage of resources from the local community into the global economy. In terms of the immediate environmental impacts of the community, there is the potential for reduction in: the production and consumption of medical prepa-rations as alternative approaches to health care are adopted; the distances travelled by members to obtain goods and services; 'food miles', ie the distance food travels from production to consumption, along with reduced inputs of fertilizers and pesticides as food is produced on a smaller scale (and usually organically) and becomes more seasonal. Moreover, Stroud LETS members influenced the wider community and to some degree its impacts through their support of local gardening and the allotments society, their participation in veggie box schemes (organic vegetable box deliveries from usually local sources) and recycling and waste minimization activities and other lifestyle choices. Seventy-seven per cent of respondents in the Stroud LETS survey were members of a veggie box scheme, expressed the desire to join one or already grew their own organic vegetables. However, the limited number of members and light trading which has continued to characterize Stroud LETS means that any such effects are likely to remain marginal.

## Community Development and Capacity Building

It is in the arena of community development and capacity building that we would expect to see significant effects of LETS schemes. While LETS are certainly a form of local economic development, it was clear that no member of Stroud LETS viewed their participation in relation to an economic ideology alone. All saw LETS as a project for enhancing social solidarity where the symbolic significance of trading outweighed the material benefits. Skills devel-opment, both for the individual and for the LETS community as a group, was also significant. Quite apart from the range of social skills which are brought into play in LETS interactions, Stroud LETS, in common with others, insisted on the participation of members in developing the rules and norms of the local market, so that there was an ongoing communal re-working of dominant codes (Melucci, 1989) and the genuine exercise of democracy. Moreover, Stroud LETS encouraged members to re-evaluate their skills and to practise these outside the immediate market, underpinning the assumption that a person's identity is not solely dependent on their paid job and/or that they are following a defined career path, but may have many skills and multiple identi-ties. LETS also validated the sharing in the community of practices and pleasures which were other than purely utilitarian, eg through massage. Thus LETS empowered individuals by acknowledging their skills, and at a commu-nal level by allowing people to gain access to each other's skills, usually hidden from view as unmarketable, or inaccessibly priced.

If one of the criteria of development towards sustainability is the ability to think globally while acting locally, then Stroud LETS emerges as a positive contribution. Interviews with LETS members indicated that their motives for belonging included an internationally expressed concern for the environment, equity and futurity, spread and shared through media of various kinds; and that their political ideologies included the replacement of the global market with fairer local alternatives. However, Stroud LETS did not extend beyond a fairly limited social milieu. Stroud LETS had the social base which has generally characterized LETS schemes (Lee, 1996). It was predominantly middle class (although not necessarily high income earners: many members were single parents etc), almost exclusively white (as indeed is Stroud itself), and with a preponderance of women generally in the 30–50 year-old age range. Moreover, links between regional LETS schemes were not identified, although most Stroud LETS members belonged to other 'alternative' networks as described above.

## DISCUSSION

Our two case studies present contrasting approaches to 'action towards sustainability in the community'; but have features in common in terms of the criteria for community sustainability which we defined earlier. Both affected only marginally the environmental impacts of the communities within which they were based; and the extent to which resource loops were closed through the activities of the initiatives was small. Limited numbers of individuals were involved in each initiative, although the changes in their patterns of resource consumption may have been significant at the individual level and their participation in WRCP and LETS self-reportedly reinforced other patterns of behaviour which supported local sustainability, such as patronage of local businesses. In terms of effects on the waste stream in the three years of the WRCP, the change in frequency of local authority-sponsored kerbside recycling collections from monthly to fortnightly and finally to weekly had a greater quantitative impact than any other observed. There are questions anyway about the scale at which various resources may realistically be cycled, and how a sustainable community may be defined, as discussed above in relation to the policy context. Quite apart from the limited effect which was achieved through the lifetime of each initiative because of the slow pace of community change in the absence of compelling external pressures, the potential for the spread of action from a core group of activists into the wider community was also probably limited by the size of social milieux (Purdue et al, 1997).

It is indeed in the field of community development and capacity building where more interesting lessons in terms of community sustainability can be found. The strength of WRCP was perhaps less immediately in stimulating genuine grassroots action towards environmental gains, but rather in reinforcing pathways of local governance towards sustainability. TRC increased in profile, staffing and power through WRCP at a time when local authorities were under great pressure both to act on waste (DETR, 1998b) and to implement Local Agenda 21 strategies in partnership with the community (DETR, 1997). It was able to draw in funds from multiple sources in the public and private sectors (notably through the Landfill Tax) to expand its local education and awareness campaigns into other communities and indeed nationally through the production of a community action 'toolkit' (TRC, forthcoming). Its development workers were increasingly able to build bridges between the highly sophisticated world of 'issues' campaigns and local community concerns, providing a politically neutral resource in terms of knowledge, know-how and enthusiasm.

However, there was also political 'safety' in the WRCP. It did not challenge current social norms nor threaten established economic activity. Although it was committed to waste minimization and as such was ahead of local authority activity which focused on the end-of-pipe solution which is recycling, it had, with limited resources, to act in concert with local authority policy and relied on consensus-building between sectors, including private businesses who were co-sponsors, for its survival. A cornerstone of the WRCP approach was inclusiveness, and this also precluded any overt radicalism. A member of one of the WAGs who challenged the overall approach of WRCP, complaining that it merely sanitized current wasteful and environmentally-threatening practice, was felt by others in the group to be undermining their work, and eventually left. It was just such an anarchic thrust which characterized the Stroud LETS community. The many who were socially committed professionals tied to the establishment were, to some degree, supporting others who were experimenting more actively with alternatives. Williams (1996b) identifies the social base for LETS as a 'disenfranchized' fraction of the middle class, in response to structural economic dislocation; we consider that, in our case study, this group may be better termed 'disenchanted' since this indicates choice and a 'values' as well as 'class' cleavage (O'Doherty et al, 1997).

Most of the literature on LETS has focused on whether they can defend localities against the flow of global capital and deliver re-distribution (Pacione, 1997; North, 1996); but our work indicates that LETS are better considered in relation to identity and the re-definition of the local community. Seyfang (1997) analyses LETS in relation to 'weak' and 'strong' sustainability (O'Riordan, 1981). Within weak sustainability, she defines LETS as a policy for local economic development which provides an additional money supply to plug gaps where cash is scarce. This model of LETS is favoured by local authorities and policy makers and indeed Robbins (1997) describes the institutionalization of LETS in Hounslow, Leicester City, Liverpool City and North Kesteven. By contrast, within strong sustainability, LETS is an empowering tool to build communities and strengthen social cohesion. Social values are put into practice, eg through providing payment for domestic or voluntary work which usually goes unrewarded, and more effective citizenship (Dobson, 1993) is encouraged. Effective environmental conservation is also encouraged through 'greener' ways of life. LETS may thus provide exactly the encouragement and support (physical as well as moral) which enables the survival of community activists and the advocates of real change and through which new ideas are generated.

Whether Stroud LETS at the time of the study could be considered to be an example of development towards strong sustainability may be questioned, because of its narrow social base and limited sphere of action. While Williams (1995) has pointed to a broadening of the social and skills mix within LETS generally, Pacione (1997) nonetheless compares the success of a LETS in a suburban area of Glasgow with the lack of success on a Glasgow council estate.

In contrast, WRCP attempted to bring about change, especially in attitudes and awareness, in very different kinds of communities, some at least of which where new ground was being broken. The empowering of advocates for change in all of these communities (with the exception of Hartcliffe where a more formal network developed) was probably the most important outcome of the initiative. Crucially relevant to skill is self-confidence (North, 1996;

Pacione, 1997); and such confidence, a form of cultural capital, North (1996) suggests may be absent from, for example, council estates because of the material conditions of working class life. It is in the support and empowerment of individuals within the community advocating change where a direct comparison may be drawn between the WRCP and Stroud LETS. These individuals play a vital role in what Etzioni (1993) has described as a 'multilogue': the slow process of discussion and debate in workplaces and pubs, through radio and the press out of which new consensus forms. A local authority might offer the householder a recycling collection service, but it is more likely to be the article in the parish newsletter or shared enthusiasm for a school project which will convince a family, as a sub-set of the community, that waste reduction is a worthwhile goal.

The difficulty which the WRCP encountered in accessing community activity in Hartcliffe exposes a key problem inherent in the New Labour policy drive towards inclusive government. Greater participation in policy-making and neighbourhood management is proposed as a tool in the fight against social exclusion (Social Exclusion Unit, 1998) but if, as identified in the WRCP, poor communities are unwilling to accept this role, the desired result will not be achieved. The SEU's *National Strategy for Neighbourhood Renewal* recognizes this problem and proposes research into how best to encourage community self-help. However, if the barriers to participation lie in poverty and exclusion themselves, community driven regeneration faces a vicious circle. Local authorities will also be grappling with this issue, since the Local Government White Paper (DETR, 1998c) promises increased powers to councils which can develop innovative practice in local democracy. The experience of the WRCP has shown that even the best-resourced communities require support if they are to take part in local management and decision-making. There are resonances here with the ongoing debate about the representativeness of council members; few people who are not retired have the time and /or energy to engage in unpaid activities which are additional to work, leisure and family commitments. However, in communities where adequate capacity exists, the WRCP offers a possible model of how it might be supported.

The full potential for influence of the WAGs had, at time of writing, yet to be tested: opportunities, in the form of a contested change of policy or development proposal which might have placed them in direct opposition to other interests, did not arise in the lifetime of the project. However, they undoubtedly influenced local authority policy, most notably in determining the spending of Landfill Tax credits and speeding the shift of focus towards waste reduction and composting in South Gloucestershire. In Bristol, the WAGs played a key role in consultation on the waste disposal contract, which contributed to the decision not to pursue incineration as the main disposal option. A further result of the WRCP was the enhanced profile and capacity of TRC which strengthened its position; it was poised to take a lead role in a recycling promotion campaign initiated by Bristol City Council and funded through the Landfill Tax.

There has tended to be an assumption, upon which Local Agenda 21 is largely predicated, that a society run through a mosaic of local communities would be sustainable. To this end, public, private and community sectors have been encouraged to work together locally towards cooperation and compromise, and indeed much government funding, eg through Single Regeneration Budget (SRB) assistance, depends upon active demonstration of such partnership. While the WRCP case study in many ways epitomizes this approach and has indeed been eagerly taken up by local authorities, Stroud LETS presents quite a different kind of example. Evaluating its relationship with sustainability as defined in current central government policy, as though it were an economic tool, denies its nature; it is an expression of life politics which runs outside the system and does not pay its taxes, validated by norms which are international in direction and scope and ideological rather than strategic. In terms of cultural sustainability, while Local Agenda 21 may lead the community towards a certain level of state-orchestrated conformity, however benign, LETS may challenge this conformity. They have a real role in strengthening civil society in that they create an 'action zone' outside the state. This conundrum lies at the heart of the current uneven movement towards democratization, where there is a tendency for funding and accountability to remain central although responsibility is devolved down eg in SRB projects; real democracy is by its very nature inconvenient, risky and expensive to manage. Thus the institutionalization of LETS noted above, where local authorities have supported their development, may sanitize them, turning them from instruments of expression to instruments of function at the community level.

Our case studies, then, raise huge questions about the nature of democracy and the changing nature of community which are very relevant to any discussion of sustainable communities. While certain functions of sustainability may be 'designed in', eg better waste minimization practices, the freedom to experiment at the community level and to generate new responses to old problems is also prerequisite. The role of local authorities must be to support this experimentation through empowering individuals and the various types of community to which they belong, so that responsibility – and indeed accountability – are apportioned appropriately, and contributions of every kind may be recognized.

# 11 COMMUNITY GOVERNANCE

*Murray Stewart*

## INTRODUCTION

The principles underlying sustainability are well understood and rehearsed extensively in Chapters 1 and 3. Such principles are increasingly visible in formal governmental papers on neighbourhood or community level democracy, and are percolating through the systems of government into practical initiatives. *Opportunities for Change* (DETR, 1998f) and *Sustainable Regeneration: Good Practice Guide* (Rogers and Stewart, 1998) are but two documents which exemplify both the direction of governmental thinking and the principles which underlie sustainability. These principles include recognition of the importance of equity at local, national, and international levels (in relation both to current inequalities and to the needs and aspirations of future generations), the threat to carrying capacity of resource depletion, the centrality of consultation, empowerment and partnership as the means of mobilizing, informing and encouraging change in attitudes and behaviour, and respect for the diversity and the strength which can be built from the coexistence of difference and variety.

These principles have in general been applied to environmental and to a growing extent economic issues. There is increased recognition, however, of the interrelationship of social, economic and environmental sustainability, and extension of the principles of sustainability into new areas of social life. Cultural sustainability for example can be explained in terms of a respect for heritage of language, religion, ethnicity, art and music, leading to stability and continuity in local life. This chapter, however, explores a further avenue, that of institutional sustainability – involving extension of the principles of sustainability to the issue of 'community governance'. This embraces issues of community based decision-making, of power and of management in local areas or neighbourhoods. There is increasing awareness of the need to build sustainable institutions capable of governing the community on principles and practice of lasting benefit.

The concept of carrying capacity is familiar in the environmental field – the realization that there is a limit to the extent to which the bio-system can cope with pressures upon it and that asking that system to carry more than it can is unsustainable. The notion of capacity can be equally applied to issues of governance. The idea of governmental 'overload' is well known, and recognizes that attempts by the State to manage more than it reasonably can results in bureaucratic seizing up, administrative inertia and governmental inefficiency. Both in theory and in applied practice there is thus great interest in the issue of 'capacity' and capacity building as it applies to community governance.

On the theoretical side considerable interest has emerged in the concept of 'social capital' – networks of interpersonal and intergroup relations built on values of trust, mutuality, and reciprocity. Grounded originally in economic ideas about the optimal organization of firms, and reflecting the concern of economic analysis about minimizing the transaction costs of the market, the notion of social capital sees informal networks as the basis for trust maximization and risk minimization. Robert Putnam in his studies of Italy (1993) concluded that the strength of the economy – and the local economy in particular – was a function of its capacity to generate locally based links which enhanced local savings and their recirculation in the community, which facilitated lending to local community business, which enhanced the local multiplier effect through better relationships between large and small firms. The arguments around the concept of a sustainable local economy (Gibbs, 1991; LGMB, 1993) involve moving towards a circular form of development rather than continuing traditional linear models. They emphasize the potential of 'closure', the prevention of leakage from the local economy by increasing local purchasing, the retention of savings, the recirculation of capital, and the protection against external expropriation of benefits. There are, of course, limitations to the closure of local economies, but the concept emphasizes principles of integration, self reliance and the non-exploitation of resources from other places, principles which are central to any definition of local sustainability.

The significance of a strong local social economy and the need to recirculate economic activity within localities to secure a sustainable local economic base has been reflected in the emergence of formal guidance not simply about community consultation and involvement but latterly about support for capacity building towards community based organization. In 1997 a good practice guide on community involvement in urban and rural regeneration (DETR, 1997b) heralded explicit reference – in a later annex to the 1998 Single Regeneration Budget (SRB) *Bidding Guidance* – to the importance of community based activities – Credit Unions, Local Exchange Trading Systems (LETS), Community Enterprise and Development Trusts. Capacity building was equally emphasized with up to 10 per cent of SRB funding allowable for capacity building.

The European Commission has initiated a programme of community investment which explicitly refers to social capital, and capacity building is a major feature of much of the thinking about local regeneration. Policy initiatives emphasize the role of such a localized bias to regeneration and revitalization of communities and, as well as the latest SRB policy advice, thinking on the New Deal for Communities highlights the growing scope for community-based experimentation in governance.

This brings the discussion back to the principles of sustainability, to the concept of capacity, to recognition that capacity building for sustainable institutions must be a central feature of planning for new communities, and to the potential for community governance.

# THE SCOPE FOR COMMUNITY GOVERNANCE

'Community' is one of the overused and abused words in the language of public policy – disputed amongst theoreticians as well as applied to almost any initiative which allows the state to withdraw resources or support to local services. But the basic distinction between communities of interest and communities of place is well recognized as well as the fact that individuals and groups may be part of multiple and often overlapping communities. This book is concerned primarily with communities of place – and indeed with the governance of place, in this case at the neighbourhood or ward level.

The term governance (and its difference from government) also causes confusion. The latter term – *government* – is the activity of the formal governmental system which takes place within specific administrative boundaries, involves the exercise of particular powers and duties by formally elected or appointed bodies, and uses public resources in a financially accountable way. Government is perhaps best seen as the formal presence and representation of the State in the locality. The business of government is conducted under clear procedural rules, involving statutory relationships between politicians, professionals and the public.

*Governance* is a much looser process of steering (*gubernator* – the rudder) localities which often involves issues transcending geographical or administrative boundaries, which is multi-sectoral, and in which networks, alliances, and coalitions play an important part. Such networks are informal (although they may be formalized into structural arrangements such as partnerships) and are often ambiguous in their memberships, activities, relationships and accountabilities. Governance is the process of multi-stakeholder involvement, of multiple interest resolution, of compromise rather than confrontation, of negotiation rather than administrative fiat.

The scope for community governance is inevitably limited by external political and administrative structures – the general relationship between state and civil society and the more particular patterns of relations between nation state, local authority and community (parish, commune etc). The variations are enormous. Danish local government for example is highly decentralized with a strong local democratic culture built into the national value system. By comparison the UK, although in many respects a pioneer of localism, has experienced a highly centralized system over long periods of time due as much to the history of a Westminster based unitary state as to the particular centralizing tendencies of the Conservative government of the 1980s and mid 1990s. France, again by contrast, experiences a mixture of strong central state with strong localism arising from the respective roles of l'Etat and commune in French political and administrative history.

Above all the potential for area based governance is influenced by the fiscal arrangements which determine the resources available to local communities. In general throughout mainland Europe the units of local government are smaller than in the UK, with some financial autonomy resting at a more local 'commune' level. The role of the lowest level of local government in the UK – the parish – is often overlooked. Even if the Parish/Town Council lacks powers and duties it should not be overlooked that it holds precepting revenue raising autonomy. Parish Council expenditure, for example, has never been capped!

The extent of formal powers and duties, however, offers only a partial explanation of the position of community governance. More significant is the cultural history and traditions of central local relations and the in-built regard which exists for local democracy. Here again national cultures vary significantly but it is possible to identify a shifting climate for community governance across both western Europe and the newer post-communist countries of Eastern Europe. This shift of political/administrative climate stems from a number of factors:

- the EU has emphasized the role of citizenship, community development and subsidiarity as the foundation of a strong Europe across a wide range of policy areas;
- shifts to an enabling governance – rather than government – have enhanced the potential for a community role, emphasizing institutional pluralism, and pointing to influence rather than formal power as the basis for good government;
- there has been more formal empowerment of local interests with increased rights of complaint, redress, and appeal against administrative incompetence or bureaucratic insensitivity. In housing services and elsewhere there has been a growth of participative and managerial structures;
- there has been a revival in thinking about communitarianism, together with the world-wide debate about the significance of social capital;
- communities of place have become more significant in policy terms with the spreading application of area and/or estate based initiatives.

In examining the implications of these trends for community governance it is possible to identify a number of influences affecting future directions. On the one hand at a political and philosophical level the whole nature of community and democracy remain under active discussion, exerting pressure on the role of local government. On the other hand innovative developments in community and neighbourhood management are emerging reinforced by the decentralization of local management and services. The remainder of this chapter discusses each of these issues in turn.

## COMMUNITY AND DEMOCRACY

The underpinnings of community-based governance lie in part in philosophical arguments about the inherent importance of bottom-up ways of life, but lie also – at least in the UK – in dissatisfaction with big government and with formal representative democracy. This is in part reflected in concerns about electoral participation and voter turn out. Although there are complex explanations for differential turn out relating both to the nature and timing of electoral systems, and to structural and attitudinal factors, the evidence points clearly to low turn out (40 per cent on average) in local government elections in the UK (Rallings et al, 1994). There is some evidence, however, to suggest that turn out increases as ward size diminishes reflecting perhaps knowledge of the candidate, the influence of friends and family or lesser distances to travel to vote. There are also studies, however, which suggest that the smaller the ward the more likely there are to be uncontested elections (Masterson and Masterson, 1980). There thus appears to be stronger identification with smaller local areas than with larger areas.

Investigation of some of the basic propositions about community and identity – that local attachment provides for a basic human need, that modernization has extinguished the traditional community as a source of identity, and that attachment to community of place has declined suggests that 'there is a clear focus of attachment on the most local area' (Young et al, 1996). For many people, however, there is no channel for the release of this sense of local identity into structures of governance. The many studies of disadvantaged neighbourhoods, and most recently the diagnosis of the Social Exclusion Unit, however, make less of exclusion from governmental systems than they might. Whilst it is recognized that 'not enough has been done to build up skills and institutions at neighbourhood level' (Social Exclusion Unit, 1998) there are few specific proposals in the Government's analysis for strengthening the position of such local capacity. Equally the White Paper on modernizing local government (DETR, 1998j) makes little mention of the role of parishes or decentralized forms of governance, concentrating for the main part on improving the quality of the democratic and service oriented activities of the local authority.

This may be because radical shifts in the balance of influence and power towards local communities threaten the most powerful of existing institutions. Nevertheless communitarianism continues to receive attention (Etzioni, 1998) reinforcing the basic principles of democratic subsidiarity – 'Generally no social task should be assigned to an institution that is larger than necessary to do the job'. Additionally the emergence of debate about social capital and the moves needed to strengthen and mobilize it to the benefit of neighbourhoods and local communities (Putnam, 1993) reflect recognition of the potential strength of community capacity to plan, manage and deliver local governance.

## THE PRESSURES FOR COMMUNITY GOVERNANCE

There has long been tension between representative democracy and new forms of participative democracy which involve communities in direct access to power. Elected councillors have been slow to accept that they might not be the sole spokespersons for their localities, whilst professionalism has created a monopoly of power which has inhibited the devolution of responsibility to more localized communities. Parish Councils have little power (although with direct precepting powers they do possess some legitimacy), whilst in Scotland Community Councils have been predominantly consultative. Current thinking has moved local government to a new interpretation of community leadership (Clarke and Stewart, 1999) but there again the culture shift is towards a listening, shaping, influencing council rather than towards a devolution of power. In the same vein, whilst the Government's proposals for modernizing local government contain clear messages about a more responsible community role, with a new duty of community leadership, the emphasis remains on the role of the local authority in initiating and leading community based service planning and delivery (DETR, 1998j). Some councils have of course made significant strides towards redefining the culture of governance with widespread use of innovative new participative mechanisms (Lowndes et al, 1998). These range from the well established complaints and suggestions schemes, through a variety of consultative forms relating to service needs and provision, into new forms of community based debate and investigation. Public meetings are being overtaken by more sophisticated forms of discussion from focus groups to community visioning and citizens' juries.

The impetus to building new forms of community oriented governance comes from a variety of sources. There is no doubt that the requirement for partnerships involving public, private and community sectors as partners to bidding for funds (as for Single Regeneration Budget funding for example) has enhanced local government understanding of the benefits of a community perspective. It is also clear that community involvement in such partnerships has helped to remove a number of stereotypes about the nature and capacity of community representatives. Nevertheless the bulk of the evidence (Hastings et al, 1996; DETR, 1997b) suggests that community involvement remains tokenistic, that it is undertaken too speedily to be sustainable and that once the bid is in and won or lost, the community reverts to junior partner status.

Other pressures for a more active culture of community governance have come from a variety of sources. The Local Government Review, and in particular its descent into the use of community surveys as the arbiter of change, stimulated a number of councils to promise a new community orientation to governance as the price for gaining or retaining status under the review. Thus Gloucestershire for example, promised a new structure of community assembly areas and local service points if the County Council retained its status (Gloucestershire County Council, 1992). The availability of new technology has allowed the development of localized service points offering information and access in one stop shops. A number of authorities again are considering the extension of their networks of communication into post-offices, health centres and so on. Elsewhere service failures – or even an occasional crisis – have driven new efforts to enhance structures of community involvement, but the thrust of this has been towards more effective service management rather than to democracy (Lowndes et al, 1998). 'Best Value' includes a focus on achieving best value through public engagement, and:

> 'A *number of pilots are seeking to situate best value within broader strategies intended to improve community governance and democratic accountability. They see engagement as a process of dialogue which builds trust in the authority ... and tend to emphasize more deliberative forms of engagement, often at neighbourhood level'* (Martin, 1998).

## COMMUNITY AND NEIGHBOURHOOD MANAGEMENT

Cultural change in the larger organization of government has an important impact on local communities, and can go some way to building an empowered and self-regulating system. But there is also evidence that the most convincing route towards credible neighbourhood governance lies in the direct involvement of residents. Historically this route has been trodden most heavily – albeit slowly – through the growth of tenant management in social housing. Area management and estate committees have a long history (Dale and Derricourt, 1989) but without significant delegated powers of either management in general or budgets in particular were seen to be weak and remained tied to the culture and mechanisms of local government (Zipfel, 1989). Estate Management Boards gave tenants more control (Dickson and Robertson, 1993; Steele et al, 1995), whilst Tenant Management and Ownership Cooperatives began to vest power and ownership with tenants. Estate Action gave the formation of tenant management a further impetus in England and the spread of resident democracy has been extended through the establishment of Resident Boards and the drawing up of estate agreements (Cole and Smith, 1996; Aldbourne Associates, 1994).

If housing has seen the majority of innovation in influencing management from within the community, there are parallel examples in economic development, community safety and public health. Community Enterprise has a long history, not least in Scotland, where support for community business, generated a wide range of initiatives in the peripheral estates of Scottish cities. Drawing heavily on a long tradition of cooperative enterprise stemming from Robert Owen (New Lanark) and the Rochdale Cooperative in the mid-19th century (Pearce, 1993), the evolution of Scottish experience remains the most significant for community business experimentation in the 1980s. There are mixed messages about community business. Many of the jobs created are concentrated – inevitably perhaps – around the estates and many relate to the maintenance of the housing stock, upkeep of the environment, protection of property and local services. Thus painting, decoration, minor repairs, landscaping and maintenance of grounds, contract cleaning, security, launderettes are typical of the local jobs available. Many are low skilled, many are part-time, many are low paid. Thus the job profile in many ways reproduces the employment structure of the estate – unskilled, low paid and largely male jobs. Some community businesses recruit strongly from the local area (see Watson, 1994) and demonstrate high levels of targeting on local need; others, however, show far less local recruitment and move to the position where in order to win contracts and stay in business it is necessary to recruit labour more openly in the market (McArthur, 1993).

The most recent 'movement' is that of LETS (Local Exchange Trading Systems). LETS represents the attempt to establish a non-money economy within the present general economic system by an extension of bartering. It allows people in the system to trade with each other using a form of 'local' currency. A LET is simply a directory of services which can be provided by members, and trading takes place without the need for any money; members credit each other using a local cheque book. Again the nature of the work involved is often local – cleaning, repair work, gardening, childminding – and essentially responds to community needs, depending upon a recognition of mutual needs and provision of services in the locality. Whilst not organizationally within any system of governance, LETS do generate services by local people and for local people; they thus substitute for the formal activities of government. The scope for LETS to operate at estate level as an alternative economic system for local services remains to be developed, but the essence of the initiative is essentially built around values of community and mutuality, concepts which figure strongly in community empowerment.

It has been noted that current regeneration policy guidance endorses the extension of such local economy schemes. Most recently the proliferation of area based initiatives reflects the intention of government to offer communities a much stronger voice in local service delivery and management. Education Action Zones, Health Action Zones, Pioneer Legal Service Partnerships, offer a greater say to local residents whilst neighbourhood management as advocated by the Social Exclusion Unit (1998) pushes strongly towards direct neighbourhood management. The characteristics of the latter are devolved powers, a Neighbourhood Board (resident dominated), a neighbourhood manager and possibly other local staff working to the Board, a neighbourhood budget, and service agreements with local government departments or other service providers. The neighbourhood in effect becomes less a recipient and more a commissioner of local services. The implications are for far greater decentralization of direct management of a wide range of maintenance and management services – housing, cleansing, waste collection and possibly disposal, environmental management, libraries and information – with education, social services and even policing not far behind.

## LOCAL GOVERNMENT DECENTRALIZATION AND COMMUNITY GOVERNANCE

Much of the impetus towards a more community oriented governance has come from the experience of decentralization within local government. Two interpretations of decentralization are commonly applied. The first is a geographical interpretation which addresses the physical dispersal of operations to local – often one-stop or first-stop shops – whilst the second focuses on the delegation of a greater degree of decision-making authority to lower levels of management or governance (Hambleton et al, 1996). A second distinction made is between managerial decentralization (directed primarily at improving service quality) and political decentralization (aiming to enhance local democracy and the quality of governance).

Increasingly local authorities have begun to use decentralized structures both to enhance democracy and service delivery and to offer new roles to local elected members as cabinet government begins to take hold in local government. Recent research on integrated working (Stewart et al, 1999) illustrates the 'localization' approach in different ways.

Sheffield has developed a city-wide area basis for working involving area member panels, area officers, and the preparation and analysis of information on an area basis. Local forums have been established, co-terminosity with health is being pursued, and an 'area' culture is being developed. Not all areas have the same needs, are of the same size, or receive the same treatment. Sheffield, however, believes it is important not to identify only a few areas but to cover the city with an area system as a key element of corporate working and for the pursuit of integration of service delivery.

In Newcastle local accountability groups have been established in many of the most deprived areas. These consist of local councillors, officers and local community representatives. Each group has a small budget to spend in the locality. This bottom-up approach to problem solving was felt to be especially necessary in sensitive areas of the city. Originally the groups concentrated on looking at issues around disaffected youth but have now widened their remit. Initially some members were cautious about the initiative, feeling it threatened their roles, but they have been won over as the groups have proved successful.

In Mendip the small and medium sized town character of the district has led to the establishment of Town Managers who provide the focus both for translating top-down district-wide policy frameworks into local service delivery, and for bottom-up local inputs into service planning. The Town Manager role in Mendip has increased in visibility and status and now provides an important focus for service integration, as well as offering the potential for making service planning more community oriented and re-orienting officers to a more user responsive culture.

## COMMUNITY LEADERSHIP

The importance of leadership has been underplayed in the research on area based community governance. Numerous studies (Thake and Staubach, 1993; Thake, 1995; Power and Tunstall, 1996), have highlighted the importance of community empowerment, stressing the centrality of engaging local communities in regeneration, of offering real stakes in the change process, and of integrating fully into civil society those marginal to its norms and values. The same studies, as summarized by Taylor (1995) have pointed out the difficulties associated with the participation of local people in partnerships – difficulties over representation, accountability, continuity, and commitment.

Hastings et al (1996) point to the negative perceptions held about 'career activists'; Macfarlane (1993) calls participation a 'minority sport'. Stewart and Taylor (1995) identify a range of dangers which offset the potential for resident empowerment on estates and begin to address the role of individuals arguing that 'it is necessary to unpack what is being asked of local people'. Fordham (1996) argues that capacity building and sustainable community empowerment relies on long term investment in people, whilst Roberts et al (1996) point to 'new personalities' as one catalyst for partnership.

Little research, however, focuses explicitly on the role and function of community leaders even if particular estate-based research (Scottish Office, 1996; Hastings et al, 1996) highlights the combination of power and vulnerability located in community leaders as they engage in multi-organisational partnership working. Thake (1995) focuses upon sustainable community regeneration organizations operating within disadvantaged urban communities, basing his analysis on the experience of 20 'community regeneration organizations' (CDTs; sponsored regeneration agencies; housing associations; housing trusts; charitable foundations; settlements and faith communities). He points to two overriding objectives. The first is to bring about social and economic regeneration within their neighbourhoods and the second is to develop a sustainable organization.

Building on a strong US literature (Flora and Flora, 1993; Flora et al, 1997; Henton et al, 1997), Atkinson (1997) argues that social entrepreneurs will be as important in the next decade as business entrepreneurs were in the 1980s. Social entrepreneurs are like business entrepreneurs in the methods they use – but they are motivated by social goals rather than material profits. Their great skill is that they often make something from nothing, creating innovative forms of active welfare, health care and housing which are both cheaper and more effective than the traditional services provided by government. Atkinson (1997) redefines professionalism identifying new roles (like neighbourhood officers) which help people to gain the confidence to formulate and express shared goals, and help them also to press these goals upon the city authorities and ensure they are acted upon:

> *'Just as the private economic sector depends on risk taking, visionary people to construct new companies, products, services and wealth, so the third sector need social entrepreneurs. The role, once less vital, used perhaps to be fulfilled by the village school. Today, a new breed of determined professional is needed who is employed by the active citizens of the neighbourhood forum to bind together and empower the fractured community.'*

The concept echoes the thinking on planning for real, the contribution of which to neighbourhood based change has been significant for years (Gibson, 1993), whilst Thake (1995) argues '...at the centre of every successful community regeneration organization is a new type of professional person: the social entrepreneur'. His definition gives them many of the same attributes as private sector entrepreneurs, namely being able to see and to develop the potential of under-utilized resources (human, financial and physical), being personable, charismatic and energetic, capable of motivating those around them. Social entrepreneurs have an organizational flair and persuasive negotiation skills, are adept at utilizing the plethora of grant regimes available to localities, and differ from the private entrepreneur in that the purpose of their involvement is to create assets, resources and surpluses which make the community richer. Whilst much of the emphasis is from the US there is growing support for the development of social entrepreneurs in the UK (Thake and Zadek, 1997). Leadbetter (1997) calls for 2000 social entrepreneurs by the year 2000, and the Community Action Network Centre (Baird, 1998) as well as the School for Social Entrepreneurs (Young, 1998; Young and Smith, 1998) are already turning out 'graduates'.

Additionally there is much positive reference in the literature to the potential role of front line workers – health visitors (Bowes and Domocos, 1998), community police (Crandon, 1998), community wardens (Hadley, 1998), youth workers (France and Wiles, 1997), town centre managers (Stewart and Goss, 1999), and neighbourhood managers (Social Exclusion Unit, 1998c). Traditionally recognized as having considerable discretion on the ground, front line staff offer potential for reshaping the local services in the light of local preferences. Local knowledge helps create social control.

# CONCLUSION

The major conclusion from this chapter must be that it is in the interaction between internal and external cultures that a new community culture can be grown. The traditional practices of local government are under pressure with 'community leadership' the watch word of current best practice (Clarke and Stewart, 1999). The need to modernize, however, is a force for change and many authorities are responding to the need for decentralization and devolution. It is in the shift of responsibility for functions and tasks that community empowerment in local governance is likely to emerge. Out of the material presented above five main conclusions emerge with implications for practical action.

First there is increasing evidence of community governance as an integral part of local management and decision-making with community involvement gradually being organized in ways which suit communities rather than local government. Secondly we can see shifts in representative roles with elected members taking a different, and less proprietorial, stance to local communities than hitherto. Thirdly structures of accountability and management performance review are being redrawn to include the scale and extent of devolution as a key indicator of best value. Fourthly there is a wider rehabilitation of civil society with recognition of the function of social capital accepted as the basis for a more reciprocal and mutually supportive approach to local governance. Lastly there emerges the need to resist the consolidation of small units of government (parishes, communes etc) and to retain and enhance the examples of community-based governance which combine small scale representative democracy with more participative styles of management devolution.

# PART IV
# MANAGING RESOURCES LOCALLY

# 12 THE COMMUNITY ENERGY UTILITY

*Trevor Houghton*

## INTRODUCTION

In the postwar period, energy supply has been controlled first by large nationalized monopolistic utilities, then replaced by large privatized utilities. In each case control is very remote from the energy user giving little incentive for the consumer to take responsibility for the adverse impacts of the use of energy in their home or business. During the late 1990s, efforts to introduce competition into domestic energy supply have opened the possibility for energy utilities with community stakeholders, energy purchasing cooperatives and other 'community-based' structures dealing with energy. A variety of legal structures are being utilized that give the community a range of different roles in the ownership and management of energy systems. This chapter sets out to demonstrate that community stakeholding is a key element to achieving greater sustainability.

## THE CHANGING ORGANIZATION AND OWNERSHIP OF ENERGY SUPPLY

At the turn of the millennium, the UK energy supply industry is in a period of dramatic transformation affecting both organization and ownership. In the space of little more than 15 years we have seen the big state owned energy supply monopolies broken up and privatized. The organization of energy supply has moved from a position where central and long term planning predominated to the current situation where the short term thinking of competition and market forces has a much stronger influence on what power stations are built and which energy resources are used. The demise of nuclear power and the contraction of the UK coal industry can be partly put down to private ownership and the new pressures of the liberalized energy market.

The state owned monopolies operated in a very paternalistic fashion towards energy users. The managers of these monopolies, primarily engineers, believed they knew what was best for the country and generally opted for large scale centralized systems. Liberalization has resulted in a more customer orientated management. This is made up of individuals with primarily marketing skills, but whose main motivation is maximizing the dividends of their share-holders by selling more energy. In neither situation, state owned monopoly or privatized utility does the energy end user have much incentive to take greater responsibility for the impacts of their energy use. The liberalization of energy markets does however give energy users the possibility of choosing to buy from sustainable energy sources; in the same way as we are encouraged to buy recycled paper and to use timber from sustainably managed forests. The gradual stripping away of monopoly powers has created the possibility for small scale initiatives to operate, buying and selling energy on more equitable terms.

Many of the changes in the organization of energy supply have been made possible by technological developments in information technology and metering of energy. The complex trading arrangements that now exist in the gas and electricity markets would not have been possible without the ability to track and transfer data relating to distribution of fuel and the millions of transactions as customers pay different suppliers for their energy. The current market structures would not have been possible without the microchip.

These same technological developments also improve the feasibility of operating a small scale energy utility. In particular remote metering and computerized billing systems can cut down on operating costs. Sophisticated metering can also give advantage to a utility that can accurately predict and record energy demand from its customers over time. This will enable the utility to purchase energy at the lowest cost.

## Sustainable Energy in the Liberalized Energy Market

The concept of sustainable development embraces concerns for protecting the environment, equitable distribution of resources within a sound economy. Such concerns do not fit that well with the operation of liberalized markets. The experience in the UK is that liberalized markets are not meeting social and environmental needs. A massive switch from coal to gas fired power stations has had some environmental benefits. But these benefits have been a side effect of the drive for more economically efficient generating technology that delivers enhanced dividends to the shareholders. Renewable energy technologies have by contrast needed the incentive of the NFFO subsidy[1] mechanism in order to attract the interest of the big electricity companies.

Competition does tend to make companies more customer orientated but this does not apply to all customers. Companies are orientated towards their desired classes of customers which can leave out those that are expensive to supply. These unwanted customers include those on low-income who want to use frequent cash payment methods, customers with special needs and those living in remote rural areas. As a result it has now been recognized by the UK Government that it will be necessary to impose social and environmental duties on the privatized utilities through regulation. In contrast, energy utilities with community stakeholders do more naturally take on environmental and social responsibilities in response to their end user stakeholders. This means that they should require less regulation and it is an argument for a more relaxed licensing regime for such utilities.

---

1 NFFO stands for Non Fossil Fuel Obligation. This is a mechanism whereby renewable energy projects are subsidized by a levy on the sales of fossil fuelled electricity.

# THE COMMUNITY UTILITY VERSUS THE CONVENTIONAL UTILITY

Currently in the energy sector, there is a flurry of takeovers and mergers resulting in larger and larger multi-utility companies ultimately owned by multinational conglomerates. There is a view that in the next millennium there will be no more than half a dozen large multi-utility companies in the UK, each with interests in energy generation as well as supply and distribution selling both gas and electricity. These same companies are also likely to be selling water, telecoms and a number of other services. This takes decision-making in these utilities further and further away from the energy user. At the same time, on the fringes of these developments, there are an increasing number of small scale initiatives, some led by local authorities and others by community businesses, that are showing an alternative approach which is described here as 'the community utility'. Table 12.1 summarizes the main features and differences between these two types of utility. A number of case studies illustrating this approach are given later in this chapter. They all have the common feature of being local initiative driven by local needs.

**Table 12.1** *Comparison Between Conventional and Community Energy Utilities*

|  | Conventional energy utility | Community energy utility |
|---|---|---|
| Generating plant | Large scale and remote from customers | Small scale and locally based |
| Customer base | Very large with tens of thousands of customers | Relatively small, usually a few thousand customers and could be much smaller |
| Legal structure | Public Limited Company, subsidiary to multinational parent company | Variety of legal structures including joint venture companies, co-operatives and charities |
| Control | Main control lies with the multi-national parent but shareholders also influence decisions through their desire to maximize dividends | Day to day control could be in the hands of a commercial management. Energy end users having a substantial stake in the utility. Local authority may also be a stakeholder as an agent for the community |

# SUSTAINABLE ENERGY RESOURCES IN SUSTAINABLE COMMUNITIES

While the 'traditional' renewable energy sources such as wind, solar, and hydro can be valuable sources of energy to a sustainable community, the most readily accessible resources that could be considered as 'renewable' are waste products. The use of waste products for generating heat and electricity can be seen as a way of recycling and reusing these resources:

- *Organic wastes* such as sewage, putrescible municipal waste, waste food processing etc. These are materials where disposal is becoming increasingly expensive (as a result of the Landfill Tax) and heavily environmentally regulated. New solutions are needed. Anaerobic digestion can be seen as a way of processing waste into a 'cleaner' and more useful material and as a way of producing heat and generating electricity.
- *Combustible wastes* such as scrap wood, paper and card, car tyres etc. While direct reuse and recycling must remain the preferred option for dealing with these wastes, there is still potential to combust some of these wastes. Conventional waste to energy incineration is very controversial in the UK but other closed system technologies such as pyrolysis plants are more generally acceptable. Small scale heat-only plants also have a place.
- *Waste heat.* Towns and cities radiate heat but still many people live in cold and unhealthy homes. Harnessing the waste heat from offices and process industries is a largely untapped energy resource but it requires the infrastructure to collect the heat and transport it to the end user. This requires the development of district heating networks.

In all cases it is easier and more economic to utilize these energy resources in new developments where the infrastructure can be designed in from the start and integrated with sewage treatment and household waste disposal etc. In all cases utilizing these resources would link a sustainable settlement to its surrounding. The settlement could become a waste sink for its surroundings – every town should have one! At the same time it might produce more energy than it needs and become an exporter of energy to the surroundings.

The first case study (Box 12.1) shows how an inner urban area is being served by a community based utility that is providing low cost energy services. This energy utility is a commercial company but one whose business is the provision of services to *local* domestic and business customers and is driven by their needs.

## ENVIRONMENTAL RESPONSIBILITY

While community involvement is no guarantee that a new power plant will gain planning permission in the UK planning system it will greatly enhance its prospects. The second case study (Box 12.2) shows how the development of a community utility's generating plant is determined by local decision-making. In Denmark, where local utilities can be wholly or part owned by their customers, it is not uncommon for a vote at a public meeting to be the main planning approval needed. The weighing up of personal energy needs and environmental concerns becomes very real when the source of your energy is on your doorstep and you have a stake in energy developments. The result is that environmentally benign energy sources and the cleanest energy conversion technology become the obvious choice.

Bringing energy supply closer to the user both in terms of location and control can also have a positive effect on people's awareness of the environ-

---

## BOX 12.1 ENVIROENERGY LTD

### Description

EnviroEnergy Ltd is an example of where a large community energy utility has been established by a local authority in order to manage an existing community heating scheme. It was set up as a joint venture company with a private sector partner taking the lead role. It was formed in 1995 by Nottingham City Council and Energy and Technical Services Group plc and manages a sizeable Combined Heat and Power (CHP) and community heating scheme.

The main energy source for the scheme is a waste to energy incinerator run by WasteNotts Ltd (a private company which is part of Yorkshire Water plc). The incinerator provides steam which is used in EnviroEnergy's own steam turbines to generate electricity which is then sold to East Midlands Electricity plc for distribution through the grid. The heat from this plant is provided to a variety of customers including nearly 5000 households (or all tenures), commercial customers including two large shopping centres, a hotel, council buildings, government buildings, university buildings and a separate steam supply to a large pharmaceutical company.

### The Local Authority as the Agent of the Local Community

Because this company was set up by the local authority there were extensive consultations with their own tenants and other consumers of the heat on the form it should take. The tenant consultation also covered the issues of payment billing and affordable warmth.

The private sector partner bought in new investment and commercial expertise to transform a loss making operation into viable local enterprise.

EnviroEnergy has a board made up of three City councillors and three members from ETS. It is set up as a 'private sector influenced company' and so the City Council has a 19.9 per cent shareholding with ETS holding 80.1 per cent of the shares. The general manager appointed by the company was a former District Housing Manager for the St Ann's Estate where most of his domestic customers live.

To protect the consumer interest a shareholder agreement was established which ensures that certain matters such as changing the nature of the business or altering prices outside an agreed formula, needs a unanimous decision. There is also a 'Consumer Charter' and a proposed Ombudsman to deal with disputes.

The City Council tenants connected to the community heating scheme are benefiting from a low cost, controllable heat supply (in 1996, 2.34p/kWh of useful heat as compared to 2.41p/kWh if provided through individual gas central heating).

The future for EnviroEnergy is likely to be as an Energy Service Company which might include services such as insulation measures for domestic customers.

---

mental and other implications of their end use of energy and other resources. This includes their demand for energy in absolute terms and over time. For example, poor energy design in buildings or inefficient appliances could mean that the local power station has to have a larger capacity than would be economic and hence managing peaks in demand begins to have more meaning.

---

### BOX 12.2 THE RY HEATING PLANT

*Description*

The district heating plant at Ry in Denmark, serves 13,000 households and operates on a mixture of fuels. It has two boilers which can operate on wood pellets or coal and another back-up boiler which burns oil. The unusual feature of the plant is that the return water is heated in a 'solar field'. This is an array of flat plate solar collectors which provides 1270MWh of heat for the plant out of a total production of 36,000MWh. 28,000MWh of heat is sold to customers with the remainder being lost in transmission.

The solar field is an European Commission demonstration project and has received a large amount of financial support (European funding provided 49 per cent of 6 million kroner capital costs). The solar collectors are all of a similar design and are manufactured by a Swedish company. The output temperature from the solar collectors is between 80°C and 90°C.

*Local Control and Local Resources*

Local consumers own the heating plant and they ultimately give the approval on any major initiative proposed by the plant managers. For instance the decision to take on the solar project was taken by an extraordinary meeting of consumers.

The Ry plant is situated in an area of dense forest, so wood is a local resource. Its use is supported by taxation on fuel which effectively make it competitive against conventional fuel such as coal.

---

## SOCIAL RESPONSIBILITY

Local control brings two very positive gains in managing debt and dealing with arrears for a community run utility when compared to a conventional utility. The first is that failure to pay for your energy when you are able, will reflect on your standing in the community. The evidence in housing shows that in tenant run housing cooperatives there is a far lower level of rent arrears than among other social landlords. This suggests that if you are in debt to a utility in which you and your neighbours have a stake, you will be far more motivated to pay up as soon as you can. This will reduce the debt management costs of the local utility.

Where there is a genuine problem for a household in managing to pay for its energy services, a community run utility is likely to be more responsive to their needs. At the most basic, this might mean providing a payment method that aids the consumer in effectively managing their household budget. Recent experience with the introduction of domestic gas competition has seen a reduction in the cash payment methods available to consumers of new suppliers and the growth in price differentials between prepayment meter and Direct Debit tariffs. These trends are evidence of an erosion of basic services in terms of choice of payment method to the poorer sections of society which makes them more vulnerable to debt problems. These trends are associated with energy utilities that are motivated primarily by the need to satisfy their shareholders who in most cases have little interest in social responsibilities.

---

### BOX 12.3 ST PANCRAS HOUSING ASSOCIATION

*Description*

St Pancras Housing (SPH) is a housing association providing housing services in London and Hertfordshire. It has a housing stock of nearly 3000 units. In one development in Euston, London, the housing association has in effect become a community energy utility. SPH installed a combined heat and power (CHP) unit to provide electricity, space and water heating to 95 dwellings, ten commercial units and its own offices.

Not only has SPH installed the CHP unit but it has taken over ownership of the electricity wires serving these energy consumers from London Electricity. SPH has installed its own modern electronic meters which are linked to a computer billing system in their offices. This means SPH is now operating its own micro electricity distribution company. Sales of electricity produce an income stream of £45,000 per year. This income stream is helping to pay for the CHP unit which also provides heat to all the energy users.

*Community Decision-Making*

SPH consulted its tenants about how they would like to pay for their energy services the costs of which had been considerably reduced by the installation of the very efficient CHP unit. In a ballot, the tenants decided to take their savings by having no standing charge. This meant that they still had a strong incentive to reduce their energy costs. Tenants are able to pay for their electricity by quarterly bill or standing order and SPH have also installed a cash deposit machine to enable small cash payments.

---

More fundamentally, a community utility will be strongly motivated by its community stakeholders to provide affordable energy services and, particularly, affordable warmth. The ability of the utility to provide affordable energy services is greatly enhanced where there is a direct link with the provision of housing, such as a utility which has local authority or housing association stakeholders. The case studies in Boxes 12.3 amd 12.4 are examples of where the prime motivation for setting up the projects has been to provide affordable energy services. The Poolsbrook case study also shows how a community utility can be an element in the regeneration of an area that has been blighted by the demise of heavy industry.

# THE LOCAL ECONOMY

The creation of a community energy utility is a way of stopping spending on energy leaving an area for some anonymous multinational utility with no stake in the locality. In the UK most of the electricity companies are now owned by parent companies based in the US.

The most obvious economic pay off for taking responsibility for energy might be lower costs for energy services. However a more significant benefit could be that fuel bills are paid to a local enterprise which will in turn stimulate the local economy and provide local employment. Typically about 4 per cent of disposable income is spent on fuel. This means that a community of a 1000

---

## BOX 12.4 POOLSBROOK, ERIN AREA COMMUNITY HEATING (PEACH)

At the time of writing, PEACH is a project that has only reached the feasibility study stage. The project is based around the Erin Void, a former opencast coal working, now a landfill site, in the most easterly part of the Borough of Chesterfield.

The basic concept is to establish a combined heat and power plant and heat only boilers serving a district heating network that provides heat to local housing and community buildings and electricity to the grid. Initially the CHP unit and the boilers will be fuelled by natural gas but as the landfill site becomes operational this will be supplemented and eventually replaced by landfill gas. While the technological aspects of the project are tried and tested the organizational and financing aspects are novel.

The largest part of the capital funding for the project is to come from the Landfill Tax Credit Scheme. This scheme allows Landfill operators to retain up to 20% of the Landfill Tax that has been collected and to use these funds to finance environmental and community projects within ten miles of the landfill site. The funding is channelled through an 'environmental body', in this case the South West England Environmental Trust. The organization receiving funding must be a not-for-profit body. The PEACH project will be run by a non-profit-distributing energy service company or ESCO. The ESCO will not only supply heat and generate electricity but will use part of its operating surpluses for energy efficiency improvements to local housing.

The ESCO will be established after public consultation. It is seen by the Local Authority as a vehicle for bringing affordable warmth to a very deprived area with high levels of unemployment and poor housing.

---

households and associated small businesses and shops is likely to have an annual energy bill in excess of one million pounds sterling. The next case study (Box 12.5) is still at its early stages but it shows how a small rural community of 1000 households is seeking to switch to a more sustainable energy supply.

# BARRIERS TO THE COMMUNITY ENERGY UTILITY

While liberalization of the energy markets is removing many legal and regulatory obstacles to the development of community energy utilities some important barriers remain.

The true costs of distributing energy locally, without the use of the supergrid, needs to be reflected in the 'use of system charges' imposed on local generators. As local generators only need the local distribution grid to deliver their electricity to the end user, they should be charged for this alone. The alternative for some community utilities has been to take ownership or to install their own distribution system (as in the St Pancras Housing case study). Either route means that the community energy utility would be able to undercut the prices of the big utility companies.

Community energy utilities are likely to be in reality community energy service providers ie organizations that are concerned with providing heat, light, refrigeration etc at an affordable price from sustainable sources. As such they will be as involved in controlling energy demand as well as energy supply.

---

## BOX 12.5 A PROPOSAL FOR AN ENERGY PURCHASING COOPERATIVE

The proposal is to form a renewable electricity purchasing cooperative made of house-holders and small businesses in the parish of King Stanley in Gloucestershire.

The project is led by the Stroud Valleys Project which is a charitable community trust and is financially supported by Stroud District Council and the Countryside Commission. The King Stanley Initiative is a body established through the parish council to formulate and implement a sustainable development strategy for the parish and is representing the local community interest in the development of the cooperative.

The cooperative will be made up of electricity consumers living in the parish who come together to pool their purchasing power to obtain 'sustainable energy services' at a competitive price. As a community organization of households and small businesses working together, they will be able to negotiate finance and credit facilities on more favourable terms than could be obtained by individuals. Their common interest is a desire to improve the environment by using their consumer power. Their objective is to obtain services at a price that is comparable or less than those generally available to an individual consumer and to gain greater local control over their energy supply.

An important aspect to this proposal is to test out the metering and billing systems that would be required. This aspect and the whole area of contracting for renewable energy supply would be carried out initially through the Renewable Energy Company (a licensed Second Tier supplier specializing in the supply of electricity from renewable projects).

At the time of writing work has started on the setting up of the cooperative including a local consultation process comprising of a number of public meetings with various interest groups in the parish; and the setting up of a network of neighbour-hood representatives to take on the role of promoting the cooperative to their neighbours and passing on information.

The formation of the cooperative will support existing local renewable energy projects and stimulate the market for new developments of green energy sources. In the longer term it is intended that the cooperative could become involved in improv-ing energy efficiency by such actions as bulk buying energy efficient appliances.

---

Current regulations stipulate that contracts between energy suppliers and their customers can be cancelled at 28 days notice. This is to ensure effective compe-tition. It also has the effect of discouraging the energy service approach. This requires a longer term commitment from the 'customer' towards their energy supplier who may have installed capital intensive measures to reduce energy demand, the costs of which need to be recovered over a number of years. There is therefore a need for a different form of contractual relationship between customers and energy service providers. This becomes more justifiable with a community energy utility where the division between customer and supplier is blurred as the customer is likely to also be a stakeholder in the utility.

Local authorities are important agents of local communities and in many cases have the know-how to establish and run community energy utilities. They currently lack the financial resources and face problems in terms of their legal powers. Central government needs to address these kind of obstacles to enable local authorities to take on this role on behalf of their communities.

*Forms of Stakeholding*

The case studies given here utilize a variety of organizational forms with a range of stakeholders. The stakeholders include not only organizations that are agents of the community, including housing providers (such as local authorities and housing associations) and parish councils and community development organizations, but also providers of finance and technology such as plant operators and installers of district heating networks.

This combination is necessary to ensure the technical and management expertise to run the utility is linked to the needs and requirements of the end-users. A community energy utility can be 'commercial' and seek to run an enterprise that will generate surpluses. In contrast to a conventional utility, these surpluses are ploughed back into the community often in the form of energy efficiency measures – several of the case studies demonstrate this feature.

# CONCLUSION

The community utility could become a vital element of new sustainable settlements or the revitalization and renewal of run down areas. The possibility of community stakeholding in the energy supply systems serving an area is perhaps an unexpected spin-off from the liberalization of the energy markets in the UK. The case studies cited demonstrate how community stakeholding is a driver for true sustainability without paternalistic external regulation. A successful community energy utility has the potential to bring together the three main strands of sustainable development – environmental and social responsibility within a sound economy.

# 13 THE FOOD PRODUCING NEIGHBOURHOOD

*Rob Hopkins*

## INTRODUCTION

The basic premise of this chapter is simple. It is that it is an essential component of any settlement which is striving for sustainability that it should be able to produce as much of its food needs as it can, and that affordable organic and ethically sourced produce should be available to everyone. Our cities and any new urban development should be green oases, creating abundance and beauty rather than the sterile landscapes of tarmac and low maintenance shrubs which characterize most modern developments.

This chapter will argue the case for a rethink of how urban development is conceived and implemented, focusing on strategies applicable to both new and existing sustainable neighbourhoods. It will firstly explore the case for a reappraisal of how we feed urban communities, looking at the way in which the food system currently fails both human communities and the environment. This is followed by a look at some principles upon which to base an approach for reversing this, as well as a look at permaculture, a design system which offers many useful insights for the actualization of these approaches. It will then go on to look at a range of approaches for providing the inhabitants of the neighbourhood with fresh produce, from people's back gardens up to ethical supermarkets. The chapter closes with an examination of ways in which designers can best promote urban food production through design, and a look at the management issues that arise from this.

## WHY GROW FOOD IN TOWNS?

Urban food growing projects are not a luxury but a necessity which arises from the need for solutions to a wide range of problems. Often these problems aren't seen as being linked, but any urban neighbourhood which professes to be sustainable must recognize the need for an approach to providing food for its residents which acknowledges and tackles them all.

## 'Food Miles'

The environmental impacts of the food system are profound, and are showing very little sign of lessening. Recent studies of the phenomenon which has been dubbed 'food miles' have shown that the impacts of food are not limited solely to its production. A study by Stefanie Böge of the Wuppertal Institute in Germany analysed the distances that each element required to make a pot of strawberry yoghurt had to travel before the final product reached the supermarket. The final figure was 3494km (Douthwaite, 1996). Each phase of production consumes considerable amounts of energy, a system only made possible by subsidized cheap fossil fuels, resulting in a heavy dependence on fossil fuels (making the importing countries very vulnerable to fluctuations in supply) and a major contribution to global warming.

## The Globalization of the Food Industry

Since the 1940s, food has become an internationally traded commodity, and the advent of GATT (the General Agreement on Tariffs and Trade) has greatly increased the control of transnational corporations over the way our food is produced and distributed. Transnational corporations control huge areas of the food market – for example, Cargill controls 60 per cent of the world trade in grains (Kneen, 1995). As well as the environmental impacts of the food system, there are also the social and cultural ones. Much of the food consumed in western supermarkets, particularly fresh fruit and vegetables, have been grown as monocultural cash crops in countries with high levels of poverty. The whole issue of debt repayments and the activities of transnational corporations are a very important part of the whole picture. As Tom Athanasiou observes in his recent book *Slow Reckoning*, the 1984–85 Ethiopian famine which claimed over one million lives didn't interrupt the export of green beans to UK supermarkets (Athanasiou, 1996).

## Biodiversity Loss

Modern agriculture has had a devastating effect on global biodiversity. This is firstly due to it having modified landscapes and habitats for agriculture, draining wetlands, clearing forests and hedgerows, ploughing up permanent pasture and so on, thereby massively reducing the ecological niches for many species. The second area of concern is the massive loss of diversity in what it grows. Although there are over 6000 apple varieties that can be grown in the UK, the bulk of apple production utilizes just nine varieties. The same is true across the board, variety in all areas of production is rapidly being eroded. It is only in growers' back gardens that certain varieties of fruit and vegetable now exist, through schemes such as the Henry Doubleday Research Association's Seed Savers and others.

## Global Warming

That global warming is now underway is a fact disputed now by very few people. Even the most optimistic scenario, the 'Fossil Free Energy Scenario' prepared by the Boston Centre of the Stockholm Environmental Institute which is modelled on the reduction of carbon dioxide emissions to zero by the year 2100, predicts a global temperature rise of 2.7 degrees Fahrenheit (Athanasiou, 1996). Any urban eco-village must minimize greenhouse gas emissions in all areas of its activities, and reducing the amount of energy required to get food onto its residents' plates is an integral part of this.

## Food Poverty

Malnutrition is not just a problem of developing countries. A recent report by the Low Income Project Team for the Department of Health stated that poverty has resulted in malnutrition on a scale unseen since the 1930s (Jones, 1996). Around one-fifth of UK citizens suffer from problems of food poverty and it is a situation made worse by town planning. The cheapest food is to be found in out-of-town supermarkets, yet without a car, these stores remain virtually inaccessible.

## Landscapes of Monotony

It is an indication of our separation from the land and from our agricultural past that we fail to make the connection between food and land. Henry David Thoreau wrote in 1854 that the farmer 'knows Nature, but as a robber' (Thoreau, 1992). The same could be said of our modern-day developments, which replace very little of the habitats and diversity they destroy. We should be aiming to create landscapes which are as varied as the original landscape, indeed more so.

## The Challenge

Clearly the above as well as many other problems such as the environmental impacts of intensive agriculture, health impacts of agrochemicals and the lack of education about cooking and healthy eating, combine to form a whole which demands our attention and action. However, as the environmental impact of their choices and decisions are not felt or perceived at the site itself or even in the locality, both the developers and the residents live in the illusion that such impacts do not exist. It is the assertion here that for any urban eco-neighbourhood to be able to be truly sustainable, it should, indeed must, develop strategies for feeding its inhabitants which respond directly to the challenges outlined above.

# APPROACHING SUSTAINABLE FOOD STRATEGIES

The growing of food in cities is clearly an appropriate response to a wide range of challenges. I would go so far as to state that sustainable urban food production is a vital component of any sustainable neighbourhood project, indeed of any urban development at all. As Christopher Alexander states in his seminal work *A Pattern Language* (1977):

> *'Parks, street trees, and manicured lawns do very little to establish the connection between us and the land. They teach us nothing of its productivity, nothing of its capacities. Many*

*people who are born, raised, and live out their lives in cities
simply do not know where the food they eat comes from or what
a living garden is like. Their only connection with the productivity of the land comes from packaged tomatoes on the
supermarket shelf. But contact with the land and its growing
process is not simply a quaint nicety from the past that we can
let go of casually. More likely, it is a basic part of the process of
organic security. Deep down, there must be some sense of insecurity in city dwellers who depend entirely upon the supermarkets
for their produce.'*

## Eight Principles of Urban Food Production

In order for such urban food growing projects to become truly effective and
sustainable, they should observe the range of principles outlined below:

1   *Promote local wealth:* benefits must accrue to the local community in
    terms of cheaper food, paid jobs or the utilization of local skills. Food
    growing must be seen as being of benefit not only aesthetically or in terms
    of its wildlife value, but also in terms of financial benefit.
2   *Be environmentally sustainable:* although not all community gardens and
    other urban food growing projects prohibit the use of chemicals, many do.
    It is essential that just in the same way that intensive broadscale agricul-
    ture needs to examine its inputs and outputs in terms of their
    environmental impact and sustainability, so too should food production
    on any other scale.
3   *Use and build upon existing community networks:* urban areas usually
    have existing community groups, existing gardening societies and other
    community groups. To avoid 'reinventing the wheel' it is important that
    this network be tapped into as much as possible, and other groups are
    drawn in too.
4   *Promote and conserve biodiversity:* it is essential that any food growing
    project protect and enhance biodiversity – it should make use of
    'heirloom' seed varieties, avoid using F1 hybrid seeds and aim to save its
    own seeds. Biodiversity can also be encouraged by the creation of or the
    protection of existing green corridors to allow wildlife to move freely
    between different areas.
5   *Be affordable to all:* if the produce grown within a community is not
    affordable to that community then it becomes elitist and has failed in its
    principal aim, to provide the local community with fresh, affordable,
    locally grown produce.
6   *Integrate water, waste, employment, recreation, housing, energy genera-
    tion, wildlife and so on into a whole system:* through the application of
    intelligent and thoughtful design, an urban food growing project can
    achieve a number of aims. For example, food growing can be designed
    into buildings (see below), productive gardens can also purify waste water
    (through the integration of constructed wetland systems), can be social
    focus points for communities, can include playgrounds and can be part of
    a carefully planned network of urban 'wildlife corridors'.

7   *Nurture ethnic and cultural diversity:* urban areas generally include a wide mixture of ethic groups, and as Tara Garnett of the National Food Alliance notes, 'by growing food from their own culture, many people of ethnic origin can begin to reclaim and revalue their cultural identity' (Garnett, 1996).

8   *Contribute to an overall move towards sustainable development in the community:* food growing projects should ideally be part of a wider programme of measures dealing with recycling, transport, employment and a range of other issues. One of the simplest places to begin is with a composting programme for the composting of local organic wastes. Local authorities should put together whole packages of such measures designed to achieve this, viewing the separate parts as part of a whole rather than piecemeal projects. The various projects can be linked by an 'umbrella' organization which oversees the sharing of information and funding, and which regularly brings the different groups together to share their experiences.

## Permaculture, a Design Approach

Originally conceived in Australia in the 1970s as a 'perennial agriculture for human settlements', permaculture has evolved into a system for the conscious design of sustainable productive systems which integrate housing, people, plants, energy and water with sustainable financial and political structures. It offers an excellent approach to the design of the sustainable urban neighbour-hood which is working to actualize the eight principles above. Permaculture (from *perma*nent agri*culture* or *perma*nent *culture*) takes nature as its model, observing that natural systems, typified as climax forest, require no inputs bar sun and rain, create no pollution, have a huge natural biodiversity, are productive on an array of levels or 'niches', are permanent and are massively productive in terms of biomass. It aims to maximize the number of 'cycles', seeing any inputs not provided by another part of the system as unnecessary work created, and any output which do not form the inputs for another part of the system as pollution created.

Permaculture is founded on three ethics. The first, 'Earthcare', advocates strategies which repair and regenerate both the planet and all its living species. The second, 'peoplecare', states that the objectives of Earthcare cannot be separated from the repair of human communities and societies, and that not only is the simultaneous tackling of the human and the natural crises currently facing us desirable, the two are actually inseparable. The third ethic is that of 'fair shares', which means that any permaculture project must also play its part in making the world a more equitable place. This principle is often also described as meaning the giving away free of any surplus produce.

In relation to the planning of an urban neighbourhood, permaculture is often seen as being solely concerned with gardening. One often sees a small area of a larger piece of land being designated for permaculture, meaning a food garden, while the rest of the site is excluded from the design. However, permaculture offers an excellent tool for the integrated design of the whole urban eco-neighbourhood, founding the whole development on good ecological design and a sense of ethics.

Food production would not be seen in isolation from the other aspects of the development. Creating cycles of waste and water, maximizing the number of functions they perform creates many niches for food growing.

# FEEDING THE NEIGHBOURHOOD

Any strategy for the sustainable provision of food should be inclusive of all the members of the community and should aim to cater for their wide range of needs. I have therefore identified a range of strategies, which, when put together, would provide all of the members of the eco-neighbourhood (and beyond) with clean, fresh and affordable food.

## 'Grow your Own'

Clearly the best way of providing food in the urban eco-village would be for people to grow a large proportion of their own food needs. In countries where food is in short supply or where there is much poverty there is a clear motivation for the urban food grower. The United Nations Development Programme estimates that world-wide 800 million people are involved in urban agriculture (Smit, 1996). While this figure is very encouraging, it must be remembered that much of this is in poorer countries, and the challenge to be addressed in the planning of a European urban sustainable neighbourhood remains how one is to inspire in modern day western urban dwellers an interest in food growing. There are no figures for the amount of people actively growing food in the back gardens of the UK. How does one define food growing anyway? Is a window box of herbs food growing, or do we mean a certain amount of vegetables? To my knowledge, no-one has yet attempted to put a figure on this, the closest figure is probably that one in every 45 households has an allotment (Crouch, 1996).

## Productive Gardens

Back gardens can be highly productive and not necessarily involve a lot of work. A good example of this is the small intensively used urban garden of Michael and Julie Guerra in Hatfield in Hertfordshire. The garden, like many urban gardens, originally had very little topsoil and consisted almost entirely of concrete slabs and lawn. They prepared a permaculture design for the site and then 'created' the back garden over a weekend; all the raised beds were made and the paths were laid. A huge diversity of species was planted (with a high proportion of perennial species) and every available growing space utilized. The Guerras state that during the summer months their weekly food bill averaged £3 a head and required only about two hours work a week. The total annual productivity of their garden has been estimated as producing the annual equivalent of 15 tons of food per acre (Garnett, 1996). They are aiming, through the use of more cold frames to extend their growing season and wish to install a 'grey-water' system, which they feel would double the garden's productivity. It is an excellent example of just how productive a back garden can be.

## BOX 13.1 TEN PRINCIPLES OF PERMACULTURE DESIGN

There are ten design principles which Mollison (1988) defines as being central to permaculture design. The first, *'relative location'*, states that it is how elements of the design are sited in relation to other elements that is important, along with how many beneficial connections are established between them.

The second, *'multiple function'*, states that each element of the design should be sited/designed/selected to perform at least three functions. Tree planting can provide a windbreak, a harvest of fruit, nuts or coppice timber, animal fodder, soil stabilization, reduced heat loss from houses and a wildlife habitat.

The concept of *'multiple sources'* is that it is sensible and prudent to not rely on just one source of anything, for example relying solely on tap water for irrigation is a risky strategy, a combination of rainwater harvesting, ponds, diversion ditches, moisture-retaining mulches and grey water reuse is much more sensible.

Mollison's fourth principle is *'zone, sector, slope'*. Zone refers to placing elements of the design according to frequency of use, for example a herb bed needs to be nearer the house than a walnut tree. Sector refers to the analysis of the site so as to enable the control and utilization of the energies entering/passing through the site – cold winds, summer/winter sun etc. The utilization of slope is also important, it enables the designer to allow gravity to do much of the work which bad design requires the use of external energy to do.

*'Energy cycling'* aims to harvest nutrients and energy which would otherwise be lost from the design by building in as many cycles as possible.

*'Using biological resources'* means using the natural qualities of things, for example chickens like to scratch so put them onto vegetable beds in winter to turn them over, eat weed seeds and slugs.

*'Stacking'* is based on observations of natural systems as three-dimensional systems (eg forests) rather than one dimensional (a field of wheat, a lawn), and trying to replicate this where possible.

The eighth principle is that of *'diversity'*. Permaculture landscapes contain a very high diversity of plants, and protection of biodiversity is seen as being a high priority. Diversity is also important socially and economically – a wide range of small businesses being far preferable to one big employer.

*'Edge'* notes that in natural environments productivity increases at the edges between different ecosystems. In permaculture garden design, edges of ponds and beds tend to be curved and crenellated so as to maximize this effect.

Finally *'small scale'*. This means, in terms of gardening, starting at your back door and keeping a garden intensive and small. The application of permaculture design can result in highly productive intensive small gardens, keeping them small makes them easier to manage, easier to water and more pleasurable to work in.

### Allotments

In a very high density urban settlement, particularly one which makes use of a high level of flats or maisonettes, provision must be made for those with no access to a garden. This could be done through the provision of allotment spaces nearby, preferably within 200 metres of the house. This model has been used in many places, including Odense in Denmark, where allotments provide an attractive area around the flats and provide an important outdoor social focus for residents. Vancouver in British Columbia has built many high density housing developments as housing cooperatives and surrounded them with extensive gardens and other horticultural activities to great effect. Any new allotment space created as part of the neighbourhood should prohibit the use of biocides from the outset.

### Rooftop Gardening

Lack of garden space need not be an obstacle to the urban gardener. Garden spaces in such situations could also be created through imaginative building design. The use of rooftops for food production offers many benefits, it reduces rainfall runoff, 'greens' urban environments, increases wildlife interest, improves air quality and adds to the insulation of a house. It doesn't necessarily require strengthening of roofs, regular soils and composts can be used, and perlite and vermiculite can be added where lighter soils are required. St Petersburg in Russia now has 15 rooftop gardens growing a range of fruit and vegetables. The produce has been found to have lower levels of heavy metals than vegetables bought at the city market (Gavrilov, 1996). Switzerland is the first country to legislate in favour of rooftop gardens, a recent bylaw states that new buildings must be designed to relocate the greenspace covered by the building's footprint to their roofs, and existing buildings must green 20 per cent of their roofs. Rooftop gardening is now becoming an accepted element of urban ecological projects, for example the Halifax EcoCity Project in Adelaide is designed to include rooftop gardens to 'provide places to relax, grow food and nourish neighbourliness'. (Urban Ecology Australia, 1995)

### The Question of Yields

The issue of how much food a city could actually produce is still one in need of much research. At present the most productive system seems to be bio-intensive gardening, being developed in the US with considerable success. Yields have been recorded in a range of 2–16 times the US commercial mechanized levels, and in terms of home gardens, bio-intensive gardens have been highly successful too. It has been estimated that on an area of 100 square feet, with just 20 minutes input per day can produce up to 322lbs of vegetables and soft fruit during a four to six month growing season (Todd and Todd, 1994). This system uses only a quarter of the land used to grow vegetables conventionally.

## Local Food Growing Initiatives

### Community Gardens

Some residents of the eco-village may want to grow some of their food but they may not have a garden, they may be too busy to commit themselves to an intensively productive garden, or they may feel that, as yet, they don't have sufficient skills or knowledge to undertake vegetable growing on their own. One way of addressing this is by including a community garden. Community gardens are more established in the US but there are also some working models in the UK. Growing food together with others is increasingly becoming seen as a valuable tool for community development, as Georgia Ashby of Philadelphia Green, one of the US's largest community gardening programmes says 'gardening is the catalyst that brings residents from behind locked doors

## BOX 13.2 DAVIS HOMES, CALIFORNIA. CASE STUDY OF A FOOD PRODUCING NEIGHBOURHOOD

Davis Homes is a small housing subdivision of 240 homes on 63 acres near Sacramento, California. It was designed by Paul Calthorpe and Michael and Judy Corbett with the aim of being as self-sufficient as possible in food and energy. It was a highly innovative development in many ways, not least for its approach to food production.

The suburb is surrounded by a greenbelt of fruit trees; almonds, pineapple guavas, figs and plums (Kourik 1986). Each neighbourhood within the development has its own orchards. The fruit trees were all part of the original design and were paid for by the developers. They are maintained by a crew which works for the home-owners association and are paid partly by income from selling the trees' produce, which fetches a high price at the local markets. Many of the orchards are under-planted with clover instead of grass which needs less maintenance and which fixes nitrogen to the trees. The landscaping of the area as a whole features a wide range of edible and otherwise useful plants, leading to levels of plant and animal diversity approaching those of natural ecosystems (Kourik, 1986).

In terms of individual food gardens, at its outset the creation of an atmosphere of abundance and the encouragement of individuals to grow food, resulted in over 80 per cent of the homes having food gardens, averaging 55 feet by 85 feet in size (Kourik, 1986). In recent years however, much of this has declined as new people move in and as peoples' lifestyles change, and where once there were abundant gardens there are now lawns. Davis Homes is a good example of one of the main problems with urban food growing initiatives – how does one keep them going once they've started? The rapid turnover in allotments in urban areas is testimony to this. People may start a garden but then may have children, may get a new job, may simply get bored of gardening.

It is the broader landscaping concept that has been most successful in the long term though Davis has the feel more of a food forest than a housing project, and has proved very popular to home-buyers. Indeed, the problem if anything has been that it has proved so popular that house prices have risen to far in excess of the original prices, resulting in many of the original residents leaving. However, the project does prove that there is great demand for such development and indeed it is extraordinary that it is still the only development of its type in the US.

As a model for integrating productive landscaping, energy efficient housing (all the houses are designed to maximize passive solar for space and water heating), waste reduction (70 per cent of the population sort their rubbish for recycling; Girardet, 1992) and water conservation, Davis Homes is highly innovative and illustrates that food production can be a highly successful component of well-designed ecological housing projects. It also illustrates however the potential pitfalls of sustaining urban food production over periods of time (see Appendix 2, Davis).

to work together' (Hamilton, 1996). Community gardens can be any size and can be run in a variety of ways. A community centre may involve local residents in growing food, some of which may then be distributed among local people, either free or at reduced cost, or vacant land or the land of a community centre or church may be divided into plots.

At Springfield Community Gardens, a permaculture project in inner-city Bradford funded by City Challenge, volunteers grow food which is then given to a local social club for the elderly or is sold in local shops. At Calthorpe Community Gardens in central London, local people use plots to grow produce and are provided with seeds, tools and compost. The 'Green Thumb Community Gardening Programme' in New York is the largest municipally run community gardening project in the US, leasing, free of charge, over 1000 plots totalling over 125 acres (Garnett, 1996). It leases city owned land to local groups to turn them into flower and vegetables gardens, being provided with materials by the project. They also run a number of other successful projects, including the 'Urban Orchards' programme, which has planted nearly 2000 fruit trees since 1984, and 'Education in the Garden' which aims to involve local children and their schools in gardening.

Community gardens bring many benefits. According to Australian community gardening activists and permaculture designers Neal Bodel and Martin Anda:

> '...the values of community gardens are manifold. They provide opportunities for the public to garden, grow food, and work with nature, while at the same time living in a medium density urban environment. They provide a space for learning, social activity, cultural exchange, community art and "community science". They can provide a place of beauty for contemplation, or a pleasant stroll. In short, they are productive, empowering and regenerative of the human spirit.'

An urban sustainable neighbourhood could include one or more community gardens. They could either be operated as allotments or by a system in which one received produce in relation to how many hours work one had put in. The exact model adopted would be unique to each project.

## The Urban Market Garden

Most of our towns and cities used to be ringed with market gardens which supplied the local population with a percentage of their fresh fruit and vegetables. In some places this is still the case, for instance in China, 14 of the 15 largest cities are surrounded by belts of farmland leading to their being largely self-sufficient in food. The cities are designed to be as compact as possible, leaving the maximum amount of farmland possible (Girardet, 1992). However, the process of development usually results in such land being viewed as a 'soft touch' for developers. This happens world-wide, from the pressure from supermarkets on urban greenspace in the UK to the pressures on land caused by the massive urban expansion projects currently underway in China.

The revival of the urban market garden is an important aspect of the urban eco-neighbourhood. These days, with a heightened demand for fresh organic produce and the dire need for employment opportunities in urban areas, the recreation of some urban market gardens seems more promising. It is unlikely, however, that they would be able to meet all of the fruit and vegetable needs of the neighbourhood. How then could the land be most productively used?

The most logical approach to focus on crops which don't travel or store well. Staple crops like carrots, parsnips, onions and leeks take up a lot of space, are easy to store and can be produced very efficiently by nearby organic farmers. More worthy of attention is a wide range of salad crops, tomatoes, sweetcorn, soft fruits, green leafy vegetables and herbs. These are more productive on less ground and bring in good financial returns.

Problems could arise in terms of whether the gardens would need a heated greenhouse to enable all-year round production, and if so, how that heat is to be produced sustainably? I once visited a Combined Heat and Power (CHP) plant in Denmark, the interior of which was extremely warm all year round, and wondered why no-one had thought of this as a food-growing space...it was warm enough to produce a wide range of produce all year round. The application of sensible design could easily result in an 'edible CHP', and as many ecological planners now look to CHP as the most efficient way to heat new neighbourhoods and settlements this is a potential area for a further research.

Market gardens can be operated as a private business concern, as a cooperative, or by other groups, such as part of rehabilitation schemes for prisoners or as part of occupational therapy for the handicapped or those with psychiatric problems. Ruskin Mill in Nailsworth, Gloucestershire, for example, runs courses for young people with behavioural problems and learning difficulties which give training and experience of a wide range of crafts and skills, an integral part of which is food growing. Students work in the organic market garden, tend the sheep and cows, work in all aspects of the vegetable shop and also in the Mill's café, preparing and serving the food. In this way, the organizers state, 'disaffected young people can take part and take pride, in every aspect of food production from growing and rearing to harvesting and marketing, from preparing and presenting to eating and celebrating the end result' (Garnett, 1996).

### Involving the Next Generation

If the neighbourhood includes or is near to a school, involving the children in food production is very important. Michael Littlewood, an international environmental design consultant, has proposed that schools embrace the challenges of sustainable development and 'start not only teaching "designing in harmony with nature" but practising it too' (Littlewood, 1996). The creation of productive landscapes combining 'green' buildings, intensive food gardens, productive ponds, coppice woods, orchards, small livestock and so on would be an invaluable tool in terms of environmental education, as well as promoting healthy eating, providing life skills and what Neil D Hamilton calls 'agricultural literacy' (Hamilton, 1996). It could involve all areas of schools activity and produce could then be sold to local residents or parents. There are some schools experimenting with food growing projects, but as yet there are none who have taken this approach to the whole landscaping. Tara Garnett also suggests that schools, when awarding catering contracts, specify that food must be sourced locally where possible (Garnett, 1996).

### The City Farm

As the focal point for the development, a city farm can combine a number of uses. It can provide environmental education, a venue for courses and

---

### BOX 13.3 THE SUSTAINABLE FOOD CENTRE, AUSTIN, TEXAS

The Sustainable Food Centre has been developing innovative ways of supplying inner city urban dwellers with fresh organic produce as well as supporting local farms. The Centre encourages local stores to support local farms and to stock local produce. As a part of this they run a 'Buy Texas' campaign which now includes over 750 companies in promoting local produce (Colloff, 1996, p1).

They also set up the Eastside Community Farmers' Market where, during the summer months, farmers sell fresh produce to the residents of the poor East Side community. This led to a two acre site next to the Farmers' Market being developed as the Eastside Community Garden, making allotments available for individuals, families and organizations. Any surplus fruit and vegetables grown in the garden can be sold at the Farmers' Market.

The Centre has also pioneered a number of innovative food related projects. Their Cocina Alegre Food School teaches people healthy cooking on a low income and they are also considering an agricultural apprentice scheme for local teenagers. The Food Centre illustrates a combination of local food growing, involvement of local farmers and the involvement of and education of the local population.

---

meetings, a café as well as selling its produce. It could also be a community composting centre, it could include a reed bed/aquaculture system to purify and then utilize local waste water and it could provide workshop spaces for local small businesses. Through a careful examination of the surrounding community's needs and skills, a city farm could be designed to perform a large number of tasks.

## Beyond the Neighbourhood – Bringing the Food to the People

### Community Supported Agriculture

It is highly unlikely that a combination of all of the above would be able to produce all of a town or city's inhabitants' food needs. It is also important to consider the eco-village in terms of its effect on the surrounding rural community as well as the urban one. Therefore, support of local organic farmers is essential. One of the best ways of doing this is community supported agriculture, the most successful recent manifestation of which is generally known as 'vegetable box schemes', also known as 'standard ordering systems'. Here, weekly deliveries of boxes or bags of fresh, seasonal, locally grown vegetables are delivered to a number of drop-off points across the city. Buyers have no control over what produce they receive, but for many people this is one of the attractions of the scheme. There is also a more complicated version, the 'combined ordering system', which gives people more choice over what they receive and includes other organic produce as well as vegetables (Pullen, 1992).

It would also be possible to link the eco-village with an organic farm on the outskirts of the city. The farmer would have the benefit of a regular buyer of his produce and would be able to plan what to grow and when through discussion with the residents. The residents for their part would have a regular supply of fresh produce from a grower they know. This relationship has proved very successful in many places for individuals and smaller groups of people via veggie box schemes, and an urban eco-village seems the ideal opportunity to establish this twinning on a larger scale.

### Farmers' Markets

One problem some people find with the veggie boxes however, is that they have little say over what comes in the boxes, for a three week period every year they may have rather a lot of a vegetable that they don't like. One way around this is through the establishment of farmers' markets. In the US, farmers' markets are very successful and are growing rapidly. By the end of 1993 there were 1755 local farmers' markets in the US, enabling over 3.5 million consumers to obtain at least a portion of their food from them (Hamilton, 1996). Farmers' markets are now beginning to appear in the UK, the first started in September 1997 in Bath. It was organized by a collection of local community groups and the local council's Agenda 21 unit. The first market was attended by over 4000 people and was widely reported by the media. One stallholder was reported as saying 'Its such a lovely atmosphere. Its fun to be here, much busier than I had expected. Its like being on holiday, with people laughing and talking to each other. It feels so open and cheerful' (Tutt and Morris, 1998).

### Farmer–Consumer Cooperatives

An approach which has proved very successful in Japan and elsewhere is that of farmer-consumer cooperatives. In Japan the concept is now firmly established, with over 660 producers providing over 11 million people with food (Clunies-Ross and Hildyard, 1992). The system is quite simple. Groups of six to 13 families make a bulk order once a month of a range of produce, which is then delivered at different times depending on its perishability. One of the principles of the system is that only one variety of each product is available, this gives the cooperative more leverage in terms of bulk buying as well as in asking producers to ensure the produce is chemical-free.

### Ethical Shopping

Conventional shops too have a role to play. If the neighbourhood is to have its own food shop, it can be encouraged to source local produce and seek to sell as high a percentage of ethically and sustainably produced foodstuffs as possible. The model developed by the Out of this World, the 'ethical grocers chain', is a good model for how large stores can put ethical concerns as their priority. Out of this World is a consumer cooperative which is owned by its 15,000 members who are both shoppers and shareholders. Out of this World selects its produce in accordance with five main criteria which are 'that products make a positive contribution to healthy eating, animal welfare, fair trade, environmental sustainability and the local community' (Out of this World, 1997). Their shops, of which there are now a number throughout the UK, also seek to stock locally grown produce where possible.

## CONSIDERATIONS FOR DESIGNERS

What can be learned from the above, and what can the principles of permaculture add to our approach to designing food strategies for the eco-neighbourhood? What follows are some strategies for designers and developers to consider at the planning stages.

Designers should strive to integrate approaches to food, housing, water, energy and waste, considering how all the elements can be interconnected to create the maximum amount of cycles and the highest level of productivity. If density is to be high, consideration should be given to ways of compensating for this, for example in terms of productive parks, rooftop gardening and so on. When designing the layout of the whole development, designers should maximize the number of housing plots with south facing gardens, and preferably plant trees to the north side to create sun traps.

Tree planting should be made up of fruiting or otherwise useful species, with species needing more attention placed nearer to housing. Trees should also be sited to perform a variety of functions, windbreaks, privacy, soil stabilization and so on.

If food growing is made the focal point (physically) of the development, surrounding housing can be designed so that the area is always overlooked, thus reducing vandalism and creating a feeling of connection to nature for the residents. Another way to deter vandalism and theft is to remove the labels from fruit and other high value trees; if people don't know what a tree is, it is harder for them to sell on to other people.

The concept of 'multiple function' outlined above can also be applied to ponds and lakes. If the site has an area which is susceptible to flooding, this could be made into a lake, which could be designed to produce food and other useful crops, as well as being part of a sewage purification system. This lake could also be sited to reflect winter sun into buildings, provide a leisure facility and irrigation for other food gardens. An aquaculture city farm, for instance, could serve many different functions. If the development is along the edge of a river, lake or docks, John and Nancy Jack Todd propose that food could be grown on floating barges which could 'line the harbours and sell their produce of fish, flowers, vegetables and herbs' (Todd and Todd, 1994).

A system of composting and recycling would vastly reduce the amount of waste generated by the residents and provide compost and other materials to enrich the soil. Designers can allocate a recycling area as well as an area for composting, in an area accessible to all but shielded by trees so as to contain any possible smells and visual intrusion. The design of the development cannot make people separate their waste for recycling but house design can include adequate kitchen space for a number of different bins. Community recycling schemes can much reduce the amount of waste households produce. The WyeCycle scheme in the village of Wye in Kent estimates that households making full use of the scheme can reduce their waste by 90 per cent (Hoyland, 1996). Community Compost, a community composting project in the Forest of Dean, collects waste from two villages, kitchen waste once a week and garden waste once a month. The resultant compost is sold to local people, and the scheme also sells biodynamic vegetables grown at Oaklands Park, a nearby

Camphill Community through a box scheme that runs alongside the waste collection. The scheme has created part-time employment for two people (Hoyland, 1996).

## MANAGEMENT ISSUES ARISING

To create a sustainably fed neighbourhood or to retrofit an existing one based on the above is clearly feasible, as well as desirable. The first question that arises however is whether there is a market for such neighbourhoods. It is my belief that there would be a very strong interest in them, that their time has arrived. In terms of new social housing projects which not only tackle homelessness but also address many of the other chronic problems affecting urban areas such as malnutrition, unemployment, poor water quality, lack of greenspace and so on, the 'business-as-usual' approach is clearly inappropriate. Intelligently designed urban agriculture can tackle many of these problems. A number of other considerations then arise which can be looked at in three stages. The first is those which relate to the initial stages of the development, the second is those of relevance to the establishment phase and the third is those which relate to the project once it is up and running.

### Initial Stages of Development

In some developments the issue may arise of who the neighbourhood's residents are to be. Either an approach can be taken such as at the Lebensgarten urban ecological community in Germany and in some co-housing projects, where people are chosen who are already sympathetic to the project's aims. The alternative, which would be the case on larger developments, particularly those with a social housing element, would be trying to involve and educate incoming residents. If the developers knew who the residents were to be, they could involve them in the design process. There could also be a course and a 'user's manual' given to people on arrival, to teach them about the site design and how they might live and operate in a way most in harmony with the aims of the development. This is an approach which is now used with great success in rural eco-villages in Australia such as Crystal Waters and Kookaburra Park.

Setting goals for the amount of food you intend to grow and obtain from other sources as well as setting out how, practically, this will grow with time is a very useful practice. This will keep the project realistic and also keep it moving towards a goal. The Los Angeles Eco-Village project for example, have set themselves the initial goal of increasing neighbourhood organic food production to provide 10 per cent of the diet for 20 people (the eco-village group), and to obtain another 10 per cent of their diet via neighbourhood food buying cooperatives.

### Establishment

When the village's food gardens are being created, employ as many future residents as possible to do the work. This is only really possible in a centrally planned development though, a private sector development could involve local community/volunteer groups. One approach used by Catherine Sneed in her urban gardening work with ex and current prison inmates in San Francisco is to get prison inmates from particular neighbourhoods to plant trees in those neighbourhoods. 'No-one messes with our trees!' she says.

Each site will be different in terms of whether gardens will need to be fenced. Where it is necessary, aim through design to fence as sensitively as possible. Screen fences with fruiting hedges and try to use wood instead of metal.

Other approaches which may prove useful at this stage in the development are giving free trees to residents from an on-site tree nursery and involving local schools in tree planting. It is important too during the construction phase of the development that care is taken not to damage any existing trees, hedges or natural features and that great care is taken to compact only the minimum of soil.

There may be concern also about contamination of soil and the health risks associated with growing vegetables in an urban environment. Care should be taken to screen roads so as to form a barrier for pollutants. Lead, one of the most harmful pollutants in terms of human health, does not travel very far from roads and is quite easily screened out.

### Up and Running

If the development contains low-cost housing, developers may like to consider ways to retain it as low cost, a development of this kind will be very popular and house prices will rapidly rise. The project may therefore start out with some affordable low cost housing but end up ten years later with exclusive expensive homes. It is also important to make every effort to involve residents in the management of the project.

## Conclusion

I have argued here that for the designers and developers of an urban sustainable neighbourhood to take clear and effective strategies to the sustainable provision of its residents' food is both essential and practical. If the development is to truly become a part of the solution to our current ecological decline then it must address the whole area of food and land use. People like greenery, they like contact with nature. It is a simple point but one which much modern development seems to forget. There is a strong argument that almost the entire population has a strong desire or even psychological need for contact with nature (Johnston, 1990) and there is an equally strong argument that separation from nature is a major factor in anti-social behaviour.

Although much can be done at the design stage, the main challenge is residents' lifestyle choices and patterns of behaviour remaining true to the ecological aims of the development. If the developers, be they private or public sector, are truly committed to the project being an 'ecological/sustainable neighbourhood', it is important that they offer some sort of education or awareness raising programme to incoming residents. As has been mentioned earlier, the running of a permaculture design course would fulfil this role excellently.

The time is right for developments which take an innovative approach to how it feeds its residents. The aim of many new developments seems to be to site them within easy reach of existing jobs, rather than creating new jobs as part of the development. To adopt the integrated approach outlined in this chapter creates a wide range of niches for employment creation, both in the production of produce and then secondary 'spin off' jobs processing that produce into higher value items.

The range of approaches and possibilities which I have set out here are practical and tried and tested. The more they are implemented and proliferated, the more commonplace they become, until, we can hope, we reach a point where, to quote Christopher Alexander, 'it becomes as natural for families to have their own vegetables as their own air' (Alexander, 1977).

# 14 Planning Local Movement Systems

*Tony Hathway*

*'Motor vehicles create new distances which they alone can shrink – they create them for all, but can shrink them only for the few'* Ullich (1974)

This chapter focuses on movement within neighbourhoods. It starts by examining the wider issues, such as the growth of motor vehicle travel that has dominated towns and cities in recent years. This is followed by a review of policies and guidance that have been introduced to guide us towards a new, environmentally friendly approach to transport. The main body of the chapter explores local movement patterns and the opportunities for implementing new access strategies. This includes a review of options and measures to promote walking, cycling, public transport and provide for essential vehicle movement. The chapter concludes with advice on producing a coordinated set of proposals.

## More Movement at a Price

A visitor from another planet might reasonably conclude that the last few decades have been dedicated to satisfying the urban dweller's passion for movement by motor vehicle. Enormous investment has been poured into building and widening roads, creating vast areas for the parking of cars and designing residential and shopping areas to cater for the needs of the motor vehicle. The character of towns, villages and the countryside has been radically altered. The pleasure of walking and cycling has decreased as journeys have become less direct, more dangerous and polluted. Many recent developments put the vehicle first leaving people to negotiate their way past motor vehicles in unpleasant surroundings to reach their destination. All too often, public spaces have become compounds for cars rather than places for people.

Fortunately there is a desire to move away from this concept of providing free and unlimited movement for vehicles. A more rational approach is emerging which focuses on providing access for people whilst causing minimum damage to communities, our heritage and the environment. However, this will not be an easy task as it entails reversing a very strong trend of accelerating traffic growth in recent years. People are now travelling further and more often than in the past. Since 1965 there has been a 25 per cent increase in the number of journeys over one mile and the distance travelled has increased by 75 per cent (POST, 1995). Car ownership has grown dramatically making it the dominant form of personal transport. In 1956, less than one in four households owned a car. By 1994 more than two in three owned at least one car (DETR, 1997a). There is now a growth in multiple car households as partners and older children acquire their own vehicles. Almost no households owned two or more cars in 1956 but by 1994 nearly one in four did so. This increase in car ownership has resulted in seven out of ten journeys of a mile or more being made by car (RCEP, 1994). As a result travel by bus and coach now accounts for only 6 per cent of distance travelled. Other surveys confirm a decrease in walking and cycling journeys.

There is no doubt that the motor vehicle brings great advantages to its users. The challenge that now faces governments, communities and individuals is how to maintain this high quality of movement alongside a high quality of life. Many people are aware of the detrimental effects that excess mobility is having on their lives. Subjective responses by the human senses are sufficient indicators to demonstrate the extent that our quality of life is being eroded:

- *sight:* removal of attractive buildings and natural habitats and their replacement with dull, stained road surfaces, signs, lines, and traffic clutter; unattractive bridges, car parks; light pollution at night;
- *sound:* peaceful locations disturbed by the drone of traffic, revving engines, slammed doors, horns, sirens and alarms;
- *smell:* fumes from passing traffic, idling engines, fuel and amateur car repairs;
- *touch:* obstruction by parked vehicles causing nuisance to the partially sighted, elderly, infirm, parents with young children; dirt and grease on walking surfaces; physical impact and personal injury from moving vehicles;
- *taste:* grit and unpleasant tastes from air pollution, ingestion of harmful substances such as lead and particulates containing carcinogens;
- *sixth sense:* psychological and emotional reactions to traffic such as fear and intimidation.

There are other less obvious repercussions on lifestyle arising from the type of journey that people make. The young and the elderly and those without a car or driving licence may face difficulties in leading a full and independent life. Older people may find it difficult crossing heavily trafficked roads or using pedestrian bridges and underpasses. Parents may be concerned about the safety of allowing their children to cycle to school or visit friends near a busy road. As more and more people make journeys by car and have the opportunity to travel further, there is a chance that local shops and facilities will close putting further pressure on those who rely on these essential facilities. Furthermore, this increased motorization is sterilizing one of our most valuable assets – land. In England alone, in the second half of the 1980s an area equivalent to the size of Bristol was taken for road building and parking (DETR, 1998b).

The implications of increased motorized travel are not just experienced locally but have repercussions globally. Transport pollution contributes to global warming. About one-fifth of the carbon dioxide in the atmosphere arising from human activity can be attributed to motor vehicles (World Bank, 1996). Road Transport also produces one-third of the CFCs which contribute to depletion of the ozone layer. It is also responsible for half of the nitrogen oxides which lead to continental scale acidification and ecological damage (World Bank, 1996). Whilst individuals and communities can make their own contribution to tackling these problems, a positive lead is required at national level.

## POLICIES AND TARGETS FOR A BETTER FUTURE

The need to recognize and tackle the worsening global environmental issues was taken up by a number of international task forces in the 1980s and 90s. The United Nations Conference on Environment and Development which was held in Rio in 1992 ('the Earth Summit') pulled together many key issues and has led to the subsequent setting of both national and local objectives and targets. One of the most thorough examinations of transport policy in the UK was carried out by the Royal Commission on Environmental Pollution, who proposed eight objectives for transport policy:

1    To ensure that an effective transport policy at all levels of government is integrated with land use policy and gives priority to minimizing the need for transport and increasing the proportion of trips made by environmentally less damaging modes;
2    To achieve standards of air quality that will prevent damage to human health and the environment;
3    To reduce carbon dioxide emissions from transport;
4    To reduce noise nuisance from transport;
5    To improve the quality of life, particularly in towns and cities, by reducing the dominance of cars and lorries and providing alternative means of access;
6    To increase the proportions of personal travel and freight transport by environmentally less damaging modes and to make the best use of existing infrastructure;
7    To halt any loss of land to transport infrastructure in areas of conservation, cultural, scenic or amenity value unless the use of the land for that purpose has been shown to be the best practicable environmental option;
8    To reduce substantially the demands which transport infrastructure and the vehicle industry place on non-renewable materials (RCEP, 1994).

The Royal Commission recommended quantified targets for moving towards their objectives. The UK Government has produced several helpful strategies such as the UK National Air Quality Strategy and the Transport White Paper (*A New Deal for Transport*) which guide future policy. These identify some targets and suggest others for the future:

*   *greenhouse gases:* legally binding target to reduce emissions to 12.5 per cent below 1990 levels by the period 2008 to 2012 and a domestic aim to

reduce carbon dioxide emissions by 20 per cent by 2010;
- *air pollution:* National Air Quality Strategy encompasses health-based objectives for a range of pollutants to be met by 2005;
- *EU vehicle and fuel quality standards:* to reduce toxic emissions and noise from new vehicles;
- *cycling:* double cycling by 2002, doubling again by 2012;
- *accidents:* reducing deaths and injuries from road accidents by one-third (DETR, 1998).

Local transport policies will be expected to meet these targets and reflect other government guidance. The Traffic Reduction Act (1997) requires local authorities to identify the future amount of traffic in their areas. The background guidance to the Act originally set a target of a 10 per cent reduction in the level of traffic by 2010. Local authorities may indicate their commitment to change by setting their own standards/targets in the five year local transport plan. Examples are as follows:

1  To reduce the proportion of journeys undertaken by car from x per cent to y per cent in the urban area and from p per cent to q per cent in the town centre by year n;
2  To increase the proportion of passengers carried by bus from x per cent to y per cent by year n;
3  To increase the tonnage of freight carried by rail (water) from x per cent to y per cent by year n;
4  To increase cycle use to x per cent of all urban journeys by year n;
5  To reduce cycle (pedestrian) deaths from x to y by year n.

The UK Government in its Transport White Paper states that it 'wants transport to contribute to our quality of life not detract from it'. The main emphasis of the 'new deal' has been to guide transport decision making towards an integrated transport policy (DETR, 1998b):

- integration within and between different types of transport;
- integration with the environment;
- integration with land use planning;
- integration with policies for education, health and wealth creation.

The recent introduction of these new objectives, targets and guidelines from national and local government provides encouragement for the design of eco-friendly settlements. However, the real test is to provide a level of eco-friendly movement to, from and within the settlement that meets the individual needs of all who live within and visit it.

## UNDERSTANDING LOCAL MOVEMENT PATTERNS

A successful, sustainable settlement is most likely to consist of a wide mix of people of different age, income and background. As part of their normal lifestyle they will make a variety of journeys. For example, children will travel to nursery school, primary school, secondary school, college. Older people will visit shops and places of recreation and entertainment. Some people will be self employed and require occasional journeys to collect/deliver materials. Other journeys will be made to meetings or a place of business away from the settlement. In addition, visitors will need to enter the settlement to meet residents and deliver/collect small and large packages. All of these journeys have the potential of creating conflict with the underlying principles of an eco-neighbourhood. The key to success is to:

- encourage people to walk and cycle;
- reduce the number of journeys that are made by motor vehicle;
- keep journeys as short as possible;
- combine motorized journeys so that the maximum number of people travel together (ideally on an efficient public transport system).

This will happen only if there is a successful understanding of the travel needs of the local community. A start can be made by listing the range of journeys that are required to maintain a satisfactory quality of life. Some journeys are not just made for the functional purpose of travelling between A and B but contain other benefits eg a chance to meet people or take some exercise. Other journeys may have arisen out of habit and may no longer be necessary eg driving a child to school. It is worth spending time to get this information right as it provides the essential building blocks of a sustainable transport policy. It may seem a lengthy process but a lot of effort is put into considering other aspects of development. It is worth comparing the amount of time that is devoted to studying the energy consumption and emissions of individual buildings with the time allocated to researching an energy efficient transport policy that meets every essential need. An accurate list of journeys by purpose is an essential pre-requisite of an efficient transport strategy.

Successful transport measures should evolve from the needs of the people using it, rather than letting the transport infrastructure determine how people behave. The optimum travel patterns can be developed from an understanding of: the type of person(s) travelling; the purpose of the journey; the length of journey; the time of day; and, whether the journey is independent or part of a chain of linked trips.

The type of people travelling can be considered in as much detail as appropriate but it is important to ensure that all key types of journeys are considered by both residents and visitors:

- *residents:* eg parent with pushchair, unaccompanied children, family group, single adult, older people, mobility impaired;
- *visitors:* eg residential and business visitors, deliveries and collections, service/maintenance and emergency vehicle visits.

Defining the purpose of the journey will help establish any constraints on the traveller such as carrying heavy shopping or delivering large parcels. It can also assist in identifying probable common destinations for journeys. Care should be taken against jumping to conclusions about the effect these journeys have. It is widely assumed that the journey to work by commuters is the major cause of traffic pollution but more journeys are made for shopping and social purposes than for commuting. Commuting by car accounts for less than one in ten of all journeys (FOE, 1998).

Once the number and types of journey have been identified they can be further examined to asses the most appropriate method of travel. Key factors here are the length of journey and time of day. Shorter journeys can be made attractive to those travelling on foot or by cycle. The time of travel can be compared to explore the opportunities for shared journeys (either between individuals or on an organized basis). However not all journeys will be independent. Some trips will lead to or from another location as part of a chain of visits making sharing more complex.

Each individual will choose the method of travel that best meets their needs. This will depended on a number of factors that the individual will examine to assess how the opportunities and constraints presented by different transport options influence them.

# PLANNING FOR NON-MOTORIZED AND MOTORIZED TRANSPORT OPTIONS

## *Walking*

Walking is an essential and frequently used method of transport. Over 80 per cent of journeys under one mile long are made on foot (IHT, 1997). Virtually all trips contain an element of walking. Journeys by public transport and car involve walking even if it is just to get to the bus stop or car park. Unfortunately, little attention is often paid to these important journeys. This may in some part be due to the National Travel Survey, which only considers journeys in excess of one mile (1.6km). The routes that are designed to be followed by pedestrians are often obscure or require a detour to avoid traffic. More direct 'unofficial' routes can place the pedestrian at greater risk or involve walking on unattractive surfaces. The walker is left feeling that priority is given to the motor vehicle and that the pedestrian is only considered when all other decisions have been made. Very often it is the most vulnerable members of society, the young and old, who are placed at greatest risk by taking the obvious short cut.

Most walking journeys are fairly short in length, with almost three-quarters less than one mile and 40 per cent less than half a mile long (Hillman and Walley, 1979). This means that if people are to be encouraged to walk, facilities should be located within easy walking distance. The generally accepted preferred maximum walking distance when planning facilities is a quarter of a mile or 400 metres (Barton et al, 1995). However, the decision to walk will not just be influenced by distance. Factors such as safety, convenience, comfort and quality of environment will all play a part. One of the main reasons given by parents for not letting their children walk unaccompanied to school is fear of traffic accidents or abduction by strangers. Older people also feel threatened by large vehicles moving close to them or by cycles suddenly appearing next to them. Failing sight, hearing and mobility can make crossing the road a major hazard for the elderly.

This perceived threat from traffic can lead to a change in social activity. Parents will not allow their children to visit friends who live on the far side of a busy road. Older people will change their shopping habits and only visit facilities on their side of the road. This leads to an effect called community severance. These effects have been well researched and illustrated by Appleyard (1986) and Clark et al (1991). Whilst this concept is carefully considered by the government in the design and upgrading of new roads it is important to monitor the build up of traffic on lesser roads to prevent the traffic on these becoming a barrier to pedestrian movement.

Pedestrian routes need to be attractive to the user. Not every person will value the same experience. Whilst a direct route will be appreciated by those in a hurry this can appear very boring to those with more time to spare. Young children will want to explore, hide behind bushes, climb on walls and steps. Older people may prefer a flat or gentle gradient with the opportunity to rest now and again in an attractive location where they can observe activity or a peaceful view. The design of successful pedestrian routes will take all of these (sometimes conflicting) characteristics into account whilst avoiding places and features that might encourage anti social behaviour. Generally as a pedestrian route becomes busier, people feel safer and the risk of anti social behaviour declines.

Problems can arise when pedestrian routes meet vehicular traffic. There are four ways of resolving potential conflicts:

1   *Horizontally:* a segregation strip or verge in a different material can provide a comforting feeling of protection. In very busy areas some form of railing or barrier may become necessary;
2   *Vertically:* the traditional kerb provides some protection but a slightly higher raised footway can lift the pedestrian above the worst fumes and give greater security. In the past, pedestrian bridges and underpasses have been designed for the benefit of the motor vehicle leaving the pedestrian with a change in gradient and extra distance to travel. This need not be the case. Structures can be built that keep the walkway direct and flat whilst the traffic is taken over or under the pedestrians. Some good examples exist in Beijing (Hathway 1994 and Shen, 1994);
3   *Time:* light controlled crossings allow time for the pedestrian to cross the road. Newer designs of pedestrian crossings (puffins) can monitor the number of pedestrians waiting by the kerb and also hold the traffic on red until the last person has crossed. This is of particular benefit to older people. Temporary street closures are possible at predetermined times of the day (eg for shopping) or time of year (eg play streets);
4   *Share:* vehicles and pedestrians can use the same surface area. By reducing the speed of traffic priority can be given to safe and comfortable pedestrian movement. There are now many examples of traffic calmed roads, mews courts and bus-only streets where pedestrians and vehicles mix together successfully.

The fundamental principles of good pedestrian planning are:

- a legible network of routes that will be well used and meet at recognized focal points;
- clear signing and sufficient night time lighting to encourage use;
- careful design of surfaces and surrounding vegetation to create a pleasing and interesting environment whilst not encouraging antisocial behaviour;
- routes that are relatively direct, avoid significant changes in level and provide easy access for pushchairs and wheelchairs;
- enhanced personal security by placing routes so that they are overlooked by nearby buildings (eyes on the street);
- avoiding conflict between pedestrians and traffic, with the pedestrian route taking design priority at crossing points.

## Cycling

The cycle offers enormous potential for travel within neighbourhoods. It is the quickest method of travel over short distances. It is virtually pollution free and requires much less land than motor vehicles. A four metre wide cycle path can carry five times the number of people catered for in cars on a road twice as wide and ten cycles can be parked in the space required by one car (Cleary and Hillman, 1992). For many years, sales of new cycles have exceeded new car registrations. It is estimated that there are now nearly 20 million cycles in the UK but sadly few of these regularly find their way onto the roads (Bicycle Association, 1996). A depressing fact is that cycle mileage has fallen by 13 per cent in ten years despite investment in new cycles and facilities. The result is that cycle use currently accounts for just 2 per cent of all journeys (National Travel Survey, 1994–96).

Two major concerns seem to deter many people from cycling – safety and security. Many new cyclists feel justifiably threatened by motorized traffic. Riding a cycle on normal roads is ten times more dangerous than travelling by car. Having spent several hundreds of pounds on a new cycle the owner will want to park it in a secure place. Theft is a major problem. Some 200,000 cycles are reported stolen each year (as many again are not reported) and usually less than 10 per cent are recovered (DoT, 1996). Further deterrents to cycling are the effort required to cycle up steep hills and the effects of inclement weather. This is often not helped by the lack of convenient facilities to (shower and) change clothes on arrival.

This current downward trend in cycling could be tackled by investing in proper facilities for cycling. Cycle routes can be built away from other traffic or directed along normal roads where traffic calming has reduced the speed of motor vehicles. This might encourage the 90 per cent of children who own cycles (Hillman et al, 1991) to use them. In Odense, where over 50 per cent of teenage children cycle to school, new safe routes have been introduced along calmed roads and short lengths of separate track. This has led to the number of accidents being reduced by 82 per cent (Anderson, 1997). Safe routes to other facilities could lead to a considerable growth in cycling. A report by the Cyclists' Touring Club (Rowell and Fergusson, 1991) suggests that 40–50 per cent of all non-walking journeys of less than three miles could be undertaken by cycle.

The fear of theft would be lessened by the provision of secure cycle parking stands and lockers. In high use areas, supervised cycle parks with weather protection can be provided. Leicester Bike Park has 100 racks in a locked room. Japan has taken cycle parking very seriously by providing nearly 9000 specially designed cycle parks of which 829 are multi-storey and 35 fully computerized (PADECO, 1994).

The cost of providing most facilities for the bicycle can be relatively small. The engineer for Stevenage, who built 24 miles of segregated cycle route in the town, claimed that he provided 'motorways for the price of footpaths'. Cycle lanes, marked by a white line, can give cyclists some advantage on busy roads but not all drivers allow sufficient clearance. Cycle lanes should be wide enough to avoid intimidation from motorists and allow clearance around obstacles near the kerb. A minimum width of 1.5 metres, preferably 2.0 metres is recommended (IHT, 1997). Cycling in bus lanes can make the rider feel safer but there is no substitute for a completely segregated cycle track. in some cases cyclists and pedestrians can share the same route but care needs to be taken to avoid conflict with the more vulnerable pedestrians eg the partially sighted.

A major concern of many cyclists is the negotiation of complex junctions. Signal controlled junctions can include special provisions for cyclists such as advanced stop lines or 'cycle by-passes' to help cyclists filtering left or going straight ahead. Generally it is best to keep cycle routes away from difficult junctions and provide crossing points in a less dangerous position. Special light controlled crossings can be provided solely for the use of cyclists or combined with pedestrians as a 'Toucan' crossing. Guidance on measures to assist cycling is provided in documents by the Bicycle Association (1996) and ARUP (1997).

Many opportunities exist in an eco-friendly environment to encourage the use of cycling. Several cities have experimented with 'public cycles' that can be used by anyone. These are usually brightly painted and released by inserting a coin into a lock. Copenhagen has provided 2000 'city bikes' (Eir, 1994). Sandnes in Norway with 200 public cycles is carefully monitoring the success of their scheme (Eikland, 1997). The newest 'cycle club' schemes use smart card technology to reduce theft and irresponsible use. Facilities are provided in several countries to attach cycles to busses and trams. In Hanover and Stuttgart trailers are towed behind the vehicle (Brunsing, 1997). In Havana, Cuba, a conventional bus has its seats removed and ramps installed to convert it into a cycle bus. It carries 3.2 million cycles and riders a year (Hathway, 1994). Pedal power can also provide pollution free public transport. Pedicabs, which are a highly geared and sophisticated form of rickshaw operate in New York and are being introduced into other western cities (Hook, 1994). Other novel concepts include cargo cycles (for delivering heavy loads) and wheelchair trikes (Roelofs, 1996).

By incorporating these various opportunities it is possible to plan a cycle network that attracts a growing number of users. However it is important at the outset to identify the main users and destinations. How many trips are to work, school or for recreation? Where are the locations that will attract cyclists – college, shopping centre, railway station? The following criteria for cycle network design are summarized from *Sustainable Settlements* (Barton et al, 1995):

- is direct access provided along segregated or traffic calmed routes?
- are routes as continuous as possible with few stops, particularly at junctions?

- are separate lanes or paths provided where there is a potential conflict with motor traffic?
- is diversion from the most direct line kept to a minimum?
- are routes comfortable, with attention given to grade, surfaces and micro-climate?
- are routes attractive, interesting, well maintained and free from fumes, noise and turbulence caused by traffic?
- are routes linked to conveniently located cycle parks or secure sheds that protect from theft and rain?

### Access to Public Transport

Public transport has declined in recent years as more and more people have made journeys by car. Bus travel was the most used form of transport in the 1950s but local buses now only account for 6 per cent of journeys and 4 per cent of distance travelled (RCEP, 1997). If more people are to change back to public transport we need to understand how they make their choice of travel. Four groups of characteristics can be identified that influence choice: type of person; journey characteristics; the transport system; and external influences.

### Type of Person
- *Personal characteristics* such as age, gender, health, ability to drive, occupation and self importance all influence the decision to use public transport;
- *Household influences* include availability of a car, income, size of family group.

### Journey Characteristics
- *Purpose* eg journey to work, business trip, shopping, visiting friends, recreation;
- *Length of journey*, letting the train take the strain on a long journey;
- *The time of travel* eg during the day or at weekends can discourage or encourage car use.

### Transport System
- *Route:* does a public transport service travel to that destination?
- *Cost:* is the perceived cost of a public transport journey cheaper than the cost of driving and parking a car?
- *Speed:* which method of transport will give the quickest door to door journey time including waiting and walking time?
- *Comfort:* will the vehicle be clean, comfortable and pleasant to travel in? Are waiting and interchange facilities comfortable?
- *Reliability:* can the car or public transport service be relied upon to reach the destination at the desired time?
- *Safety:* does the method of travel offer threats to personal security or injury?
- *Information:* is information available on service frequency, waiting time, possible delays?

## External Influences

- *Access:* is it easy to travel to and from the bus stop or car park? are there steps, steep gradients or busy roads to negotiate?
- *Weather:* is there protection from adverse weather conditions whilst walking to and waiting for the service?
- *Environment and health:* is there a positive decision to use the journey to improve one's health or the quality of the environment?
- *Density of development:* are there sufficient potential users in close proximity to provide a frequent, viable service?

Most of the decisions that influence the provision of a good public transport system will be beyond the control of a relatively small group of residents in an eco-neighbourhood. It is therefore very important that the initial location for the settlement is selected to take maximum advantage of neighbouring public transport services. There might be some opportunity to influence the type of public transport vehicle that is used eg electric powered, hybrid magnetic motor or flywheel driven. Where conventional buses are used, priority should be provided on normal roads. Bus lanes are capable of reducing bus journey times by up to 30 per cent and bus emissions by up to 35 per cent (Bayliss, 1990). Further improvements can be made with the introduction of selective vehicle detection (SVD) which allows priority at junctions. SVD is widely used on trams and buses in French, German and Swiss cities. In the Ruhr area of Germany, average speeds have increased by a further 20 per cent with SVD (OECD, 1994). The main local consideration within the settlement will be to make access to the service as convenient and attractive as possible.

Some helpful planning and design principles to encourage public transport use include:

- bring public transport services into the heart of the settlement and group major activities along its route;
- ensure that every home is within 400 metres of a stop/boarding place;
- provide direct, safe and attractive routes to boarding places avoiding major changes of level;
- position boarding places where they can be easily recognized and observed;
- provide seats and protection from inclement weather at boarding places plus secure cycle parking facilities at major stops;
- reduce the risk of delay to public transport services by providing segregated or priority routes for public transport vehicles;
- keep users informed with a good passenger information service (preferably interactive).

## Providing for Cars and Other Motor Vehicles

Whilst some residents may decide to have nothing to do with motor vehicles, provision will still have to be made for essential and unexpected traffic. Visitors will arrive by car, deliveries will be made and residents will probably move the contents of their home in a large van. More importantly the emergency services will require relatively unhindered access to all parts of the settlement. However, the motor vehicle consumes vast areas of valuable space. A study in Germany estimated that the space needs of a car are around 11 square metres (msq) when parked and 169msq at a speed of 50km/h. This compares with an average living space of 35msq plus 0.5msq of open space per head (Ullrich, 1997). The introduction of smaller vehicles and motorcycles can assist but this balance between vehicle dominated space and peopled space has to be addressed. The challenge will be to create external spaces that reflect the ethos of the neighbourhood and allow human activity to take place without threat or disturbance from motor vehicles. This can be achieved with minimal adverse effect by limiting the number of vehicles and controlling their movement.

Vehicles will only be able to stay in the settlement if there is somewhere for them to stop. The deliberate design of the number and location of parking spaces will enable the number of vehicles to be controlled. Careful design of other communal spaces can make illegal parking either physically difficult or embarrassingly antisocial. Some new settlements such as those in Edinburgh, Berlin and Bremen are planned to be car free. Even in these cases some parking provision has to be made to avoid over-spill parking in surrounding streets. It will be important to differentiate between essential *operational parking* – which will allow the normal business of the settlement to be carried out; *social parking* – which provides space for visiting doctors, health visitors, family and friends; plus parking spaces for *residents*.

One method of reducing or eliminating the need for residents to have their own car is to form a community transport group. This allows drivers to be trained to operate a community bus or operate car share schemes. Another concept is the 'car club'. This works with a pool of communal vehicles which can be hired by members of the community as and when required. Instead of the usual practice of residents' cars sitting unused for long periods of time, a smaller selection of vehicles (of various shape and size – some may be electric powered) can be used far more effectively. The UK's first car club in Edinburgh provides up to 24 vehicles parked in three locations. It is modelled on clubs rapidly attracting members in Germany, Austria, Switzerland and The Netherlands. In Berlin there are over 3000 members of car sharing clubs. Experience from Germany also suggests that members of car clubs who were previously car owners reduce their mileage by half (DETR, 1998b).

There is now wide experience on methods that can be used to control vehicles within settlements. Buchanan (1963) highlighted the concept of environmental areas in his report *Traffic in Towns*. This idea of creating small areas free of extraneous traffic has been developed by the Dutch with 'Woonerven' and in Germany with 'Wohnstrassen' or 'living street'. The approach is to allow vehicles into the area but to reduce their speed so that the safety of pedestrians becomes a priority. This is done by avoiding long straight roads and introducing horizontal and vertical deflections to keep speeds low. The opportunity can also be taken to plant trees and vegetation within the street and remove the conventional kerbs and footway. A good example of calming traffic to create an interesting and pedestrian friendly environment exists at Poundbury in Dorset. The lessons from this scheme have been adopted by the UK Government in their guidance *Places, Streets and Movement* (DETR, 1998i).

Current regulations allow traffic to be calmed to 20mph on certain streets and for 20mph zones to be created. This can create substantial social benefits by increasing activity on the street. The effect of slowing traffic has led to a significant reduction in accidents. In 20mph zones the frequency of accidents has reduced by about 60 per cent and accidents involving children by 67 per cent (Webster and Mackie, 1996). In Denmark and a few other European countries, traffic speeds have been halved again to create 10mph (15kph) zones. The UK Government acknowledge that these 'home zones... could prove to be a valuable tool in improving the places where people live and children play' (DETR, 1998b). A drop in some vehicle emissions occurs (usually $NO_x$) in traffic calmed streets but the level of improvement will depend on the frequency and spacing of calming measures. For major improvements in air quality most motor vehicles have to be removed.

Key considerations for motor vehicle access include:

- limit the number of parking spaces and prioritize essential parking needs;
- locate and design parking areas so that they are safe and secure but not visually obtrusive;
- give priority to pedestrians, cyclists and public transport on the movement network;
- design vehicle trackways to limit the speed of vehicles to 20mph or 10mph as appropriate;
- create places that are safe and attractive to people where vehicle circulation does not dominate the layout;
- allow efficient access for emergency vehicles, refuse collection and deliveries.

## COOPERATION AND COORDINATION

This chapter has highlighted a variety of measures that can be used to encourage walking, cycling and the use of public transport whilst reducing the reliance on private motor vehicles. The way in which these different ingredients are selected and combined will depend on the people who use them, the nature, size and character of the neighbourhood and the structure of the wider area in which it is located.

A successful movement strategy will be very hard to implement unless it 'gets inside the heads' of the users and is planned to meet their needs. Too often transport systems have been designed to meet the requirements of the provider rather than the user. It is vital that the users (residents and visitors) are involved at a very early stage and continue to participate in the process as ideas develop and detailed proposals evolve.

The various measures that are selected for implementation will need to be carefully coordinated. They will also benefit from rigorous testing to ensure that they do not disadvantage specific groups or create solutions that are unviable, either within or beyond the boundaries of the neighbourhood. The following tests illustrate the main areas of evaluation:

- *operation:* is access provided to all facilities? Are the routes direct, convenient, easily managed by all groups? Are they integrated with other transport systems and land uses?
- *environment:* are there adverse effects on humans, the natural environment/planet? Tests can be made against human senses or the DETR criteria of noise, air quality, landscape, biodiversity, heritage, water;
- *equity:* are any groups disadvantaged by the strategy? Will everyone be safe and feel secure? Is there provision for the mobility impaired?
- *viability:* can the capital and running costs be afforded? Is it technically feasible? Can it be implemented? Will it receive support?

This testing process will highlight the strengths and weaknesses of different parts of the strategies. Combining the best features should lead to a successful pattern of movement for everyone involved.

A further dilemma will be to decide on the extent to which the neighbourhood relates to and anticipates change in the surrounding area. Residents will probably still be heavily dependent on facilities elsewhere. It is unlikely that colleges, hospitals, specialist shops and employment will all be provided nearby. Whilst the need to travel to these facilities may reduce in the future as society changes to embrace new ideas such as distance learning, information technology, home deliveries and the opportunity of working from home, travel outside of the neighbourhood will still be an important function of daily life. The big challenge will be to decide how far the neighbourhood can progress with a radical movement strategy in advance of complementary measures being introduced in the surrounding area.

A start has to be made somewhere and small scale examples of good practice within neighbourhoods which have strong community support are more likely to succeed than large scale, long term, area wide strategies. If sufficient neighbourhoods initiate eco-friendly measures, strong pressure will build up to develop sympathetic area wide transport links. Rather than wait for all the surrounding pieces of the jigsaw to be in place, why not make a start at neighbourhood level? One small step within the neighbourhood could lead to a giant leap forward for the whole area.

# 15 COMMUNITY SAFETY AND ACTUAL NEIGHBOURHOODS

*Henry Shaftoe*

## INTRODUCTION: CRIME AND LOCALITY

Cities and large conurbations, originally developed as places of safety and civilized behaviour, have, in many instances, become fearful and insecure environments for their inhabitants (see Ellin, 1997).

In a historic reversal of fortune, many people now flee to the relative safety of the countryside and rural villages. How can we recreate community safety in our cities?

Community safety is an essential prerequisite for a stable and sustainable neighbourhood. A neighbourhood or locality is doomed if it is perceived or experienced as unsafe. Most 'quality of life' surveys show that crime and fear

**Figure 15.1** *Urban Centre, South Wales*

of victimization are two of the top deleterious ingredients of urban living (see, for example, Burrows and Rhodes, 1998).

This chapter proposes that the safest neighbourhoods are those that incorporate many of the environmental and social qualities that emulate those found in the traditional village. It is further argued that by careful design, management and community development it is possible to develop and sustain village-like communities in inner-city environments. These will be termed 'actual neighbourhoods' to differentiate them from areas that may be physically labelled as neighbourhoods but do not actually function as such.

There has been an increasing interest in developing areas designated as 'urban villages'. Often these urban villages will consist of one or more 'actual neighbourhoods' but, as we shall show, for this to happen, the social infrastructure and dynamics are as important as the physical structure.

The notion of actual neighbourhoods functioning within urban villages reconciles well with current thinking on community safety. The higher per capita crime rates in cities and large towns, compared to rural areas, is usually explained by the anonymity and high mobility within cities. Self contained, cohesive communities offer much higher levels of informal surveillance and social control. It has also been found that crime and antisocial behaviour are less prevalent where people feel they have a stake in, or 'ownership of', their neighbourhood.

It should be noted, however, that the term 'crime' covers a multitude of sins and that the proliferation of new urban villages will not necessarily impact on all categories of offence. The development of actual neighbourhoods should be most successful at preventing 'locational' crimes such as burglaries, thefts and street robberies. Actual neighbourhoods, characterized by good social networks may also be better able to control 'abuse' offences such as assaults (domestic and sexual), drug misuse and racially motivated crimes, although these are often tied to broader social policy and developmental issues which cannot primarily be tackled at the neighbourhood level.

## Urban–Village Safety

Despite the ubiquity of crime as entertainment, people loath being in, or living in, neighbourhoods where they feel unsafe. But risk of being a victim of crime varies significantly according to location. One of the most dramatic variations in crime rates becomes apparent when urban and rural figures are compared. For example, the people in the predominantly urbanized South Wales police force area (which includes Cardiff and Swansea) experience more than double the number of crimes per head than neighbouring Dyfed/Powys, which is almost entirely rural. Moreover, the crime rate in rural mid-Wales (Dyfed/Powys) has also experienced one of the sharpest drops in crime rates of anywhere during the late 1990s. A similar contrast can be found between many other urban and neighbouring rural locations.

The 'white flight' from many inner-city areas of the US has now moved beyond the suburbs and out into more rural locations, as those who can afford to, venture ever further to find a safe haven for their families. It is unlikely to be pure chance that gives predominantly rural Norway a much lower per-capita crime level than densely urbanized Holland.

**Figure 15.2** *Child's Play, South Wales*

The irony of all this is that cities were originally built as places of safety. The early cities of Roman, Greek and other civilizations were safe refuges from the threats and violence of their rural hinterlands. Up until the 17th century most European cities were still walled to guard against ill-intentioned outsiders. And yet by the mid-19th century the enemy was within and the good burghers of inner city London had to set up the first police force to control the rising tide of theft and thuggery in the city streets.

It has been suggested (see for example Ravetz, 1980) that 20th century cities actually provoke criminal behaviour amongst their citizens, who, alienated by the bleak, impersonal and oppressive built environment, turn to vandalism and violence in response.

Nowadays the lesson seems to be: if you want to reduce your chances of being a victim of crime, go and live in the country and many of those who can afford to, do exactly this. Clearly, for practical reasons, this is not a feasible option for the majority of the population. So perhaps our task should be to firstly identify what factors in the rural environment appear to make them more secure against crime and secondly, see what we could do to re-create these factors in an urban environment.

## WHY IS THERE LESS CRIME IN RURAL AREAS?

First of all a clarification – crime is not just lower in rural areas because there are fewer people; per capita rates are significantly lower. In 1995 the police recorded about 328,000 crimes in the Greater Manchester area, whereas in mid-Wales, the Dyfed/Powys police had only about 19,400 crimes on their books. Even comparing them on a per-capita basis Manchester clocked 12 crimes per 100 residents as against mid-Wales' 4 crimes per 100 – a three-fold difference. However, all is not perfect in the countryside – for example racist attitudes are often more entrenched in rural areas, which on occasion can lead to horrendous outbursts against ethnic minority people who have settled or trade in villages and small towns.

There could be a number of explanations for the urban/rural variation in crime rates:

1  *'Maybe urban police forces record more crime, whereas there is more "hidden" crime in rural areas.'* There is evidence (in the British Crime Surveys) to suggest that much more crime occurs than is ever recorded by the police, but nothing to suggest that this is proportionately more likely to be the case in rural areas. In fact, if anything, less crime might be reported in urban areas, where the police are more likely to be over-stretched and less accessible to residents;

2  *'There is more poverty in urban areas, so people are more likely to steal to get what they want or need.'* There are heavier concentrations of poverty in urban areas (on large housing estates and inner city areas) but there are many poor people living in rural areas too – agricultural work is one of the lowest paid industries and there are relatively high levels of rural unemployment in some parts of the country;

3  *'There is more relative inequality in cities, so people steal to get even'.* Partly true, but the difference between the landed gentry in their country seats and the farm labourers in their council houses and tied cottages could hardly be more polarized;

4  *'There is more to steal in towns and cities.'* In absolute terms this is true, but there are still plenty of pickings for the determined rural thief and the items in question are often less secured or supervized (eg farm equipment and livestock, or contents of holiday cottages);

5  *'Everything is too spread out in the country. This makes crime more difficult to commit, particularly as offenders and victims tend, statistically, to reside a short distance from each other.'* Yes, research has established that 'journeys to crime' are comparatively short (eg Davidson, 1981) and rural areas are more dispersed than urban areas. But within these dispersed areas the dispossessed and the affluent often live in close proximity (think of the typical village or hamlet with the manor house and the tied cottages or the executive commuter homes and the council houses) and the motor car has effectively reduced journey times for almost everyone;

6  *'Cities attract deviants, drug addicts and ne'er-do-wells who thrive in the urban anonymity and are less visible in densely populated environments. Such people therefore migrate from the rural to the urban.'* Yes, there is an element of truth in this – people who deviate from the norm are much more visible in rural areas and can often be better supervized, formally or informally, in such an environment. However it is important to recognize that many types of deviation are perfectly legal (eg: growing dreadlocks or being a 'traveller') and the innate conservatism of many rural areas can be prejudicial and repressive;

7  *'Everyone knows everyone else and their business in villages and rural areas, so any suspicious activity is likely to be visible and noted.'* Yes, this kind of informal surveillance is much stronger in small communities,

whereas in the big city there are too many goings-on to keep track of. Although, conversely, in spatial terms there are potentially more 'hidden corners' in rural areas where, at the far end of a farm track, it may be possible to engage unseen in some illicit activity;

8 *'There is a much bigger turnover of residents and visitors in towns and cities, so routine, predictable and legal activity is less likely to be the dominant pattern; rural communities tend to be much more stable, so anything out of the ordinary or unpredictable (and possibly illegal) will stand out.'* Yes, indeed this links to and reinforces point 6, although the down side could be rural intolerance (as in 5);

9 *'Urban living is more stressful so people get violent.'* Yes, urbanites tend to live faster, more pressurized existences which are more likely to bring them into confrontational proximity with other stressed-out urbanites (see Newman and Lonsdale, 1996). However, it may be significant that the two worst massacres in the UK during the last 20 years (Hungerford and Dunblane) both occurred in semi-rural areas;

10 *'There are more escape routes and hiding places in the confused maze of the big city.'* Yes, this seems to be true; geographically rural areas offer more possibilities for secretion yet, paradoxically they are more visible. It is significant that the IRA, when preparing for terrorist bombing campaigns on the UK mainland, generally (but not exclusively) chose to hide their arms and explosives in anonymous urban locations;

11 *'Residents feel more proprietorial in villages and rural areas; in towns and cities many people feel the neighbourhoods and public spaces are outside their control.'* Yes, this seems to be generally the case – there is often a stronger sense of community and unity in self-contained villages, reinforced by the village pub, store and hall. As a result, residents are more likely to take combined action against a perceived threat.

**Figure 15.3** *Tetbury, Gloucestershire*

The real picture that makes up the difference between urban and rural crime rates is likely to be made up of elements from most of the statements listed above, as well as possible other factors not discovered. In terms of crime and social conditions, nothing is ever simple!

## CAN WE RECREATE RURAL QUALITIES IN URBAN ENVIRONMENTS?

If we cannot all go to the country, can the country come to the city? It should be possible to bring many of the social and situational factors that benefit rural living (and relative safety) into the urban fabric, thus creating actual neighbourhoods as opposed to seamless tracts of urban development where people live and work. Points 6 to 11 in the above list could all have implications for the way we plan, design and manage our towns and cities. As Lynch (1981) summarizes:

> *'The pleasures of living in an identifiable district which has quiet, safe streets and daily services easily accessible nearby, and within which one can organize politically when the need for control arises, are surely a legitimate feature of good settlement.'*

Although it was grounded in a different motivational source, the urban villages movement appears to address many of these issues and could therefore lead to the unintended, but very welcome, added benefits of less crime and fear for residents. The urban villages movement in the UK was an attempt to tackle ecological and design problems in the bland suburban sprawls that were enveloping most cities during the 1970s and 1980s (Urban Villages Group, 1992). A similar movement has developed in the US under the banner of 'new urbanism' (see Katz, 1994). Instead of single use and single tenure housing estates, the Urban Villages Forum (along with the new urbanists) argues for a wider mix of uses, activities and tenures within new developments, to encourage people to interact more easily and to discourage unnecessary car journeys. Although proposed as a form of development to facilitate economic, environmental and social sustainability, it becomes obvious from the points raised in the previous section, that such an environment should also lead to sustainable reductions in crime and improvements in community safety.

Christopher Alexander in his book *A Pattern Language* (1977) anticipated the notion of the urban village with his pattern for a community of 7000. He proposes: 'Decentralize city governments in a way that gives local control to communities of 5000 to 10,000 persons. As nearly as possible, use natural and historical boundaries to mark these communities'. Alexander then proposes the 'neighbourhood' as a smaller residential unit of about 500 inhabitants, with a cluster of neighbourhoods grouped to form a community (or in the new terminology: an urban village).

Specifically, an urban village or 'pattern for a community' is expected to have the following characteristics, all of which can help to enhance community safety (see also Urban Villages Forum):

- a population small enough to make up an identifiable 'community' where people will mostly recognize each other, but large enough to support a range of neighbourhood services and facilities (Alexander, 1977);
- a strong sense of place, with basic amenities within easy walking distance of all residents; this will define the physical design and spatial coverage of the neighbourhood (Alexander, 1977). The sense of place can be enhanced by giving a physical focus or point of convergence where local people can gather and interact. Traditionally this has been the village green, town square, community centre or sub post office/corner shop;
- a variety of uses, such as shopping, leisure and community facilities along-side housing, so that people do not have to travel far out of their neighbourhood for day-to-day needs and activities, although some of these facilities might be shared with adjacent neighbourhoods (perhaps positioned along the boundaries between several neighbourhoods) to make them viable. Small business workshops and homeworking support facilities could also be provided. All these will encourage more social inter-action, stability and cohesion;
- a choice of tenures (both residential and commercial) and housing types to enable a mixed and balanced community, with neither concentrations of disadvantagement or privilege. Also a variety of housing types, so that old and young, families and singles, able and less able can all live as neigh-bours; this will allow extended family networks to remain in the area, as there will be accomodation for every life stage;
- a high level of involvement by local residents in the planning and onward management of the new development. This gives people a sense of control and 'ownership', and means that they have a stake in the future well-being of 'their' community. This involvement and control can take a number of forms, with 'the more the merrier' as a guiding principle. At the minimum this might consist of a Neighbourhood Watch scheme and an annual neigh-bourhood consultation meeting; preferably there would be a democratically elected neighbourhood forum, 'parish council' or commu-nity development trust, plus a neighbourhood services office with resident representatives on the management board and a whole range of mutual aid groups such as parent support networks, LETS, a youth programme with local young people on the management committee, a food coopera-tive or perhaps even a community shop and café.

All these measures should contribute to a safe and sound neighbourhood (or cluster of neighbourhoods) with good informal social controls and active surveillance possibilities, to inhibit crime and antisocial activity.

Above all, an 'actual neighbourhood' has to have a stable population where the majority of people feel they are settled and have a long-term commitment to maintaining an acceptable quality of life in that neighbourhood (see Hirschfield and Bowers, 1997). If people regard the neighbourhood as a 'transit camp' or temporary home, then they are unlikely to invest time and effort in developing networks and will not care too much about undesirable aspects of life in the area. This is noticeable in areas occupied by large numbers of students (passing through) or by families living on unpopular housing projects who are hoping to be transferred to somewhere better. In some respects this requirement for stability militates against the increasing mobility of the job market. In the future people may have to make a conscious choice between staying in a friendly and active neighbourhood and reducing their promotion chances, or living a transitory life full of insecurities in all senses of the word.

## BOUNDARIES AND EDGES

The major remaining urban village or 'actual neighbourhood' issue is that of the 'edges' of the development and what happens in adjacent areas. This is one major difference between the urban village and its rural equivalent. In the country, a village will almost certainly be surrounded by fields, which act as a neutral and relatively safe buffer zone. In the town or city it is likely that the actual neighbourhood will be mostly surrounded by other populated or activity areas, from whence predatory incursions may occur. Edges of neighbourhoods are often the most vulnerable to crime, because easy forays and escapes are possible and strangers or irregular activity are less apparent than in the core. The crude solution is to build a wall round the neighbourhood and indeed this happens in the US and in areas of extreme sectarian conflict such as parts of Belfast and Londonderry. There are early signs of this approach in Britain with, for example, the Brindley Place development in central Birmingham enclosing its residents behind a continuous barrier of walls and access controlled gates (Figure 15.4).

**Figure 15.4** *Brindley Place, Birmingham*

'Gating' is a drastic solution with many undesirable side effects, not least of which is the creation of a divided society and the gradual erosion of the civil liberty to enjoy all urban spaces as a member of the general public. Walled-in neighbourhoods or gated suburbs can also heighten fear among residents who may feel they are under permanent siege and are frightened to emerge from their fortified enclave (Ellin, 1997). A more humane and inclusive approach to the 'edge' problem is to install symbolic barriers (using different surfacing materials or a 'finger park' for example). But the best solution is clearly to make sure that any urban village is part of a comprehensive community safety plan for a town or city and not an isolated oasis in otherwise hostile territory.

Lynch (1960) suggests that edges of neighbourhoods can be 'uniting seams' rather than isolating barriers. This can be the case when an edge is defined by a substantial routeway to a town core or to the country, or where it is a linear provider of services that could not be sustained by single neighbourhoods. So in fact the edge or seam can be an asset rather than a liability, offering access routes and major attractions, such as cinemas, restaurants and sports centres which need more than a population of 5000 to make them viable.

## Can it Happen?

There are a number of difficulties in implementing this utopian vision of actual neighbourhoods. Above all is the perfectly understandable desire of those with choice and means to select their own preferred living environments. Many people like to live in the aspirational suburbs where all neighbours are of the same social class and family status. They do not want to live next to poorer people or students or hostels for people with learning difficulties. Significantly though, most people on low incomes would not complain if they were offered accommodation in a prosperous neighbourhood! Even among the less well off sectors of society there are respectable working class neighbourhoods and 'sink' estates. Nobody wants to live next to a 'problem family' with kids excluded from school and perhaps dabbling in drugs. There seem to be two stark choices: either we can let the free market heighten the polarization of neighbourhoods into rich and poor, black and white, families and singles (US style) or we can go for a social interventionist approach where there are incentives for people to live in mixed areas and people with needs get proper levels of support and supervision (Scandinavian style). One encouraging trend in England is the 'return to the cities'. For most of the past half century people with choice have headed for the suburbs, with the consequent abandonment of the central core to the poor and the homeless. Recently there has been a noticeable reverse in this trend in cities such as Bristol and Norwich where there has been a deliberate policy to make city centre living an attractive and realistic proposition. (Scotland and most other European countries have always managed to maintain a good mix of inner city housing) Such an approach on its own has a valuable function in terms of extra informal surveillance at all hours. Combine this with a planned community infrastructure (as in Bordesley Urban Village in Birmingham – Figure 15.5) and there is a real possibility of re-establishing the actual inner city communities championed by Jane Jacobs (1961).

Putting aside (for the purposes of this discussion) new-build urban villages such as Poundbury in England and Seaside in the US, there are some notable examples of existing neighbourhoods that have been redeveloped physically and rehabilitated socially, where crime has been reduced and the perception

**Figure 15.5** *Bordesley Urban Village, Birmingham*

of safety increased. A common thread that runs through these success stories is the input of local people in the revival of 'their' neighbourhoods and the control they are able to exert both over the redevelopment and the management and maintenance of the improvements. Another common thread seems to be a sense of human scale whereby people can identify with and feel part of a community, where they are known and can recognize neighbours and where many of their needs are catered for within the neighbourhood. In other words, people feel that they belong to an actual neighbourhood rather than a conglomeration of buildings and spaces that have no personal or social 'meaning' to them.

## CASE STUDIES

It could be argued that the 'model villages' developed in the UK by philanthropically inclined industrialists for their workers, during Victorian times, were the precursors of urban villages. The well known ones include: *New Lanark* (Robert Owen), *Bournville*, Birmingham – Figure 15.6 – (Cadbury), *New Earswick, York* (Rowntree) and *Port Sunlight, Wirral* (Lever Brothers).

These model villages were all built to high standards, with integral community facilities, village greens and, significantly, they still remain popular, desirable and safe areas to live in. For example, New Earswick, built by Joseph Rowntree for his chocolate factory workers, is still a clearly defined 'community', despite being swallowed up by suburban residential expansion. The Joseph Rowntree Housing Trust continues to invest in appropriate facilities for the area and has recently built a new community centre and a small group of 'lifetime homes', enabling residents to stay within their homes in the village even when they grow old and frail.

**Figure 15.6** *Bournville, Birmingham*

## Eldonians' Housing Cooperative, Liverpool

Residents of a run-down high crime area in inner-city Liverpool resisted the council's plan for clearance and came up with their own design and management proposal, which succeeded. Since completion of the new scheme, managed by the residents, there has been virtually no crime, in stark contrast to neighbouring areas.

## Hallwood Park, Runcorn

This is the new name for the neighbourhood that is now located on the former site of Sir James Stirling's award winning Southgate housing estate. After much campaigning, residents of Southgate were given a major say in the re-design of their new community.

## Niddrie House, Edinburgh

Another high crime location where local people, working with sympathetic architect and community worker, have been able to create a new community, which not only has been physically rehabilitated, but also has a community shop, playgrounds, a community centre and local employment initiatives. Niddrie House has the difficulty mentioned earlier of being an enclave in a wider area of disadvantagement. A neighbouring estate had previously been physically rehabilitated at huge expense with very little long term improvement in quality of life or crime reduction, because as one resident observed 'they changed the buildings but the people are the same' (There had been no real involvement or engagement with local people and their social needs).

**Figure 15.7** *Egebjerggard, Copenhagen*

## Egebjerggard, Denmark

A new 'village' on the outskirts of Copenhagen, which has been deliberately designed to create and sustain a sense of community and safety, using both physical and social methods. The homes are designed to offer good natural surveillance and are grouped to define mini-neighbourhoods with their own built-in community facilities. Danish housing law requires 10 per cent of all development to be given over to community space; as a result Egebjerggard has a wealth of neighbourhood facilities which provide the infrastructure for local people to get together and 'bond' (Figure 15.7).

## Casa Loma, Los Angeles

Instigated by a grass roots group of Latina women, Casa Loma is remarkably similar to The Homes for Change development in Manchester. Casa Loma consists of 110 apartments built as a high density courtyard scheme in the Belmont neighbourhood of downtown Los Angeles, one of the poorest and most troubled sections of the city. Inside Casa Loma's physical structure is a 'complete community' which provides residents with a chance to lead safe and stable lives. Within the complex are a comprehensive range of services and facilities to provide for: child care, after-school, teenagers, elders and training and counselling for all.

## Ancoats Urban Village and 'Homes for Change' Cooperative, Manchester

Ancoats Urban Village is a redevelopment of a declining industrial area and the cooperative at Hume (Figure 15.8) has been built on the cleared site of one of the highest crime estates in the country. It is a self-contained high density development consisting of 50 apartments and 16,000 square feet of workspace. Since occupation in 1996 there have been no break-ins.

**Figure 15.8** *Homes for Change, Manchester*

## Crown Street and Merchant City, Glasgow

Both these high quality neighbourhoods have been regenerated from declining inner-city parts of Glasgow. Crown Street is on the site of the Gorbals, one of the worst slums in the city, which was massively redeveloped in the sixties. Despite being built to the designs of Sir Basil Spence, one of Britain's most acclaimed postwar architects, the 'new' Gorbals blocks were not a success and highlighted the shortcomings of mass clearance and monolithic housing redevelopment. Crown Street is part of the 'third wave' of development in the Gorbals, attempting a more human scale and integrated development. Merchant city is part of central Glasgow and had become very run down in the sixties and seventies. As well as attracting new retail, service and leisure facilities the council has ensured that 1200 flats have been part of the overall redevelopment.

## City Heights Urban Village, San Diego, US

This is one of the most ambitious 'urban village' projects so far, entailing the redevelopment of nine blocks of one of San Diego's most deprived suburbs. This is a public/private venture aiming to produce a pedestrian friendly neighbourhood based on the wishes and participation of its multi-ethnic population. Significantly, all the major community facilities (school, library, recreation centre, police station) have been built before the housing, so that the infrastructure needed to support an active and safe community is already in place before the majority of residents move in.

## Royds Community Association, Bradford

This is a resident led and controlled rehabilitation programme covering three formerly disadvantaged peripheral housing estates with a combined population of 12,000. The Community Association has secured a £108 million Single Regeneration Budget over seven years and is ensuring that improvements to the area are being defined, determined, managed and implemented (60 per cent of the construction workers are residents of the area) by local people. Part of the strategy is to divide up the huge area of housing into identifiable communities with defining physical features such as public art and 'village centres'. As neighbourhoods were improved, crime levels fell by anything between 30 per cent and 90 per cent. As the Chair of the Royds Community Association said, 'people are now taking responsibility for their own actions and their children's actions'.

# SUMMARY AND KEY PRINCIPLES

To make our cities more liveable, we need to ensure that they *are* safe and that they *feel* safe. The analysis and case studies given previously suggest five key principles for creating actual neighbourhoods that can minimize fear and maximize safety:

1 *Quality:* cheap mass housing solutions have proved to be expensive in the long run. Some schemes built in the 1960s have already been demolished, or expensively refurbished. There is also the psychological proposition that brutal, neglected environments encourage (or at least do not inhibit) brutal and uncaring behaviour;

2 *Diversity (and self-sufficiency):* viable and thriving neighbourhoods need to be able to accommodate a whole range of occupants and activities. Single use, monolithic areas have proved to be less safe and secure than mixed use neighbourhoods. Diversity should extend to housing (for all ages, tenure types and incomes) and core amenities (shops, workshops, leisure, care and education), so that the neighbourhood is self-sufficient without being totally insular;

3 *Identity:* the neighbourhood should be the right size (probably no more than 5000 people and one kilometre from end to end) on a human scale and have enough particular character to give it a clear identity that residents and users can relate to and 'bond' around;

4 *'Ownership':* through involvement and control of the neighbourhood's destiny, residents should feel that they have a stake in the neighbourhood's present and future conditions and quality of life. In this way they will care for their neighbourhood and their neighbours and are more likely to ensure that other people behave accordingly (or that something happens if they do not);

5 *Stability and continuity:* if residents and users regard the neighbourhood as a 'transit camp' then they are unlikely to invest much time and effort in ensuring that it becomes, or remains, a good place to live. Through choice of living arrangements and 'lifetime' homes people should be encouraged

**Figure 15.9** *Security, Los Angeles*

to remain in their area. The same stability and continuity should be offered by service providers in the area. For example the community constable should remain working in the same area for as long as possible (at least three years) and, ideally, would live there too (as happens in Japan).

All the demographic trends indicate that we are living in an increasingly urbanized world and that this is unlikely to reverse in the foreseeable future. The city has numerous advantages both from the points of view of sustainability and civilization generally. It is paramount therefore that we reverse the decline into fear and insecurity experienced by the inhabitants of many conurbations.

If we fail to create and maintain actual neighbourhoods where people feel safe and secure, by default we will deteriorate into the alternative scenario where those that can afford to, flee to the countryside or fortified enclaves, leaving the less advantaged to inhabit the mean streets and housing of an increasingly rotten city. This has already happened in some US cities, with dire economic and social consequences. We do not all have to go the way of Detroit; there is still time to return our cities to their original functions of civilization, safety and enlightenment.

# 16 Towards Sustainable Communities

*Hugh Barton*

*'Whatever you can do, or dream you can, begin it! Boldness has genius, power and magic. Begin it now.'* Geothe, *Dichtung und Wahrheit*, circa 1825

## General Conclusions

This final chapter acts as a summary and a launch-pad. It is clear that the significance of 'neighbourhood' in people's lives has faded, but the wish to reverse the trend is very widely shared. Technological evolution, community development programmes and exemplary neighbourhood projects all suggest there is potential to reinvent locality, but success so far has barely touched the generality of situations. The knowledge/skills base needs further development and much wider dissemination, however, the key issue is not knowledge but *will*. There is a prevailing lack of determination on the part of the public and private sector agencies who shape the physical environmental to convert the noble (over-rehearsed) rhetoric of sustainable development into practice. Political and institutional inertia still prevails and impedes the discovery of neighbourhood strategies that are effective in the contemporary situation. Following Geothe's injunction the answer is not wait and see (in which case we remain part of the problem) but *begin now*. Uncertainties and conflicts of interest can only be resolved by boldly taking steps forward, opening up the neighbourhood option. This chapter sets out some of the spheres where action is appropriate, emphasising process rather than product: first, by empowering local communities and forming partnerships for action in the context of 'neighbourhood action plans' (NAPs); second, by changing the prevailing culture of local decision-makers, professionals and development companies; third, by government policy catching up with its expressed aims, particularly in terms of fiscal priorities and institutional remits.

At the policy level there a gulf between rhetoric and reality. Government sees neighbourhoods as essential building blocks of the sustainable city, and is beginning to promote policies of transport demand management, mixed land use and urban intensification which in principle should assist. However, some policies inevitably pull in different directions (for example the maintenance of urban open spaces and the pressure to find brownfield housing sites) and the lack of integration between government departments is reflected in the lack of coherence at local level. Economic development priorities, for instance, lead to land hungry car dependant business parks, often on greenfield sites, whereas PPG13, in line with urban form theory, suggests mixed use centres at public transport nodes, embedded within residential townships. The development industry, aided and abetted by the planning system, is producing new residential areas which seriously compromise the principle of neighbourhoods, leading to a fragmented, increasingly privatized environment characterized by high car reliance, wasted resources and pollution intensity. Such localities marginalize the interests of those who are tied to the local place, increasing social exclusion and the risk of mental illness. Except in the small protected home-zones (often cul-de-sac, sometimes gated) these residential areas present a hostile environment for pedestrians, exacerbating problems of community safety.

## COMMUNITY DECISION-MAKING

A central thrust of Local Agenda 21 is that all the main stakeholders in a city, or a locality, need to be involved in decision-making processes in order to achieve policy consistency, shared ownership and commitment. As Stewart points out (Chapter 11) there are few specific proposals in the government's analysis for strengthening such capacity at the local level, and this may be because radical shifts in the balance of power towards local communities threaten existing powerful institutions. Nevertheless the principle of subsidiarity has many adherents. Proposals for greater community self-determination come not only from communitarian and radical environmental sources but from the diagnosis of the Social Exclusion Unit (1998) and rather generalized references in DETR guidance (DETR, 1998a, c). The range of techniques used to achieve greater community participation and agency collaboration – including LA21 fora, citizen's juries, focus groups, regeneration partnerships – reflects the widespread support.

A vexed question is how subsidiarity can be achieved at the level of the whole neighbourhood. Genuine community decision-making can occur at *project* level, witness the LETS in Stroud (Chapter 10), the community-initiated eco-village schemes (Chapter 5) and the Easton community centre (Chapter 9). But at neighbourhood level there are, according to Alexander – though not Plato – too many people to get actively involved (see Chapter 8). And there are perceived threats to the authority of elected members, jealous of their right to be the channel between people and local authority.

If localities are to be awarded any extra powers then this probably depends on new neighbourhood or ward policy frameworks. Some agencies are promoting a new-style neighbourhood action plan (NAP) interpreting slimmed-down local authority statutory documents in coordinated, holistic detail at the local level (Johnson, 1999). Elements of such NAPs could be given authority (even with current legislation) through Supplementary Planning Guidance attached to local or unitary Plans. The problems, though, are the sheer cost and complexity of cash-strapped local authorities producing NAPs for every neighbourhood, and the difficulty of galvanizing every relevant department and agency to attend a series of local meetings. There is also the question of the representativeness of those community members who choose to sit on local committees.

In practice only some places are likely to be able to resource and manage local devolved democracy effectively. The strategy therefore should be to initiate structural and attitude changes that will in the longer run deliver greater community capacity. Stewart (Chapter 11) suggests shifting structures of accountability and management performance review, and supporting new forms of community-managed trusts and collaborative fora (obligatory already for many regeneration projects). The move towards local resource management, especially for energy and water, could prompt action. When residents groups have the obligation (and self-interest) to manage their own water supply, sewage garden or renewables-based CHP plant, then social skills and community commitment may spill over into broader neighbourhood arenas.

If NAPs are not a practical proposition then the critical level remains the whole municipality. Integrated corporate plans have been proposed, drawing the strands together at that level. Coventry city is reinventing the idea of an overall *corporate plan* a generation after the previous attempt foundered on political rocks. But the nub of the question is attitude. The decision processes at district-wide level need to reflect the spirit of the neighbourhood approach, with effective involvement of local people, and to reflect sustainability goals with minimal bureaucratic barriers between social, economic and environmental agencies. The training and orientation of the professionals involved – inclusive, normative and rational; not exclusive, procedural and functional – are central to success.

## SHIFTING HEARTS AND MINDS

Changed attitudes among the many interests (local bureaucracies, politicians, business people, citizens etc) can only come if there is convergence of understanding. 'Sustainable development', while an *intellectually* powerful construct, has little *emotive* power – not sufficient in most situations to win hearts and galvanize action. An alternative banner is needed. 'Quality of life' is rather woolly, but perhaps 'health', in the broad World Health Organization (WHO) meaning, has some force. Health is explicitly anthropocentric, where sustainable development is sometimes falsely sidelined as a 'purely' environmental issue. Health of our community, health of the city, health of the planet, health of our children – all have a convincing ring, and health relates very well to the reasons for reinventing neighbourhoods: local work, safety, community, equity, accessibility, climate stability, clean air and water etc.

The vision of healthy neighbourhoods, shared by many, has been strongly promoted by the WHO and, recently, the UK Department of Health and Social Security. Linking the health and environment agenda together begins to provide a constituency of political support that can make things happen. Cities such as Glasgow and Sheffield in the UK, Toronto and Seattle in North America, Athens and Copenhagen in Europe, have embarked in just such a journey under the auspices of the WHO Healthy Cities programme. If health and environment could also be partnered by *economic development*, then the triumvirate of sustainable development would be complete. The policies of economic regeneration of dying localities and of boosting small, indigenous businesses as a means of increasing local economic resilience, links to the project of reinventing neighbourhoods. In principle, therefore, there could be support for a sustainable neighbourhood strategy from a wide range of stakeholders.

Coordination of any sustainable and healthy neighbourhood programme needs to occur in relation to service coordination, utilities and development policy. *Service coordination*, ideally linking health, social services, community development, education, housing, leisure and police agencies is something that the Healthy Cities programme exemplifies. *Integrated utility plans*, affecting electricity, district heating, waste and recycling agencies, are exceptional in the UK but commonplace in Sweden and Denmark. Coordinated *planning and development strategies* are illustrated, for example, in The Netherlands, where housing, transport, land use and environmental control functions are closely entwined. The next section concentrates on aspects of this third area.

## REORIENTATING THE PLANNING SYSTEM

In the UK the development plan system provides a potentially valuable means of coordinating policy as it applies to neighbourhoods; and government guidance is ostensibly strongly in favour of a neighbourhood approach. The barriers to implementing sustainable neighbourhoods through the planning system no doubt consist of a range of attitudinal, bureaucratic, market and political factors, but I will focus here on specific features of the current plan system that were discussed originally in Chapter 1, and are particularly inhibiting: the short-term planning horizon (at present 2011); the fixed trend forecasts for that date; and the focus on brownfield housing capacity and greenfield NIMBYism at the expense of any real attention to the nature of the development itself.

The government is now tentatively suggesting (DETR, 1998a) that development options or contingency plans could be considered over a 25 year period. This would be a welcome shift of emphasis. In 25 years there is likely to be a substantial growth increment (of the order of 25 per cent) and most existing buildings will receive significant investment to adapt them or renew them. In this situation the problem of planning for future growth and change becomes recognized as much bigger and more serious than the premature 2011 end date allows, and the policy options open for consideration are commensurately more radical. There is the opportunity for fundamental thinking about sustainability principles and how best to achieve them, matching the concern for intergenerational equity. If at the same time local planning authorities were to focus attention on a 'localization and quality-of-life strategy' that could be subsequently be picked up for individual NAPs, then public cynicism in the wake of LA21 participation might prove misplaced.

In many ways the political argument (often vociferous locally) over greenfield and brownfield development is a sterile one. Reuse of urban land is a widely accepted priority. But the popular belief that therefore greenfields can

be saved does not necessarily follow. Existing urban dwellers, given the opportunity to influence events through LA21 or NAPs, vote to enhance local
environmental quality, and they fight to defend playing fields, allotments and
backlands against the flood-tide of development pressure. Equivalently in edge
of town and village situations local residents campaign to 'save our valley' and
say 'no more houses'. This exposes the tension between the Local Agenda 21
sympathy for greater citizen control, and the goal of sustainable development.
As ever, in the absence of clear guidelines, it is the well-organized, articulate
groups who successfully promote or defend their territory, and the interests of
the under-represented (often poorer) groups and of future generations are
sidelined. The intense debate over sites deflects attention from fundamental
issues: given that a certain site can be considered for development, what form
should that development take? How can its development be used to foster
neighbourhood services and identity? Even more basic: in the context of the
local area, whose needs should be met?

The revitalized art of neighbourhood planning could provide sensible
answers. Working on the principle of sustainable development it could give
shape and limits to local public debate (as in the Charette process – see
Chapter 1). This approach would take the needs of local communities (all
sectors, now and anticipated for the future) as a starting point, and analyse
settlements – and within them neighbourhoods – as dynamic ecosystems
providing the human habitat. In that context land reuse/release (brownfield or
greenfield) occurs not merely to satisfy strategic housing estimates but to
enable the settlement to evolve more sustainably and provide a healthy quality
of life for residents and other users. An honest and explicit strategy of sustainable neighbourhoods could produce very different locational, use and density
patterns to those of current development conventions. It would certainly
provide a logic and rationale for incremental development control that is
currently lacking.

By way of example, consider the typical city suburbs. According to one
recent report – *Sustainable Renewal of Suburban Areas* (Civic Trust, 1998) –
the established suburbs are declining almost unnoticed as high mobility
allows residents to frequent superstores at the expense of local shops, and
health, leisure and community facilities are lost due to centralization on
large sites. These suburbs are not at a *critical* state which demands intervention with regeneration projects, but they are pre-critical where every
development control decision is tending to reinforce malign trends. The
report suggests mechanisms for increased local control, and, in line with
suggestions in Part II of this book, recommends increasing densities near
services and bus routes, and diversifying the housing stock to provide for the
full range of households.

Applying similar principles to the area of Bristol North Fringe that was
evaluated in Chapter 1, a radical overhaul of planning policy is needed.
Intensification, with higher density commerce and housing (including building on existing car parks) could help pay for necessary public transport
infrastructure. This would reduce the pressure for more greenfield development (often on inappropriate sites with low accessibility). The purpose would
be to transform the North Fringe from a market-led unsustainable sprawl into
a coherent, healthy town (Barton et al, 1999).

*Diversity* is a key thread through the sustainability maze. Within localities social diversity, built-form and land use diversity, transport modal choice, landscape variety and biodiversity are interwoven. *Stakeholder* diversity is also a critical factor. If a strategy for healthy and sustainable neighbourhoods is to be successful, then the first and critical stage is that of building alliances, drawing an appropriate range of agencies and representatives of local people into engagement with the issues and the opportunities.

## CHANGING GOVERNMENT POLICY

It has been obvious throughout the discussion that government holds the key to the move towards more sustainable neighbourhoods. The DETR has in the mid/late 1990s comprehensively overhauled planning guidance, and the rhetoric of sustainability is beginning to be matched by action through the plan approval and planning appeals systems. Some related areas of government are also showing signs of embracing the new local approach – particularly in relation to health and urban regeneration. However, there are fundamentals of government fiscal and regulatory policy that need to shift if moves towards localization, neighbourhoods and greater subsidiarity are to be generally successful. The tax system still taxes things which we want – eg employment, and urban renewal (through VAT) – rather than taxing the things we do *not* want – eg pollution and the use of non-renewable resources – thus sending the wrong messages to the market. Local sustainable practices need encouragement specifically through the way energy, food and materials are taxed and regulated.

More specific to the development process is the issue of the way the market for land inhibits reallocation from high value to low value uses (eg from housing land to open space within the urban green network), while giving no benefit to the public purse when the reverse happens (eg through intensification policies). The Dutch approach to capturing development value for the community has something to commend it.

Institutional remits set by government are also key factors contributing to inertia. While deregulation has in general helped to increase the efficiency of resource use and increased the options open to consumers (for example in the field of energy – Chapter 12), the underlying motivation remains anti-sustainability. Companies are competing to sell more rather than cooperating to conserve. So innovative resource-efficient schemes involving partnership and sharing of information are sometimes stillborn because of claimed commercial confidentiality. And creative transport strategies, for example, are difficult to implement. In some situations local authorities should be given a stronger hand by government to coordinate other agencies. But it is within the local authorities and other state agencies themselves that the biggest changes in priority need to occur. For the neighbourhood project to work government needs to adjust the remits given to education, health and other social services so they give much greater weight to *client accessibility*. In other words rather than treating the client's costs (children getting to school, old people getting to health centre and post office) as unrewarded externalities they are incorporated in the social and environmental accounting systems of the agencies.

Environmental management systems and other techniques of environmental and social audit are beginning to show the way forward.

# ROUNDING OFF

This book has shown that on many different counts there are admirable reasons for trying to rejuvenate localities as living, active, place communities based around common services and local resource management. But the trends in the other direction remain powerful, and innovative neighbourhood scale projects are still very rare. There is a widespread desire amongst Local Agenda 21 coordinators, community developers, urban designers, health professionals and a wide body of public and political opinion to reverse that trend. Achieving it relies on concerted effort from a plethora of agencies – public, private, voluntary and community sectors. The planning system is in a good position to facilitate and coordinate the process, and government has begun the reorientation of policy. Reshaping fiscal and regulatory signals will need to be accompanied by retraining of professionals and other actors involved: a root and branch reworking of deeply ingrained habits of thinking and acting.

These habits, evinced by the way public policy is normally conceived and implemented, stem in part from the discredited reductionist view of the human environment (ie an approach which analyses the parts and assumes the whole is the sum of the parts). This false consciousness is illustrated, for example, by the way in which agreements over largely spurious housing figures take precedent over issues about the quality of life; by the way potential housing and commercial sites are treated as tradable commodities by the market/planning system, with the needs and values of affected groups often secondary; by the way resources of water, energy, land and air are treated as inexhaustible flows rather than part of a complex ecosystem which includes humankind. Sennett (1970) saw this tidy, zoned, atomized, linear view of the world as symptomatic of an adolescent's approach, and called for adult recognition of the complex and uncertain reality.

A holistic, egalitarian, inclusive set of values and conceptual models would be reflected in changed ways of making decisions, and in changed decisions – both at institutional and personal level. Perhaps what the book has demonstrated is that at the level of the neighbourhood there is a surprising degree of consensus about what it would be desirable to achieve, and an impressive range of exemplary projects. Change is sluggish because of the innate conservatism of bureaucracy and the market. But, as Goethe enjoined us – whatever you can do, or dream you can, *begin it*. Boldness has genius, power and magic in it.

# APPENDIX 1
## SURVEY OF ECO-NEIGHBOURHOODS WORLD-WIDE

*Deborah Kleiner and Hugh Barton*

## RESEARCH METHOD

The research process used to compile this appendix involved:

1 Literature search;
2 Internet search;
3 Personal interviews with people working in the 'eco-village' field.

Often a trail was initiated, perhaps beginning with a personal interview, leading to an Internet search, leading to personal communication with another party.

The main and most successful method of identifying case studies was via the Internet. The Global EcoVillage Network (GEN) has individual websites for each of the many offices. Most of the eco-villages listed are small-scale and it seems often to be the case that large scale developments are not listed. Each GEN office was sent an e-mail explaining our work and asking for further details of any eco-villages not listed on their websites. Some GEN offices were extremely helpful in passing on useful information. GEN Europe have been compiling a list similar to this of all eco-villages and had no qualms about sending us a copy of their unfinished work in return for a copy of ours. Many of the eco-villages listed, however, were very small-scale, some with only one member (http://www.gaia.org).

Another useful website is 'Intentional Communities' (http://www.ic.org/iclist.html) which has a frequently updated alphabetical list of intentional communities. Some of these are very small, often co-operative housing but some of the large sites are also listed.

## PROBLEMS ASSOCIATED WITH FINDING CASE STUDIES

There were problems associated with finding case studies as well as difficulties in defining criteria for selection. The main difficulties encountered are listed below:

1    The Internet is an extremely useful source of identifying sustainable commu-
     nities. However there are numerous websites to sift through with some being
     purely one person's dream of a sustainable settlement which had not yet
     shown any signs of realization;
2    Letters were sent to numerous contact addresses found either on a website or
     from a book reference. The response rate to these letters was around 20 per
     cent and replies were not received from that 20 per cent for at least a month.
     E-mails were also sent sometimes as a duplication to a letter. The response
     rate was higher but was still extremely poor. The reason for this was usually
     that there had not been a contact person on the letter, the letter was lost in
     the system or that the 'eco-village' was too busy to reply. It seems that most
     successful eco-villages receive numerous enquiries and have neither the money
     or time to respond to all of the enquiries they are sent;
3    Once contacts had been established there was concern from some contacts
     about exactly what would be written about their community. Some felt that
     they needed to know more about the book before sending information. This
     was extremely time consuming and costly;
4    As there is such a range of eco-villages in terms of scale, it proved difficult to
     define a minimum size. Some communities referred to themselves as an 'eco-
     village' when they were a small housing cooperative of say 30 people which
     did not necessarily meet sustainability criteria. However, there are some cases
     where a small cooperative does meet sustainability criteria associated with an
     'eco-village';
5    Another problem associated with selection criteria is 'how far towards sustain-
     ability should a settlement have gone – at what point do they count?';
6    A difficulty in a few cases was deciding whether a seemingly 'green' develop-
     ment is actually eco-friendly or whether only one particular aspect is. For
     example a televillage may qualify as a sustainable settlement due to the
     reduced commuting aspect but have all other sustainability criteria been
     addressed?

## CRITERIA FOR SELECTION

Due to the wide scope of research, encompassing a world-wide search for eco-
villages, three criteria were used in selecting case studies to list in this appendix:

1    Eco-village size/scale;
2    Eco-village stage (ie if the development was only at the initial concept stage
     without any local authority consultation to establish the likelihood of going
     ahead, it has been omitted);
3    Clearly fulfilling a number of sustainability criteria (see list in Appendix 2).

It is likely that there are a number of sustainable neighbourhoods that have been
omitted from the following list. The author apologises for this; every effort has
been made to ensure that the list below is as comprehensive as possible.

# Alphabetical List of Eco-Neighbourhoods
/ = information unavailable

| | |
|---|---|
| *Name of eco-neighbourhood:* | **Anningerblick, Austria** |
| *Initiator:* | Developer S-Wohnbau Gesellschaft – Vienna |
| *No. of residents/dwellings:* | 140 residential units |
| *Size:* | 32,771m$^2$ |
| *Type of neighbourhood:* | Urban greenfield |
| *Stage:* | Built |
| *Special features:* | Part financed by Austrian housing programme |
| *Contact:* | Developer – S-Wohnbau GmbH/S-Bausparkasse, Vienna |
| *Source:* | GEN Europe, D–31595 Steyerberg |

| | |
|---|---|
| *Name of eco-neighbourhood:* | **Arcosanti, Arizona, USA** |
| *Initiator:* | Arcosanti Foundation |
| *No. of residents/dwellings:* | 7000 people |
| *Size:* | 4060a (25a built up) |
| *Type of neighbourhood:* | Prototype town (high desert) |
| *Stage:* | Building started |
| *Special features:* | Demonstration of Paolo Soleri's theory of 'arcology', an integration of architecture, ecology and urban planning |
| *Contact:* | Jackie Engel Acosanti, HC 74 Box 4136, Mayer, AZ 86333, USA |
| *Source:* | Website: http://www.arcosanti.org/ |

| | |
|---|---|
| *Name of eco-neighbourhood:* | **Auf dem Schafbruhl, Germany** |
| *Initiator:* | Karlsruher Lebensversicherung AG, Germany |
| *No. of residents/dwellings:* | 111 residential units |
| *Size:* | 1.3ha |
| *Type of neighbourhood:* | Urban |
| *Stage:* | Built |
| *Special features:* | Subsidized 40 per cent loan from government |
| *Contact:* | Joachim and Barbara Eble tel: 030 852 08 10 |
| *Source:* | New Sustainable Settlements, EAUE, Bismarckallee 46–48, D–14193 Berlin, Germany |

| | |
|---|---|
| *Name of eco-neighbourhood:* | **Auroville, India** |
| *Initiator:* | 'The Mother', with support from Government and NGOs |
| *No. of residents/dwellings:* | 1300 people – planned to grow into a town of 40,000 |
| *Size:* | 25 km$^2$ |
| *Type of neighbourhood:* | New town – bio-region |
| *Stage:* | Established but growing |
| *Special features:* | Part of whole existing city approach – working with surrounding settlements |
| *Contact:* | Auroville Secretariat, Bharat Nivas, Auroville 605 101, Tamil Nadu, India |
| *Source:* | Website: http://www.auroville-india.org and Auroville UK, Chichester |

*Name of eco-neighbourhood:* **Bamberton, Canada**
*Initiator:* Development corporation
*No. of residents/dwellings:* 12,000 residents
*Size:* 1560 acres
*Type of neighbourhood:* New urban (town)
*Stage:* Planned
*Special features:* One job per household
*Contact and source:* Bamberton, 3rd Floor, 506 Fort Street, Victoria, British Columbia V8W 1E6 Canada. Tel: (+604) 3891 1888

*Name of eco-neighbourhood:* **Bottom Village, North Yorkshire, UK**
*Initiator:* Camphill Village Trust
*no. of residents/dwellings* 300+ people
*Size:* Several km²
*Type of neighbourhood:* Rural therapeutic community
*Stage:* Complete
*Special features:* Sheltered living and working community for mentally handicapped producing much of its food and household needs, biodynamic agriculture, sustainable forestry, water management, rural crafts. Note: Bottom is included here as representative of a whole set of Camphill Villages across the world
*Contact and source:* Camphill Village Trust, Bottom Village, Danby, North Yorkshire, UK

*Name of eco-neighbourhood:* **Boughton Energy Village 2001, Notts, UK**
*Initiator:* Newark and Sherwood District Council
*No. of residents/dwellings:* 1288 households
*Size:* 150a
*Type of neighbourhood:* Brownfield development
*Stage:* Planned
*Special features:* Incorporated into a current residential area. Zero $CO_2$ emissions
*Contact and source:* Ollerton and District Economic Forum, Stan Crawford, Sherwood Lodge Annexe, Sherwood Drive, New Ollerton, Nottinghamshire, NG22 9PP, UK

*Name of eco-neighbourhood:* **Ballerup Kommune, Denmark (2 schemes Osterhoj and Egebjerggard)**
*Initiator:* EU supported
*No. of residents/dwellings:* Around 700 households
*Size:* 40a and 50a
*Type of neighbourhood:* Urban greenfield
*Stage:* Planned – part built
*Special features:* Integrated home and workplace, side by side
*Contact and source:* Ballerup Kommune, Teknisk Forvaltning, Radhuset, DK 2750, Denmark

| *Name of eco-neighbourhood:* | **Civano, Tucson, USA** |
|---|---|
| *Initiator:* | / |
| *No. of residents/dwellings:* | 5000 people |
| *Size:* | / |
| *Type of neighbourhood:* | Urban greenfield |
| *Stage:* | Planned – zoning approved |
| *Special features:* | Aims to become world leading solar energy centre |
| *Contact and source:* | Website: http://www.civano.com e-mail: info@civano.com |

| *Name of eco-neighbourhood:* | **Crestone/Baca, Colorado, USA** |
|---|---|
| *Initiator:* | Manitou Foundation – created by H & M Strong to manage land grants |
| *No. of residents/dwellings:* | 328 homes built – 5527 lots available |
| *Size:* | 20 square miles |
| *Type of neighbourhood:* | Rural wilderness |
| *Stage:* | Part built |
| *Special features:* | Aims to support establishment of centres of the world's wisdom, traditions and religions |
| *Contact:* | Manitou Institute, PO Box 118, Crestone, CO 81131, USA |
| *Source:* | Website: http://www.gaia.org/manitou/ mi_obj_hx.html |

| *Name of eco-neighbourhood:* | **Centre for Alternative Technology, Wales, UK** |
|---|---|
| *Initiator:* | Charity |
| *No. of residents/dwellings:* | 30 people plus temporary residents |
| *Size:* | Several hectares of old quarry and tip |
| *Type of neighbourhood:* | Rural visitor centre |
| *Stage:* | Built |
| *Special features:* | Demonstration project run as cooperative, energy and water autonomous |
| *Contact and source:* | CAT, Llyngwern Quarry, Machynlleth, Powys, Wales, UK. Tel: (+44) (0)1654 702400 |

| *Name of eco-neighbourhood:* | **Crickhowell Televillage, UK** |
|---|---|
| *Initiator:* | Acorn Televillages |
| *No. of residents/dwellings:* | 30 |
| *Size:* | / |
| *Type of neighbourhood:* | Rural |
| *Stage:* | Built |
| *Special features:* | Part of network of televillages that will be set up by Acorn |
| *Contact:* | Ashley Dobbs, Acorn Televillages Ltd, The Televillage, Crickhowell, Powys NP8 1BP, UK Tel: (+44) (0)800 378848 |
| *Source:* | Website: http://ctr.cstp.umkc.edu/ NevadaTelecommunity/ |

| | |
|---|---|
| *Name of eco-neighbourhood:* | **Crossroads Co-Op, UK** |
| *Initiator:* | Community |
| *No. of residents/dwellings:* | / |
| *Size:* | 183ha |
| *Type of neighbourhood:* | Rural |
| *Stage:* | Ongoing |
| *Special features:* | Medieval inspiration – a village for living and working |
| *Contact:* | Crossroads |
| *Source:* | Website: http://www.crossroads.org.au/cross-roads_residences.html |

| | |
|---|---|
| *Name of eco-neighbourhood:* | **Crystal Waters, Australia** |
| *Initiator:* | Community |
| *No. of residents/dwellings:* | 200 people |
| *Size:* | 259ha |
| *Type of neighbourhood:* | Rural permaculture |
| *Stage:* | Built and ongoing expansion |
| *Special features:* | Permaculture village |
| *Contact and source:* | Max Lindeggar, Regional Coordinator, Global Eco-village Network, 59 Crystal Waters, ms 16, maleny qld 4552, Australia. Tel: (+61) 7 5494 4741. Fax: (+61) 7 5494 4578. E-mail: lindegger@gen-oceania.org |

| | |
|---|---|
| *Name of eco-neighbourhood:* | **Dancing Rabbit Ecovillage, Missouri, USA** |
| *Initiator:* | Community |
| *No. of residents/dwellings:* | 500–1000 residents |
| *Size:* | 280a |
| *Type of neighbourhood:* | Rural |
| *Stage:* | Pioneering stage |
| *Special features:* | Plans to be locally self-reliant small town |
| *Contact:* | 1 Dancing Rabbit Lane, Rutledge, MO 63563, USA. E-mail dancingrabbit@ic.org |
| *Source:* | http://www.woodwind.com/dancing-rabbit |

| | |
|---|---|
| *Name of eco-neighbourhood:* | **Davis City, USA** |
| *Initiator:* | City Council |
| *No. of residents/dwellings:* | 50,000 people |
| *Size:* | 101.6sqm |
| *Type of neighbourhood:* | Existing city being greened |
| *Stage:* | Ongoing |
| *Special features:* | / |
| *Contact and source:* | Davis California, Planning and Building Dept., 23 Russell Boulevard, Davis, California 95616, USA |

| | |
|---|---|
| *Name of eco-neighbourhood:* | **Dreamtime Village, USA** |
| *Initiator:* | Community |
| *No. of residents/dwellings:* | Six buildings currently with aims to grow |
| *Size:* | 80a |
| *Type of neighbourhood:* | Rural |
| *Stage:* | Ongoing |
| *Special features:* | Rural experiment in combining permaculture with hypermedia arts |

| | |
|---|---|
| *Contact:* | Dreamtime Village, Rt 1 Box 131, LaFarge, WI 54639, USA |
| | E-mail: dtv@mwt.net |
| *Source:* | Website: http://www.net22.com/dreamtime/ index.shtml |

| | |
|---|---|
| *Name of eco-neighbourhood:* | **Earthaven Eco-village, North Carolina, USA** |
| *Initiator:* | Community |
| *No. of residents/dwellings:* | Currently 30 with aim for 120–160 people |
| *Size:* | 325a |
| *Type of neighbourhood:* | Rural |
| *Stage:* | Building started and ongoing |
| *Special features:* | Demonstration project |
| *Contact:* | Earthaven, PO Box 1107, Black Mountain, NC 28711, USA. Tel: 704–298–2399. |
| | Email: info@earthaven.org |
| *Source:* | Website: http://www.earthaven.org/us/intro/htm |

| | |
|---|---|
| *Name of eco-neighbourhood:* | **Ecolonia, The Netherlands** |
| *Initiator:* | The Netherlands Agency for Energy and Environment |
| *No. of residents/dwellings:* | 280 buildings |
| *Size:* | / |
| *Type of neighbourhood:* | Urban |
| *Stage:* | Ongoing |
| *Special features:* | Demonstration project |
| *Contact:* | Novem Siottard, Swentiboldstraat 21, PO Box 17, 6130 AA Sittard, The Netherlands |
| *Source:* | Novem publications 'Ecolonia' and 'The Road to Ecolonia' |

| | |
|---|---|
| *Name of eco-neighbourhood:* | **The Farm, Tennessee, USA** |
| *Initiator:* | Community |
| *No. of residents/dwellings:* | 250 residents |
| *Size:* | 1750a |
| *Type of neighbourhood:* | Rural Eco-village |
| *Stage:* | Built |
| *Special features:* | Over 300 acres restored to productive organic agriculture |
| *Contact:* | The Gate, 34 The Farm, Summertown TN 38483, USA |
| *Source:* | Website: http://www.faia.org/farm/general/ farmfaq.html |

| | |
|---|---|
| *Name of eco-neighbourhood:* | **Findhorn Bay Community, Scotland, UK** |
| *Initiator:* | Community – Eileen and Peter Caddy, Dorothy Maclean |
| *No. of residents/dwellings:* | 350 people |
| *Size:* | 20ha |
| *Type of neighbourhood:* | Rural |
| *Stage:* | Built but ongoing |
| *Special features:* | Eco-centre |
| *Contact:* | E-mail: ecovillage@findhorn.org |
| *Source:* | Website: http://www.mcn.org/findhorn |

*Name of eco-neighbourhood:* **Gorgie Car Free (Edinburgh), Scotland, UK**
*Initiator:* Housing Association (Canmore)
*No. of residents/dwellings:* 120 flats
*Size:* 1.4a
*Type of neighbourhood:* Urban new build
*Stage:* Planning permission received
*Special features:* Car free
*Contact and source:* Canmore Housing Association, Canmore House, 193 Dalry Road, Edinburgh, EH11 2EB, UK

*Name of eco-neighbourhood:* **Greenwich Millennium Village, UK**
*Initiator:* Government and private sector
*No. of residents/dwellings:* 1377 residents
*Size:* 13ha
*Type of neighbourhood:* Urban village, brownfield
*Stage:* First planning permission granted
*Special features:* Pre-manufactured homes, low energy and CHP, cycleways, LRT
*Contact and source:* Canmore Housing Association, Canmore House, 193 Dalry Road, Edinburgh, EH11 2EB, UK

*Name of eco-neighbourhood:* **Grunenstrabe 17, Bremen, Germany**
*Initiator:* Community
*No. of residents/dwellings:* 43 people
*Size:* 850m²
*Type of neighbourhood:* Urban renewal
*Stage:* Complete
*Special features:* Building included 500 DIY hours per person – no car park
*Contact:* Dipl.-ing Architekt, Pit Klasen, Holbeinstrabe 12, 28209 Bremen, Germany
*Source:* Pit Klasen – personal communication

*Name of eco-neighbourhood:* **Gyurufu, Hungary**
*Initiator:* Community
*No. of residents/dwellings:* 19 people, growing
*Size:* 1000ha – only 250ha bought so far
*Type of neighbourhood:* Rural
*Stage:* First house under construction
*Special features:* Emphasis on IT and telecommunication.
*Contact:* E-mail: bela@borsos.zpok.hu

*Name of eco-neighbourhood:* **Halifax, Australia**
*Initiator:* Community organization
*No. of residents/dwellings:* 800–1000 residents
*Size:* 2.4ha
*Type of neighbourhood:* Ecopolis – urban redevelopment and rural renewal
*Stage:* Planned
*Special features:* Car free – in heart of Adelaide
*Contact:* The Halifax Project Management Team, c/o Urban Ecology Australia inc, PO Box 3040, Grenfell St, Adelaide, Tandanya Bioregion, SA 5000, Australia

| | |
|---|---|
| *Name of eco-neighbourhood:* | **Hocamkoy, Turkey** |
| *Initiator:* | Mainly University students |
| *No. of residents/dwellings:* | Undecided as yet |
| *Size:* | / |
| *Type of neighbourhood:* | Rural |
| *Stage:* | Ongoing |
| *Special features:* | Restoration of barren landscapes and aim to provide solutions to large scale migration of villagers who have settled in slums |
| *Contact:* | Hocamkoy Movement, Kircicydedy Sok. No 5/2 G.O.P., 06700 Ankarra, Turkey |
| *Source:* | Website: http://hocamkoy.metu.edu.tr/ whoarewe.html |

| | |
|---|---|
| *Name of eco-neighbourhood:* | **Hockerton Earth-sheltered Housing, Leicestershire, UK** |
| *Initiator:* | Self-build group |
| *No. of residents/dwellings:* | 7 dwellings |
| *Size:* | / |
| *Type of neighbourhood:* | Rural |
| *Stage:* | Ongoing |
| *Special features:* | Self-build, earth-sheltered solar buildings; hoping to be self-sufficient in energy; sewage treatment in reedbeds |
| *Contact:* | / |
| *Source:* | / |

| | |
|---|---|
| *Name of eco-neighbourhood:* | **Ithaca, USA** |
| *Initiator:* | Centre for Religion, Ethics and Social Policy |
| *No. of residents/dwellings:* | 30 homes built – aim for 500 residents |
| *Size:* | 176a |
| *Type of neighbourhood:* | Urban greenfield |
| *Stage:* | Part built |
| *Special features:* | / |
| *Contact:* | Ecovillage at Ithaca, Anabel Taylor Hall, Cornell University, Ithaca, NY 14853, USA |
| *Source:* | Website: http://www.cfe.cornell.edu/ecovillage/ guide.html |

| | |
|---|---|
| *Name of eco-neighbourhood:* | **Jarlanbah Permaculture Hamlet, Australia** |
| *Initiator:* | Community |
| *No. of residents/dwellings:* | 43 dwellings |
| *Size:* | 12ha |
| *Type of neighbourhood:* | Rural |
| *Stage:* | 30 home sites sold |
| *Special features:* | Education centre on 2ha site |
| *Contact and source:* | E-mail: jhunter@nor.com.au PO Box 188, Nimbinb NSW 2480, Australia |

| | |
|---|---|
| *Name of eco-neighbourhood:* | **Kitezh Childrens Eco-Village, Russia** |
| *Initiator:* | Community |
| *No. of residents/dwellings:* | 50 people |
| *Size:* | 90ha |
| *Type of neighbourhood:* | Rural |
| *Stage:* | Ongoing |
| *Special features:* | Community of foster families for orphan children |
| *Contact:* | Ecologia Trust, Scotland |
| | E-mail: ecoliza@rmplc.co.uk |
| *Source:* | Website: http://communities.gaia.org/kitezh |

| | |
|---|---|
| *Name of eco-neighbourhood:* | **Kolding, Denmark** |
| *Initiator:* | Kolding Council |
| *No. of residents/dwellings:* | 129 dwellings |
| *Size:* | / |
| *Type of neighbourhood:* | Urban Renewal |
| *Stage:* | Complete |
| *Special features:* | Local biological sewage treatment plant/pyramid |
| *Contact and source:* | The Urban Renewal Company, Byfornyelsesselskabet Danmark, Lasbygade 65, DK–6000 Kolding, Denmark |

| | |
|---|---|
| *Name of eco-neighbourhood:* | **LA Ecovillage, USA** |
| *Initiator:* | Community |
| *No. of residents/dwellings:* | 500 people |
| *Size:* | 2 blocks acres |
| *Type of neighbourhood:* | Neighbourhood redevelopment |
| *Stage:* | Ongoing |
| *Special features:* | / |
| *Source:* | Website: http://www.context.org/iclib/ic29/arkin.htm |
| *Contact:* | Mary Maverick, 3551 White House Place, Los Angeles, CA 90004, USA |
| | Tel: (+1) 213/738 1254 |
| | E-mail: crsp@igc.apc.org |

| | |
|---|---|
| *Name of eco-neighbourhood:* | **Kookabura Park Eco-village, Australia** |
| *Initiator:* | Community |
| *No. of residents/dwellings:* | 60 people |
| *Size:* | 190ha/485a |
| *Type of neighbourhood:* | Rural |
| *Stage:* | Building |
| *Special features:* | Focus on natural health education |
| *Contact and source:* | Grant Davies, 3 Kookaburra Park, m/s 368, Gin gin, qld. 4671, Australia. E-mail: grant@ic.org |

| | |
|---|---|
| *Name of eco-neighbourhood:* | **Ladakh, Western Himalayas, India** |
| *Initiator:* | Ancient settlement |
| *No. of residents/dwellings:* | / |
| *Size:* | / |
| *Type of neighbourhood:* | Rural |
| *Stage:* | Established for over 1000 years |
| *Special features:* | Autonomous settlement following ancient tradi- |

| | |
|---|---|
| *Stage:* | Base house established and development plans drawn up |
| *Special features:* | Aim to set up a research station for studies of traditional techniques |
| *Contact:* | / |
| *Source:* | Website: http://www.gaia.org/nevo/objectives.htm |

| | |
|---|---|
| *name of eco neighbourhood* | **Okotop, Dusseldorf, Germany** |
| *Initiator:* | Community |
| *No. of residents/dwellings:* | 200 homes |
| *Size:* | 160,000m$^2$ |
| *Type of neighbourhood:* | Urban fringe |
| *Stage:* | Funding awarded by City of Dusseldorf and enterprise foundations |
| *Special features:* | 1/3 government rented flats, 1/3 private flats, 1/3 single family dwellings |
| *Contact:* | fachochschule anhalt, postfach 1458, d–06354 kothem. anhalt, Germany |
| *Source:* | ELASA 1996 |

| | |
|---|---|
| *Name of eco-neighbourhood:* | **Ouje-Bougoumou cree, Canada** |
| *Initiator:* | Community |
| *No. of residents/dwellings:* | 650 |
| *Size:* | 1000km$^2$ |
| *Type of neighbourhood:* | Remote rural |
| *Stage:* | Built |
| *Special features:* | District heating fuelled by waste wood from sawmills |
| *Contact:* | Paul Wertman. 24 Bayswater Ave, Ottawa, Ontario, Canada K1Y 2E4, E-mail: ouje@magi.com |
| *Source:* | Paul Wertman e-mail 17/10/97 |

| | |
|---|---|
| *Name of eco-neighbourhood:* | **Plants for a Future, UK** |
| *Initiator:* | Non-profit group |
| *No. of residents/dwellings:* | 10 people (and growing) |
| *Size:* | 84a |
| *Type of neighbourhood:* | Rural |
| *Stage:* | Awaiting planning permission |
| *Special features:* | Resource centre for information on useful plants |
| *Contact:* | The Field, Penpol, Loswithiel, Cornwall, PL22 0NG, UK. Tel: (+44) (0)1208 873 553 |

| | |
|---|---|
| *Name of eco-neighbourhood:* | **Puchenau II, Linz, Austria** |
| *Initiator:* | Municipality |
| *No. of residents/dwellings:* | 5000 people |
| *Size:* | 1.5km x 100–150m wide |
| *Type of neighbourhood:* | Urban |
| *Stage:* | Mix of public and private funding |
| *Special features:* | District heating |
| *Contact:* | Municipality of Puchenau, Nr Linz, Upper Austria |
| *Source:* | New Sustainable Settlements 1994 |

tions. Traditional agriculture produces enou
food in growing season to last whole year.
Modernization now threatens this lifestyle.
Projects are now set up to tackle problems

| | |
|---|---|
| *Contact:* | ISEC, Apple Barn, Week, Totnes, Devon TQ9 UK. Tel: (+44) (0)1803 868651 or Ladakh Ecological Development Group, Leh, Ladakt 194101, India |
| *Source:* | Website: http://www.gaia.org/ladakh.html |

| | |
|---|---|
| *Name of eco-neighbourhood:* | **Lebensgarten Steyerberg, Germany** |
| *Initiator:* | Community |
| *No. of residents/dwellings:* | 86 |
| *Size:* | 4ha |
| *Type of neighbourhood:* | Rural renewal |
| *Stage:* | Built |
| *Special features:* | Part of ecovillage network |
| *Contact and source:* | Website: http://www.gaia.org/lebensgarten |

| | |
|---|---|
| *Name of eco-neighbourhood:* | **Little River, New Zealand** |
| *Initiator:* | Community |
| *No. of residents/dwellings:* | 400 (80 units to be built) |
| *Size:* | / |
| *Type of neighbourhood:* | Rural renewal |
| *Stage:* | Existing community – rest at paperwork stage |
| *Special features:* | Built within an existing community bringing the ecovillage concept into the mainstream model |
| *Contact and source:* | Catherine Edmeades University of Auckland, Private Bag 92019, Auckland, New Zealand E-mail c.edmeades@auckland.ac.nz |

| | |
|---|---|
| *Name of eco-neighbourhood:* | **Lykovryssi, Athens, Greece** |
| *Initiator:* | Greek/German programme |
| *No. of residents/dwellings:* | 435 families of workers |
| *Size:* | 7.2ha |
| *Type of neighbourhood:* | Urban fringe |
| *Stage:* | Complete |
| *Special features:* | Demonstration project to find out more about rational use of energy, about utilizing solar energy to provide heating and hot water for residential use and to test various active and passive systems in terms of technical performance as well as economic and social acceptability |
| *Contact:* | Alexandros N Tombazis, 85 Marathonodromou Str., GR–154 52 Psychico, Greece |
| *Source:* | Declan Kennedy – GEN Europe and Landscape Design Sept 1996 and ELASA 1996 |

| | |
|---|---|
| *Name of eco-neighbourhood:* | **Nevo Ecovillage, Karelia, Russia** |
| *Initiator:* | Community |
| *No. of residents/dwellings:* | 12 residents at present |
| *Size:* | 26ha |
| *Type of neighbourhood:* | Rural |

| | |
|---|---|
| *Name of eco-neighbourhood:* | **Rosneath Farm Eco-Village, West Australia** |
| *Initiator:* | Community |
| *No. of residents/dwellings:* | 71 lots |
| *Size:* | 144ha |
| *Type of neighbourhood:* | Rural |
| *Stage:* | Ongoing |
| *Special features:* | Each lot will be 1/2 acre to preserve 60ha of forest and streams and 60ha of farming land. Each family will run their own farming operation (beekeeping/wine making/marron farming/orchards etc) |
| *Contact:* | Warwick Rowell, Rosneath Farm, PO Box 250, Dunsborought 6281, WA |
| *Source:* | Website: http://communties.gaia.org/rosneath-farm/ |

| | |
|---|---|
| *Name of eco-neighbourhood:* | **Sherwood Energy Village, UK** |
| *Initiator:* | Community |
| *No. of residents/dwellings:* | 65 dwellings |
| *Size:* | 50ha |
| *Type of neighbourhood:* | Urban brownfield |
| *Stage:* | Not built – funding applied for |
| *Special features:* | Former colliery site – contaminated land |
| *Contact:* | Sherwood Energy Village, Sherwood Lodge Annexe, Sherwood Drive, New Ollerton, Nottinghamshire NG22 9PP, UK |
| *Source:* | Carla Jamison at Sherwood Energy Village E-mail: sev@netcomuk.co.uk |

| | |
|---|---|
| *Name of eco-neighbourhood:* | **Sirius, Massachussetts, USA** |
| *Initiator:* | Community |
| *No. of residents/dwellings:* | Around 40 people |
| *Size:* | 93a |
| *Type of neighbourhood:* | Rural |
| *Stage:* | Formed in 1978 by former members of Findhorn |
| *Special features:* | Primary activity – each member's personal spiritual growth |
| *Contact:* | E-mail: clrwater@valinet.com |
| *Source:* | Website: http://siriuscommunity.org/ecovillage1.html |

| | |
|---|---|
| *Name of eco-neighbourhood:* | **Solheimar, Southern Iceland** |
| *Initiator:* | / |
| *No. of residents/dwellings:* | 100 people |
| *Size:* | 250ha |
| *Type of neighbourhood:* | Rural |
| *Stage:* | Built |
| *Special features:* | First community where able and disabled people live and work together |
| *Contact and source:* | Solheimar, 801 selfoss, Iceland. Tel +(354) 486 4430 |

| | |
|---|---|
| *Name of eco-neighbourhood:* | **Solta Eco-village, Yugoslavia** |
| *Initiator:* | 10–15 houses |
| *Size:* | / |
| *Type of neighbourhood:* | Urban renewal |
| *Stage:* | / |
| *Special features:* | Network of eco-settlements to integrate recreational and educational aspects of tourism with traditional ways of life in Solta |
| *Contact:* | Mr Milivoj Burica, Director of Jugoplasika, 58 430 Grohote, Island Solta, Yugoslavia |
| *Source:* | Website: http://www.context.org/ICLIB/IC29/Cluster.htm |

| | |
|---|---|
| *Name of eco-neighbourhood:* | **Svanholm Collective, Sealand, Denmark** |
| *Initiator:* | Community |
| *No. of residents/dwellings:* | 120 residents |
| *Size:* | 988a |
| *Type of neighbourhood:* | Rural eco-village |
| *Stage:* | Built |
| *Special features:* | Intentional community – common ideals concerning ecology, income sharing, communal living and self government |
| *Contact:* | Visitors group, Svanholm gods, 4050 Skibby, Denmark |

| | |
|---|---|
| *Name of eco-neighbourhood:* | **Tir Gaia Solar Village, Wales, UK** |
| *Initiator:* | David Stephens, private |
| *No. of residents/dwellings:* | 200 people, 60 dwellings |
| *Size:* | 9a |
| *Type of neighbourhood:* | Greenfield, next to town of 2000 |
| *Stage:* | Permission received |
| *Special features:* | Active and passive solar features |
| *Contact and source:* | David Stephens, Tir Gaia solar village, Rhayader, Powys ID6 5AG. E-mail: david@sustain.force9.co.uk Website: http://www.sustain.force9.co.uk |

| | |
|---|---|
| *Name of eco-neighbourhood:* | **Torsted vest, Denmark** |
| *Initiator:* | Horsens town with citizens |
| *No. of residents/dwellings:* | / |
| *Size:* | 130a |
| *Type of neighbourhood:* | Urban greenfield |
| *Stage:* | Started |
| *Special features:* | Developers encouraged to experiment with local wastewater treatment, use recycled material in roads etc, give residents opportunity to grow local food as well as other ecological perspectives. |
| *Contact:* | Horsens Kommune, Radhustorvet 4, 8700 Horsens, Denmark |
| *Source:* | City Architect Henrik Bertelsen, Horsens Kommune |

| | |
|---|---|
| *Name of eco-neighbourhood:* | **Torup, Denmark** |
| *Initiator:* | community |
| *No. of residents/dwellings:* | 85 people |
| *Size:* | 13ha |
| *Type of neighbourhood:* | Rural, greenfield development |
| *Stage:* | Built but ongoing |
| *Special features:* | Co-housing structure |
| *Contact:* | Soren Fritzsche, Okologisk Landsbysamfund, Hagendrupvej 6, Torup, dk–3390 Hundested, Denmark. Tel: (+45) 4798 3668 E-mail: moondome@centrum.dk |
| *Source:* | 'The eco-village at Torup' leaflet |

| | |
|---|---|
| *Name of eco-neighbourhood:* | **West Harwood, Lothian, Scotland, UK** |
| *Initiator:* | Local authority and private sector |
| *No. of residents/dwellings:* | 12 houses |
| *Size:* | 90ha |
| *Type of neighbourhood:* | Rural resettlement |
| *Stage:* | Complete |
| *Special features:* | Reafforestation and small-holdings |
| *Contact and source:* | New Lives, New Landscapes |

| | |
|---|---|
| *Name of eco-neighbourhood:* | **Whyalla, Australia** |
| *Initiator:* | City Council |
| *No. of residents/dwellings:* | Unknown |
| *Size:* | 15ha |
| *Type of neighbourhood:* | City centre new core site |
| *Stage:* | Planned |
| *Special features:* | Part of whole existing city approach |
| *Contact:* | Ecopolis pty. ltd E-mail: urbanec@dove.mtx.net.au |
| *Source:* | Website: http://www.eastend.com.au/ ~ecology/whyalla |

| | |
|---|---|
| *Name of eco-neighbourhood:* | **Wilhelmina Gasthuis-Terrein, Amsterdam, The Netherlands** |
| *Initiator:* | Municipality and Local Group |
| *No. of residents/dwellings:* | 86 dwellings |
| *Size:* | 12ha |
| *Type of neighbourhood:* | Urban renewal |
| *Stage:* | Complete |
| *Special features:* | Regeneration of hospital grounds and buildings |
| *Contact:* | / |
| *Source:* | Declan Kennedy, GEN Europe |

## APPENDIX 2

## CASE STUDIES OF ECO-NEIGHBOURHOODS

*Deborah Kleiner*

This appendix includes the following case studies:

- rural eco-villages:
  Crystal Waters; West Harwood; Little River; Crickhowell Televillage;
- urban greenfield:
  Ithaca; Ecolonia;
- urban renewal:
  Halifax; Kolding; Canmore Car Free Development; Sherwood;
- eco-towns:
  Davis; Auroville.

These case studies are an attempt to illustrate the vast range of eco-neighbourhoods in existence. The geographical spread of the selected case studies reflects the fact that initiatives are being developed all over the world. All of the case studies are either already established or are well developed and very likely to get planning permission. It is clear that the case studies illustrate both good and bad practice and the summaries are by no means intended as recipes for successful sustainable neighbourhoods. They are purely providing a taster of the innovations that exist. The following are outlines of the schemes with the main themes pulled out and evaluated. The criteria against which these developments are evaluated are:

- *energy:* local supply of heat/electricity – heat loss reduction in building and neighbourhood design;
- *water:* minimizing demand, maximizing reuse, on site treatment and good infiltration;
- *transport:* pedestrian and cycling permeability, means of reducing car reliance;
- *activities:* localized work/workspace, community based services and facilities, local food/fuel production;
- *landscape:* design for wildlife, recreation, pollution control, organic recycling process;

- *building:* for long life, low energy, loose fit, materials conservation, reuse, low embodied energy;
- *layout:* for conviviality, distinctiveness and delight, integrated functional solutions;
- *implementation:* self build/private market/social agencies, eco-sensitive construction process;
- *management:* of housing, land and services/activities, maximizing user control, maintaining sustainability attributes.

It would be unfair to the initiators of these case studies to give an in-depth critique without visiting each development. It was not possible to visit each case study to interview residents and relevant bodies. This would have provided a much greater possibility for evaluation. Therefore, it is hoped that the descriptions given provide a basis for the reader's own evaluation.

# TYPE 1: RURAL ECO-VILLAGE

## Crystal Waters – Queensland, Australia

### Aims and Origins

Crystal Waters was evolved by a group of people with a keenness to take responsibility for their needs and to live more sustainably. The residents of Crystal Waters aim to create a viable internal economy and for people to be free to express their own beliefs.

Initiated in 1985, Crystal Waters was not developed for speculation. The four designers set up a Trust Fund, encouraging would-be residents to lodge sufficient funds. Having reached this goal, the $250,000 profit was handed over to the cooperative and used for community buildings and the visitors camping area.

### Description

Crystal Waters permaculture village is 260ha of land, now home to 200 residents who are committed to working with rather than against nature. It is located 1.5 hours drive north of Brisbane with Maleny, the nearest settlement being 27km away. Maleny is a small town with a population of around 3000 with a small supermarket, doctors, dentists and a hospital. The nearest urban centre is Caloundra which is an hour's drive away. The infrastructure is in place with 70 houses completed or under construction and ten more to be built.

Currently, over one third of residents are children, the adults being mainly 30–45. The dwellings are varied in style and value with a few using renewable energy systems for electricity and hot water. Residents have 18 by-laws to abide by covering issues such as vehicle speed, flora and fauna protection, children and invitee behaviour, prohibition of keeping animals etc.

A village area has been incorporated into the design which will become the commercial centre for the community. So far the kitchen, a restaurant, a shop and information centre are complete which are used by the community.

There are many businesses and occupations at Crystal Waters with the main business being in the building trade. Occupations range from accountants and architects to mail order businesses and university lecturers. Most residents work from home but a few have part time work in Maleny with some people travelling to Brisbane a couple of days a week. Some people are on pensions, some unemployed or unemployable. Many residents grow their own food in their permaculture gardens and 80 per cent of the land is available for sustainable agriculture, forestry, recreation and habitat. Very few residents make an income solely from farming the land. Large parts of Crystal Waters were cleared in the 1960s and in recent years trees have been planted by residents. In the future, these trees will contribute to firewood and construction timber requirements as well as providing wildlife habitat.

### Comment

Crystal Waters tackles many sustainability issues admirably with the design based on permaculture ethics ensuring that all these issues are addressed. As long as new as well as existing residents are as committed to working with nature, the current plethora of sustainable features are likely to be maintained. A minor concern is the fact that Crystal Waters is considerably isolated from other communities. Autonomy cannot be a goal if the population remains at 250, as the nearest doctors, dentists and supermarkets are 27km away. While the village is already exemplary, Lindegger envisions it eventually becoming not only more self-reliant, but non-parasitic in terms of its food production and energy use. The key to sustaining Crystal Waters' accomplishments will be in nurturing not just a permanent agriculture, but a permanent culture as well (http://www.context.org).

## West Harwood, Lothian – Scotland

### Aims and Origins

Lowland crofting is a local authority initiative which aims to create a well wooded landscape whilst providing upmarket houses and allowing farmers to retire from farming with a premium.

One aim of a new lowland croft development at West Harwood is to improve economic prospects by enhancing the area's image and attracting business managers to the area. Other aims are to improve the environment for wildlife and provide public access to the countryside.

### Description

On 90ha of extensive overgrazed marginal farmland, with drained watercourses, 12 low density houses with gardens now stand amongst 40ha of four year old mixed woodland with 5km of public paths. West Harwood is the first development of this kind, now complete and with two more schemes in the pipeline. 50 per cent of the so called 'crofters' (inhabitants) at West Harwood have some form of business based at home but none make a living entirely from the land. The 'crofters' are generally middle aged local couples who have done well enough economically to be able to afford £45,000 for the serviced plot of land. Practically all the residents at Harwood are using their plots as amenity gardens, some with vegetable patches. Around half the plots contain an acre or so of new woodland which are currently being managed by the developers but in the future by individual residents. A couple of residents keep ducks, geese and hens and some intend to keep horses.

The West Harwood scheme has some ecologically beneficial features such as a biological reedbed sewage treatment system. 'Crofters' are obliged to join a residents association and are responsible for managing common facilities such as sewers, roads, hedges.

## Comment

Lowland crofting allows new housing to be built on degraded farmland which might not ordinarily be redeveloped according to existing planning policy. West Harwood fails on some sustainability criteria as it is a low density out-of-town commuter development, inhabited by affluent urbanites with high car usage (Young, 1997). Although the developers of West Harwood (New Lives, New Landscapes) are striving for more sustainable development, they are restricted by local authority policy. For example, the developer believes lowland crofts should be located closer to existing settlements/infrastructure. This conflicts with West Lothian Council whose policy is that farms that are close to towns and villages would create an 'unacceptable impression of suburbanization' (West Lothian Council, 1997). They also lack social cohesion, being spread too thinly and are too small to maintain autonomy in terms of inhabitants needs.

Although low density housing is not as energy efficient, lowland crofts could be forgiven as West Lothian lacks upmarket housing which may detract businesses from the area. West Harwood is a stepping stone towards a potentially sustainable dual concept of providing housing and reforestation.

## Little River – New Zealand

### Aims and Origins

Little River is an existing community of 400 people in a network of valleys in Canterbury, New Zealand. Currently Little River's water supply is polluted and inadequate and traditional farming has become uneconomic. These problems have led to the conception of a new eco-village within the existing community. After a thorough consultation process, Little River are aiming for an eco-village with the addition of 80 new households. The concept came from a Local Agenda 21 process by 'Common Ground and Sustainable Cities Trust' funded by the District Council.

### Description

A community trust was set up in June 1997 chaired by the local shop/café owner, Stewart. The shop is used as an information point where Stewart and his wife update the 'Little River Blackboards' daily. The trust have agreed on a number of sustainable outcomes which include; access for all, health, safety, community, art/richness/identity, equity, vitality, tolerance, prosperity, affordability, empowerment, energy conservation, regeneration, biodiversity, personal achievement, cleanliness, environmentally benign settlements and self-determination.

The village centre will include cluster housing with both communal and private space. Each cluster will have space for local food production. The housing will be diverse with a range of tenures and housing types. All buildings will be sited to maximize passive solar gain and residents will be encouraged to come off the grid. Water will be collected on roofs for landscape irrigation and possibly for household consumption. Permeable surfaces will be used wherever possible returning water to the ground to maintain healthy waterways. Waste water will be treated in a Bio Centre which produces hydroponically grown crops, fish and clean water as its end products. Heat will be generated and transferred to an indoor community swimming pool.

The village is designed to minimize car use and is compact to ensure all amenities can be reached by foot within ten minutes. A public access strip will connect the currently inaccessible river with the village. A strong identity is planned for the village by way of the 'Little River Brand'. All goods produced in the village that meet specific criteria will be awarded the quality stamp and products will be marketed regionally, nationally and internationally. Children are an integral part of the consultation process and their most crucial needs are for a cycle and walking path separated from the main road as well as for a meeting place.

## Comment

The initiative of Banks District Council to commission a strategy for community empowered change has undoubtedly provided a catalyst for change that may not otherwise have existed. The team, namely 'Common Ground and Sustainable Cities Trust', have been sure to consult and involve the community during the strategy development. Due to this approach, the project has become more 'bottom-up' than 'top-down', a healthy sign that any change will be more likely to benefit the residents at Little River. The community appear to have been extremely accepting of the 'study team' with many offering their spare rooms to the consultants. This has given the team a true insight into the heart of the community.

The proposal for Little River has considered a vast range of sustainability issues with an admirable focus on village identity in the form of the 'Little River' brand on locally produced products. The design team have come up with innovative solutions to the sustainability challenge.

## Crickhowell Televillage, Brecon Beacons National Park, Wales

### Aims and Origins

The concept of televillages has not yet come to fruition in the UK. 'Acorn Televillages' seem to have cornered the market for this new approach to low transport developments. Acorn's base is at one of its' first developments at Crickhowell in the Brecon Beacons National Park. Unfortunately, we do not have comprehensive information on Crickhowell, mainly due to Acorn's opinion that 'it would be foolish to pass on the knowledge which we have spent several million developing' (Dobbs, 1997). However, the concept of homeworking is potentially a solution to the commuter problem.

### Description

When complete, Crickhowell will consist of 30 homes, workspace, workshops, a telecentre and a café. All houses will be linked into a fibre optic network which forms a Local Area Network (LAN) within the televillage. Although most homes are detached, flats as well as one bedroom terraces are included. Car parks have been kept to the edge of the site, to discourage traffic within the site. There do not appear to be any water features or wildlife spaces but there has been a major focus on the 'village' feel. The houses are designed to be adaptable to living and working requirements with an attempt to use local craftspeople for small touches such as lightfittings. It is stated in the Acorn brochure that homes are some of the most energy efficient. The brochure shows an 'example' of an Acorn home referring to the use of more wall insulation than a typical home. Acorn have sold and built all of the smaller units in Crickhowell and are currently selling and building the houses in the £149,000 upwards price range (Acorn, 6th June 1998).

*Comment*
Overall, Acorn has responded admirably to trends and aspirations to shift towards self-employment and to achieve a better quality of life. It would seem that Acorn have tackled the sustainability issues of localized work, a means of reducing car reliance as well as convivial and distinctive homes. In order for this development to become truly sustainable there are many other issues that can be considered such as local energy supply, self-build, eco-sensitive construction, a wider housing choice etc. Combine Acorn's approach with some of the permaculture features from villages such as Crystal Waters and this development would be closer to a sustainable autonomous settlement than many. However, a problem often associated with developer led schemes is the lack of community involvement. Acorn's brochure shows no evidence that the televillage ideals have come from the community. Some recent research has shown that there has been some scepticism from local residents towards the televillage. This is not helped by the fact that there has been no input from local organizations prior to the development (Paternoster, 1998). This research has also shown that the televillage is 'plagued by its own success as a residential development' (Paternoster, 1998) as many have chosen to purchase their retirement or holiday home there. Thirty-six per cent of residents work from home full time with 54 per cent wanting to work from home.

# TYPE 2: URBAN GREENFIELD

## *Ithaca – New York USA*
### *Aims and Origins*
Launched under the auspices of The Centre for Religion Ethics and Social Policy, the first newsletter was produced in August 1991 following a public presentation of ecovillage visions to 100 members of the local community. A foundation was formed with the basic idea of a pedestrian village of neighbourhood clusters.

A document involving the input of 100 people was developed with guidelines for site development. These guidelines consist of clear goals which are written as 11 headings; residential neighbourhood, village centre complex, visitor's centre, ecovillage education and research centre, agricultural, transportation and circulation, natural resources and recreation, water and waste-water, solid waste, energy, building materials and social. Each of these aspects have two to five aims with objectives to match such as to reduce the amount of solid waste generated on-site, to encourage pedestrian and cycle circulation, to form of a sense of community, create a gateway to the village, develop on-site employment opportunities, minimize water use, promote reuse, recycling and composting as well as many other vital goals, all relating to Ithaca's sustainability potential, (http://www.cfe.cornell.edu.ecovillage.guide.html, 1997).

## Description

The 176a site is consciously located on a bus route at the edge of the Ithaca city, two miles west of downtown Ithaca. The Danish co-housing model has been used in constructing the first neighbourhood of 30 homes with the second group at planning stage. Elements that define co-housing are:

- individually owned houses (sometimes rather smaller than typical);
- a common house with large dining room and kitchen and other shared facilities (laundry, teenager's den, crèche etc);
- some shared meals each week;
- pedestrian friendly neighbourhood, parking away from houses;
- resident management, often using consensus processes;
- emphasis on community, with high levels of interaction;
- a careful balance of private and shared spaces. (McCamant and Durrett).

Private self-contained homes cluster around shared space and the common house. Open space is maintained as well as agricultural land within the urban area. There is a large kitchen, laundry, workshops etc in the common house which the residents can use. The roads are very much pedestrian oriented with parking away from the housing. The common house will be used by residents for work in eight office spaces allowing residents more leisure, and less commuter time. Houses are super-insulated with passive solar and common energy centres for all homes. The third neighbourhood is being designed initially by architectural students provided with design criteria.

In choosing to be close to the city centre, land costs were relatively high and strict zoning regulations had to be adhered to. The land cost $400,000 which was paid for by way of various loans. The house prices range from $80 to $150,000 depending on the design and size (Osborne, 1997).

## Comment

Liz Walker is the Director of Ithaca eco-village and she feels that 'the biggest single challenge to making this into a mainstream movement is to streamline the process of creating community. We need a hybrid model between the way co-housing groups are currently organized and the way that standard development takes place.' (Osborne, 1997). Newsletters have been valuable in keeping subscribers up to date and making it feel like a live project.

Attempts to locate this new settlement close to existing services, have created penalties, in terms of land prices. This issue is one that many other central urban sustainable settlements may come up against.

## Ecolonia

### Aims and Origins

The Netherlands Agency for Energy and the Environment (NOVEM) initiated Ecolonia as a demonstration project with finance from the Dutch government. The main goal of Ecolonia is to foster the integration of sustainable building into mainstream house building in The Netherlands (NOVEM, undated).

### Description

One hundred and one sustainable buildings were designed including housing and offices which are now occupied. The dwellings are built in an energy-saving and environmentally conscious way. Ecolonia forms part of an expansion plan in Alphen aan den Rijn, a medium sized Dutch municipality between Amsterdam, The Hague, Rotterdam and Utrecht. Town planning expert Lucien Kroll was invited to produce the design for an area which incorporates 300 dwellings within which Ecolonia has a central location. Kroll favours urban development which creates a relationship between the occupant and their surroundings. He feels that smallness of scale is an important element in this because a person can be more easily motivated to become aware and concerned about his place in nature (NOVEM, undated). The plan devotes much attention to open space with buildings positioned in a way that streets and squares are created.

The houses themselves incorporate many aspects of passive solar and energy efficiency but all have different themes. Water plays a major role in Ecolonia with a lake occupying a central position creating a functional element that excess water is fed into. There is a variety of architectural styles, which is carried through to the materials used in the dwellings. There is a gateway to the development in the form of higher buildings creating a type of entrance gate. He has absolutely avoided uniformity with features giving residents a sense of place such as a tower in one of the narrow streets. Water saving features have been built into houses with bath water recycling and compost toilets. There are nine different housing types designed by nine architects each incorporating particular features. Some devote additional attention to health and safety due to the limitation of chemical pollution of interior air, the front steps, attention to ease of cleaning, limited pollution from building materials used, central dust extraction etc. Others are designed with an energy saving heat wall using natural materials with a non-standard heating system.

### Comment

An evaluation and residents survey has been carried out by NOVEM which shows that the main goal of the development was fulfilled. However, it seems that the residents were not consulted early enough which is shown by the fact that 22 kitchens were removed and replaced by residents' preferred choice of kitchen design. This could of course have been prevented by offering choice. Many residents did not appear to have the 'environmental aspect' at heart, they just wanted somewhere to live. Initial residents were provided information on the aims of 'Ecolonia' by Novem but the next generation of residents have slipped through the net. Unless the initial residents pass on the 'instruction booklet', new owners may not understand the original concepts of the design of their new home and village (NOVEM, undated).

Another problem encountered by NOVEM was the lack of communication between the municipality departments. Eventually the director of urban development managed to get the various departments to cooperate but perhaps if they had been involved earlier this could have been avoided (NOVEM, undated).

On a more positive note, seven out of the nine house types met energy consumption targets, water consumption is 22 per cent below the Dutch average and architectural diversity is appreciated by residents. Residents were interviewed and generally they are happy with their house but some are dissatisfied about one or two features. One in ten houses have no clear separation between public and private areas and many residents have erected fences. Ecolonia was not targeted to 'green' residents but many claim they are more 'environmental' now than before living here.

## TYPE 3: URBAN RENEWAL

### Halifax
### Aims and Origins
The central idea is to turn a currently contaminated 2.4ha city block into part of an eco-city. The site is owned by the council and was vacated in 1993 giving an opportunity for this community-driven vision. The community's representative is the non-governmental organization Urban Ecology Australia who have been backed by the council for a one-year option on the site. The development will use 'Ecopolis Development Principles' which are drawn from a document put together as part of the Ecopolis' ecological city proposal. It refers to an urban ecology checklist developed by Paul Downton and covered in his paper *Ecological Cities* (1990). Ecopolis development principles are only fulfilled where a human settlement achieves all of the following fundamental objectives in an effective and integrated way:

- restore degraded land;
- fit the bioregion;
- balance development;
- halt urban sprawl;
- optimize energy performance;
- contribute to the economy;
- provide health and security;
- encourage community;
- promote social equity;
- respect history;
- enrich the cultural landscape;
- heal the biosphere by contributing to the repair, replenishment and improvement of air, water, soil, energy, biomass, food, biodiversity, habitat, ecolinks and waste recycling.

### Description
In the centre of Adelaide in the Tandanya Bioregion in South Australia the city owned 2.4ha block has been vacant since 1993. Ecopolis Pty Ltd drew up an

initial sketch to Adelaide City Council to register an interest in the now vacant site. Soon after a management team was set up to initiate the formal structures to proceed with the project. The three structures set up were Halifax EcoCity Land Trust, EcoCity Developments Ptd Ltd and The Residents and Users Group. The Land Trust own the land and control finances. The Development Board take the place of the conventional developer and the Residents Group deal with conflict resolution and community demands.

The original design proposes a community of 800–1000 people in a mixed use development. Buildings will be energy efficient with three to five stories, using stabilized earth, concrete and timber construction. Every dwelling is designed involving architects in consultation with members of the incoming community. Structures will be heated and cooled using passive solar working with vegetation, with solar water heating and electricity generation. Storm and grey water is collected and used with composting toilets capturing the nutrient value of sewage, and using methane as a fuel. The development is described as a piece of eco-city as it is not designed to stand alone but to be connected to the existing city.

Cars are kept out of the way with parking mainly underground. The streets belong to the pedestrian.

Adelaide City Council have been slow to clean up the site, so in the meantime, Urban Ecology have acquired a separate piece of land where five townhouses are being constructed. This project known as the Bourne Court development will be trialling 90 per cent of the technologies planned for the Halifax EcoCity but will be a different legal structure (held under community title). September 1998 was the date set by the council for the Halifax project site to have been cleaned to residential standards.

### Comment

A solution has been found at Halifax, in a good working relationship with the council, being prepared to clean up contaminated land for this development. It is not clear whether the land price was prohibitive, being central, as it was in Ithaca.

As development has not yet started it is not possible to comment on whether the design has been effective. Paul Downton has covered all sustainability issues with a real feel for creating a 'sense of place'.

## Kolding Ecological Renewal

### Aims and Origins

Kolding is a town of 50,000 in Jutland, Denmark. In 1992, a Danish urban renewal company presented Kolding city with a proposal to start an integrated urban renewal project. The purpose of the experiment is to combine collected experience with new developmental themes and to gain experience with known techniques by testing them in a larger context (Kolding Municipality, 1993).

### Description

The whole scheme cost 66 million Dk Kr which mostly followed the standard Danish urban renewal procedure of 50/50 contribution from the Municipality and Ministry. The first block to be renewed consists of 40 three-storey houses with 129 apartments and six businesses. As well as the district heating system being used, some houses also have solar collectors with passive solar through glass facades. Rainwater is collected on roofs with half of the houses using it for toilet flushing. The inner area of the block is communal and incorporates play areas for children. Many of the new fences are living with willow crossed with a light wooden structure. The inner courtyard is pedestrianized but with some parking underneath a solar cell pergola with future potential for solar driven cars to be charged. The electricity produced is currently used for communal needs such as outdoor lighting.

The municipality was able to get 100 per cent extra funding for an experimental addition to the renewal scheme. This is an outstanding feature, known as the bioworks which takes the form of a pyramid at the centre of the block. This treats waste water on a pond/algae system. A gardener is paid to run the bioworks garden which is paid for out of the water treatment savings. He also earns money selling the plants that are grown there.

## Comment

Rents have increased since the renewal although each individual's rent depends on their ability to pay. This project has unusually had a 'top-down' approach in contrast to Danish practice over the past 20 years. The inhabitants feel that they should have had more opportunity to organize themselves in working groups as well as more meeting space being made available. Aside from this, the renewal has given the block a new focus, with residents seeing their water treatment as the symbol of their neighbourhood (Kennedy, 1996).

## Edinburgh Car Free Development

### Aims and Origins

Canmore Housing Association are developing a 1.4ha site in Edinburgh city centre which will be designed as a 'car-free' energy efficient development. The project aims to allow those people that choose to live without a car, to live in a healthier and more pleasant environment. The concept of car free housing started in Edinburgh's Planning Department which Canmore took on as a millennium project. Scottish Homes (Canmore's principal funder) supported the idea giving a grant to buy the site and a design competition was arranged in conjunction with the Royal Institute of Architects in Scotland. Edinburgh City Council have granted planning permission after lengthy delays, as the car free approach is not without controversy even within the City Planning Department. The Council took advice from the Queen's Council who advised them that it would be impossible to enforce the car-free ruling. They felt that people's rights were being infringed too far, especially by ruling that residents could not even park outside the site. A Section 75 agreement is now in place, covering the control of the private access road around the new flats and ensuring that residents, apart from those with a physical handicap, do not attempt to bring cars on the site. The site however, still needs to have emergency vehicle access, so road construction consent has been applied for which is also a lengthy procedure. The council have imposed a combination of agreements as Canmore's partner organization Malcolm Homes Ltd will sell 26 of the flats.

They are party to the Section 75 agreement which will be applied to owner occupiers through the Title Conditions.

## Description

The competition winning scheme by local architects Hackland and Dore, are based on the traditional Edinburgh tenement block, incorporating a courtyard adapted to maximize solar gain. One hundred and twenty flats will be built within two, four storey blocks surrounded by pedestrian street and cycle route. The building materials have been sourced to be maintenance free, recyclable and of minimal environmental impact. The structure will be clad with a breathing wall using warmcell insulation with an indicated SAP rating of 96. Units are predicted to require space heating with a minimal annual cost. Heating will come via a district heating system with the main source being excess condensate from the local distillery. Provisions are being put in place for the retrofitting of photovoltaics for lighting. Run off water will be treated using a reedbed system which has the capacity to be retrofitted for domestic grey water.

## Comment

It is clear the Councillor Begg (Edinburgh Council) has made great efforts to take Edinburgh into the lead in trying to put the car in its place. This scheme has shown that the planning process, even with the council's support, is not an easy path towards sustainable settlements. Planning permission having been granted will hopefully make the next car-free development's path alot smoother. The mutual support between all partners involved seems to have given the project momentum with the competition element enabling at least six potential designs to be studied in depth. Canmore's development will mark the millennium, as hoped for, by taking a 'quantum leap' in housing terms into the 21st century.

### Sherwood Energy Village

#### Aims and Origins

Sherwood Energy Village is a development proposal for nearly 100 acres at the former Ollerton Colliery site in North Nottinghamshire. The origins of the development are at the heart of the community which has been faced with many changes by the closure of the pit in 1994. It follows in the footsteps of another community led project which has seen a disused pumping station being saved from the bulldozer. It has now been turned into a net zero $CO_2$ centre comprising workspace, offices, exhibition centre and visitor attractions powered by a combined heat and power biomass generator.

British Coal sold the site for £1 with a legacy in tow of a £2 million bill for cleaning up the site. A public meeting was held which 160 people attended to discuss the community's visions for the site. The main aim is to transform a derelict brown-site into a non-polluting, living, playing and working sustainable village to replace the jobs lost by pit closure and to offer children a future. Criteria has been set for development to encourage best practice in building materials and techniques, utilization of renewable energy sources and for ethical business investment.

### Description

The vision has been developed from community consultation and the concept interpreted on a visual plan designed by architects. The village will be a net zero $CO_2$ emission autonomous enterprise. Heat and energy will be generated by a biomass plant utilizing oil from wood by a process called pyrolysis. It is hoped that there will be three or four wind turbines on site providing electricity for 3000 to 4000 people and powering electric vehicles for use on site. A mineral railway line runs through the site but is no longer used. It is hoped that this line can be used again and a new station built on the site for commercial and passenger traffic. This line may be linked into the local Robin Hood line at a reasonable cost.

Sherwood Energy Village is the business name registered as an Industrial and Provident Society formed by members of the community in the district. This is a democratic structure in which all members have one vote regardless of how many shares are held.

### Comment

To turn a negative impact such as the sudden loss of the main employer in Ollerton, into a positive impact such as re-creation of employment is a challenge in itself. It is admirable to see the efforts to not only re-create employment but to consider the long-term impact of new development on a town with a history of community involvement. It would seem that for a town like Ollerton, which still holds on to its historical community spirit, the footings for creating a sustainable community have come about with greater ease. The community there is *au fait* with consultation and cooperative development. Therefore the fundamentals already exist to enable 'environmentally-minded' pioneers like Stan Crawford and Carla Jamison (the coordinators) to plant the seeds for sustainable growth. Many other sustainable developments have a number of hurdles to jump before reaching the stages Ollerton were at when the Energy Village idea first came about. In terms of the development itself, Sherwood Energy Village has considered renewable energy, energy efficiency, local economy, leisure, tourism, transport and many other issues. The proposed master plan and more comprehensive guidelines will no doubt develop as soon as funding can be found.

# TYPE 4: ECO-TOWNSHIPS

## Davis

### Aims and Origins

The 1974 General Plan gained Davis a national reputation for community efforts in energy conservation. The plan addressed issues such as recycling, solar energy use, affordable housing mix and planning for cycle and transit (City of Davis, 1996). Davis has since then distinguished itself for its long standing high level of citizen involvement in policy decisions. The city has 370 paid city employees and a 376 strong volunteer committee to advise on decisions. The 1994 two year General Plan revisions integrated 15 committees of 20 members each and involved hundreds of other citizens. Although the level of public involvement slowed the process, the City maintains this in the aim of greater community acceptance and commitment.

## Description

The city of Davis is located 50 miles north-east of San Francisco separated from surrounding cities by agricultural land. Davis is a small scale, university city with a community of 50,000 people. A high percentage of the population is linked to the University. Amongst Davis's distinctive qualities is the fact that it has an unusually high level of 'green' amenities, transport alternatives to the car, and neighbourhood services.

Davis's qualities have origins in the city's earliest planning policies in 1958 and reaffirmed as the city grew. The open space system is a long-term vision to integrate and link habitat areas, wetlands, agriculture, paths and parks. As well as continuous and connected open space, the 'Davis Greenbelt' is partially implemented surrounding the city's urban development. This could take another 20 years to complete and this concept has come under increased scrutiny with objections being raised by farmers.

The city accommodates the motorist but not to the cyclist's, pedestrian's or transit user's detriment. The city's management measures have brought about peak hour traffic reduction and single occupant reduction. Most streets are designated 'greenstreets', intended to provide more space for pedestrians and cyclists. With an estimated 40,000 cycles in use, 25 per cent of all personal trips are made on cycle.

One notable innovation is the 'Village Homes' scheme completed in 1975 which encompasses 70a with 208 residential units. It is unique in that streets are narrow and meandering, the ground surfaces are permeable, it is higher density, has mixed housing and energy efficient homes, uses street trees for shading and has a strong neighbourhood association. A more recent project known as 'Aspen' is an adjacent 110a site with 587 residential units, a 15a district park and a school. An interesting ecological aspect of Aspen is its' wildlife pond, open drainage and greenbelt and cycleway system.

## Comment

Although Davis's local plan requires new developments to have mixed housing, it remains a privileged exurban town. The success of Davis has been public involvement which has been recognized as the backbone for many of the social and environmental improvements.

With but a few more challenges to complete, it is the opinion of some that Davis's liveability, sustainability and sense of community and place can be enhanced (Loux and Wolcott, 1994). One such challenge may be Davis's relatively low density, making local services harder to sustain.

## Auroville

### Aims and Origins

'The Purpose of Auroville is to realize human unity', (The Mother, Auroville Press, 1997). Auroville is the dream of 'The Mother' who had a vision in 1965 of a universal town where all nations could live together in peace. Auroville has had the endorsement of the General Conference of UNESCO since 1966 and most recently in 1983. Various governmental and other organizations have funded parts of the development.

## Description

Today, Auroville is a growing community of 1300 people from all over the world, consisting of 80 settlements. It is located on the south-eastern coast of India, 160km south of Madras and surrounded by 13 existing villages with a total population of 40,000.

Internationally acclaimed for its wasteland reclamation, Auroville has transformed near barren land into a lush green area. With significant improvements to the area's life-support, over two million forest and hedge trees, fruit and fuel wood trees have been planted. Not only are Aurovillians actively pursuing the exclusion of pesticides but they are encouraging the surrounding village farmers to re-introduce sustainable agricultural practices.

Auroville has two crèches, two kindergartens, two primary schools and one high school. 700 children from surrounding villages are also benefiting from the educational programme which is based on a child centred approach with a free choice system allowing students to choose their own subjects for study.

There are many systems of primary health care in Auroville, such as homeopathy, acupuncture, massage and others. The Auroville Health Centre has basic medical facilities, a dental care unit and a pharmacy and serves surrounding villagers as well as Aurovillians.

## Comment

Auroville is concerned not only with environmental sustainability but psychological and spiritual sustainability as well. Social stability is only achievable when individuals are at peace with themselves. People at Auroville appear to follow the ways of Sri Aurobindo who believes that people in their present condition are transitional beings and therefore spiritually inherently unsustainable. People therefore are encouraged to follow a spiritual path in order to overcome this problem.

Life at Auroville is mainly land-based and the solutions that have come about for land regeneration have been extremely successful. Socially, it started as an experiment and there is no evidence to show that the residents have suffered due to this. With the coming together of people from many different cultures, living with existing communities, it is likely that social cohesion is a challenge. The biggest impact of Auroville is probably the effect its existence has on surrounding villages. With educational programmes, compost programmes, lobbying against pesticide use etc, inhabitants close to Auroville have been helped to follow more sustainable lifestyles.

# BIBLIOGRAPHY

Acutt, M and Dodgson, J (1996) 'Policy Instruments and Greenhouse Gas Emissions from Transport in the UK', *Fiscal Studies*, Vol 17, No 2, pp65–82

Addenbrooke, P, Bruce, D, Courtney, I, Hellewell, S, Nisbett, A and Young, T (1981) *Urban Planning and Design for Road Public Transport,* Confederation of British Road Passenger Transport, London

Albrow, M (1996) *The Global Age*, Polity Press, Cambridge

Aldbourne Associates (1994) *Can Housing Managers Learn to Dance?*, Report for the Joseph Rowntree Foundation, Aldbourne Associates

Alduns, T (1992) *Urban Villages: A Concept for Creating Mixed-use Urban Developments on a Sustainable Scale*, Urban Villages Group, London

Alexander, C et al (1977) *A Pattern Language: towns, buildings, construction,* Oxford University Press, New York

Anderson, T (1997) 'Safe Routes to School in Odense, Denmark' in Tolley, R *The Greening of Urban Transport*, Wiley, Chichester

Appleyard, D (1986) 'Evaluating the Social and Environmental Aspects of Transport Investment', *Transport Sociology*, Pergaman Press, Oxford

Argyle, M (1996) 'The Effects of Relationships on Well-being' in Baker, N (ed) *Building a Relational Society*, Arena, Aldershot

Arnstein, S (1969) *A Ladder of Citizen Participation*, JAIP, Vol XXX, No 4, pp216–224

ARUP (1997) *The National Cycle Network, Guidelines and Practical Details*, Sustrans, Bristol

Athanasiou, T (1996) *Slow Reckoning: the ecology of a divided planet*, Secker and Warburg, London

Atkinson, D (1994) *The common sense of community,* DEMOS, London

Atkinson, R (1994) *Radical Urban Solutions: urban renaissance for city schools and communities*, Cassell, London

Baird, M (1998) 'Social entrepreneurs' *The Guardian*, 5th August 1999

Baker Associates and the University of the West of England (1999) *Urban Capacity in SW England*, South West Regional Planning Conference, Exeter

Balcombe, R J and York, I O (1993) *The Future of Residential Parking*, Transport Research Laboratory Report, Crowthorne

Bane, P (1994) 'A Garden Growing Wild: the Promise of a Bioregional Agriculture', *Raise the Stakes: The Planet Drum Review*, No 22, Winter 1993–1994

Banister, D (1992) 'Energy Use, Transport and Settlement Patterns' in Breheny, M (ed) *Sustainable Developments and Urban Form*, Pion, London

Banister, D (1996) 'Reducing the need to travel: the research evidence', *Oxford Planning Monographs*, Vol 1, No 2, Oxford Brookes University, Oxford

Barton, H (1987) *The potential for increasing the energy-efficiency of existing urban areas through planning policy*, unpublished M.Phil thesis, Faculty of the

Built Environment, University of the West of England, Bristol

Barton, H (1988) *Is Energy-integrated Land Use Planning Possible in Britain?*, Town and Country Planning WP, No 10, UWE, Bristol

Barton, H (1992) 'City Transport, Strategies for Sustainability' in Beheny M (Ed) *Sustainable Development and Urban Form*, Pion, London

Barton, H (1997) 'Environmental Capacity and Sustainable Urban Form' in Farthing, S (ed) *Evaluating Local Environmental Policy*, Avebury, Aldershot pp78–96

Barton, H (1998) 'New Zealand Doublethink', *Planning Practice and Research*, Vol 13, No 4, November 1998, pp453–459

Barton, H and Bruder, N (1995) *A Guide to Local Environmental Auditing*, Earthscan, London

Barton, H, Davies, G and Guise, R (1995) *Sustainable Settlements – A Guide for Planners, Designers and Developers*, University of the West of England and Local Government Management Board, Luton

Barton, H, Claydon, J and Lambert, C (1999) 'New Vision for Outer Sprawl', *Planning*, 26 March

Bayliss, D (1990) *Urban Traffic Management, Transport Policy and the Environment*, European Conference of Ministers of Transport, OECD, Paris

Bell, C and Newby, H (1971) *Community studies: an introduction to the sociology of the local community*, George Allen and Unwin, London

Bentley, I, Alcock, A, Murrain, P, McGlynn, S and Smith, G (1985) *Responsive Environments: a manual for designers*, Butterworth, Oxford

Best (1981) *Land Use and Living Space*, Methuen, London

Bicycle Association (1996) *Cycle Friendly Infrastructure*, CTC, Godalming

Birley, T (1983) 'Planning and Energy Use: Towards Energy Efficiency in the Built Environment', *The Planner*, February 1983, pp42–48

Bishop, Jeff (1986) *Milton Keynes: The Best of Both Worlds? Public and Professional Views of a New City*, SAUS Occasional Paper 24, Bristol University

Blowers, A (ed) (1993) *Planning for a Sustainable Environment*, Earthscan, London

Bodel, N and Anda, M (1996) *Places For Food Production, Places For People*, (a talk to the 6th International Permaculture Convergence), Permaculture Association of Western Australia

Bowes, A M and Domocos, T M (1998) 'Health Visitors work in a multi-ethnic society: a qualitative study of social exclusion', *Journal of Social Policy*, Vol 27, No 4, pp489–506

Boyd et al (1945) *Homes for the People*, HMSO, London

Boyle, G and Harper, P (1976) *Radical Technology*, Wildwood House, London

Breheny, M (1992a) 'The Contradictions of the Compact City: A Review' in M.Breheny (ed) *Sustainable Development and Urban Form*, Pion, London, pp138–159

Breheny, M (1992b) 'Towards Sustainable Urban Development' in Mannion, A M and Bowlby, S R (eds) *Environmental Issues in the 1990s*, John Wiley and Sons Ltd, London, pp277–290

Breheny, M and Archer, S (1998) 'Urban Densities, Local Policies and Sustainable Development', *International Journal of Environment and Pollution*, Vol 10, No 1, pp126–150

Breheny, M, Gent, T and Lock, D (1993) *Alternative Development Patterns: New Settlements*, Department of the Environment, Planning Research Programme, HMSO, London

Breheny, M and Rockwood, R (1993) 'Planning the Sustainable City Region' in Blowers, A (ed) *Planning for a Sustainable Environment*, Earthscan, London, pp150–189

Brindley, T, Rydin, Y and Stoker, G (1989) *Remaking Planning*, Unwin Hyman, London

Bristol City Council (1998) *Local Food Links*, Sustainable Cities Team at CREATE, Bristol

Broady, M (1968) *Planning for People*, Bedford Square, London

Building Research Establishment (1975) *Energy Consumption: a study of energy consumption in buildings, and possible means of saving energy in housing*, CP 56/75 BRE, Garston

Brunsing, J (1997) 'Public Transport and Cycling: Experience of Modal Integration in Germany', in Tolley, R *The Greening of Urban Transport*, Wiley, Chichester

Buchanan, C (1963) *Traffic in Towns*, HMSO, London

Bulmer M (1986) *Neighbours: the work of Philip Abrams*, Cambridge University Press, Cambridge

Bunker, S, Coates, C, How, J and Jones, W (1997) *Diggers and Dreamers*, D&D Publications, London

Burns, D, Hambleton, R and Hoggett, P (1994) *The Politics of Decentralisation*, London, Macmillan

Burns, D and Taylor, M (1998) *Mutual aid and self help: coping strategies for excluded communities*, The Policy Press, Bristol

Burrows, R and Rhodes, D (1998) *Unpopular Places? Area disadvantage and the geography of misery in England*, The Policy Press, Bristol

Burton, P (1997) *Community Visioning: An Evaluation of the 'Choices for Bristol' Project*, The Policy Press, Bristol

CAG Consultants and Land Use Consultants (1997) *Environmental Capital: A New Approach*, Countryside Commission, English Heritage, English Nature and the Environment Agency, Cheltenham

Calthorpe, P (1993) *The Next American Metropolis: Ecology, Community and the American Dream*, Princetown Architectural Press, NY

Carley, M (1996) *Sustainable Transport and Retail Vitality*, Historic Burghs Association of Scotland, Edinburgh

Castells, M (1991) *The Informational City: Information Technology, Economic Restructuring and Urban-Regional Process*, Blackwell, Oxford

Castells, M (1996) *The rise of the network society*, Blackwell, Oxford

CEC (1990) *Green Paper on the Urban Environment*, Commission of the European Community, Brussels

CEC (1994) *The Social Europe Report; Supplement 3: Teleworking*, EU, Brussels

Central Statistical Office (1997) *Annual Abstract of Statistics*, The Stationery Office, London

Cervero, R (1989) *America's Suburban Centres: the Land Use–Transportation Link*, Unwin Hyman, London

Cervero, R (1994) 'Transit-Based Housing in California: Evidence on Ridership Impacts', *Transport Policy*, Vol 1, No 3, pp174–183

Champion, T, Atkins, D, Coombes, M and Fotheringham, S (1998) *Urban Exodus*, CPRE, London

Chanan, G (1992) *Out of the Shadows: Local Community Action in the European Community*, European Foundation for the Improvement of Living and Working Conditions, Dublin

Chaplow, S G (1996) 'Havana's Popular Gardens: Sustainable Urban Agriculture', *World Sustainable Agriculture Association Newsletter*, Fall 1996, Vol 5, No 22

Cherry, G (1996) *Town Planning in Britain Since 1900*, Blackwell, Oxford

Chesterfield Borough Council (1998) *Poolsbrook – Erin Area Community Heating*, Chesterfield BC

City of Davis (1996) *City of Davis General Plan Update: Public Review Draft*, November 1996, City of Davis, Davis, CA

Civic Trust (1998) *Sustainable Renewal of Suburban Areas*, Civic Trust, Manchester

Clark, J, Hutton, B, Burnett, N, Hathway, T and Harrison, A (1991) *The Appraisal of Community Severance*, TRRL, Wokingham

Clarke, D (1973) 'The Concept of Community Re-examined' in *Sociological Review*, 21, pp32–38

Clarke, M and Stewart, J (1999) *Community governance, community leadership, and the new local government*, Report for the Joseph Rowntree Foundation York, York Publishing Services

Cleary, J and Hillman, M (1992) 'A Prominent Role for Walking and Cycling', in Roberts, J (ed) *Travel Sickness*, Lawrence & Wishart, London

Clunies-Ross, T and Hildyard, N (1993) *The Politics of Industrial Agriculture*, Earthscan, London

Cohen, Anthony P (1986) *Symbolising Boundaries: Identity and Diversity in British Cultures*, Manchester University Press, Manchester

Cole, I and Smith, Y (1995) *From Estate Action to Estate Agreement*, The Policy Press, Bristol

Colloff, P (1996) *Sustainable Food: Buying and Growing Locally*, Greenbeat, http://earth.tec.org/greenbeat/jan96/extra.html

Combined Heat and Power (CHP) Group (1979) *Heat Loads in British Cities*, Energy Paper No 34, HMSO, London

Constanza, R, Norton, B and Benjamin, D (1992) *Ecosystem Health: New Goals for Environmental Management*, Island Press, Washington DC

Copenhagen Municipal Corporation (1993) *Copenhagen Municipal Plan 1993*, The Lord Mayors Department, Municipal Corporation, Copenhagen

Crandon, L (1998) 'Community Leader', *Police Review*, 30 January 1998

Crouch, D (1996) 'Close to the Land and Holding your Ground', *Permaculture Magazine*, Issue 12

Crow, G and Allan, G (1995) *Community Life: an introduction to local social relations*, Harvester Wheatsheaf, New York

Crowe, S (1963) *Tomorrow's Landscape*, Architectural Press, London

Cullen, G (1961) *Townscape*, Architectural Press, London

Curtis (1996) 'Reducing the need to travel: strategic housing location and travel behaviour in Oxfordshire', *Oxford Planning Monographs*, Vol 1, No 2, Oxford Brookes University, Oxford

Dale, J and Derricourt, N (1989) 'Dilemmas in Housing-Oriented Community Development' *Community Development Journal*, Vol 15, No 1

Dauncey, G (1996) *Eco-community Design*, Context Institute, webmaster@ context.org

Dauncey, G (1993) 'A new town economy for the information age', *Town and Country Planning*, December, pp342–343

Davidson, J (1988) *How Green Is Your City*, Bedford Square Press, London

Davidson, R (1981) *Crime and Environment*, Croom Helm, London

Dennis, N (1968) 'The Popularity of the Neighbourhood Community Idea' in Pahl, R *Readings in Urban Sociology*, Pergamon Press, Oxford

DoE (1993) *The Environmental Appraisal of Development Plans: a Good Practice Guide*, HMSO, London

DoE (1994a) *Planning Policy Guidance Note 13: Transport*, HMSO, London

DoE (1994b) *Sustainable Development: The UK Strategy*, HMSO, London

DoE (1994c) *Climate Change: The UK Programme*, HMSO, London

DoE (1994d) *Mineral Policy Guidance Note 1*, HMSO, London

DoE (1995) *PPG13 A Guide to Better Practice: Reducing the Need to Travel Through Land Use and Transport Planning*, HMSO, London

DoE (1996a) *Indicators of Sustainable Development for the United Kingdom*, HMSO, London

DoE (1996b) *Household Growth: Where Shall We Live?*, HMSO, London

DETR (1997a) *Developing an Integrated Transport Policy: Factual Background*, HMSO, London

DETR (1997b) *Involving Communities in Urban and Rural Regeneration: a guide for practitioners*, Pieda plc for DETR, HMSO, London

DETR (1997c) *Land Use Change in England No 12*, HMSO, London

DETR (1997d) *Sustainable Local Communities for the 21st century: Why and how to prepare an effective Local Agenda 21 strategy*, DETR, LGA, HMSO, London

DETR (1997e) *United Kingdom National Air Quality Strategy*, HMSO, London

DETR (1997f) *Planning Policy Guidance Note*, HMSO, London

DETR (1998a) *Planning for Communities of the Future*, HMSO, London

DETR (1998b) *A New Deal for Transport: The Government's White Paper on the Future of Transport*, HMSO, London

DETR (1998c) *Planning for Sustainable Development: Towards Better Practice*, HMSO, London

DETR (1998d) *Building a Sustainable Future: Homes for an Autonomous Future*, DETR General Information Report 53, HMSO, London

DETR (1998e) *General Information Report 51, Taking Stock – private financing of energy efficiency in social housing*, Energy Efficiency Best Practice Programme, BRECSU, Watford

DETR (1998f) *Opportunities for Change: Consultation paper on a revised UK strategy for sustainable development*, HMSO, London

DETR (1998g) *Modern Local Government: In Touch with the People*, Cm 4014 HMSO, London

DETR (1998h) *Less Waste More Value*, HM Government Consultation Paper, DETR, London

DETR (1998i) *Places Streets and Movement: A Companion Guide to DB 32*, HMSO, London

DETR (1998j) *Modern Local Government – In Touch with the People*, HM Government White Paper, HMSO, London

DHSS (1998) *Our Healthier Nation: A Contract for Health*, HMSO, London

DoT (1996) *Department of Transport Statistics; Cycling in GB*, HMSO, London

Dickson, J and Robertson, I (1993) *Taking Charge*, Housing Unit, London

Dobson, R (1993) *'Bringing the Economy Home from the Market'*, Black Rose Books, Montreal and New York

Douthwaite, R (1996) *Short Circuit – strengthening local economies for security in an unstable world*, The Lilliput Press, Dublin

Duany, A and Plater-Zybeck, E (1991) *Towns and Town-Making Principles*, Howard University Graduate School of Design, Rizzoli, New York

Duck, S (1992) *Human Relations* Sage, London

EA.UE (1994) *Building for Tomorrow: International Workshop on Ecological Settlements*, Barcelona, April 1994, European Academy of the Urban Environment, Berlin

Ecologist (1972) 'The Blueprint for Survival', *Ecologist Magazine*, January 1972

ECOTEC (1993) *Reducing Transport Emissions Through Planning*, HMSO, London

Eikland, M (1997) 'The Introduction of a Public Bike in Sandnes Norway', in Tolley, R, *The Greening of Urban Transport*, Wiley, Chichester

Eir, B (1994) 'A Healthy Traffic Plan For The City', in Wijk, F and Bouma, H, *Proceedings of Car Free Cities Conference*, Amsterdam

Elkin, T, McLaren, D and Hillman, M (1991) *Reviving the City. Towards Sustainable Urban Development*, Friends of the Earth/Policy Studies Institute, London

Ellin, N (ed) (1997) *Architecture of Fear*, Architectural Press, Princeton

Essex County Council (1998) *The New Essex Design Guide*, Essex County Council, Colchester

Etzioni, A (1993) *Spirit of Community*, Crown Books, New York

Etzioni, A (1998) 'A Communitarian Perspective on Sustainable Development', in Warburton, D (ed) *Community and Sustainable Development*, Earthscan, London

European Landscape Architecture Students Association (ELASA) (1996) *The role of Landscape Architects in Improving the Sustainability of Human Settlements for the Future*, Cheltenham & Gloucester College of Higher Education, Cheltenham

EU Expert Group on the Urban Environment (1995) *European Sustainable Cities Part II*, ESDG XI, Brussels

Evans, B (1994) 'Planning, Sustainability and the Chimera of Community', *Town and Country Planning*, April, pp106–108

Eve, R A, Horsfall, S and Lee, M E (eds) (1997) *Chaos, complexity and sociology*, Sage, Thousand Oaks

Fairlie, S (1996) *Low Impact Development*, Jon Carpenter, Oxfordshire

Faludi, A (ed) (1973) *A Reader in Planning Theory*, Pergamon Press, Oxford

Farthing, S and Winter, J (1985) *Consumer Reaction to Innovative Aspects of the External Residential Environment*, paper given to a conference on Housing Layout in the 1990's, RTPI SW Branch, July 1985, Bristol

Farthing, S and Winter, J (1988*) Residential density and levels of satisfaction with the external residential environment* Faculty of the Built Environment WP11, UWE, Bristol

Farthing, S, Winter, J and Coombes, T (1996) 'Travel Behaviour and Local Accessibility to Services and Facilities', in Jenks, M, Burton, E and Williams, K (eds) *The Compact City. A Sustainable Urban Form?*, E&FN Spon, London, pp181–189

Fielding, T and Halford, S (1990) *Patterns and Processes of Urban Change in the United Kingdom: Reviews of Urban Research*, HMSO, London

Finnegan, R (1989) *The Hidden Musicians: Music making in an English town*, Cambridge University Press, Cambridge

Flora, C B and Flora, J L (1993) 'Entrepreneurial Social Infrastructure – A Necessary Ingredient', *Annals of the American Academy of Political and Social Science*, 529, pp48–58

Flora, J L (1996) 'Social capital and communities of place', *Rural Sociology* 63, No 4, pp481–506

Foley, D (1960) 'British Town Planning: One Ideology or Three', *British Journal of Sociology*, Vol II; also reproduced in Faludi (1973) g v pp69–93

Fordham, G (1995) *Made to Last: Creating sustainable neighbourhood and estate regeneration*, Joseph Rowntree Foundation, York

Forest of Dean District Council (1998) *Residential Design Guide*, University of the West of England for FoD DC, Coleford, Gloucestershire

France, A and Wiles, P (1997) 'Dangerous Futures: Social Exclusion and Youth Work in Late Modernity', *Social Policy and Administration*, Vol 31, No 5, pp59–78

Friends of the Earth (1998) *Curbing Shorter Car Journeys*, FOE, London

Fulford, C (1996) 'The Compact City and the Market', in Jenks et al, *The Compact City: a Sustainable Urban Form*, E&FN Spon, London

Garlick, R (1988) 'Routefinder to lead recycling schemes', *Planning*, 22 May

Garnett, T (1996) *Growing Food in Cities. A report to highlight and promote the benefits of urban agriculture in the UK*, SAFE Alliance/National Food Alliance, London

Garreau, J (1991) Edge City: Life in the New Frontier. Doubleday, New York

Gavrilov, A (1996) *Rooftop Gardening in St. Petersburg, Russia*, paper published by City Farmer, Canada's Office of Urban Agriculture, www.cityfarmer.org

Geddes, P (1915) *Cities in Evolution: an Introduction to the Town Planning Movement and the Study of Civics* (1968 edition), Ernest Benn, London

Gibberd (1953) *Town Design* Architectural Press, London

Gibberd, Frederick et al (1980) *Harlow: The Story of a New Town*, Publications for Companies, Stevenage

Gibbs, D (1991) 'Greening the Local Economy', *Local Economy* 6.3

Gibson, T (1993) *Danger: Opportunity: A Report to the Joseph Rowntree Foundation on Meadowell Community Development for the Neighbourhood Initiatives Foundation*, Telford

Gibson, T (1984) *Counterweight: the Neighbourhood Option*, TCPA, London

Giddens, A (1990) *The Consequences of Modernity*, Polity Press, Oxford

Giddens, A (1998) 'Giddens on the Third Way', *The Observer*, September 13, London

Gilchrist, A (1995) *Community Development and Networking*, Community Development Foundation, London

Gillespie, A (1992) 'Communications Technology and the Future of the City', Breheny, M (ed) *Sustainable Development and Urban Form*, Pion, London

Girardet, H (1992) *The Gaia Atlas of Cities – new directions for sustainable urban living*, Gaia Books, Stroud

Glass, R (1959) 'The Evaluation of Planning: Some Sociological Considerations', *International Social Science Journal*, Vol XI, No 3

Gloucestershire County Council (1992) *Report to the Local Government Commission of England*, GCC, Gloucester

Goodman, R (1972) *After the Planners*, Penguin, Middlesex

Gordon, P and Richardson, H (1990) 'Gasoline Consumption and Cities: a reply', *Journal of the American Planning Association*, Vol 55, pp342–345

Greater London Council (1965) *The Planning of a New Town* ('The Hook Book'), GLC, London

Greentown Future Residents (1981) *Greater Proposal for Development of Crownhill Site*, submitted to Milton Keynes Development Corporation, Milton Keynes

Guerra, M (1993) 'An Island in Commuterville', *Permaculture Magazine*, Vol 1, No 3

Guy, S and Marvin, S (1996) 'Transforming Urban Infrastructure Provision – The Emerging Logic of Demand Side Management', *Policy Studies*, Vol 17, No 2, pp137–147

Hadley, J (1998) Civvy Street, *Police Review*, 26 June 1998

Hall, P et al (1973) *The Containment of Urban England*, Vol II, Allen and Unwin, London

Halpern, D (1995) *Mental Health and the Built Environment*, Taylor and Francis, London

Hambleton, R, Hoggett, P and Razzaque, K (1996) *Freedom within Boundaries*, Local Government Management Board, Luton

Hambleton, R (1997) 'Clinton, Blair and the New Urban Agenda', Royal Town Planning Institute, proceedings of Town and Country Planning School 1997

Hamilton, N D (1996) 'Tending the Seeds: the Emergence of a New Agriculture in the United States', *Drake Journal of Agricultural Law*, Spring 1996

Hanson, C (1996) *The Cohousing Handbook*, Hartley & Marks, Washington

Hanson, S (1982) 'The Determinants of Daily Travel-activity Patterns: Relative Location and Sociodemographic Factors', *Urban Geography*, Vol 3, No 3, pp179–202

Hastings, A, McArthur, A, McGregor, A (1996) *Less than equal ? Community organisations and estate regeneration partnerships*, Policy Press, Bristol

Hastings, C (1993) *The new organisation – growing the culture of organisational networking*, McGraw-Hill, London

Hathway, T (1994) 'Chinese Recipes for Sustainability', *Planning Week*, Vol 2, No 35, RTPI

Headicar, P & Curtis, C (1995) *Residential Development and Car-based Travel: does Location Make a Difference?*, Oxford School of Planning, Oxford Brookes University

Henton, D, Melville, J, and Walesh, K (1997) *Grassroots Leaders for a New Economy: How Civic Entrepreneurs are Building Prosperous Communities*, Jossey-Bass Inc, San Francisco

Hillman, M, Adams, J and Whitelegg, J (1991) *One False Move*, Policy Studies Institute, London

Hillman, M and Whalley, A (1983) *Energy and Personal Travel: Obstacles to Conservation*, Policy Studies Institute, London

Hillman, M and Whalley, A (1979) *Walking is Transport*, Policy Studies Institute, London

Hirschfield, A and Bowers, K J (1997) 'The Effect of Social Cohesion on Levels of Recorded Crime in Disadvantaged Areas', *Urban Studies*, Vol 34, No 8

Hoggett, P (1997) 'Introduction', in Hoggett, P (ed) *'Contested Communities'*, Vol 3, No 17, Policy Press, Bristol

Hook, W (1994) 'Pedicab Buisiness Inaugurated', *Sustainable Transport*, Vol 1, No 3, ITDP, New York

Hough (1995) *Cities and Natural Processes*, Routledge, London

Houghton-Evans, J (1975) *Planning Cities: Legacy and Portent*, Lawrence and Wishart, London

Houghton, T and Kleiner, D (1996) *A Scoping Study into Community-based Renewable Projects*, ETSU, Harwell

Houghton, T, Winter, G and Anderson, M (1997) *Gas Competition – a better deal for all?*, National Right to Fuel Campaign, London

Howard, D (1990) 'Looking Beyond the Technical Fix', *Town and Country Planning*, Vol 59, No 12, pp343–345

Hoyland, R (1996) 'Community Composting Network', *Permaculture Magazine*, Issue 13

HRH The Prince of Wales (1989) *A Vision of Britain*, Doubleday, London

Hulme Regeneration Ltd (1994) *Hulme Guide to Development*, HRL, Manchester

IHT (1997) *Transport in the Urban Environment*, Institute of Highways and Transport, London

Illich, I (1974) *Energy and Equity*, Marion Boyars, London

IUCNNR (1991) *Caring for the Earth*, International Union for the Conservation of Nature and Natural Resources, Gland

Jacobs, J (1961) *The Death and Life of Great American Cities*, Random House, USA

Jamieson, G, Mackay and Latchford (1967) 'Transportation and Land Use Structures', *Urban Studies*, Vol 4, pp201–217

Jenks, M, Burton, E and Williams, K (eds) (1996) *The Compact City: a Sustainable Urban Form?*, E&FN Spon, London

Johnson, B (1999) 'Ask Your Neighbour', *Planning*, 5 February, p13

Johnson, J (1996) 'Sustainability in Scottish Cities', in Jenks, M et al, *The Compact City: a sustainable urban form?*, E&FN Spon, London

Johnston, J (1990) *Nature Areas for City People. A guide to the successful establishment of community wildlife sites*, London Ecology Unit

Jones, J (1996) 'Poverty Triggers UK Diet Crisis', *Observer*, London

Katz, P (1994) *The New Urbanism – Toward and Architecture of Community*, McGraw-Hill Inc, New York

Kemp, D (1993) *Employment, Work and Social Trends in Australia and Their Implications for Urban Form*, Queensland Department of Business, Industry and Regional Development, Brisbane

Kennedy, M (ed) (1994) *New Sustainable Settlements in Europe*, European Academy of the Urban Environment (EA.UE), Berlin

Kennedy, M and Kennedy, D (eds) (1997) *Designing Ecological Settlements*, Dietrich Reimer Verlay, Berlin

Kitamura, R, Mokhtarian, P and Laidet, L (1997) 'A Micro-analysis of Land Use and Travel in Five Neighbourhoods in the San Francisco Bay Area', *Transportation*, Vol 24, pp125–158

Kleiner, D (1997) 'The Potential of Community Renewable Projects in Britain', unpublished dissertation, Faculty of the Built Environment, University of the West of England, Bristol

Kneen, B (1995) 'Invisible Giants – Cargill and its Transnational Strategies', *The Ecologist*, Vol 25, No 5, September–October 1995

Korten, D (1995) *When Corporations Rule the World*, Earthscan, London

Kourik, R (1986) *Designing and Maintaining your Edible Landscape Naturally*, Metamorphic Press, Santa Barbara, California

Krier, L (1984) *Houses, Palaces and Cities*, Academy Editions, London

Kuhl, D and Cooper, C (1992) 'Physical Activity at 36 years: patterns and childhood predictors in a longitudinal study', *Journal of Epedemiology and Community Health*, Vol 46, pp114–119

Kuhn, M (1997) Rooftop Gardening Fact Sheets, available from Rooftop Gardens Resource Group, c/o Grow T.O.gether Community Gardeners, Ontario, Canada

Landry, C and Bianchini, F (1995) *The Creative City*, Demos/Concordia, London

Leach, G (1976) *Energy and Food Production*, IPC, London

Leadbetter, C (1997) *The rise of the social entrepreneur*, Demos, London

Lee, R (1996) 'LETS and the social construction of local economic geographies in South East England', *Environment and Planning A*, Vol 28, No 8, pp1377–1394

LGMB (1992) 'Earth Summit: Rio 92 Supplement No 2', *Agenda 21 – a Guide for local authorities in the UK*, LGMB, London

LGMB (1993) *A Framework for Local Sustainability*, LGMB, London

Littlewood, M (1996) 'Utopia at a Green School', *Tree News*, Spring 1996

Littlewood, M (1998) *The Forest Village*, leaflet available from Troutwells, Higher Hayle, Roadwater, Watchet, Somerset, TA23 0RN

Llewellyn-Davies (1994) *Providing more Homes in Urban Areas,* Joseph Rowntree Foundation, Policy Press, London

Llewellyn-Davies (1997) *Sustainable Residential Quality: new approaches to urban living*, DETR, London

Llewellyn-Davies (1998) *Sustainable Residential Quality: new approaches to urban living*, LPAC, London

Lowndes, V, Stoker, G, Pratchett, L, Wilson, D, Leach, S and Wingfield, M (1998) *Enhancing Public Participation in Local Government*, DETR, London

Lukeman, F (1964) Geography as a formal intellectual discipline and the way it contributes to human knowledge, *Canadian Geographic*, Vol 8

Lynch, K (1960) *The Image of the City*, MIT Press, Boston

Lynch, K (1981) *A Theory of Good City Form*, MIT Press, Cambridge, Massachusetts

MacFarlane, R (1993) *Community involvement in City Challenge: A good practice report*, NCVO Publications, London

MacIntyre, A (1981) *After Virtue: A Study in Moral Theory,* Duckworth, London

Making Cities Liveable (1996) *Newsletter*, MCL, May 1996

Martin, S (1998) *Achieving Best Value through Public Engagement*, Warwick/DETR Best Value Series, Paper 8, Warwick: The Local Government Centre

Marvin, S and Guy, S (1997) 'Creating Myths rather than Sustainability: the transition fallacies of the new localism', *Local Environment*, Vol 2, No 3, pp311–318

Masterson, R and Masterson, E (1990) 'The Scottish Community Elections: the Second Round', *Local Govenment Studies 6*

McArthur, A (1993) 'Community Business and Urban Regeneration', *Urban Studies*, Vol 30, Nos 4–5

McCamant, K and Durret, C (1988) *Co-housing – a contemporary approach to housing ourselves*, Ten Speed Press, Berkely, California

McGill, J (1999) *Local Sustainable Development: Preliminary Results of a National Survey*, unpublished, Faculty of the Built Environment, University of the West of England, Bristol

Mellor, J R (1977) *Urban Sociology in an Urbanised Society*, Routledge and Kegan Paul, London

Mellor, J R (1982) *Images of the City: Their Impact on British Urban Policy*, Open University Press (Block 1 Unit 2 of Course D202), Milton Keynes

Melucci, A (1989) *Nomads of the present: Social Movements and Individual Needs in Contemporary Society*, Hutchinson Radius, London

Melucci, A (1996) *Challenging codes: collective action in the information age*, Cambridge University Press, Cambridge

Milton Keynes Development Corporation (1992) *The Milton Keynes Planning Manual*, Chesterton Consulting, Milton Keynes

Mollison, B (1988) *Permaculture: A Designer's Manual*, Togari Publications, Australia

Morris, W (1996) 'Mixed Use Development: Design to Reduce Travel and Generate Employment', *PTRC Planning for Sustainability*, PTRC Education and Research Services Ltd, England

Morris, W and Kanfman, J (1997) *Mixed Use Development: New Designs for New Livelihoods*, Department of Tourism, Small Business and Industry, Brisbane

Morton, J (1994) *From Southgate to Hallwood Park – 25 Years in the life of a Runcorn Community*, Merseyside Improved Houses, Liverpool

Moughtin, C (1996) *Urban Design: Green Dimensions*, Butterworth-Heineman, Oxford

Mumford, L (1968) *The Urban Prospect*, Secker & Warburg, London

Næss, P (1993) *Transportation Energy in Swedish Towns and Regions*, Scandinavian Housing and Planning Research, Vol 10, pp187–206

Netherlands Agency for Energy and the Environment (1992) *Ecolonia: demonstration project for energy-saving and environmentally-aware building and living*, NOVEM, Sittard, The Netherlands

Newman, P and Kenworthy, J (1989) *Cities and Automobile Dependence*, Gower Technical, Aldershot

Newman, S and Lonsdale, S (1996) *Human Jungle*, Ebury Press, London

Newton, P N (ed) (1997) *Reshaping Cities for a More Sustainable Future – Exploring the Link between Urban Form, Air Quality, Energy and Greenhouse Gas Emissions*, Research Monograph 6, Australian Housing and Research Institute, Melbourne

North, P (1996) 'LETS: a Policy for Community Empowerment in the Inner City?', *Local Economy*, Vol II, No 3

Novem (undated) *Ecolonia*, Novem, Sittard

Novem (undated) *The Road to Ecolonia*, Novem, Sittard

Oc, T and Tiesdall, S (1997) *Safer City Centres – reviving the public realm*, Paul Chapman Publishing

O'Doherty, R, Purdue, D, Durrschmidt, J and Jowers, P (1997) 'Cultural Innovation in Alternative Milieux: LETS as CED', *Regional Studies Association: Community Economic development: Linking the Grassroots to Regional Economic Development*, Proceedings of the Annual Conference, November 24–27

OECD (1994) *Road Transport Research: Congestion Control and Demand Management*, OECD, Paris

O'Riordan, T (1981) *Environmentalism*, London, Pion Press

Osbourne, P and Davis, A (1996) *Safe Routes to School Demonstration Projects*, PTRC Education and Research Services Ltd, London

Out of this World (1997) *Out of this World – Natural Food Collection* 1997, http://www.organic-networks.com/outinf.html

Owens, S (1984) 'Energy and Spatial Structure: a Rural Example', *Environment and Plannning*, Vol 16, pp1319–1337

Owens, S (1986) *Energy, Planning and Urban Form*, Pion, London

Owens, S (1990) 'Land Use Planning for Energy Efficiency', in Cullingworth, J B (ed) *Energy, Land and Public Policy* Transaction Books, New Brunswick, pp53–98

Owen, S (1992) 'Energy, Environmental Sustainability and Land Use Planning', in Breheny, M (ed) *Sustainable Development and Urban Form*, Pion, London

Owens, S and Cope, D (1992) *Land Use Planning Policy and Climate Change*, HMSO, London

Pacione, M (1997) 'Local Exchange Trading Systems as a Response to the Globalisation of Capitalism', *Urban Studies*, Vol 34, No 8, pp1179–99

Padeco (1994) *Non-motorized Vehicles in Asian Cities*, Report for World Bank, New York

Parliamentary Office of Science and Technology (1995), *Transport: Some Issues In Sustainability*, POST, London

Paxton, A (1994) *The Food Miles Report; the dangers of long distance food transport*, The SAFE Alliance, London

Pearce, J (1993) *At the Heart of the Community Economy: Community Enterprise in a Changing World*, Calouste Gulbenkian Foundation, London

Percy-Smith, J (1998) *What is the Role of Community Leaders?*, Paper presented to ESRC Seminar, University of the West of England, 21 July (unpublished), Bristol

Perri 6 (1997) *The power to bind and lose: tackling network poverty*, Demos, London

Perry, C (1939) *Housing for the Machine Age*, Russell Sage Foundation, New York

Peterborough Development Corporation (1970) *Greater Peterborough Master Plan*, PDC, Peterborough

Pharoah, T (1992) *Less Traffic Better Towns*, Friends of the Earth, London

Pilisuk, M and Parks, S H (1986) *The Healing Web*, NE University Press of New England, Hanover

Pinch, M (1994) 'Evaluation of the Travel Impact of Rural Workshops in Cornwall', unpublished MA dissertation, Faculty of the Built Environment, UWE, Bristol

POST (1995) *Transport: Some Issues in Sustainability*, Parliamentary Office of Science and Technology, London

Potter, S (1990) *Land Use and Transport*, paper prepared for the Milton Keynes Forum, Energy and Environment Research Unit, Open University, Milton Keynes, available from the author

Potts, M (1993) *The Independent Home – Living well with Power from the Sun, Wind and Water*, Chelsea Green Publishing Company, Vermont

Power, A and Tunstall, R (1995) *Swimming against the tide: Polarisation or progress on 20 unpopular council estates*, Joseph Rowntree Foundation, York

Pullen, M (1992) *Linking Farmers and Consumers*, International Society for Ecology and Culture, Bristol

Purdue, D, Durrschmidt, J, Jowers, P and O'Doherty, R (1997) 'DIY Culture and Extended Milieux: LETS, Veggie Boxes and Festivals', *The Sociological Review*, Vol 45, No 4, pp645–667

Putnam, R (1993) 'The prosperous community: social capital and public life', *The American Prospect*, Vol 13, pp35–24

Putnam, R (1995) *Making Democracy Work*, Princetown University Press, Princetown

Rallings, C, Temple, M and Thrasher, M (1994) *Community Identity and Participation in Local Government*, Commission for Local Democracy Research Report 1, London

Ravetz, A (1980) *Remaking Cities – Contradictions of the Recent Urban Environment*, Croom Helm, London

Relph, E (1976) *Place and Placelessness*, Pion, London

Rickaby, P (1985) *Towards a Spatial Energy Model*, Centre for Configuration Studies, Open University, Milton Keynes

Rickaby, P, Steadman, R and Barrett, M (1992) 'Patterns of Land Use in English Towns: Implications for Energy Use and Carbon Dioxide Emissions', in Breheny, M (ed) *Sustainable Development and Urban Form*, Pion, London

Rij van c K (1994) *Urban Environment and Sustainable Development*, Heidemij Advies BV, The Netherlands

Roberts, I (1996) 'Safety to School?', *Lancet*, Vol 347, June 15, p1642

Roberts, J, Elliot, D and Houghton, T (1991), *Privatising Electricity – the politics of power*, Belhaven Press, London

Roberts, V, Russell, H, Harding, A, and Parkinson, M (1995) *Public/Private Voluntary Partnerships in Local Government*, Local Government Management Board, Luton

Robbins, C (1997) 'A New Approach to Regeneration: LETS as Local Authority Policy', *Regional Studies Association: Community Economic development: Linking the Grassroots to Regional Economic Development*, Proceedings of the Annual Conference, November, pp34–36

Roelofs, J (1996) *Greening Cities*, Bootstrap Press, New York

Rogers, C and Stewart, M (1998) *Sustainable Regeneration*, Good Practice Guide, DETR, London

Roth, U (1977) 'The impact of settlement patterns on low temperature heating supply systems, transportation, and environment', (paper to the International Congress of the IFHP) *Towards a More Humane Technology*, IFHP, The Hague

Rowe, J (1998) *Bath and North East Somerset Local Agenda 21 Issue Commission: Interim Evaluation*, report to BANES Unitary Authority, May 1997

Rowell, A and Fergusson, M (1991) *Bikes not Fumes,* Cyclist's Touring Club, Godalming

Royal Commission on Environmental Pollution (1994) *Eighteenth Report: Transport and the Environment*, HMSO, London

Royal Commission on Environmental Pollution (1997) *Transport and the Environment: Developments Since 1994*, HMSO, London

Royal Town Planning Institute (1991) *Traffic Growth and Planning Policy*, Royal Town Planning Institute, London

Rutten Communicatie-advies (1995) *The Road to Ecolonia: Evaluation and Residents' Survey*, NOVEM, Sittard, The Netherlands

Schumacher, F (1972) *Small is beautiful*, Abacus, London

Scottish Office (1996) *Partnership in the Regeneration of Urban Scotland*, Central Research Unit HMSO, London

Scottish Development Department (1973) *Threshold Analysis Manual*, HMSO Edinburgh

Scrase, A J (1983) *Planning History*, Bristol Polytechnic (Joint Distance Learning Diploma in Town & Country Planning, Block 1 course units), Bristol

Sennett, R (1970) *The Uses of Disorder: Personal Identity and City Life*, Penguin, Middlesex

Sennett, R (1994) *Flesh and Stone: The Body and the City in Western Civilisation*, Faber and Faber, London

Seyfang, G (1997) 'Creating Community Currencies: LETS Build Sustainable Local Economies', in *Regional Studies Association: Community Economic develop-*

*ment: Linking the Grassroots to Regional Economic Development*, Proceedings of the Annual Conference, November 28–29

Shen, D, Liu, X and Luo, C (1994) 'A Study of Non Motorized Passenger Transport in China', in *Proceedings of International Symposium on Non Motorized Transportation*, Beijing Polytechnic University, Beijing

Sherlock, H (1990) *Cities are Good for Us*, Transport 2000, London

Skelcher, C, McCabe, A, and Lowndes, V (1996) *Community networks in urban regeneration*, Bristol, Policy Press

Smit, J (1996) *Urban Agriculture, progress and prospect 1975–2005*, The Urban Agriculture Network Cities Feeding People Series Report 18, Washington

Smith, D and Stewart, J (1997) 'Probation and Social Exclusion', *Social Policy and Administration*, Vol 31, No 5, pp96–115

Social Exclusion Unit (SEU) (1998) *Bringing Britain Together: a national strategy for neighbourhood renewal*, Cm 4045, HMSO, London

Stacey, M (1969) 'The myth of community studies', *British Journal of Sociology*, Vol 20, No 2, pp134–47

Stead, D (1994) 'Reducing Travel Distances Through Land Use Planning', unpublished MA dissertation, Faculty of the Built Environment, University of the West of England, Bristol

Stead, D (1999) *Planning for Less Travel – Identifying Land Use Characteristics Associated with more Sustainable Travel Patterns*, unpublished PhD Thesis, Bartlett School of Planning, University College London, London

Stead, D and Davis, A (1998) 'Increasing the Need to Travel? Parental Choice and Travel to School', *Proceedings of Seminar C – Policy, Planning and Sustainability*, 26th PTRC European Transport Forum, Uxbridge

Steele, A, Somerville, P, and Galvin, G (1995) *Estate Agreements*, report for the Joseph Rowntree Foundation, Department of Environmental Health and Housing, University of Salford Forum, Loughborough, pp75–88

Stewart, J, Greer, A and Hoggett, P (1995) *The Quango State: an Alternative Approach*, Commission for Local Democracy, London

Stewart, M and Collett, P (1998) 'Accountability in Community Contributions to Sustainable Development', in Warburton, D (ed) *Community and Sustainable Development: Participation in the Future*, London, Earthscan

Stewart, M and Taylor, M (1995) *Resident empowerment in estate regeneration*, Policy Press, Bristol

Stockholme Regioplane-och trafikkontoret (1998) *Programme for Regioplan 2000 for Stockholme Ian*, Katarina Tych, AB Stockholm

Taylor, M (1995) *Unleashing the potential: bringing residents to the centre of estate regeneration*, Joseph Rowntree Foundation, York

Taylor, N (1973) *The Village in the City*, Temple Smith, London

Tebbutt, M (1995) *Women's talk? Social history of gossip in working class neighbourhoods*, Scholar Press, Aldershot

Thake, S (1995) *Staying the Course; the role and structures of community regeneration organisations*, York Publishing Services in association with the Joseph Rowntree Foundation, York

Thake, S and Staubach, R (1993) *Investing in People – Rescuing Communities from the Margin*, Joseph Rowntree Foundation, York

Thake, S and Zadek, S (1997) *Practical People Noble Causes: How to support Community-based Social Entrepreneurs*, New Economics Foundation, London

The Edge (1995) 'Eco-Community Design: the New Canadian Town of Bamberton Put all the Pieces Together', *The Edge*, Issue 19, Oct–Dec 1995, Stroud, Gloucester

The Recycling Consortium (1999) *Community Waste Action Toolkit*, The Recycling Consortium, Bristol

Thérivel, R and Partidário, M R (1996) *The Practice of Strategic Environmental Assessment*, Earthscan, London

Thérivel, R, Wilson, E, Thompson, S, Heaney, D and Pritchard, D (1992) *Strategic Environmental Assessment*, Earthscan, London

Thomas, D N (1995) *Community Development at Work: A Case of Obscurity in Accomplishment*, Community Development Foundation, London

Thomas, L and Cousins, W (1996) 'A New Compact City Form: Concepts in Practice', in Jenks, M et al (eds) *The Compact City: a sustainable urban form?* E&FN Spon, London

Thoreau, H D (1992) *Walden – or Life in the Woods*, Shambhala Pocket Classic Series, Shambhala, Boston and London

Tibbalds, F (1992) *Making People-friendly Towns*, Longman, London

Tjallingii, S (1995) *Ecopolis: Strategies for Ecologically Sound Urban Development*, Backhays Publishers, Leiden

Todd, J T and J (1994) *From Eco-Cities to Living Machines – principles of ecological design*, North Atlantic books, Berkley, California

Tolley, R (1997) *The Greening of Urban Transport*, Wiley, Chichester

Tomalty, R (1994) 'An Ecosystem Approach to Growth Management', *Environments*, Vol 22, No 3, Canada

Town and Country Planning Association (1986) *Whose Responsibility? – Reclaiming the Inner Cities*, TCPA, London

Trevillion, S (1992) *Caring in the community – a networking approach to community partnership*, Longmans, Harlow

Turrent, D, Dogget, J and Ferraro, R (1981) *Passive Solar Housing in the UK*, a report for the Energy Technology Research Unit, Energy Conscious Design, Milton Keynes

Tutt, P and Morris, D (1998) *Bath Farmers' Market – a case study*, Eco-logic Books, Bristol

Ullrich, O (1997) 'The Pedestrian Town as an Environmentally Tolerable Alternative to Motorised Travel', in Tolley, R *The Greening of Urban Transport*, Wiley, Chichester

Urban Ecology Australia (1995) *What is the Halifax EcoCity Project?*, UEA, Grenfell Street, Adelaide

Urban Villages Group (1992) *Urban Villages, A Concept for Creating Mixed Use Urban Development on a Sustainable Scale*, Urban Villages Group, London

Valleley, M, Jones, P, Wofinden, D and Flack, S (1997) 'The Role of Parking Standards in Sustainable Development', *Proceedings of Seminar C – Policy, Planning and Sustainability*, 25th PTRC European Transport Forum, Uxbridge, pp393–411

Vellve, R (1994) *Saving the Seed – Genetic Diversity and European Agriculture*, Earthscan Books, London

Waddams Price, C and Biermann, A (1998), *Fuel Poverty in Britain – Expenditure on Fuels, 1993–94 to 1995–96*, Gas Consumers Council, London

Waitakere City Planners (1997) *Seminar on Implementing a Sustainability Strategy*, May 1997, Auckland, New Zealand

Walter, B, Arkin, L and Crenshaw, R (eds) (1992) *Sustainable Cities: Concepts and Strategies for Eco-City Development*, Eco-Home Media, Los Angeles

Ward, C (1976) *Housing – an Anarchists Approach*, Freedom Press, London

Ward, C (1989) *Welcome Thinner City: Urban Survival in the 1990s*, Bedford Square Press, London

Ward, C (1993) *New Town, Home Town: The Lessons of Experience*, Calouste Gulbenkian Foundation, London

Watson, D (1994) *Tenants in Partnership – driving force for renewal of the Pembroke Street Estate, Plymouth*, Joseph Rowntree Foundation, York

Webber, M (1964) 'The Urban Place and the Non-Place Urban Realm', in Webber, M et al, *Explorations into Urban Structure*, UPP, Philadelphia, pp79–153

Webster, D and Mackie, A (1996) *Review of Traffic Calming Schemes in 20mph Zones*, TRL, Crowthorne

West Sussex County Council (1996) *Urban Capacity in West Sussex: Technical Report*, West Sussex Structure Plan 3rd Review, West Sussex City Council, Chicester

White, P (1995) *Public Transport: its planning, management and operation (Third edition)*, UCL Press, London

WHO (1999) *Health and Urban Planning: a guide to principles, process and spatial policy*, WHO, Copenhagen (unpublished draft at time of going to press, contact Hugh Barton, UWE, Bristol)

Wilkinson, R and Marmot, M (1998) *Social Determinants of Health: The Solid Facts*, HO, Copenhagen

Williams, C (1995) 'The Emergence of Local Currencies', *Town and Country Planning*, Vol 64, No 12, pp329–332

Williams, C (1996a) 'The New Barter Economy: An Appraisal of Local Exchange and Trading Systems (LETS)', *Journal of Public Policy*, Vol 16, No 1, pp85–101

Williams, C (1996b) 'Local Exchange and Trading Systems: A New Source of Work and Credit of the Unemployed', *Environment and Planning A*, Vol 28, No 8, pp1395–1416

Williams, K et al (1996) 'Achieving the Compact City Through Intensification: An Acceptable Option?', in Jenks, M et al (eds) *The Compact City: A Sustainable Urban Form?* E&FN Spon, London

Williams, R (1973) *The Country and the City*, Chatto and Windus, London

Willmott, P (1987) *Friendship Networks and Social Support*, Policy Studies Institute, London

Wilson, E (1991) *The Sphinx in the City*, Virago, London

Winter, J and Farthing, S (1997) 'Coordinating Facility Provision and New Housing Development: Impacts on Car and Local Facility Use', in Farthing, S M (ed) *Evaluating Local Environmental Policy*, Avebury, Aldershot, pp159–179

World Bank (1996) *Sustainable Transport: Properties for Policy Reforms*, World Bank, New York

World Commission on Environment and Development (the Bruntland Report) (1987) *Our Common Future*, Oxford University Press, Oxford

World Habitat Awards, (1996) Curitiba, *Urban Management Building Full Citizenship*, IPPUC, Parana, Brazil

Worpole, K (1998) *Nothing to Fear: trust and respect in urban communities*, Comedia/Demos Report, London

Wright, C and Gardiner, P (1980) 'Energy and Housing', *Built Environment*, Vol 5, No 4

Young, K, Gosschalk, B, and Hatter, W (1996) *In Search of Community Identity*, for the Joseph Rowntree Foundation, York Publishing Services, York

Young, M and Smith, J (1998) 'Social entrepreneurs: Business sense', *The Guardian*, 21st July 1998

Young, M and Wilmott, P (1957) *Family and Kinship in East London*, Routledge and Kegan Paul, London

Zipfel, T (1989) *Estate Management Boards: An Introduction*, Priority Estates Project, London

# PERSONAL COMMUNICATIONS

Auroville, Martin Littlewood, 24th October 1997

Acorn, Ashley Dobbs, e-mail 24th November 1997; 6th June 1998, telephone; informed that all small units were built and sold. Larger properties in £149,000 price range are all that's left

Canmore Housing Association, Alan Brown, 11th October 1996, 27th July 1998

Crystal Waters, Max Lindeggar, letter 24th November 1997; e-mail 20th January 1998; letter 25th July 1998

Edinburgh City Council, Alec Patterson, 13th March 1998, 27th March 1998

Little River, e-mail 10th and 20th November 1997, 1st April and 25th July 1998; letter 3rd January 1998

Halifax, Cherie Hoyle, Urban Ecology Australia, letter 20th October 1997, Paul Downton, Urban Ecology Australia, December 1996

Hackland and Dore Architects, 24th July 1998

Ithaca, e-mail 24th September 1996, 20th October and 13th November 1997

Sherwood Energy Village, e-mail 23rd January 1998

West Harwood, New Lives New Landscapes, letter 3rd December 1997, 26th July 1998; e-mail 7th November 1997, 23rd January 1998

# INDEX

Page numbers in *italics* refer to tables, illustrations and photographs